MICROECONOMICS:
Logic, Tools, and Analysis

MICROECONOMICS:
Logic, Tools, and Analysis

Stanley Kaish

Rutgers University,
Newark College of Arts and Sciences

Harper & Row, Publishers

New York, Hagerstown, San Francisco, London

Sponsoring Editor: John Greenman
Project Editor: Cynthia Hausdorff
Designer: Gayle Jaeger
Production Supervisor: Francis X. Giordano
Compositor: Monotype Composition Company, Inc.
Printer: The Murray Printing Company
Binder: Halliday Lithograph Corporation
Art Studio: J & R Technical Services Inc.

Library of Congress Cataloging in Publication Data
Kaish, Stanley, 1931–
Microeconomics.
Includes index.
1. Microeconomics. I. Title.
HB171.5.K27 330 75-31585
ISBN 0-06-043456-2

For Lois and Harvey and Steven

Contents

3 Price Elasticity of Demand 45

4 Demand Analysis: Ordinal Utility 71

5 Supply Analysis: Production 117

9 Imperfect Competition: Monopoly and Monopolistic Competition 257

10 Oligopoly 295

11 The Market for Factors of Production: Demand 329

12 The Market for Factors of Production: Supply 359

13 Putting It All Together: Exchange, Equilibrium, and Welfare 397

Preface

My goals in writing this book are quite simple. I have tried to write a book from which it is easy to learn a hard subject. There is no doubt that students find microeconomic theory difficult. There are two reasons for this. First, the subject is abstract by nature, demanding rigorous, often lengthy, chains of reasoning. These are attempted by students for whom, too often, the underlying assumptions and principles of the theory are most tenuous. A second source of difficulty stems from the fact that the course is frequently taken as a *required* part of a business or economics major, and the student has neither the time nor the inclination to give microeconomic theory the careful attention it requires.

There is no changing either of these situations. The theory remains abstract. The students remain distracted. It is not fair to pretend to change the nature of the subject by leaving out the difficult parts. Nor is it realistic to expect the busy student to give microtheory his undivided attention. It seems to me that the practical solution is to offer this difficult material in a way that can be readily understood. With that in mind, I realized that it would not be appropriate to try to produce a rigorously analytical book—a thoroughbred, if you will. Something resembling a workhorse would be more in order, not particularly fast, graceful, or elegant, but steady, patient, and willing.

Two pedagogical devices are employed to enhance the learnability of the subject: (1) A question-and-answer presentation segments the material into more easily digestible units than one finds in most texts. These questions and answers attempt to anticipate the problems that often trouble students and resolve them before they come to be an obstacle to further learning. (2) The other device is the use of many, many sequenced diagrams. Each diagram is designed to present a specific point. Captions and comments make the diagrams self-contained. A student should be able to learn the elements of the theory from the figures. They are an integral part of the presentation.

Since the spirit of this preface is honesty with regard to the goals and probable achievements of the users of the book, I would like to make a comment about end-of-chapter references to other source materials. There are none, and the reason is simple. Students who will be helped by this text are not ready to read journal articles on economic theory in the professional literature. That material is, by and large, very difficult. It usually employs tools students don't possess and assumes a familiarity with the literature that is unwarranted as far as most undergraduates are concerned. Why pretend otherwise?

Instead, I offer the following graded list of other current textbooks. All cover more or less the same topics as this text, in chapters that have more or less the same titles. However, the degree of difficulty students will have with the texts varies. Students wishing clarification or amplification on some point are advised to consult them. Please note that these are but a small sample of the total number of books available in the field. However, each is representative of a level of treatment.

Leftwich, R. H., *The Price System and Resource Allocation*, Holt, Rinehart & Winston, 4th Edition, is the easiest to understand among the reference listed here. It is a relatively thorough, patient treatment that has been refined over the four editions. Students will find it helpful for many points that need clarification.

Bilas, Richard, *Microeconomic Theory: A Graphical Analysis*, McGraw-Hill, 2nd Edition, is more ambitious than Leftwich. It is also a step up in difficulty. The graphical treatment of many subtle points in the theory is excellent. Topics extend beyond the coverage of both this text and Leftwich.

Ferguson, C. E. and Gould, J. P., *Microeconomic Theory*, Irwin, 4th Edition, is an extremely popular bridge between undergraduate and master's level graduate work. The coverage is almost encyclopaedic and the treatment is rigorously analytical. Earlier editions of this book carried a text within a text in the mathematical footnotes that frequently covered half the page. This edition appears to reduce the extent of the footnoting, although they still present the conventional major mathematical statements of microeconomics.

Mansfield, E., *Microeconomics, Theory and Applications*, Norton, 2nd

Edition, is on a level with Ferguson and Gould, but rather than emphasizing the many nuances of the theory as found in that text, Mansfield highlights modern applications of the theory in management science and welfare economics. His discussion of the applications is quite detailed. The student may find a bridge between microeconomic theory and managerial economics in this book.

Stigler, G. J., *The Theory of Price,* Macmillan, 3rd Edition, is a deceptively subtle book. It looks easy. Don't be fooled just because the pages are small and the print is big. Stigler is a major economic theorist and his book is most thought provoking and filled with insights that should make students think twice before according passive acceptance to the established doctrines.

Friedman, Milton, *Price Theory: A Provisional Text,* Aldine, is in a different league from the others listed. Nevertheless, all students can derive some benefit from this book by one of the most creative economists of our time. The range of topics is far narrower than that of the others, but the treatments are extremely original. The sketchiness is doubtless due to the fact that the book was published from lecture notes taken in Friedman's class at University of Chicago.

Recommended chapter references

Kaish	*Leftwich*	*Bilas*	*Ferguson*	*Stigler*	*Friedman*	*Mansfield*
1	—	—	—	—	—	—
2	4	3	1	4	1	3, 4
3	3	2	2, 4	3	1	3, 4
4	5	4	1, 2, 3	4	1	2
5	7	6	5, 6	7, 8	6	5
6	8	6, 7	7	7, 8	4	6
7	—	—	—	—	—	—
8	9	8	8	10	—	8
9	10, 12	9, 10	9, 10, 11	11	—	9, 10
10	11	10	12	12	—	11
11	13	11	13, 14	11, 14	7, 9, 13	12, 13
12	—	11	14	11, 14	11, 13	12, 13
13	—	12	15, 16	—	3	14, 15

Returning to the text at hand, at the end of most chapters are Questions. These have *not* been drafted with simplicity in mind. They deal for the most part with current events or present vignettes of some parts of our daily lives. The role of economic theory in shaping events, both global and personal, will become clearer to the student as he considers these questions.

At this point I would like to acknowledge my gratitude to the generation of students that has seen parts of this presentation in the form of my lectures at Rutgers. I would like to thank the many readers who reviewed the text, singling out particularly Dominick Salvatore of Fordham for many perceptive comments, the people at Harper & Row for seeing the book through from start to finish with never-flagging patience and fortitude, my wife and children for demonstrating even more patience and fortitude than the people at Harper & Row, and to Alfred Marshall, John Hicks, Edward Chamberlin, and Joan Robinson for being such damn good economists and giving the rest of us a subject about which to write.

MICROECONOMICS:
Logic, Tools, and Analysis

1 Introduction

If you have completed an introductory course in economics, you have a pretty good idea about the subject matter of economics. Since you are going on in the area, it is evident that your interest has been piqued and you want to learn more about it. Perhaps you became interested in the stock market and want to learn how to make a lot of money there. Or perhaps you have become curious about the predicament of the underdeveloped countries or want to find out why people in Delaware are better off on the average than people in Mississippi. Some students go on in economics to acquire greater knowledge about corporations or banks or labor unions or taxes. Curiosity about inflation, devaluation, unemployment, strikes, and cartels frequently works to keep students in the field of economics. If it was a desire to learn more about topics such as these, you may very well want to turn around and leave this course—or you may not. It depends on how badly you want to learn about them.

Although economics deals with all the subjects listed in the previous paragraph, it does so in a particular manner that differs from the treatment a lawyer, a historian, or a sociologist might give the same topics. The thing that keeps economics from being merely a disjointed discussion of all these semirelated subjects is the set of theoretical tools economists have developed over the years to analyze their problems. It happens, not too unexpectedly, that it is necessary to understand the tools of economic analysis before you can really understand how an economist views society. Although students of the arts and the physical sciences accept the need to master technique before going on to content, and would-be musicians play scales for years and would-be artists practice drawing perspectives, and would-be doctors learn to adjust microscopes, students of the social sciences are more impatient to get on with the "relevant" material. Unfortunately, it turns out that trying to understand economics without acquiring the techniques used by economists is the long way around, and because economics is the science of efficiency, any economist who has learned the theory will tell you it should not be done that way. Alfred Marshall referred to economic theory as an "engine of analysis." It is because of this engine that economics has developed, uniquely among the social sciences, to a point that allows discussion to go beyond description and classification and into prediction and (occasionally) control of complex activities. The purpose of this course is to teach you the general theoretical tools that economists use to examine particular topics.

Do you mean to say that we are going to learn to deal with every economic problem here in one semester?
No, this is a good course, but not that good. First of all, let us divide economic problems into two major groupings—microeconomic and macroeconomic. At best we are going to develop *some* of the tools economists use to deal with *microeconomic* problems.

What is the difference between macroeconomic and microeconomic subjects?
In broad terms, we say that microeconomics deals with individual elements of the economy and how they interact with one another. Macroeconomics deals with the aggregate of the elements and studies how it behaves as unit Micro is like a wheel within a macro wheel. Within the human body the organs are micro units interacting with one another. The whole body is a macro unit biologically, and yet socially the individual becomes a micro unit interacting with other people. In economics we think of people moving from one job to another as involving micro adjustments. The level of total employment is a macro problem. The price of beans relative to the price of bananas is a micro problem. The level of consumer prices in general is a macro problem. These are the types of differences to which we are referring here. Micro deals more or less with *relative* values and macro with *absolute* levels.

Even professional economists sometimes become confused over what are micro and what are macroeconomic price changes. For example, the inflation of the 1973–1974 period was generally thought of as a macroeconomic problem and fought with a tight money policy designed to reduce aggregate demand in the economy as a whole However, two major components of that inflation were the high prices of food and energy which occurred as a result of relative shortages in these areas. These should have been considered microeconomic problems. A program of taxes to hold down demand for gasoline and subsidies to increase supplies of both food and energy would be indicative of microeconomic policy making. Different economists recommended different policies during that time, depending on their perception of the problem.

What is theory?

A theory, sometimes called a model, is a simplified explanation of the way things work. Science presumes the existence of cause-and-effect factors underlying all natural phenomena and seeks to isolate and understand what they are and how they interact. A theory is the latest idea consistent with the available evidence of what is taking place and how. It allows us to select the causal data we want to observe, to sort it into meaningful categories, and to make predictions of outcomes. Without theory, research is just a fishing expedition and policy is a random process of trial and error. We need guidance regarding what reactions to expect when certain actions take place. Theory provides this guidance. The real world is a devilishly complex place, with all sorts of events occurring at the same time. A theory sorts the multitude of simultaneously changing variables and selects a handful as pertinent to the study of a particular problem. The important characteristic of a useful theory is enough complexity to include all the pertinent variables and enough simplicity to permit us to think about them within the limits of our human intelligence.

How do you select the variables to be included?

This, of course, is the key question. What tools do you, yourself feel you have at hand when you are trying to explain an event? Basically, all that is available are (1) existing explanations of similar events, (2) observations, and (3) reasoning ability. These are the tools available to all scientists when they attempt to explain anything. Through alternating chains of inductive and deductive logic, they gradually narrow down the variables that are important and discard those that are extraneous.

What do you mean by alternating chains of inductive and deductive reasoning?

These terms refer to two different forms of scientific reasoning. Inductive refers to reasoning that goes from specific instances to the formulation of generalizations. Deductive reasoning goes from generalizations to predictions about behavior in specific instances. Economic theorists work primarily with deductive reasoning, using general cause-and-effect principles to forecast and explain specific economic events. Some *simple* economic theories are that inflation is caused by increasing the money supply; supply and demand determine relative prices; and aggregate consumption is a function of aggregate income. Each of these *general* theories has been used as the basis of analysis of *specific* market situations.

Inductive reasoning often appears on the scene as a by-product of statistical work undertaken to verify a forecast made deductively. For example, monetary theory usually assumes that the interest rate will vary inversely with the supply of money. The way to lower interest, it is believed, is by increasing money supply. This assumption is consistent with experience in other areas of the economy. Increased supply usually lowers price. Examination of the money supply–interest rate record, however, shows that toward the end of business cycle expansions interest rates rise even as money supply grows. Here we have specific experiences. Revision of monetary theory to accommodate these experiences is an exercise in *inductive* reasoning. The revised theory, in turn, will be used to make *deductive* forecasts of future interest levels.

Economists have included these empirical findings by theorizing that, toward the end of the expansion phase of a business cycle, lenders become increasingly aware of the rapid rate of price inflation that is taking place. They become reluctant to lend at interest rates that do not keep up with the rate of inflation and insist on higher rates of return. The more the money supply is increased by the Federal Reserve System in an attempt to pull interest rates down, the faster prices rise, and the higher interest rates are driven. Monetary theory now recognizes the need to include a variable that measures lender expectations of future price levels when attempting to forecast interest rates.

Economic model building, like all scientific endeavor, requires this continuous interplay of deductive generalizations modified by inductive experience to form clearer insights into cause and effect. It is most important to realize that ignoring a variable does not make it go away. It merely leaves it uncontrolled. We are consigning the uncontrolled variables to the "all other things being equal" pile and assuming either that they do not matter or, if they do, that their values remain unchanged for the problem. This is not always a realistic assumption.

How realistic must the assumptions of economic theory be?

It is not necessary, or even desirable, that the assumptions of an economic model vividly portray the details of the economy. This would require the inclusion of too many variables in the analysis and reduce the general applicability of the theory. A useful theory cannot be custom-fit to one given situation. Rather than a photograph, we should think of a schematic drawing that outlines the major simplified qualities of a system but ignores the details. True, the omission of the detail may cause some loss in the theory's predictive power in a particular case. However, the true test of the efficacy of a theory is whether it works and is simple enough to use in a variety of instances, not how accurate are its assumptions. The criterion is very functional. If a theory predicts an outcome with sufficient accuracy to suit our purposes, then it is a good theory. The more types of cases it can predict and the fewer assumptions it needs to do it, the better theory it is. In this course, we shall deal with a deductive method that is broadly applicable to many situations, yet is based on only a handful of basic assumptions.

What are the basic assumptions of microeconomic analysis?

Unless we indicate otherwise, five assumptions are presumed to hold for our analysis. These are the following:

1. *Economic man.* This term implies that each person under discussion attempts to maximize personal satisfactions and profits. He calculates his opportunities and takes the appropriate action to serve his selfish ends.
2. *Mobile resources.* There are no artificial boundaries among economic units. Labor is free to go to work in the most profitable or enjoyable employment. Owners of capital can invest their funds where profits appear most attractive.
3. *Reliable, free flows of information.* Everyone knows where the opportunities are. What is more, there is complete and instantaneous movement of information.
4. *Diminishing returns.* There is such a thing as too much of a good thing. Adding labor to a productive activity eventually results in diminishing its productivity. Adding to consumption eventually diminishes the satisfactions realized from each additional unit of the commodity or service consumed.
5. *Divisibility of goods and labor efforts.* Fine, quantitative gradations can be made in measurement. Goods, services, and factors of production are infinitely divisible In mathematics this assumption is called *continuity.*

Given these assumptions, we shall develop a set of analytical tools that will enable us to solve a broad variety of economic problems in many areas.

FIGURE 1–1. Basic Demand and Supply

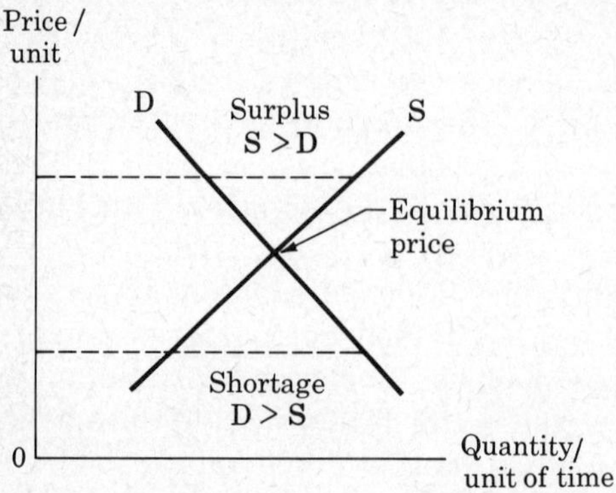

The assumption that demanders take more at a low price and suppliers offer more at a high price is usually summarized by the basic supply and demand diagram. The vertical axis shows different prices of a product. The horizontal axis shows different quantities per unit of time. The *D* curve shows the alternative quantities per unit of time that would be demanded at various prices per unit. The *S* curve shows alternative quantities per unit of time that would be supplied if different unit prices were to prevail. Their intersection is the equilibrium or market price. At prices above equilibrium, the quantity supplied exceeds the quantity demanded, and the price is bid down toward the equilibrium level. At prices below equilibrium, the quantity supplied is less than the quantity demanded, and the price is bid up toward the equilibrium level.

With what types of problems is microeconomic analysis concerned? We shall deal primarily with problems of price determination and resource allocation. We shall see how consumers divide their incomes among different goods and services; how producers decide how much of what kinds of products to make; how income gets distributed to different people in different amounts; how society provides for capital accumulation so that its total output can grow; why different production techniques are used in different countries; how labor and management bargain to determine wage rates. A common element of our approach is the use of relative prices as a mechanism to signal producers where the greatest profit opportunities lie, and to tell consumers how much they can afford to buy. Microeconomics is often called *price theory*; it should not seem strange that price is the common denominator in our analysis.

Can you give a brief overview of the manner in which we use the analytical tools?

We begin with the broad concepts of supply and demand. Any events that occur in the market are classified as affecting supply or demand for a good or service. All goods and services are traded in an abstract area called the market, and it is in this market that the forces of supply and demand converge. Demand refers to the willingness of buyers to acquire the good or service under different circumstances. Supply refers to the willingness of sellers to offer it. Employing our assumption of economic man, we assume that, all other things being equal, people prefer to buy low and sell high, so greater quantities of a commodity will be demanded at lower prices than at higher prices and greater quantities will be supplied at higher prices than at lower prices. The reasons for this are discussed in detail in Chapters 2 and 6. The basic analysis, therefore involves suppliers and demanders coming together to trade, with the demanders trying to bid price down and the suppliers trying to bid it up. The actual price at which any transaction occurs is a compromise between these opposing forces. It is a price at which the quantity that demanders are willing to take just equals the quantity that suppliers are willing to offer. It is called the *equilibrium* price. At prices above equilibrium, there will be more goods offered then are demanded, and the availability of these excess goods will produce competition among suppliers to lower their prices in an effort to find buyers. At prices below equilibrium, there will be more demanded than offered, and the competition among demanders to get a share of the inadequate offering will produce upward pressure on price. The tendency is for the price to move toward the equilibrium level and remain there (Figure 1–1).

Can you clarify what a market is?

As stated, a market exists when the forces of supply and demand come together for trading purposes. There are literally millions of separate commodity, labor, money, security, service, and what-not markets co-existing in the economy. Each has its population of buyers, sellers, brokers, and facilitators of trade. Every one of us participates in dozens of markets daily, both as demanders and suppliers. We supply our labor services in the factor of production market and our savings in the capital market. We may speculate in the stock market. On the demand

FIGURE 1–2. The Circular Flow of Income

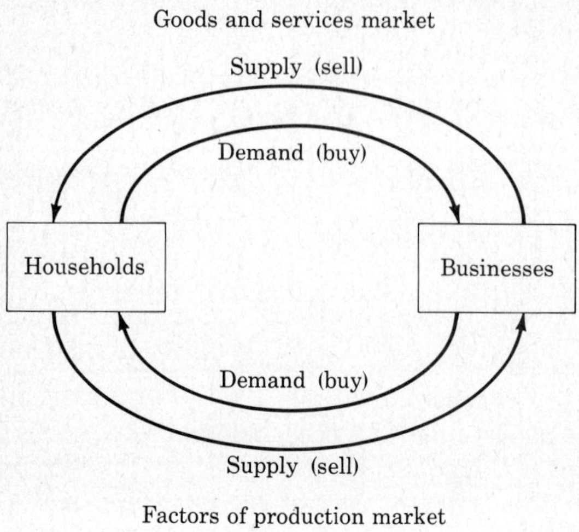

We would be remiss if we did not include the circular flow diagram. It occurs in many textbooks on many economic subjects. Here it is used to represent the notion that all of us take part in different markets as both suppliers and demanders. We offer our resources in the factor of production market and we demand commodities in the goods and services market. We cannot do one without the other. On the other hand, producers demand our resources in the factors market and supply final goods and services. They too cannot do one without the other. Microeconomic analysis studies both of these markets.

side, we participate in the various food and clothing markets, the entertainment market, the markets for travel, information, education, and so on. All of these markets are interlocked. Most personal income (ability to buy) comes from the sales of our labor services in the factor markets. Additionally, we must recognize that the level of price in any one goods market shapes the amount of money a buyer has left to spend in all of the others. Markets are therefore very much a part of our daily lives and, whether we recognize it or not, we are continuously and intimately involved with the forces of supply and demand (Figure 1–2).

Must a market be a place?

No, a market merely requires the convergence of information. Sometimes for convenience the market will have a geographic location, but this is unusual. Fresh fruits and vegetables may be traded at a produce market in each city. Ownership of the major corporations in the form of common stock is traded at a specific place, such as the New York Stock Exchange. However, for the most part, markets are merely flows of information where the buyers and sellers make known their intentions and willingness to trade. For example, although the New York and American stock exchanges house transactions in the securities of major corporations, the common stock of the smaller companies is traded on the over-the-counter market, which is a network of telephone communications between brokers representing buyers and sellers. The market for business services frequently consists of the purchasing agents and salesmen for using and supplying firms. They may deal with one another for years without ever coming face to face. Printing, containers, wire, stationery, and many, many other intermediate industrial products that are used by businesses around the world are traded this way. Once again, the intent of this course is to analyze how participants in these markets behave and how prices are set.

I have read about the law of supply and demand. What is that all about?

A really detailed answer must wait until we have completed the course. Generally, what people have in mind is the notion that the impersonal forces of supply and demand in a market will establish a "proper" price for a product and that any other price cannot be sustained in a freely competitive market. Therefore, attempts to set a price by government edict will either fail because people will break the law and trade at other rates (black market), or else will produce dislocations in supply and demand with resultant excesses or shortages. For example, for 40 years U.S. agricultural policy legislated prices for farm goods that were above the level the forces of supply and demand would have determined. As a result of these higher-than-equilibrium prices, American agriculture produced more food for many years than American consumers wished to eat at the price. During the Phase I price freeze of 1971, the U.S. government set the prices of certain goods below the level the market would have determined. The outcome was inadequate supplies as farmers diverted their resources to products that weren't regulated or shipped their food overseas to be sold more profitably. Reference to the law of supply and demand is sometimes modified to take the form, "You can't beat the law of supply and demand." This means that the market will win out in the end.

If everyone recognizes that you can't beat the law of supply and demand, why does everyone else keep trying?
By everyone else, you must mean the government. Yes, they keep trying. We presently have numerous markets in which prices are determined by governmental order rather than by market forces. To name a few, there are the markets for rail transport, air transport, natural gas, foreign currency, mortgage money, milk, and gasoline. There are other areas where quotas and tariffs shape the flow of goods among countries. Union rules establish wage, hour, and work conditions, and minimum wage laws place floors on the rates for certain types of work. Additionally, of course, there are the many licensing regulations that limit the numbers of people working in such diverse areas as law, medicine, barbering, selling real estate and removing hair, to name but a few. Our progressive tax system then attempts to redistribute purchasing power after it is earned. There is a wide variety of interference in the workings of the free market in our economy.

Is this interference good or bad?
This sounds like a "what ought the government to do" question. Well, pure economic theory cannot tell the government what it ought to do. All it can do is forecast what will happen if the government does do particular things. It cannot evaluate the desirability of these outcomes. Such judgment is quite subjective and reflects personal values. Of course, although economic theory cannot make judgments of good and bad, economists can and do. They do it in newspaper articles, in magazines, in testimony at Congressional hearings, and in lectures to unsuspecting classrooms of students. In this role, however, they are acting as interested, well-informed, and, we hope, intelligent citizens—not as economic theorists. The business of economic theory is means, not ends. It may say that rent control is a bad way to achieve low-cost housing. It cannot say that low-cost housing should be a higher or lower priority goal than intercontinental missiles. Again, that is a matter of personal values. All of these comments lead us to the distinction between *positive* and *normative* economics. Positive economics involves what is. Normative economics involves what ought to be. Another way of expressing this is to say that positive economics is a machine for deducing the outcome of economic actions. It is our engine of analysis. Normative economics, on the other hand, is the passing of judgment on the desirability of what is. It is our purpose for the most part in this course to deal with the tools of positive economics. Normative economics depends on the output of positive economic analysis. Positive economics should be independent of normative judgments.

This brings us full circle, back to our discussion of why you are taking this course. You are probably most interested in dealing with normative economics. Your priorities tell you that prices are too high, unemployment too common, income differences too great, economic mobility too limited. These are normative judgments. How can we alter these conditions? This requires positive analysis. And that is why we study theory.

QUESTIONS

1. *A favorite expression of financial writers on days when stock prices fall is, "Sellers outnumbered buyers in the market today." How can sellers outnumber buyers, when every transaction involves both a buyer and a seller? How might this statement be better worded?*
2. *When the Nixon administration froze prices in 1971, poultry farmers destroyed thousands of baby chicks, claiming that the cost of raising them was greater than the price they would be paid. Can you show this on a supply-demand diagram?*
3. *An editorialist writes: "We have the worst of all possible worlds. Inflation and unemployment ravage the economy simultaneously. Yet the Communist world is able to achieve both stability of prices and full employment. We should emulate them and adopt their policies." What normative judgments are involved here? What positive answers can you give?*
4. *Whenever someone asks me, "What do you think we should do to correct the economic situation," I answer by asking, "What is it you want to achieve?" Am I simply being evasive, or is that a legitimate reply?*
5. *Efforts at bimetalism (use of both gold and silver as backing for the money supply) usually failed because the two metals did not keep the same relative prices set for them by Congress. Did the Congress have better luck setting the price for the single metal gold? Why is it such a difficult job for government to set prices?*
6. *Critics of governmental policy argue that by keeping the price of natural gas too low, the Federal Power Commission created a natural gas shortage. What is "too low"? Too low for what? How do low prices create a shortage?*

2 Demand analysis: cardinal utility

Utility sounds as if it means usefulness. This is not exactly what we have in mind in economics. Rather, the term refers to the desirability, or want-satisfying characteristics a good or service may possess.

Utility provides a dimension on which to measure the want-satisfying characteristics of a product. A good has length and weight and color by which we may perceive it and compare it with other goods and say that it is longer, or heavier, or bluer. It is also useful to be able to make a statement concerning its desirability. Utility enables us to describe a good or service in terms of its desirability, and it permits us to compare goods and services along this dimension.

How can we compare the utility of goods?

First, it should be noted that utility is subjective and that utility comparisons must be *intra-* rather than *inter*personal. That is, one person may compare the utility of different goods as far as he, himself, is concerned. The individual sets the standards and has his own intuitive feelings of the relative worth of different goods. However, a person can never really *know* the degree of intensity of feeling of utility the same good possesses for someone else. To suggest a simple example, if I say that apples are more desirable to me than oranges, I am making an *intra*personal comparison of utility. This is a reasonable statement. However, if I attempt to say that apples are more desirable to me than they are to you, I am making an *inter*personal comparison of utility. There really is no psychological basis for making the latter statement.

Isn't it obvious that you cannot make interpersonal comparisons of utility? Why talk about it?

Although it is seemingly perfectly obvious, we shall find that many economic policies have been developed on the premise that you can make such comparisons. For example, suppose we agree that one goal of government is to increase the total level of satisfactions (utility) of the community. Will taking away an apple from me and giving it to you raise or lower total utility? Obviously we cannot tell unless interpersonal comparisons of utility are possible. We agree that they are not, but nevertheless, policy designed to encourage income redistribution effectively takes apples (or the ability to buy them) from one person and gives them to another. Utility may seem like a trivial concept, but it underlies much social engineering in our society. Unless government is to be inert in the areas of social welfare, it must act as if interpersonal comparisons are possible even though everyone recognizes that they are not. In short, policy making requires *normative* judgments.

Granting that interpersonal comparisons are not proper, what kind of intrapersonal comparisons can be made?

A basic distinction is made between *ordinal* and *cardinal* utility measurements. Early in mathematics we encounter the idea of the ordinal and cardinal numbers. The ordinal numbers are the rank-order numbers such as first, second, third, and so on. The corresponding cardinal numbers are the integers themselves: one, two, three. Ordinal utility, therefore, involves ranking different goods as more or less desirable; using ordinal ranking we can take an assortment of goods and order them as first, second, third, and so on, in terms of desirability. However, we make no statement about the *size* of the differences in desirability. Ordinal utility does not attempt to measure the degree of preference, or to determine whether the difference between the first and second is greater than that between the fifth and sixth, or for that matter, between the second and the sixth. Ordinal utility is strictly a ranking based on one's personal preferences.

What is cardinal utility like?

As already indicated, cardinal numbers are the actual integers themselves: one, two, three, and so on. A cardinal utility scale allows one to measure the amount of utility one receives from a good. Thus, at the very least, a cardinal utility scale allows more than merely *ranking* items in terms of order of desirability; it permits *measurement* of differences in utility between different items. Not only can we say that one item is more desirable than another—we can also say how much more desirable. If we have a cardinal utility measure, we can say that the difference in desirability between the first and second items is greater than the difference between the fifth and sixth items, merely by subtracting the utilities associated, one from the other. These utility scales are therefore subject to addition and subtraction.

Are cardinal utility scales also subject to multiplication and division?
Here we get into the nature of scales and measurability. Whether or not we can say that something is twice as desirable as something else just because its cardinal utility number is twice as big depends on whether there is an absolute or arbitrary zero point. If zero refers to absolute neutrality—complete indifference as to whether you get a thing or not—then the cardinal utility scale is what is referred to as a *ratio scale* and is subject to multiplication. We can make statements such as, "This item is *twice* as desirable as that one." If there is no absolute zero, we merely have an *interval scale* subject to addition and subtraction.

Can you give examples of interval and ratio scales?
The measurement of temperature gives us a good example. Centigrade and Fahrenheit are two commonly used scales. The formula for translating centigrade measurements into Fahrenheit measurements is

$$F = \frac{9}{5}C + 32$$

Applying this conversion formula we see that when the centigrade temperature goes from 10 to 20°, the Fahrenheit temperature goes only from 50 to 68°. Now the question is, Is it twice as hot when the temperature is 20°C as when it was 10°C? Apparently not, because this very same physical change is also described by saying that the temperature went from 50 to 68°. We can only make a ratio statement such as "twice as hot" if we use the Kelvin scale, which starts from an "absolute zero" that is *physically* determined as no heat. Then 10 to 20° means twice as hot. Measures of length meet this requirement of having an absolute zero as a point of departure. Two feet are twice as long as one foot, because zero means just that. Similarly with utility: If we had an absolute zero and an appropriate scale, we could speak of a cardinal utility ratio scale.

Is cardinal utility a usable concept?
Most current thinking is that we have neither an absolute zero nor an accurate, reliable scale for quantitatively measuring utility. It is really

FIGURE 2–1. Ordinal Utility Functions

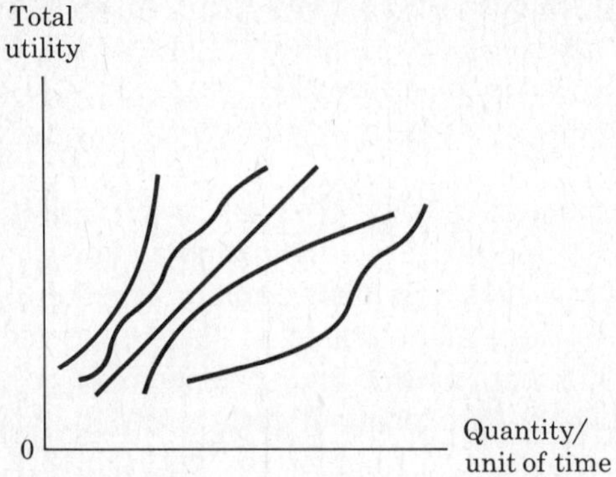

Utility functions always show total utility as an increasing function of quantity. Any upward-sloping graph has this characteristic, because it can be read to show higher utility associated with higher quantities.

a question in psychology, not economics. Can the human animal accurately and consistently measure levels of utility to the point of being able to quantify the first differences for all manner of choices confronting him? Can he say that three trips to the movies gave him 75 utils of satisfaction and a new pair of gloves gives him 43 utils and therefore the difference is 32 utils, about the same difference as he gets between an automobile that gives him 30,293 utils and a trip to Europe that gives him 30,261? From what we know about people, we tend to think that they cannot make these distinctions. They can, however, perhaps rank the four in terms of preference, thereby giving an ordinal utility judgment.

Is cardinal utility therefore a worthless concept?

No, cardinal utility occupies the curious status of being an unrealistic but nevertheless useful construct for purposes of economic theorizing. If you will pardon the pun, it is a highly utilitarian concept and hence we use it, even if it is not exactly realistic. The value of the assumptions underlying a theory should be judged by the adequacy of the result achieved by using them, rather than by their closeness to reality. Cardinal utility gets high marks by this standard.

Suggest a use for cardinal utility.

Consider a trip to the supermarket. We accept and reject different products on the basis of the dollar price asked for them. Or, at an auction we may make a bid of $10 for an item but drop out when someone else offers $11. Now, our dollar offers are in terms of cardinal numbers. We show our valuation of different things by the different amounts of money we would spend for them. What is more, we can say that steak at $3 a pound costs three times as much as hamburger at $1 a pound, as well as noting that this is a difference of $2. Thus, we employ a ratio scale for our valuation of different commodities. In fact, we behave very much as if we could make cardinal utility judgments when we are in the market. The assumption of cardinal utility enables us to develop the demand curve that is basic in economic analysis. But before discussing the demand curve, we must introduce the utility function.

What is a utility function?

A utility function is a relationship between the level of utility enjoyed and the various quantities of goods and services that produce the utility. The *ordinal* utility function ranks commodities, indicating which produce more utility and which produce less. Ordinal utility functions all share the simple characteristic of showing utility as an increasing function of quantity—that is, the more units of a commodity one has, the greater total utility that commodity gives. An old comedy routine contained the line, "I been rich and I been poor, and rich is better." The ordinal utility function manifests this sentiment. Merely specifying that a function shows utility increasing with quantity is not much of a restriction. Any relationship associating greater quantities with higher levels of utility satisfies the major requirement of an ordinal utility function (Figure 2–1).

How does the cardinal utility function differ from the ordinal utility function?

An ordinal utility relationship can be shown by any increasing function. We do not care which we use, as long as it slopes up. A cardinal utility relationship, however, requires that we specify a particular function. It must show a very definite number of utils associated with each quantity of the good. The ordinal utility function is stated generally as $U = f(x)$. This reads: Utility is a function of, or depends on, the quantity of x consumed per unit of time. The cardinal utility function must tell us *which* f or function it is (Figure 2–2).

FIGURE 2–2. Cardinal Utility Functions

Q	0	1	2	3	4	5	6	7	8	9
U	0	76	144	204	256	300	336	364	384	396

Cardinal utility functions are specific relationships showing how total utility varies with changes in quantity. For example consider:

$$U = 80Q - 4Q^2$$

where U is utility and Q is the quantity of commodity x. By substituting different quantities (Q) into the function, we compute the utility level associated with each.

FIGURE 2–3. Marginal Utility

$$300 - 256 = 44$$

Q	*U*	*MU*
0	0	—
1	76	76
2	144	68
3	204	60
4	256	52
5	300	44
6	336	36
7	364	28
8	384	20
9	396	12
10	400	4

Marginal utility (MU) is the increment occurring in total utility as units are added to the quantity one at a time. We can compute marginal utility from a total utility schedule by subtracting successive utility values. For example, the marginal utility of the fifth unit is equal to the total utility of 5 units (300) minus the total utility of 4 units (256).

What is meant by marginal utility?

The word *marginal* in economic theory is synonymous with words such as *incremental* or *additional*. Marginal is a better term because it works for decrements as well as increments and should be interpreted as involving the consequences of having either one more unit or one less.

In the case of utility, the marginal utility refers to the change in total satisfaction produced by either adding one more unit to the quantity on hand or else taking away one of the units on hand.

Why do we frequently refer to "diminishing" marginal utility?
We stated above that utility is an increasing function of quantity. There is a second condition that also applies to utility functions. The *rate* at which utility increases is presumed to decrease after some point. Although total utility rises with each increase in quantity, the extent of the increase in satisfaction gets smaller and smaller as more of the commodity comes to be on hand. Thus marginal (or incremental) utility is a *decreasing* function of quantity (Figure 2–3).

What is the basis of the assumption of diminishing marginal utility?
The assumption is largely based on armchair psychology. It just stands to reason that for a normal good our appreciation of one-unit changes in quantity will lessen as the total quantity increases. Think of the utility of money. We would rather have more than less, so obviously the total utility function of money is increasing. However, the question is, if we have only $50 and are promised another $10, is the prospect more exciting than if we have $1000 and are promised another $10? Armchair psychology says that the additional money would mean more in the first instance than in the second. Incidentally, notice that for the concept of diminishing marginal utility to make sense, we must assume at least an interval scale of total utility measurement. Marginal utility involves first differences.

How does the marginal utility function relate to the total utility function?
Let us begin by drawing the graph of the total utility function. First we assume that it is an increasing function of quantity. This means that as quantity rises, so too does total utility. Plotting quantity on the horizontal (x) axis and total utility on the vertical (y) axis, we know that the function slopes upward to the right. Second, we have asserted that at quantities farther to the right, there is a decrease in the rate at which total utility increases. Thus, although the total utility curve rises to the right, it does so at a decreasing rate. Hence it has a shape that is convex from above. Because marginal utility refers to the change in total utility relative to a one-unit change in quantity, we find that the vertical change in the curve's coordinates per one-unit horizontal change is the measure of marginal utility. This ratio also describes the *slope* of the total utility curve at different points (Figure 2–4).

FIGURE 2–4. Graph of Total Utility Function

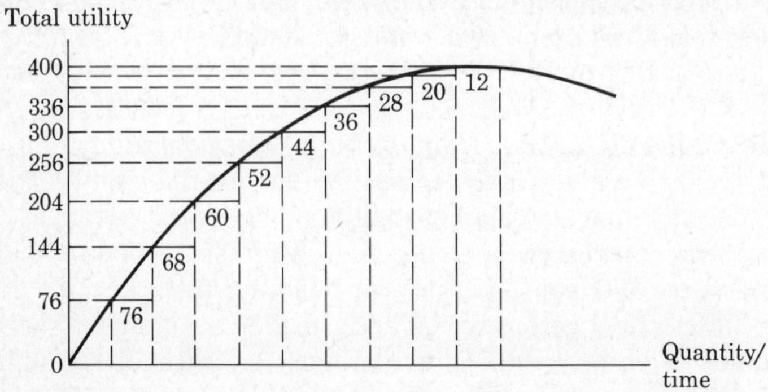

Plotting the data from Figures 2–2 and 2–3, we get a total utility curve that is increasing, but at a decreasing rate. Although it rises with each unit added, the extent to which it rises gets successively smaller. This is the meaning of diminishing marginal utility and gives the curve its characteristically humped (convex) appearance. Note that this function will reach a maximum at 10 units and then decline. This is interpreted as *satiation*, and has a zero marginal utility. Beyond this, marginal utility is negative as total utility falls due to storage or disposal problems, or interference with other activities. For most economic purposes we are not interested in this range of the curve.

FIGURE 2–5. Marginal Utility Is the Slope of the Total Utility Curve

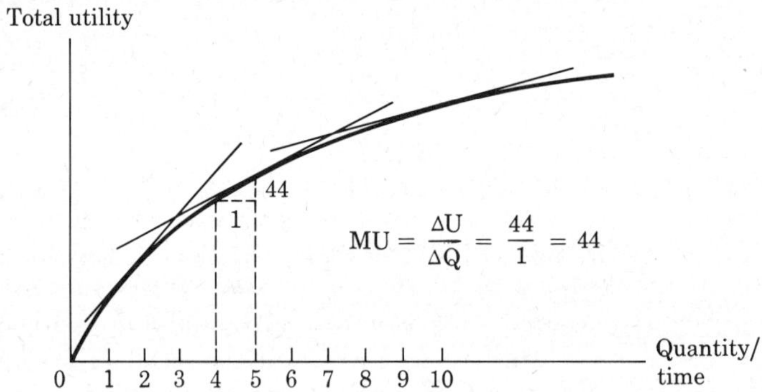

Because slope is defined as the ratio of the rise to the run or the change in the dependent variable per unit change in the independent variable, we find that slope is measured by $\Delta U/\Delta Q$.

A problem of interpretation may come up if ΔQ is larger than one unit. Then marginal utility measures the average slope between the two points on the curve. Note that the slopes get flatter at larger quantities. This is consistent with diminishing marginal utility.

Then is the slope of the utility curve equal to the marginal utility?
Yes. This is just one instance of a general relationship that we shall find holds true throughout our analysis. The slope of the total something is equal to the marginal something. That is, the slope of total utility equals marginal utility; the slope of total product equals marginal product; the slope of total cost equals marginal cost; and the slope of total revenue equals marginal revenue (Figure 2–5).

How can you graph the marginal utility curve?
One way is to measure the slope of the total utility curve at each quantity. Then plot this value up from the origin on a separate pair of axes. The scale of the marginal utility curve will be bigger than that of the total utility curve because, in the case of marginal utility, we are interested only in *per unit* changes in total utility. Thus, where the total utility scale must accommodate values of 396 and 400, the marginal utility implied would be only 4, or the difference between 400 and 396. The scale must be big enough to permit a value as small as 4 to be shown clearly. A mechanical approach is to plot the marginal utility curve directly under the total utility curve, projecting the quantities down and measuring the changes in total utility associated with those quantities (Figure 2–6).

Why is marginal utility so important?
Our entire topic is sometimes called the *marginal analysis*. The idea of *marginal* is critical, because economic decisions are made by comparing marginal units. When we decide how many units of a particular commodity to buy, we should be aware that we are deciding at the same time *not* to buy any more or any less—not even one unit more or less. Decision making in the market place is a mental trial-and-error process in which we ask ourselves: What happens to our satisfactions if we buy one unit more; what happens if we buy one unit less? Of course, the one more and one less are the marginal units. Thus our intuitive procedure is to measure the value of the marginal unit to us and determine whether or not it is worth the cost or price to use it. In the case of utility

FIGURE 2–6. Plotting the Marginal Utility Function

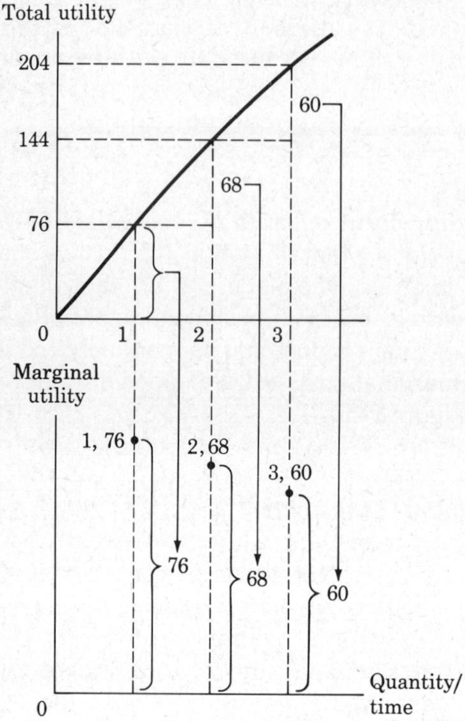

Change in total utility is plotted on separate axes. Measurement, however, is up from zero value (x axis). Note that the scale used to measure utility is bigger in the marginal utility diagram than on the total utility diagram.

FIGURE 2–7. Use of Marginal Utility for Budget Allocation

Q_X	TU_X	MU_X	Q_Y	TU_Y	MU_Y
0	0	—	0	0	—
1	76	76	1	50	50
2	144	68	2	96	46
3	204	60	3	138	42
4	256	52	4	176	38
5	300	44	5	210	34
6	336	36	6	240	30
7	364	28	7	266	26
8	384	20	8	288	22

In Figure 2–3 we assumed a utility schedule for product X. Assume now that there is also a total utility schedule for product Y as shown here. The problem is to allocate funds between X and Y so as to maximize total utility (TU on the schedule). If both X and Y cost $1 per unit, we compare the first unit of X and Y and see that X has higher marginal utility (76 vs. 50); Spend the first dollar on X. Now we examine the second unit of X ($MU = 68$) and the first unit of Y ($MU = 50$). We should buy the second unit of X. Now examine the third X ($MU = 60$) and the first Y ($MU = 50$). Buy the third X. Now examine the fourth X ($MU = 52$) vs. the first Y ($MU = 50$). Again we buy X, because it adds more to total utility. When comparing the fifth unit of X to the first unit of Y, we find that the fifth X will add 44 utils and the first Y will add 50 utils. We should therefore spend the fifth dollar on Y. Now compare the fifth unit of X with the second unit of Y (44 vs. 46). We buy the second Y and compare the fifth X against the third Y, and so on until our money is used up.

analysis, we are constrained by having only a limited amount of purchasing power. Every decision to purchase one unit of commodity X is also a decision to forego consumption of some other, alternative good. Consider units of commodity X. When deciding whether or not to buy one unit, we ask ourselves if the utility gained from it is greater than that offered by alternative products we might also buy for the same amount of money. If the utility of X is greater, we know that we wish to buy at least one unit of X. Then we ask the same question with regard to a second unit of X. The second unit is now the marginal unit. Now we are asking if the utility of the marginal unit of X is more or less than the alternatives. If more, we decide to purchase at least 2 units and examine the third, which now becomes the marginal unit (Figure 2–7).

How long do we continue to examine marginal units of X?

We continue this until the utility of the marginal unit of X falls below the utility of an alternative purchase that might be made for the same outlay. When this happens, we know how many units of X will be demanded. If 4 units of X pass the test but the fifth unit, when it becomes the marginal unit, turns out to have less utility than an alternative, we buy only 4 units of X.

FIGURE 2–8. Diagrammatic Representation of Marginal Utility Decision Making

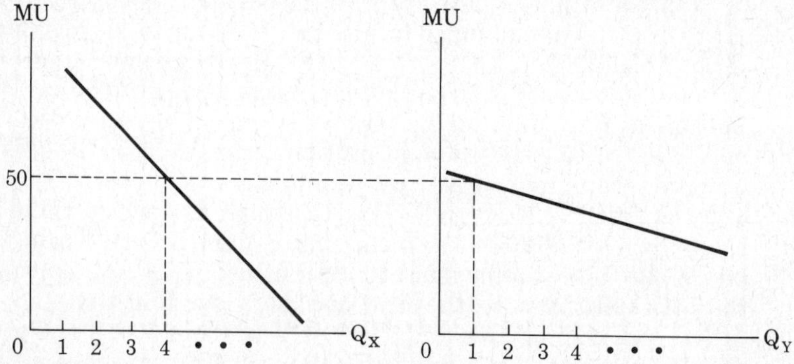

From the marginal utility schedules in Figure 2–7, we find that the marginal utility of the first 4 units of *X* is higher than that of any *Y*. If they cost the same, we shall buy 4 units of *X* before we buy 1 unit of *Y*.

How do we know that eventually some alternative will have greater marginal utility than X?
We know this because of the assumption of diminishing marginal utility. Remember that as we consider successively larger quantities of *X*, the total utility to be gained from *X* is increasing but at a decreasing rate. Marginal utility is falling. Since it falls continuously, sooner or later it will fall below the level of marginal utility available from an alternative (Figure 2–8).

What would happen if marginal utility did not diminish?
It should be obvious. If everything else remained the same and marginal utility from commodity *X* either remained the same or increased, you would find that you had no reason to stop buying incremental units of *X*. You would become an *X* freak, spending everything on commodity *X*. Actually, because people do not behave in this manner, we feel some justification in the assumption of diminishing marginal utility. Although we may not be able to measure utility directly, we do observe behavior that is consistent with the assumption of diminishing marginal utility and inconsistent with the implications of alternative assumptions.

How does one distribute one's money among different commodities?
We shall specify a definite and formal relationship shortly. Before getting to that, let us consider the logical conclusion of the process of comparing marginal units of *X* against other commodities. If after 4 units of *X* we find that the fifth unit has lower utility than the first unit of *Y* purchaseable for the same price, we shall use our next outlay of money to purchase 1 unit of *Y*. After doing this, the comparison is between the fifth unit of *X*, the second unit of *Y*, and the first dollar spent on anything else. We purchase whichever has the higher utility per dollar of expenditure and then go on to make subsequent comparisons until the money we have is exhausted. We shall probably end up with a distribution of different quantities of various commodities. They will have in common the characteristic that the marginal utility per dollar spent on any one will be no lower than the marginal utility per dollar spent on any other.

Does money have marginal utility too?
Money is assumed to have utility, both total and marginal. Its marginal utility is important because of the possibility that while considering quantities of various commodities, we may decide that none of them offers as much satisfaction as holding the money itself. That is, the marginal utility of a dollar may be higher than the marginal utility of a dollar's worth of any available commodity. In that case, we keep the money. It gives us a rationale for saving.

Does money also have diminishing marginal utility?
As far as individual total utility schedules for money are concerned, we assume that there is diminishing marginal utility. That is, everything else being equal, if I have \$100 and am given another dollar, it will mean more to me than if I have \$1000 and am given the extra dollar. Total utility is higher at \$1000 than at \$100, but not proportionately so. Note that this assumes that all other things are equal, including my personal tastes. If, by having more money, my appetite for it is increased, there is no guarantee that the marginal utility of the 1001st unit would be less than the 101st. But the same can be said of all commodities. If, by having my first glass of wine, I realize what I have missed all these years, my marginal utility for the second glass will be higher than for the first, which I may have taken with some trepidation and hesitancy. If so, my total utility curve is said to have *shifted*, and we are not talking about a movement along the curve but rather about two different points on two different curves. We shall return to the notion of *ceteris paribus*, "all other things being equal."

FIGURE 2–9. Demand Curve

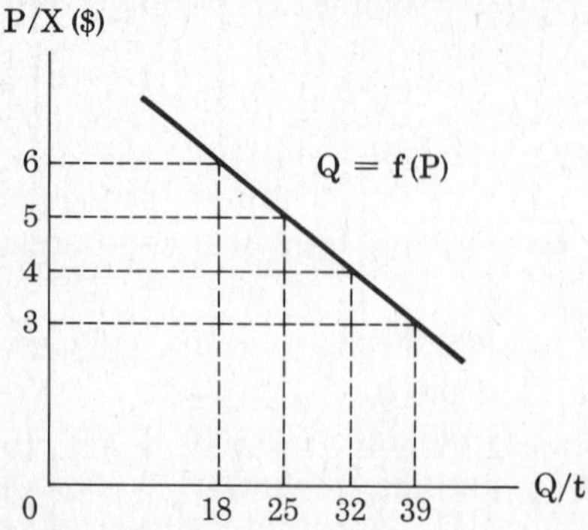

The demand curve shows the quantities per unit of time that would be taken by the market under examination if each of the alternative prices were to be asked. Important points to note are that (1) price is an average rate asked for *each* one of the units; (2) quantity is a flow of units per unit of time; (3) demand analysis assumes that the only variable is price. All other things remain constant while we consider alternative prices. Prices do not even change over time. They are alternatives at a moment in time.

Is it generally true, then, that the marginal utility of money for high-income people is less than for low-income people?

This statement is frequently accepted as true, but it is not strictly proper within the framework of our argument. Again, it may turn out to be useful for prediction, and therefore we can use it effectively. However, we should note that when we assume that for one individual the marginal utility of money diminishes with higher income, we are making an *intra*personal comparison. To say that the marginal utility of money is less for a rich man than for a poor man requires *inter*personal comparisons of utility. We discussed this and ruled it improper earlier.

What is a demand curve?

A *demand schedule* is a functional relationship showing the quantity of a good that would be bought per unit of time (i.e., per week, per month, per year) at different alternative prices asked in the market. It shows an "if . . . then" situation. If the price were $5, then 25 units would be bought; if the price were $4, then 32 units would be bought; and so on over the entire range of possible prices. That is not to say that the equilibrium price in the market will ever be $4 or $5. However, if it were, this would be the quantity taken.

The *demand curve* is the graph of this relationship. The *y* axis shows price and the *x* axis shows units of quantity. The assumption is that the prices are alternative possible prices at a moment in time, rather than a sequence of prices over time. We state this because of the likelihood that when prices change over time, new influences related to the change itself are created, and these affect the quantities taken. If price rose from $4 to $5 per unit, the consumer would react to the fact of change as well as to the level of price. If price fell from $5 to $4, there would be a different reaction. The result would be different quantities associated with the prices $4 and $5 depending on whether prices had just risen or fallen. We could not think in terms of *a* price schedule, because we would not be holding all other things constant.

Our demand schedule solves this by working with alternative prices at a moment in time (all other things being equal). When we refer to changes occurring with a price rise or price fall, we are being careless with our language. We really mean differences in quantity associated with a higher or lower price (Figure 2–9).

How does the marginal utility of money enter into a development of demand schedules and curves?

Let us assume that we know the marginal utility of money for our subject. As with other commodities, this marginal utility varies from person to person, depending on income, personality, tastes, and reference groups, to name a few considerations. Because cardinal utility analysis assumes that there is a quantitative scale of utility that can be determined for every good, there is nothing to stop us from assuming that we can come up with a utility level for money as well. Arbitrarily assume the marginal utility of money for our subject under present circumstances is 4 utils. A 4-util marginal utility of money means that whenever a person gives away a dollar he gives away 4 utils of satisfaction. If a product such as a shirt costs $10, it costs 40 utils.

Is the marginal utility of money constant?

If we treat money as just another commodity subject to diminishing marginal utility, we should recognize that after spending $10 for an item and giving up 40 utils, we have one more of the item on hand and ten fewer dollars. Theoretically, the marginal utility of the item will fall and the marginal utility of money will rise. Therefore, the marginal

FIGURE 2–10. Development of a Demand Schedule from a Marginal Utility Schedule

Q	*MU*	*Price*
1	76	19
2	68	17
3	60	15
4	52	13
5	44	11
6	36	9
7	28	7
8	20	5
9	12	3
10	4	1

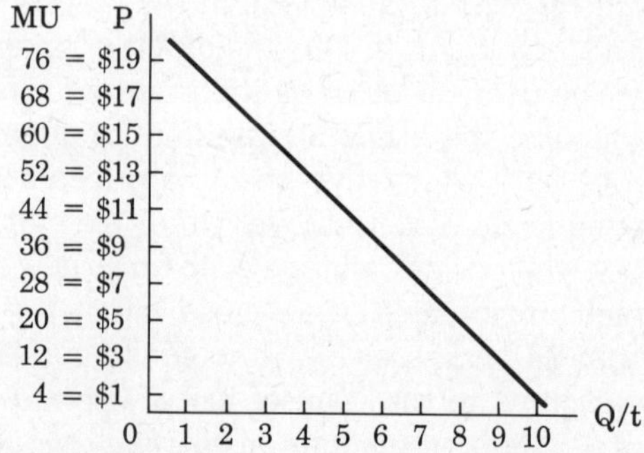

We first assume a marginal utility for money. Assume that $1 = 4 utils. We now compute the maximum price to be paid at each quantity by dividing the marginal utility of *X* by the marginal utility of money. For example, if the marginal utility of the fifth unit is 44 utils and if each dollar is worth 4 utils to me, I will not give up more than $11 for the fifth unit. However, if I pay $11 for the fifth unit, this means that the first four also cost me $11 each. Price is an average rate. Hence the price associated with 5 units is $11 on the demand curve.

utility of money should vary with each purchase, and indeed be different for each asking price, because the stock of money remaining on hand after purchase will vary. However, practitioners of cardinal utility analysis have followed Alfred Marshall's lead. He rationalized that we spend our money on so many things, and that each purchase involves such a small fraction of our total income, that marginal utility changes in money resulting from transactions are tiny enough to be ignored. Hence we treat the marginal utility of money as a constant, although in our hearts we know it should not be. However, the assumption of constant marginal utility of money makes development of the demand curve much simpler, and the loss in precision is slight.

Get back to the example of the $10 shirt

Okay. The first question is, If the shirt is priced at $10, will our subject buy it? And if he does, will he buy more than one? Well, it depends on whether or not he gets 40 utils of satisfaction from the shirt. If he does, would he get that much from a second, a third, and so on? He will buy as many shirts as he can before the marginal utility drops below 40 utils. Thus, if a shirt is priced at $10 each, we can read down our subject's marginal utility schedule for shirts until we come to the quantity that is associated with at least 40 utils. This quantity is the amount taken at price $10. Next consider alternative prices. At $5 we read down to see the number of shirts that gives a marginal utility of at least 20 utils (the number of utils given up when he gives up $5). This will be a greater quantity because of the principle of diminishing marginal utility. It takes a larger quantity to produce a lower marginal utility. Finally, we observe that larger quantities are always associated with lower prices. This relationship enjoys the somewhat grandiose title of the *law of demand* (Figure 2–10).

What is the law of demand?

The law of demand is the relationship reflected in the statement that "All other things being equal, the quantity demanded will vary inversely with the price asked." Conventionally, demand curves are drawn with price per unit on the *y* axis and quantity per unit of time on the *x* axis. Plotting a demand curve conforming to the law of demand will always result in a downward-sloping curve as we go from left to right.

Can you organize all this into a formal rule for allocating income among different commodities?

Remember that the consumer is trying to maximize total utility. Let us use the Greek letter lambda (λ) to refer to the marginal utility of money. If the price of X is P_X, the amount of utility given up for purchase of one unit of X is

$$\lambda \times P_X$$

That is, we give up P_X dollars, each of which is worth λ utils. In return for the money given up for each unit, we get the marginal utility of X. Thus, for the quantity of X bought, the following equation holds:

$$P_X \times \lambda = MU_X$$

The utility gained equals the utility given up at the margin. To buy one more unit of X would mean that MU_X would be lower (because of diminishing returns) and therefore we would be giving up more for the marginal unit of X than we gained. If this equation holds for commodity X, it also holds for commodities Y, Z, and indeed all commodities. Naturally, they have differing prices. Also they have different marginal utility schedules because the satisfactions they provide differ. The prin-

FIGURE 2–11. An Example of Spending Decisions

Suppose that you have \$27 to spend and are trying to decide how much of each of two products to buy. Also, you may wish to keep some of the money as savings. Assume the prices of the two products are

$P_A = \$4 \qquad P_B = \$2$

Assume further that the marginal utility schedules of products *A* and *B* are as follows, and the marginal utility of money equals 3 utils.

Quantity	MU_A	MU_B	*MU savings*
0	—	—	—
1	28	16	3
2	26	12	3
3	16	9	3
4	12	6	3
5	10	4	3
6	8	2	3

First we must compute the schedules showing marginal utility per dollar spent on each product, that is, *MU/P*. Then we examine the alternatives one unit at a time and assign our money in sequence to the highest return first, next highest return, and so on until the \$27 is exhausted.

Quantity	MU_A/P_A	MU_B/P_B	*MU Savings/1*
0	—	—	—
1	7	8	3
2	6½	6	3
3	4	4½	3
4	3	3	3
5	2½	2	3
6	2	1	3

The order of allocation will be

	B	*A*	*A*	*B*	*B*	*A*	*A*	*B*	*S*	*S*	*S*
MU/P	8	7	6½	6	4½	4	3	3	3	3	3

4 *A*'s, 4 *B*'s and \$3 of savings will all give 3 utils per dollar at the margin and exhaust the \$27.

ciple remains, however, that the utility given up at the margin should equal the utility gained at the margin, and therefore:

$P_Y \times \lambda = MU_Y$

$P_Z \times \lambda = MU_Z$, and so on

Notice that for each commodity this relationship of price times marginal utility of money equaling marginal utility of the product holds. If we divide both sides of each equation by the P term, we find that the following also holds:

$$\lambda = \frac{MU_X}{P_X}$$

$$\lambda = \frac{MU_Y}{P_Y}$$

$$\lambda = \frac{MU_Z}{P_Z}$$

The quantity of each product that is bought is that at which the marginal utility received per dollar spent on it is equal to the marginal utility of a dollar per se. Dollars are exchanged for products as long as it is advantageous to do so. Purchase stops when the utility of a dollar's worth of the product comes to be worth less than the utility of a dollar's worth of money. Notice that this idea applies for each good and service. Algebraically, if different values are equal to a common term, they are equal to each other. If

$$\frac{MU_X}{P_X} = \lambda$$

$$\frac{MU_Y}{P_Y} = \lambda$$

$$\frac{MU_Z}{P_Z} = \lambda$$

then

$$\frac{MU_X}{P_X} = \frac{MU_Y}{P_Y} = \frac{MU_Z}{P_Z} = \lambda$$

This last expression is a most important one. It says that resources will be allocated in such a manner as to make the marginal utility of a dollar's worth of any one product equal to the marginal utility of a dollar's worth of each of the other things bought. If this is achieved, the total utility to be gained from the limited funds available will be maximized. There are various ways to prove this, but perhaps the most convincing is to demonstrate it with numbers as is done in Figure 2–11. The individual maximizes his utility function, subject to the constraint of limited income, when $MU/P = MU/P = \cdots = \lambda$.

Can this MU/P relationship be used to develop to demand curve from the marginal utility schedule?

Yes it can. When we discussed the development of the demand schedule from the utility schedule, we logically decided that the dollar price you pay for an item should not be worth more in utility than the utility value you receive in return from it at the margin. Thus, if you know the marginal utility value of the fourth unit of X to be 52 utils and that the marginal utility of a dollar is 4 utils, it is apparent that you would not pay more than $13 for it. If you pay more, you give up more in utility than is gained in return. Computationally, this involves dividing the marginal utility of X by the marginal utility of money to get the price of X ($52 \div 4 = 13$). If we now think of this problem as merely another instance of allocating our income among alternatives, and the only alternatives are product X or money, we can set up the relationship equating the MU/P values, and solve for P_X.

$$\frac{MU_X}{P_X} = \frac{MU_\$}{P_\$}$$

What is meant by $P_\$$ in that expression? What is the price of money?

Here we are into a convention used in economic analysis. The price of the medium of exchange is assumed to be 1. Or, more simply, how much will you pay for 1 unit of money? The answer: 1 unit of money. The price of a dollar is a dollar. Solving the expression for P_X gives

$$\frac{MU_X}{P_X} = \frac{MU_\$}{1}$$

$$MU_X = P_X \times MU_\$$$

$$\frac{MU_X}{MU_\$} = P_X$$

Please give an example of that.

In the problem considered in Figure 2–10 we worked with the assumption that the marginal utility of the fourth unit was 52 utils. The marginal utility of money was 4 utils. The relationship sets up as follows:

$$\frac{MU_X}{P_X} = \frac{MU_\$}{P_\$}$$

$$\frac{52}{P_X} = \frac{4}{1}$$

$$P_X = 13$$

Thus the price the subject is willing to pay for the fourth unit is $13. Now we have a rather mechanical procedure for developing the demand curve from the marginal utility schedule.

What is meant by consumer surplus?

We have just concluded that the maximum price one will willingly pay for an item equates the utility of the dollars paid for the marginal unit of X with the utility gained from the marginal unit of X. Note that this is not the same as equating the utility of the *total* revenue paid out with the utility gained from the *total* number of units of X bought. This is a tricky point. Let us review the problem of finding the price of the fourth unit of commodity X in Figure 2–10. We calculated that if the fourth unit of X has a utility of 52 and if a dollar has a utility of 4, we shall be willing to pay no more than $13 for this fourth unit of X. It is interesting to note, however, that if we buy 4 units of X we must pay $13 for *each* of the 4 units. We therefore pay a total of $52 ($P \times Q$) for the 4 units, and if each dollar has a utility of 4 utils, we are giving up a total of 4×52 utils or 208 utils for the 4 units of X. Now, what total utility do we get in return? We observed in Figure 2–7 (the source of the data for Figure 2–10) that the total utility of 4 units is 256 utils. Although the fourth unit has a marginal utility of 52, the marginal utility of the third unit is 60, of the second unit is 68, and of the first unit is 76. The total of the marginal utilities equals the total utility, or this same 256 utils. We find, therefore, that we give up 208 utils but we get a return of 256 utils. The difference, or 48 utils in this case, is called *consumer surplus*. Obviously, the lower the asking price for a commodity, the more a consumer will buy and the greater will be the consumer surplus (Figure 2–12).

What is an aggregate demand curve?

Our discussion so far has dealt with a person's marginal and total utility schedules and from these we derived his demand schedule showing the amount of product he is willing to take at different prices. However, for most purposes we are not so much interested in *individual* demand curves as in *market* (aggregate) demand curves. These show the quantities of a product that would be taken by the entire market should various prices prevail. It is through these market demand curves, when compared to market supply curves, that we develop market prices. The

FIGURE 2–12. Consumer Surplus

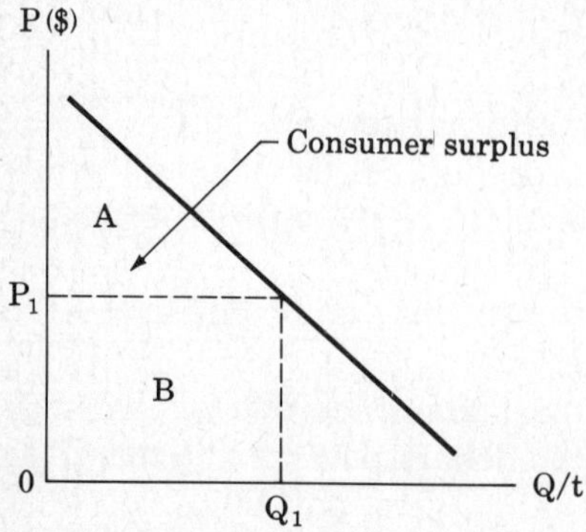

The classic consumer surplus diagram shows total utility gained as the total area under the demand curve out to the quantity bought, represented here by $A + B$. The total revenue surrendered is the rectangle B, leaving an unpaid for but nevertheless enjoyed surplus, area A. The lower the price, the bigger will be area A and the smaller will be area B.

FIGURE 2–13. The Aggregate Demand Function

Price	*A's demand*	*B's demand*	*C's demand*	*Price*	*Aggregate demand*
1	20	100	53	1	173
2	15	80	42	2	137
3	10	60	31	3	101
4	7	40	25	4	72
5	5	20	18	5	43
6	4	10	10	6	24

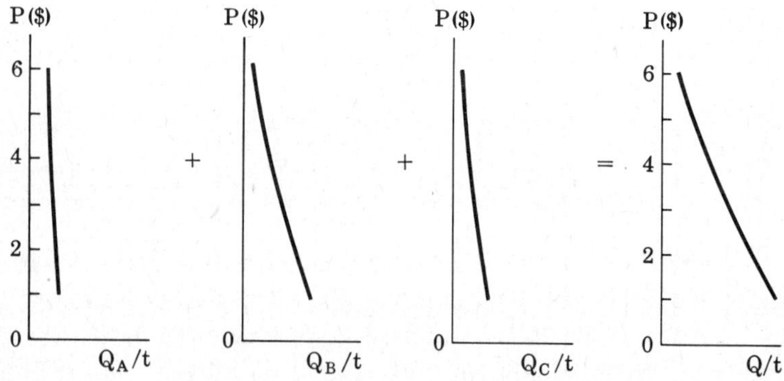

The aggregate demand function shows the total market demand at alternative prices. It is found as the horizontal summation of individual demand functions.

market demand curve is merely a horizontal summation of the individual demand curves. To use a simple example, if there are three people in the market, we add together the quantities each would take at each price and plot these total quantities against the prices. The price axis would still have the same money units, but the quantity axis would have much larger measures. If there are *n* people in the market, they would be of the order of *n* times the quantity each person takes at each price (Figure 2–13).

Does the aggregate demand curve also obey the law of demand?

Yes, the aggregate demand curve, like the individual demand curve, will be downward sloping. It is made up from individual demand curves and shares this downward-sloping characteristic. We should reemphasize that the downward-sloping demand curve assumes *ceteris paribus*, everything else being equal.

What do you mean by everything else being equal?

The theory of demand attempts to analyze how much of a commodity will be sold under different circumstances. So far we have concentrated on an examination of the role played by the price of an item in the determination of its demand. There are certainly factors other than price that will influence purchase of a commodity, and if we are to have a full discussion of demand we must consider their influence. Unless we include these non-price factors, we are apt to get confused regarding the effects of price itself. For instance, the law of demand states that, all other things being equal, the lower the price charged, the higher the quantity demanded. However, when we make empirical investigations, we find that in many markets there is actually a correlation between low prices and low sales volume. Years of relatively low price see relatively low sales volume, and years when price is relatively high see high sales. However, further examination shows that there is a correlation between relatively low prices and low disposable personal income in the overall economy. Sellers reduce their prices during periods of declining purchasing power. The quantity sold is small despite the lower market

FIGURE 2–14. Difference Between a Movement Along a Demand Curve and a Shift in Demand

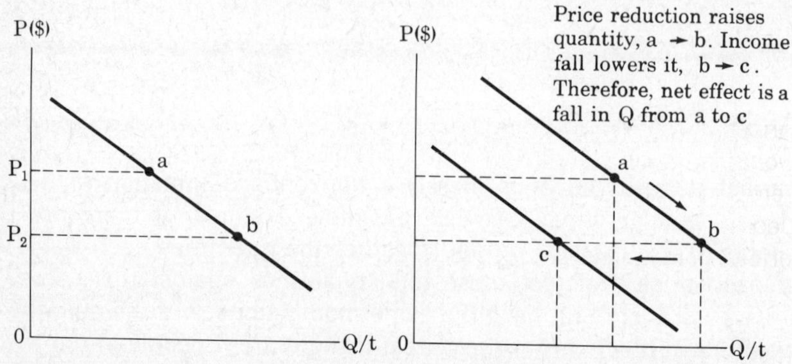

The law of demand says that, all other things being equal, larger quantities will be taken at lower prices. This is shown as a movement along the demand curve from *a* to *b*. However, if all other things are not equal, there will be a simultaneous shift of the curve itself. In the figure, we show a simultaneous fall in price that should raise *quantity* and a reduction in income that will lower *demand.* In this instance, the effect of the income fall is greater than the price decline, and the quantity taken at the new price is lower than that taken at the old, higher price.

FIGURE 2–15. Quantity Demanded as a Function of Income.

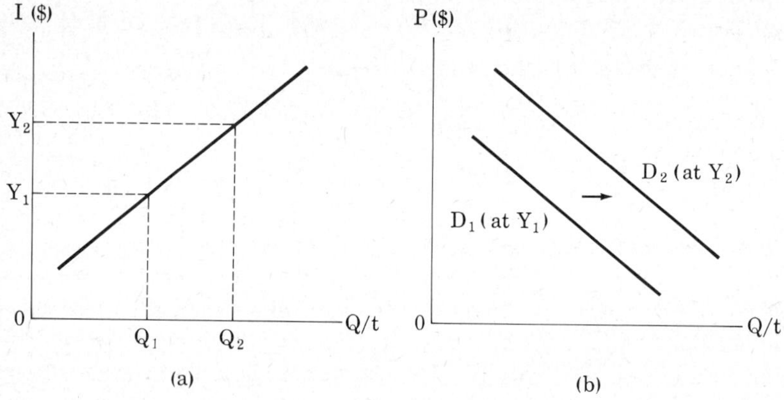

It is possible to use income (I) as the independent variable and quantity as the dependent variable. In this case, for a normal good we get an upward-sloping curve such as in (a) with higher quantities taken at income Y_2 than at income Y_1. These same events, if shown on a demand curve relating price to quantity, would be indicated through a shift of the demand curve.

price, not because of it. Had income held constant, the lower price would have increased the quantity sold. However, the income did not remain the same. It fell, and its effect was greater than that of the price decline. As a *net* result, then, we see lower quantities sold at lower prices (Figure 2–14).

It would appear, then, that income is one of the "all other things" that must be held constant. What are some others?
For purposes of quick classification, we can list the following: (1) income, (2) prices of substitute products, (3) prices of complementary products, (4) tastes. The complete demand function is a multivariate relationship:

$$Q_X = f(P_X, P_S, P_C, I, T)$$

where

Q_X is the quantity taken of X

P_X is the price of X

P_S is the price of substitutes

P_C is the price of complements

I is income

T is tastes

A change in P_X causes a movement along the demand curve. A change in any of the other variables causes a shift of the demand curve.

Please clarify the difference between a shift and a movement along a demand curve.
Remember that the term *demand curve* refers specifically to the relationship between quantity and price. We could also plot graphs showing the relationship of quantity to income or quantity to the prices of substitute or complementary products (Figure 2–15). If we did, we would be able to read the quantity associated with different incomes, or prices of substitute or complementary products, directly from the curve, just as the demand curve permits us to relate quantity to different prices. The point is that on a two-dimensional graph we can directly consider

FIGURE 2–16. Change in the Price of a Substitute Product

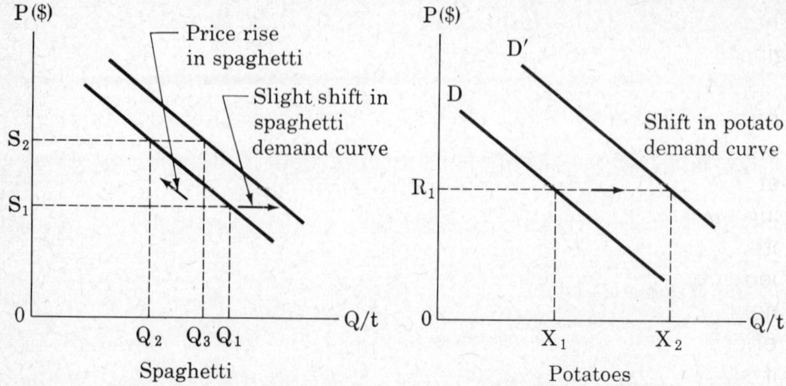

When the price of spaghetti was S_1 and price of potatoes was R_1, equilibrium quantities taken were Q_1 and X_1, respectively. An increase in the price of spaghetti to S_2 reduces the quantity taken of spaghetti. This raises the marginal utility of all starchy foods, including spaghetti and potatoes, and shifts the curves of both to the right. The shift for potatoes is shown as curve D', and the new quantity taken at the old price is X_2. For spaghetti, after the straight price effect there would be a slight increase in quantity taken as the demand curve shifts right due to a rise in marginal utility of starchy foods.

only one independent and one dependent variable at a time. The other independent variables must be held constant. However, if they do vary in our analysis, the effect is to *shift* the curve. To go back to the demand curve, if income rises while all other factors remain the same, the demand curve diagram should show different quantities associated with each price. This is found by reading values off the new, shifted demand curve.

How does a change in income affect the quantity demanded?

Normally we expect that an increase in income will increase the quantity demanded at any given price, and that a fall in income will decrease the quantity demanded at that price. The curve shifts to the right in the case of an increase and to the left in the case of a decrease in income. This occurs because a rise in income lowers the marginal utility of money, and therefore more quantity can be taken before the utility of the marginal unit falls to the level of price times the new, lower marginal utility of money.

There is another possibility. This involves a class of goods called *inferior goods*. We shall discuss the nature of inferior goods at some length when we deal with indifference curve analysis. For the moment, let us note that they are characterized by the fact that the demand curve shifts to the left when income rises. The higher the income (all other things being equal), the lower the quantity demanded. This occurs because a rise in income leads to increased purchases of some other, more desired, substitute product. Hamburger is an example of an inferior good. If income rises, there may be an increase in the purchase of steak. Should the amount of hamburger bought remain unchanged, marginal utility of the generic meat products would be lower due to the increase in the total amount of hamburger and steak. This reduction in marginal utility of meat will reduce hamburger demanded. Even though the marginal utility of money declines from the income rise, the marginal utility of the hamburger falls further. Hence less is bought.

What is the effect of price changes of substitute products?

First, we note that in a general sense all products are substitutes for all others in that they all draw from the same pool of income. If more money is spent on one good, less is left to spend on another. That is a matter of arithmetic. Here, however, we are concerned with relatively close substitutes. We have just seen that hamburger demand falls and steak sales rise because of an increase in income. Another way for steak sales to rise is through a decline in the price of steak. If this occurs and more steak is bought, the marginal utility of all meat products falls. This fall in the marginal utility of meat lowers the quantity of hamburger bought at any given price. Of course, the same reasoning—but the opposite result—holds for price increases of substitutes. Let us move on to consider potatoes and spaghetti as substitutes providing similar satisfactions in the daily menu. If the price of spaghetti rises, less will be bought. The result is that less starchy food is being bought, with a resultant rise in marginal utilities. For potatoes, whose price has not risen, this means that the marginal utility is above that of the money price being paid. The consequence will be an increase in the quantity of potatoes to lower the marginal utility again to the point where

$$\frac{MU_P}{P_P} = \frac{MU_S}{P_S} = \lambda$$

(Figure 2–16).

FIGURE 2–17. *Affect of Breadth of Definition of the Product on the Demand Curve*

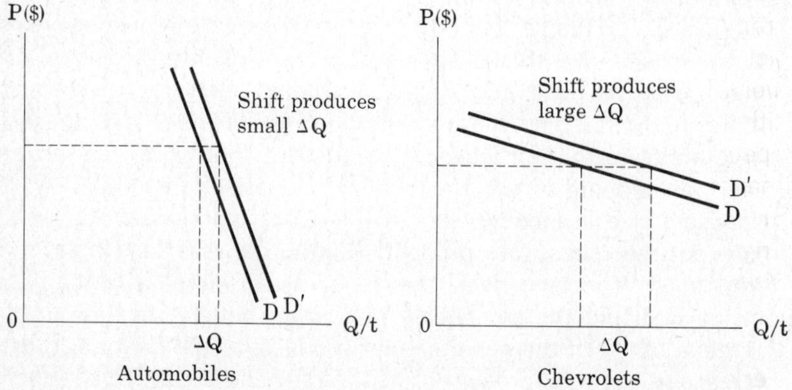

For a broad, generally defined product such as automobiles, the demand curve is quite vertical, and changes in the price of substitute products shifts the curve only slightly. If the product is defined as Chevrolets, the curve is flatter, and changes in the price of substitute products shifts the curve greatly.

What exactly is meant by "close substitutes"?

From a pragmatic point of view, close substitutes are defined as products for which the demands are very responsive to price changes in other products. As the price of one good changes, we judge the degree of substitutability by noting the amount of change occurring in the quantity demanded of another good. If, all other things being equal, there is a perceptible response in demand for product X when the price of product Y changes, we call these two products close substitutes. The term *cross-elasticity of demand* is used in quantitative treatments of substitutability.

How do you deal with different brands of a product? Are these close substitutes or really the same product?

This question brings up something very basic in demand analysis. That is the requirement that, when developing a demand schedule, it is necessary to be very careful to define the product precisely. For instance, in the case of, say, automobiles, we might discuss the demand for all automobiles, or all American-made automobiles, or all General

Motors automobiles, or all Chevrolet automobiles, or all blue and green Impalas with white sidewall tires, air conditioning, and tape decks. The product can be as broad or as narrow as desired and still fit into the framework of demand analysis. However, we must know what the product is. Similarly, we must know how extensive our market is. Is it a world market, a national market, a regional market, or what? The quantities taken will vary with the definition of the market. Also, we must specify a time period. Quantity taken is a rate of withdrawal from the market. Do we mean so many units sold per year, per month, per week, or per day? This seems obvious, but there can be much confusion engendered if we ignore these matters, and much confusion avoided if we recognize them early in the game.

Very interesting, but that still does not answer the question about brands.

Glad you reminded me. Suppose that we define our product as automobiles. What substitute products are available for automobiles in general? Not many. Public transportation, perhaps, and if the price of public transportation falls (due to subsidy by the government, perhaps), some people may decide not to own a car, thereby producing a shift in the demand for automobiles. However, we do not expect too much substitution effect from this situation, because public transportation is a reasonable substitute only for certain uses of autos. It is a "poor" substitute in that there will not be much of a shift in the auto demand curve given a fall in the bus fare Suppose, however, that we define our product as Chevrolet automobiles. What substitutes are available? Among others (including public transportation) are Fords, Plymouths, and all of the other brands that were included when the product was defined as automobiles but are excluded when the product is defined as Chevrolets. As the product becomes more narrowly defined, the number of substitutes increases. If the price of Fords falls, there will be a big shift in the demand curve for Chevrolets. Of course, the responsiveness really depends on the extent to which brand loyalty exists and the different brands are differentiated in the consumers' minds (Figure 2–17). In instances where brand names are very unimportant, the response by brand X to a price change in brand Y will be very great. The substitutability is high, and they verge on becoming the same product in everything but price. On the other hand, in product areas where brand loyalty is very great, substitutability of brands, one for the other, is not too frequent, and the sensitivity to price changes in substitutes becomes less important. The subject of substitutes comes up again when we deal with elasticity in the next chapter.

What role do complements play in this analysis?

First, let us define a *complement* as a product that is used in conjunction with another product: bacon and eggs, cars and tires, pipes and pipe tobacco, and so on. As with substitutability, the degree of complementarity varies.

Let us once again turn our attention to the example of automobiles and divide the market into full-sized and compact autos. Of course they are substitutes for one another and will respond to price changes in one another as described above. However, let us now introduce gasoline into the picture. Gasoline is a complement to all cars, but is used with them in different ratios depending on weight, engine capacity, and so on. Now, if the price of gasoline rises (due to shortage), the law of demand says that less gasoline will be demanded. If less gasoline is demanded, the tendency is for less miles to be driven and, in time, less automobiles in general to be sold (all other things being equal). Thus a rise in the price of a product shifts the demand curves of its complements to the left. A fall in the price of a product increases the quantity demanded, both of itself and its complements. The demand curve for complements thus shifts to the right.

Now, however, let us consider the relationship between full-sized and compact cars. Here we find a substitute relationship operating. An increase in gasoline prices raises the cost of operating a big car more than that of operating a small car. As far as small cars are concerned, there is a leftward shift induced by the complement effect and also a shift to the right induced by the substitute effect. The latter will probably be stronger, and the total sale of compacts will rise. However, the shift to the left for full-sized cars induced by a change in the price of a complement will be reinforced by a substitute effect that sees it losing sales relatively to compacts as well as absolutely to other forms of transportation. As we extend our focus from one product to many, the interactions become quite complex—as may be evident from just this three-product problem. An analysis that embraces all interactions among all products due to price changes in any one of them is called a *general equilibrium analysis*.

So far we have considered income, price of substitutes, and complements. What about the effect of tastes on demand?

We lump under tastes all residual factors that play a role in determining demand. Seasonal and regional considerations, events that shape fads, and, most important, advertising and demand-shaping efforts have their influences included under "tastes." Taste can be the most important demand-shaping consideration. Recall the fortunes of the Bon Vivant Soup Company after one of its products caused the death of a customer due to botulism poisoning. No possible price cut could stimulate sales, and Bon Vivant quickly became as sick as its ill-fated customer. Thus we find the demand curve shifting to the right if tastes increase desire for the good and to the left if tastes lessen the desirability of the product.

Can you sum up the effect of factors, other than price, on demand? Remember that the purpose of demand analysis is to show how much of a product will be sold under different circumstances. A given demand curve assumes that all circumstances other than price are held constant. For various prices we find specific quantities taken. If we allow other factors to vary, we shall find different quantities taken at the same prices as earlier. Hence the demand curve must shift so that a different quantity can be associated with a given price. These are the shifts in demand—the changes in behavior to reflect the new relationship between given prices and new quantities under new circumstances.

CHAPTER HIGHLIGHTS

1. *We defined utility and made a distinction between ordinal and cardinal utility.*
2. *With our emphasis on cardinal utility in this chapter, we discussed different types of scales that can be used to measure it. We took note that the first difference in total utility is referred to as marginal utility and observed that an assumption of cardinal utility functions is that they have diminishing marginal utility.*
3. *Using the marginal utility of money as a yardstick, we were able to formulate a demand curve from a marginal utility function. It slopes down to the right, reflecting an inverse relationship between price and quantity that is known as the law of demand.*
4. *A rule for allocating money among conflicting uses was formulated. Specifically, we stated that money should be allocated so that marginal utility per dollar spent on each good is equal.*
5. *The other parameters of the demand function, income, the price of related goods, and tastes, were specified. We saw that the law of demand assumes these factors to remain constant. If they vary, the effect is to shift the demand curve.*

QUESTIONS

1. *Alfred Marshall wrote: "After a time new riches often lose a great deal of their charms. Partly this is the result of familiarity which*

makes people cease to derive much pleasure from accustomed comforts and luxuries though they suffer much greater pain in their loss." Can you translate this observation into movement and shift of the demand curves? What is the implication for marginal utility?

2. A comedian once quipped, "Everybody gotta be some place." Explain how the application of this generalization to money leads to the equimarginal principle:

$$\frac{MU_X}{P_X} = \frac{MU_Y}{P_Y} = \lambda$$

3. "The supermarket does not sell taste, it sells appearance. You cannot sell a blemished apple in the supermarket, but you can sell a tasteless one." Draw a demand curve for blemished apples. Assuming that this statement is true, what implications are contained for the manufacturers of automobiles?
4. During the recession year of 1974, many companies reported record sales volume and profits. What would contribute to high profits of (a) a spaghetti company, (b) a bankruptcy lawyer, (c) an auto mechanic, (d) a bicycle importer?
5. In New York City, the administration moved to lay off 600 rookie policemen in an austerity move. The remaining 16,000 patrolmen voted instead to work for five days during the year for no pay, thereby saving enough money to keep the rookies on their jobs. Can you draw any implications about interpersonal comparisons of utility from this? If so, what?
6. An author in the New York Times, commenting on the changing tastes in food, wrote: "The painstaking efforts of Luther Burbank and such contemporaries of his as gave their names to the loganberry, the boysenberry and the youngberry are now being shoveled down the drain. It is unprofitable to handle too many varieties. Nor can large-scale dealers be bothered with items in minor demand. Since when has your supermarket offered pomegranates, persimmons, or gooseberries?" What happens to the consumer surplus of people who like pomegranates, persimmons, and gooseberries? How can it be increased?

3 Price elasticity of demand

The principle of diminishing marginal utility tells us that the demand curves for all types of products are downward sloping. The lower the price charged, the greater the quantity taken. A logical question economists ask is, How much greater? Does a reduction in price cause a relatively large, a relatively small, or an insignificant change in the quantity demanded? To answer these questions some measure of the responsiveness of the dependent variable to changes in the independent variable is needed. Two possibilities are measures of slope and elasticity.

How does slope show responsiveness of quantity to price change?

The *slope* of a function measures the *rate of change* of one variable relative to another. In the case of a demand curve, a relatively flat slope shows large changes in quantity occurring when there is a small change in price. When the curve is steep, the change in quantity relative to the change in price is smaller. The slope therefore measures the responsiveness of the dependent variable (quantity) to changes in the independent variable (price). The flatter the slope, the more the responsiveness. The greater the slope, the less the responsiveness (Figure 3–1).

Don't flat slopes usually show relatively slight responsiveness, and steep slopes, greater responsiveness?

Yes, normally graphical analysis shows the independent variable on the *x* axis and the dependent variable on the *y* axis. In math we deal with

FIGURE 3–1. Slope of the Demand Curve

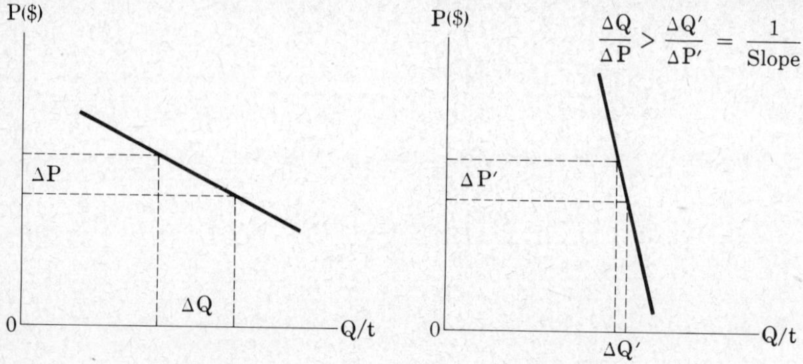

Slope is one measure of responsiveness of quantity to changes in price. In the diagram at the left, flatter slope shows greater responsiveness of quantity to price change than is the case in the diagram at the right, where steep slope shows little responsiveness. Although slope normally refers to the ratio of the change in the vertical axis variable to the change in the horizontal axis variable, we shall frequently use the term slope when actually we mean the reciprocal of the slope, that is, $\Delta Q/\Delta P$.

FIGURE 3–2. Difference Between Slope and Elasticity

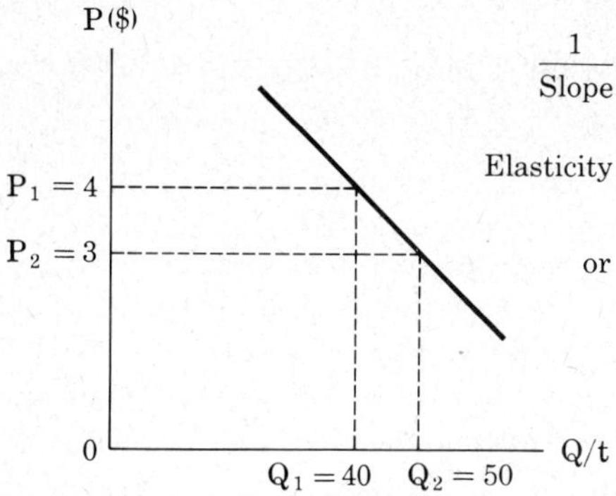

$$\frac{1}{\text{Slope}} = \frac{\Delta Q}{\Delta P} = \text{either } \frac{10}{1} \text{ or } \frac{10}{100}$$

$$\text{Elasticity} = \frac{\Delta Q}{\Delta P} \times \frac{P}{Q} = -\frac{10}{1} \times \frac{3}{50} = -.6$$

or

$$= -\frac{10}{100} \times \frac{300}{50} = -.6$$

Using the figures on the diagram, the slope may be expressed either as $-1/10$ or $-100/10$, depending on whether price is measured in dollars or cents. However, substituting into the elasticity formula gives a value of $-.6$ regardless of the units used. Here the problem creating ambiguity is whether we use P_1 or P_2 and Q_1 or Q_2 as the base value.

problems expressed as $y = f(x)$. In demand analysis, we treat price as the independent variable and quantity as the dependent variable determined by price, that is, $Q = f(p)$. Economists have followed the lead of Alfred Marshall and adopted the convention of plotting price on the y axis and quantity on the x axis. It is arbitrary, unusual, and somewhat confusing, because we must speak of the greater response as involving a lower slope and a lesser response as involving a greater slope. More mathematically inclined economists, after years of frustration, have come to grips with the difficulty by reversing the axes and plotting price on the x axis. However, this only confuses those accustomed to the conventional format. There is nothing to do but learn it.

Is slope the only measure of responsiveness of one variable to another?
No. As a matter of fact, slope is less often used than *elasticity*. When economists discuss the responsiveness of quantity to price, they generally employ the coefficient of price elasticity of demand as their measure.

What is the coefficient of price elasticity of demand?
Price elasticity of demand is another measure of responsiveness of quantity to price change. It is the ratio of the percentage change in quantity demanded to the percentage change occurring in price. This is to be distinguished from slope (or rather the reciprocal of the slope), which is defined as the ratio of the change in quantity demanded to the change in price. One involves percentage change and the other involves actual unit change.

Why bother with elasticity to measure responsiveness of demand? Why not just use the slope of the demand curve?
This is a tricky point. The problem with slope is that it involves actual measures of money and quantity, and the choice of the *units* of measure affects the slope. Suppose that we are dealing with wheat and measure price in dollars and quantity in millions of bushels. If the price of wheat goes from \$3 to \$4 per bushel and the quantity sold goes from 50 (million) to 40 (million) bushels, the slope is -10. However, suppose that we measure money in pennies. This very same price change would involve 100 cents. The quantity change is still 10 (million). The result is a slope of $-10/100$ or $-.1$. On the other hand, measuring these changes in percentage terms would give the same elasticity regardless of whether money was denominated in cents or dollars (Figure 3–2).

How would you compute elasticity in that instance?

First, set up a formula for elasticity. We have defined elasticity as the percentage change in quantity over the percentage change in price. Algebraically this is

$$\frac{\%\ \Delta Q}{\%\ \Delta P} = \frac{\frac{\Delta Q}{Q}}{\frac{\Delta P}{P}}$$

Substitute into the formula, first using dollars.

$$\begin{aligned} \Delta Q &= 10 \\ \Delta P &= 1 \\ P &= 3 \\ Q &= 50 \end{aligned} \qquad \frac{\frac{10}{50}}{\frac{1}{3}} = \frac{30}{50} = .6$$

Now do the same computation using cents.

$$\begin{aligned} \Delta Q &= 10 \\ \Delta P &= 100 \\ P &= 300 \\ Q &= 50 \end{aligned} \qquad \frac{\frac{10}{50}}{\frac{100}{300}} = \frac{3000}{5000} = .6$$

The coefficients are the same, and you can see that elasticity is independent of the units of measure. The number .6 is a ratio of ratios. It has had all the units boiled out of it.

Are there alternative ways to compute elasticity?

The formula we have used is certainly awkward looking, but it is quite useful in that it follows from the definition of elasticity. Even if you forget the details of the formula, you can reconstruct it because you know the definition to be the percentage change of quantity over the percentage change of price. There is a better computational formula, however, that follows simply from converting this "improper" four-tiered fraction into a more conventional one. First invert the denominator and multiply:

$$\frac{\frac{\Delta Q}{Q}}{\frac{\Delta P}{P}} = \frac{\Delta Q}{Q} \times \frac{P}{\Delta P}$$

Then rearrange the terms:

$$\frac{\Delta Q}{\Delta P} \times \frac{P}{Q}$$

This expression involves a slope-like term ($\Delta Q/\Delta P$) multiplied by the ratio of price to quantity (P/Q). This is the conventional formula used for elasticity.

In looking at the problem, I see that there are two prices and two quantities, the old and the new. How do you know which to substitute in the formula?

This is an ambiguity inherent in the concept of *arc elasticity*, which is what we are dealing with. Because we are comparing percentage changes in price and quantity, the question is, Which base do you use for purposes of computing the percentage? Obviously, it makes a difference, because you will get different answers if you use different bases on which to compute the percentages. For example, in the problem examined above, using the dollar measures of price the following are possibilities:

$\Delta Q = 10$	$\Delta Q = 10$	$\Delta Q = 10$	$\Delta Q = 10$
$\Delta P = 1$	$\Delta P = 1$	$\Delta P = 1$	$\Delta P = 1$
$P = 3$	$P = 4$	$P = 4$	$P = 3$
$Q = 50$	$Q = 40$	$Q = 50$	$Q = 40$
$E = \frac{10}{1} \times \frac{3}{50} = \frac{3}{5}$	$\frac{10}{1} \times \frac{4}{40} = 1$	$\frac{10}{1} \times \frac{4}{50} = \frac{4}{5}$	$\frac{10}{1} \times \frac{3}{40} = \frac{3}{4}$

No one is better than the others, and there is no real logic behind selecting one rather than another. Perhaps the solution that makes the most sense is to take the average of the prices and quantities as our measures of P and Q. Computationally you will find that you get the very same result if you simply add the prices together and add the quantities together and substitute into the formula for P and Q (Figure 3–3).

What happened to the minus sign?

Strictly speaking, the demand elasticity should always be negative in sign. Remember that it involves the slope times the ratio of P/Q. The slope of the demand curve is always negative, and so the product should be also. However, it is conventional to drop the minus sign and use only "absolute" values. The reasons are largely semantic. In comparing products we want to be able to say such things as "the coefficient of elasticity of X is greater than that of Y in the event demand for X is more sensitive to price change than demand for Y." However, if we use the minus sign we find that, logically, the bigger the number the smaller the value. That is, -10 is less than -6, but we conventionally say that the coefficient of 10 represents a greater degree of elasticity than that of 6 (Figure 3–4). To preserve our sanity we drop the minus sign and use "greater" or "less" with reference to the absolute numbers.

FIGURE 3–3. Computing Arc Elasticity

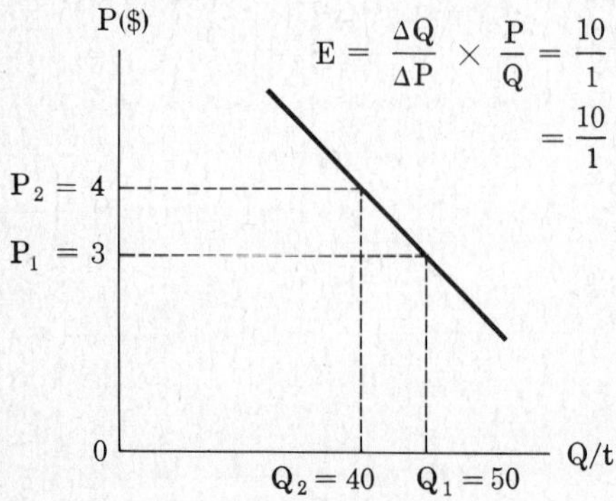

$$E = \frac{\Delta Q}{\Delta P} \times \frac{P}{Q} = \frac{10}{1} \times \frac{3.5}{45} = \frac{7}{9} \quad \text{(averaging)}$$

$$= \frac{10}{1} \times \frac{7}{90} = \frac{7}{9} \quad \text{(adding)}$$

The question of whether to use P_1 or P_2 and Q_1 or Q_2 has no real solution. The convention most frequently employed is to use the average of the two prices and the average of the two quantities. Alternatively, by adding the two prices together and the two quantities together, we can get the same answer with slightly simpler computation.

FIGURE 3–4. The Sign of the Coefficient of Elasticity

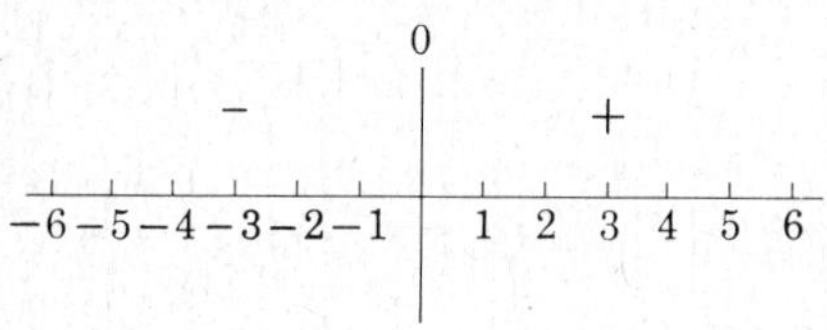

Even though −6 is less than −5, we want to call an elasticity of −6 greater than an elasticity of −5. The solution is to ignore the sign and use the absolute values.

Let us examine a linear demand curve. Is elasticity a constant throughout?

No. This is a common misconception, but it is a silly one. If you look at the formula for elasticity, you will see that it involves a slope multiplied by the ratio of price to quantity. The slope is constant all along a linear demand curve. However, the ratio of price to quantity clearly is not. At the left end the price is big and the quantity is small. This will lead to a relatively high value for elasticity. At the right end, the quantity is big and the price in small. This will lead to a small value when the P/Q ratio is multiplied times the slope (Figure 3–5).

Is this variable elasticity logical?

It is if you refer back to the definition of elasticity. It involves the percentage changes of price and quantity and these depend on the size of the base on which you calculate the percentage as well as on the amount of change. At the left end of the curve there is a high price base, so any change in price will represent a relatively small percentage change. Similarly, there is a small quantity base, so any change in quantity will involve a big percentage change. Because elasticity compares these percentages, we are comparing a big quantity percentage to a small price percentage. The result is a big coefficient of elasticity. Just the opposite prevails at the right end of the curve.

What is the range of possible values the coefficient of elasticity can take?

Again ignoring the sign, the coefficient can take on any value from zero to infinity. A vertical demand curve will have a zero value throughout, because ΔQ is zero regardless of price change (Figure 3–6). Substitution into the formula gives elasticity of zero. A horizontal demand curve will have an infinite demand coefficient of elasticity because when ΔP is anything other than zero, the change in quantity is infinitely great.

I have trouble seeing the infinite elasticity for the horizontal demand curve. Can you elaborate?

Instead of drawing the curve horizontal, draw it almost horizontal. Very flat. Now take two prices that are close together and project them over to the demand curve (Figure 3–7). You will find that the quantity differences are very great. As the curve gets flatter and flatter, the quantity differences become greater and greater until finally, when the curve is horizontal, projection of any price other than the level of the curve itself will never reach it. Change in quantity is infinitely great (Figure 3–8).

When is demand said to be "relatively elastic" or "relatively inelastic"?

We said that the range of values for elasticity was from zero to infinity. We break this continuum at the value of one (ignoring sign). Coefficient values between zero and one are said to involve demand that is rela-

FIGURE 3–5. Linear Demand Curve

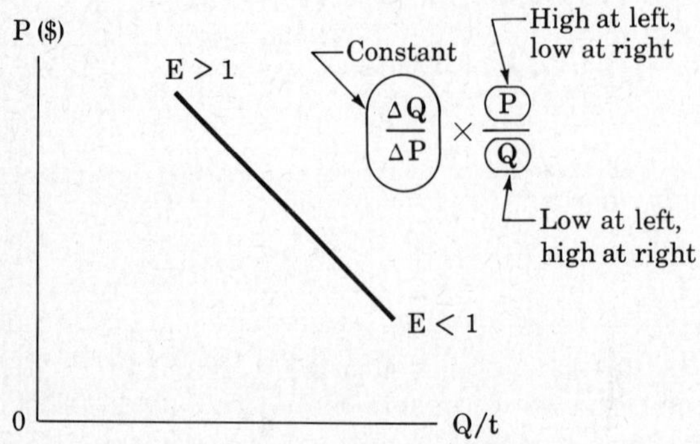

Even though a linear demand curve has a constant slope, the elasticity varies. Elasticity ranges from a high coefficient near the *y* axis, through unitary, to low values near the horizontal (*x*) axis.

FIGURE 3–6. Vertical Demand Curve

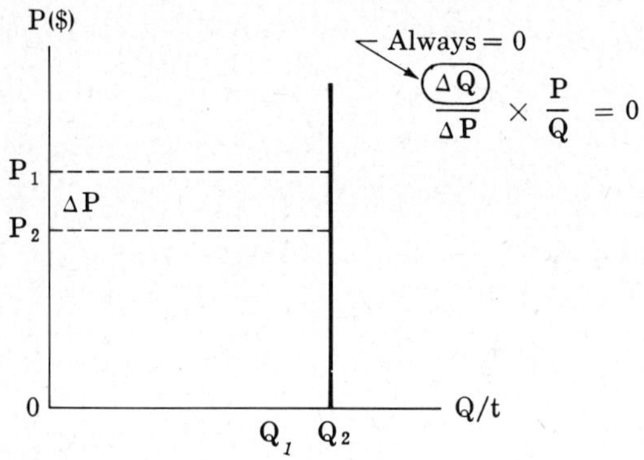

The vertical demand curve is perfectly inelastic at all points. The coefficient of elasticity is zero because by substituting into the formula, ΔQ equals zero.

FIGURE 3–7. Horizontal Demand Curve

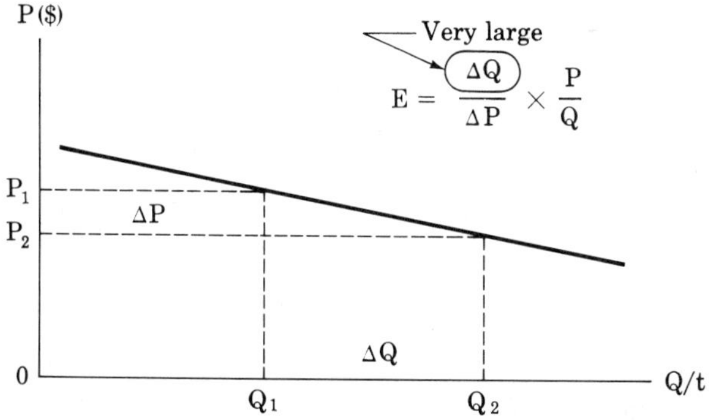

The horizontal demand curve has a coefficient of elasticity of demand of infinity. This can be seen by looking at a curve that is almost horizontal. Here a very small change in *P* produces a large change in *Q*. The more nearly horizontal, the greater the change produced in *Q*. Finally, at the limit, the change in *Q* is infinitely great.

FIGURE 3–8. Horizontal Demand Curve

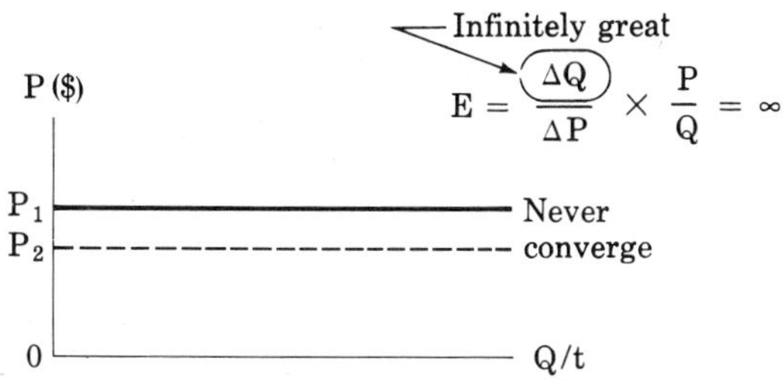

The projection of P_2 to the demand curve never touches it. The change in *Q* is infinitely great because the demand curve is parallel to the projection. They never intersect.

tively inelastic. Values between one and infinity are relatively elastic. Values of zero are said to mean that demand is *perfectly inelastic* (vertical demand curve), and values of infinity mean that demand is *perfectly elastic* (horizontal curve). If the coefficient of elasticity is one, we say that demand is of *unitary elasticity* (Figure 3–9).

FIGURE 3–9. Range of Values of Elasticity

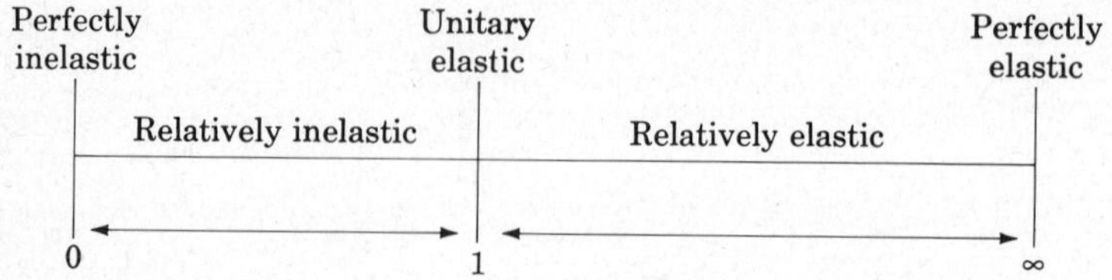

Elasticity ranges from zero to infinity (ignoring sign). There are five descriptive terms used for various values of the coefficient.

FIGURE 3–10. Total Revenue

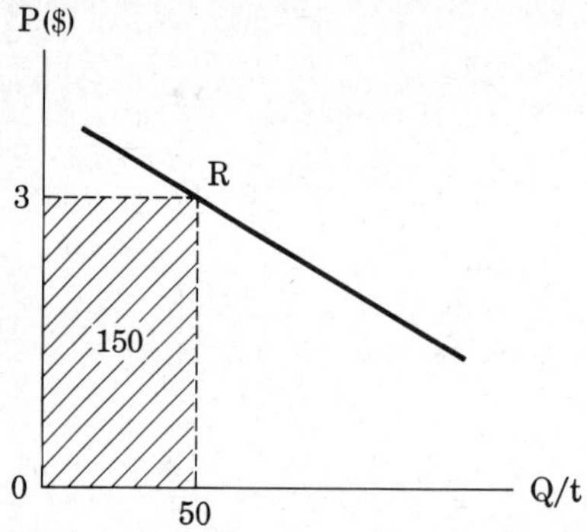

Total revenue is the area $03R50$ under the demand curve at point R. Since the area of any rectangle is equal to length times width, by definition, total revenue equals prices times quantity. On the diagram, price equals length 3 and quantity equals width 50, so total revenue equals 150, or area $03R50$.

FIGURE 3–11. Elasticity–Total Revenue Relationship

A schematic summary of the total revenue–elasticity relationship is given here.

$E < 1$ (inelastic)	$P \nearrow TR \nearrow$	$P \searrow TR \searrow$
$E = 1$ (unitary)	$P \nearrow TR \rightarrow$	$P \searrow TR \rightarrow$
$E > 1$ (elastic)	$P \nearrow TR \searrow$	$P \searrow TR \nearrow$

Why make these particular distinctions? Why not use elasticity of two or three as the breaking point? Why have any distinctions?

Again, we are measuring the ratio of percentage change of quantity to percentage change of price. When the elasticity is less than one, it means that for a 1 percent change in price we get a *less* than 1 percent change in quantity. If price rises 10 percent, quantity demanded will fall by less than 10 percent. On the other hand, if elasticity is greater than one, a 10 percent rise in price will reduce quantity demanded by more than 10 percent. If elasticity is three, a 10 percent rise in price will reduce quantity demanded by 30 percent. These relative changes in price and quantity will translate into different effects on total revenue.

What is total revenue, and what does it have to do with elasticity?

Total revenue is the term used to describe the product of $P \times Q$, or the quantity sold multiplied by the price at which each unit is sold. It is represented on the demand diagram as the area of the rectangle formed by price and quantity under the demand curve, because geometrically this area equals the price dimension times the quantity dimension. Thus if, at a price of $3 per bushel, 50 million bushels of wheat are sold, the total revenue is $150 million (Figure 3–10). Whether or not a change in price raises or lowers total revenue depends on the relative quantity changes occurring in response to price change. This in turn is indicated by the coefficient of elasticity of demand. It stands to reason that if price rises 10 percent but the quantity sold falls by more than 10 percent, there will be a decline in total revenue. On the other hand, if price rises by 10 percent and the quantity falls by less than 10 percent, there will be a rise in total revenue. Should you raise price 10 percent and suffer exactly a 10 percent fall in quantity, total revenue would remain the same. These observations are summarized as follows: If demand is relatively inelastic (*E* from zero to one), the total revenue will change in the same direction as the price change. If demand is relatively elastic (*E* from one to infinity), total revenue will change in the opposite direction from the price change. If elasticity is unitary, total revenue will be the same at both prices (Figure 3–11).

Can we generalize the total revenue–elasticity relationship further?

One further conclusion that follows from what we have indicated thus far is that the total revenue is at a maximum at the point on the demand curve where elasticity is unitary. This may seem surprising at first, but look at it this way. As long as demand is relatively inelastic, a rise in price raises total revenue; and as long as demand is relatively elastic, a rise in price reduces total revenue. We know that as we move

FIGURE 3–12. Total Revenue Maximized When Elasticity Is Unitary

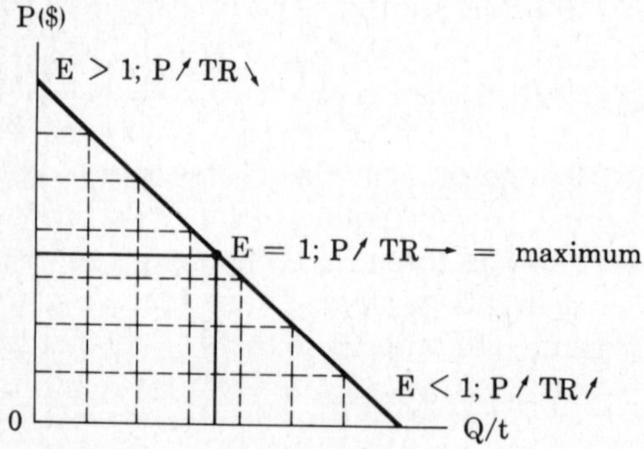

Compare the areas of the total revenue rectangles defined at different points along the demand curve. They go from small to large and to small again as you go from one end of the demand curve to the other.

FIGURE 3–13. Total Revenue Plotted Against Price

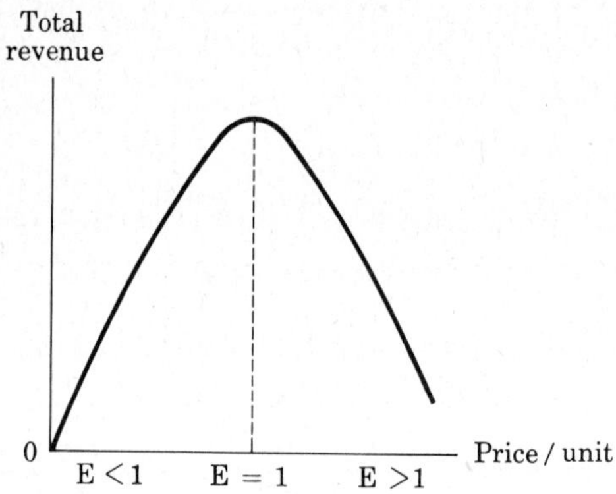

If total revenue were plotted against price, it would rise to a peak as price rises, and would then fall as price continues to rise. These fluctuations correspond to total revenue changes occurring as elasticity goes from zero to infinity.

from the lower right to the upper left of a demand diagram (price rising, quantity falling), elasticity is changing from very inelastic to very elastic. The particular point where demand changes from inelastic to elastic is the point where total revenue stops rising with each rise in price and begins to fall with rises in price. At this point total revenue is at a maximum. This is also the point of unitary elasticity (Figures 3–12 and 3–13).

Should a producer then strive to price his product at the level where elasticity is unitary in order to maximize total revenue?

Not necessarily. We shall see that a producer strives to maximize total profit, not total revenue. To compute total profit, we must have an estimate of costs of production as well as of revenue. It may be that at the output at which total revenue is maximized, costs exceed revenue and the producer operates at a loss. Total revenue is necessarily the same as total profit only in the case of zero costs. For other cases, we must wait for our discussion on costs.

What is point elasticity?

Earlier we mentioned arc elasticity in conjunction with the arithmetic difficulties encountered in deciding which base price and quantity to use. Arc elasticity involves comparison of two discrete points on the demand curve. This is why we had two different prices and quantities to worry about. The segment of the demand curve between the two points is referred to as an arc. Now picture the arc getting smaller and smaller and the two points getting closer and closer together. Eventually they will converge, and to all intents and purposes they will be the same point. Now, if we ask what the coefficient of elasticity is between these two infinitesimally close-together points on the curve, we are asking about *point elasticity* (Figure 3–14).

But if the two points are the same point, the changes in price and quantity are both zero. $\Delta Q/\Delta P$ is 0/0, and this is mathematically meaningless.

That is true. There is no way we can compute point elasticity by merely substituting directly for ΔQ and ΔP in the formula. In absolute terms their values are practically zero. However, one of the more ingenious insights of mathematics comes into play here. Remember that we described the points as *approaching* each other and the arc between them as *approaching* zero. The arc becomes infinitesimally small but does not vanish altogether. Although change in Q and change in P are

FIGURE 3–14. *Point Elasticity*

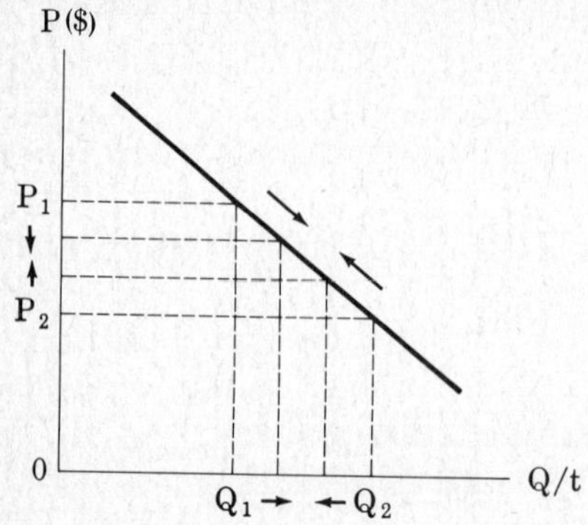

As P_1 and P_2 and Q_1 and Q_2 get closer together, we go from a problem in arc to a problem in point elasticity.

FIGURE 3–15. *Point Elasticity at Point D*

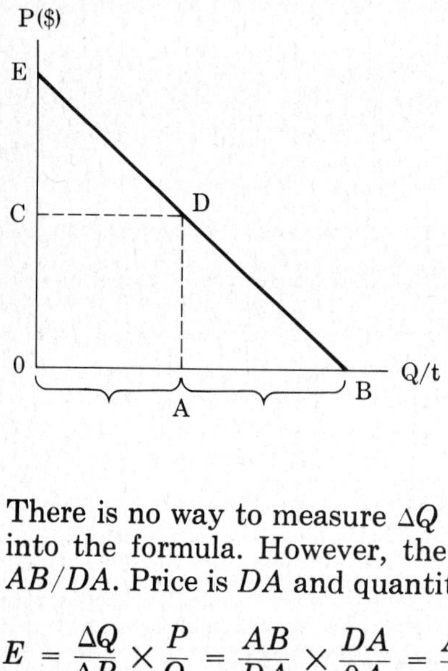

There is no way to measure ΔQ and ΔP directly and substitute into the formula. However, the ratio $\Delta Q/\Delta P = 1/\text{slope} = AB/DA$. Price is DA and quantity is $0A$, so

$$E = \frac{\Delta Q}{\Delta P} \times \frac{P}{Q} = \frac{AB}{DA} \times \frac{DA}{0A} = \frac{AB}{0A}$$

FIGURE 3–16. Three Examples of Point Elasticity Measurement

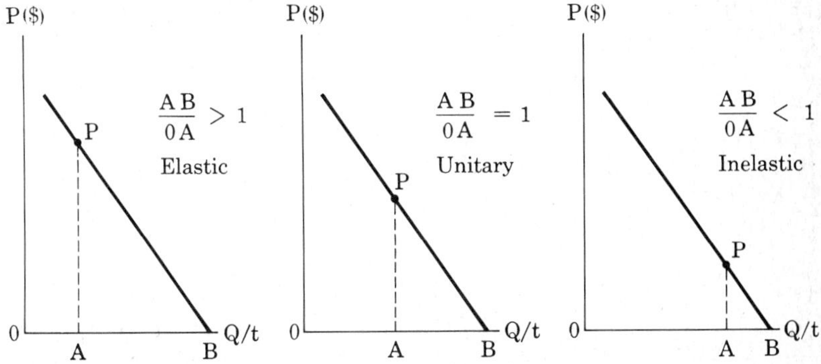

The coefficient of elasticity depends on where the point *P* is on the demand curve.

each infinitesimal, one may still be bigger than the other. For example, if change in *Q* is .0000004 and change in *P* is .0000001, each is pretty close to zero. Nevertheless, change in *Q* is four times as big as change in *P*. The secret of understanding point elasticity is to recognize that although it is impractical to try to measure ΔP and ΔQ by themselves, measuring the ratio of one to the other does give a meaningful figure. We must look at what we already know in our problem and see if there is some way we can get the ratio of $\Delta Q/\Delta P$ without actually needing either by itself. We find that the slope of the demand curve (or at least its reciprocal) gives this. The formula for elasticity is

$$\frac{\Delta Q}{\Delta P} \times \frac{P}{Q}$$

We get the $\Delta Q/\Delta P$ part from measuring the slope of the demand curve. The P/Q part is easy. These are the price and quantity values at the point. Look at Figure 3–15. By translating our formula elements into equivalent elements of the diagram, we see that the coefficient of elasticity is equal to the ratio of line segment *AB* to line segment 0*A*. Using this ratio as a guide, we can make quick estimates of relative elasticity by examining the diagram (Figure 3–16). If point *A* is nearer to point *B* than to point 0, the demand is relatively inelastic because *AB*/0*A* is less than one. If point *A* is nearer point 0, the demand is relatively elastic because the ratio *AB*/0*A* is greater than one. If point *A* is right in the middle, the elasticity is unitary because the ratio equals one. Thus the

FIGURE 3–17. Steepness of Demand Curve Indicating Relative Elasticity at a Point on the Curve

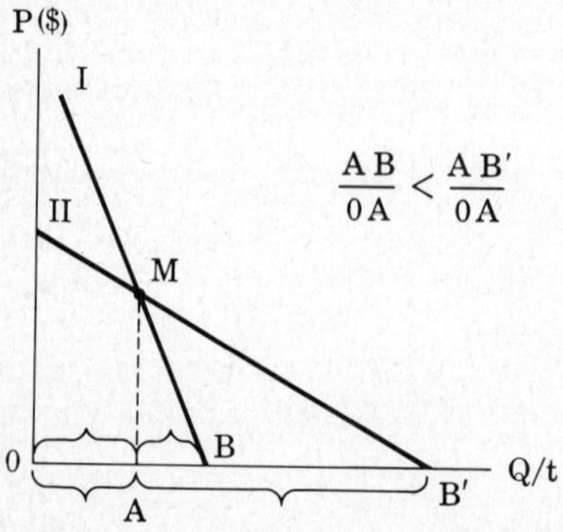

At point M, the steeper demand curve (I) has lower elasticity than the flatter curve (II). This is seen by examining the $AB/0A$ ratios.

FIGURE 3–18. Slope of Demand Curve

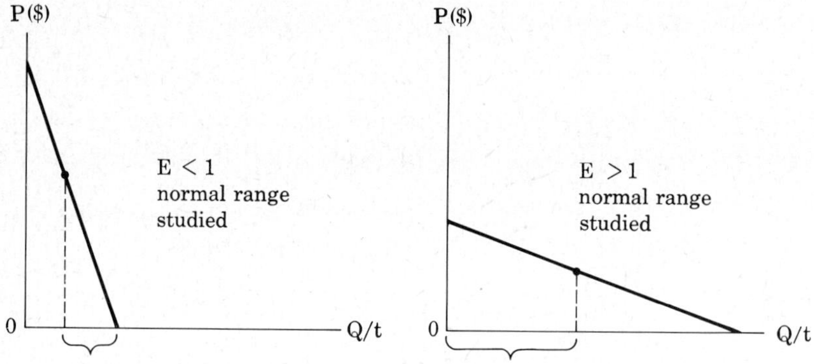

For steep demand curves the values in the "normal" range of interest are in the inelastic range. For flat curves, "normally studied" values are in the elastic range.

point of unitary elasticity is in the center of a linear demand curve, as is the point of total revenue maximization.

Can we make any generalizations about the relationship between elasticity and slope?
Students tend to assume that flat demand curves have higher elasticities than steep demand curves. This is a dangerous generalization, because we have just seen that all linear demand curves have ranges over which elasticity is greater than one and ranges over which it is less than one. In Figure 3–17 elasticity is smaller at point M on the steep curve, where the AB/OA ratio is less than one, than it is on the flat curve at point M, where this ratio is greater than one. We can say that, given a particular point on the diagram, a flat curve passing through it will have higher elasticity at that point than a steep curve passing through the point.

Why do we so frequently associate flat curves with high elasticity and steep curves with low elasticity?
Although all linear demand curves have values ranging from zero to infinity, we must ask where the observations that we are studying fall on the curve. For a steep curve, the elastic range occurs only at very high prices, way up in the upper left corner of the diagram. Chances are that we do not actually have observations involving these values. Similarly for the relatively flat curve, the inelastic values occur far to the right at very high quantities and low prices. Chances are that we do not have observations in that range either. Thus economic studies generally involve data found in the inelastic range of steep curves and the elastic range of flat ones (Figure 3–18).

Now that we have discussed all the technical nuances of elasticity, what does it all mean? How does elasticity relate to product or market characteristics?
Substitutability is the key word here. Remember that we are dealing with the response of the market to changes in the price of a product. For price rises, the law of demand says that people will buy less of the product. How much less? It depends on the alternatives open to them. If there are a number of very close substitutes the prices of which do not change, people will switch their buying to the substitutes in great numbers. Watch what happens when *one* gasoline station lowers its price. Pretty soon the cars line up at those pumps. The percentage change in quantity sold relative to percentage change in price will be high, and the demand will be relatively elastic. On the other hand, if

there are few and imperfect substitutes available, then despite a price rise buyers will be forced to remain with the product. If the only gas station open on Sunday raises its price, sales will not go down much. The closest substitute available is to fill up on Saturday, and not too many people will bother doing that.

How do you know if there are substitute products in the market?
Substitutability depends on the degree of uniqueness or differentiation inherent in the product. Where products are standardized, or graded by government agency, such as is the case with agricultural staples, there really is no uniqueness associated with the output of one grower when compared with another. An increase in the asking price by one farmer for his wheat has the effect of sending buyers to other farmers, because the wheat sold by one farmer is identical to that sold by any other farmer. In this case demand is highly elastic. In fact it is perfectly elastic, and will be shown by a horizontal demand curve. When you get into differentiated merchandise, the degree of price elasticity is lower. How much lower it is depends on the importance of the product differences to the buyer. One role of advertising is to make small differences appear important. An interesting example is the Morton Salt Company, which successfully promoted its brand of common table salt as unique and was able to sell it at a premium for many years. "When it rains, it pours."

The degree of differentiation can run from slight brand preference down to a patented, unique product characteristic. Consider the product called Antivenom. This is the sole antidote listed in the Physician's Desk Register for victims of coral snake bite. Price elasticity of demand is low indeed. The buyers don't even have the option of postponing purchase.

Won't elasticity be zero for the product of a monopolist?
Probably not. Although a monopolist may offer the only source for a particular product, there are likely to be alternative products capable of doing the same thing and performing the same service. For instance, even if the steel industry were monopolized, the demand curve would nevertheless slope downward to the right because of the existence of substitute products: aluminum, wood, fiberglass, plastic, and so on. Buyers can still go to another source.

What about the case where there is no substitute product, such as electricity? Is that demand curve perfectly inelastic?
Again, probably not. There is an alternative to using electricity and that

is conserving it. You may do without some lights or use lower wattage or less air conditioning if the price becomes higher. Remember, everyone doesn't have to do this for the curve to slope downward—only some people.

Then are there no situations in which demand is perfectly inelastic?
The only type of situation that is usually taken to indicate a vertical demand curve is a product such as a vital drug needed to sustain life: We mentioned Antivenom. Here, regardless of price, a certain amount is required, and this will receive the highest priority in the spending pattern of the afflicted person. The total quantity of the drug demanded in the market is fixed by the number of patients requiring this unique treatment, and remains constant regardless of price. Admittedly, the circumstances are unusual.

Is it true that the more specifically you define a product, the higher the elasticity?
Yes, we discussed this idea in another context in Chapter 2. It holds because the more narrowly you define a product, the more things there are that are not included in the definition and are available as substitutes. In his famous textbook, Paul Samuelson has a question that asks which has the higher elasticity, ice cream, chocolate ice cream, or Breyer's chocolate ice cream. The answer, based on the generalization just made, is that Breyer's chocolate ice cream is the product with the higher elasticity. When Breyer's chocolate ice cream is the product under analysis, all the other brands of chocolate ice cream, as well as all the other flavors, including Breyer's, are available as substitutes and the consumer is free to switch to them should Breyer's chocolate ice cream go up in price. On the other hand, if ice cream is the product under analysis, then all these other flavors and brands are part of the product and the only substitutes are non–ice cream products: sherbet, Jello, Coca Cola, and so on, none very perfect. Hence there will be low elasticity, because there will be little substitution opportunity.

How does this specificity criterion relate to the size of the market and elasticity?
It holds in the same manner. The more geographically narrow the market is for a product, the higher the elasticity of demand for that product. There are other regions where the product may be bought. One finds that the demand for grain is more elastic when the market is defined as national rather than international in scope. Foreign grain is a substitute for domestic grain, but both are encompassed within the

product called world grain. A state excise tax that raises the price of cigarettes within one state reduces sales more sharply than a federal excise tax that raises prices in all geographical areas. New Yorkers risk jail by buying large quantities of cigarettes in North Carolina to avoid the New York tax—anything to prove elasticity is greater when the market is more specifically defined.

Are there causes for elasticity other than substitutes?

Most discussions of this topic list two other indicators of relative elasticity: (1) the price of the product relative to personal income, and (2) the number of uses to which the product can be put. Taking the latter first, it appears that this is actually another wrinkle on the substitution argument. When there are many uses to which a product can be put, we find that as the price rises, different uses get priced out of the market whereas others remain. For example, consider water. Here the first impulse is to assume that demand is nearly perfectly inelastic, or at least highly inelastic. However, this impression is gained because we are thinking of drinking water. Actually, drinking is just one of many uses for water, and probably the one that will be in effect at the highest price. Possible uses of water include watering the lawn, washing the dog, cooling the nuclear reactor, and a thousand others. As Adam Smith pointed out, value in use for water is high but it is priced very low in spite of this. As the price goes up we can picture watering the lawn less frequently and finally stopping altogether, washing the car less frequently and finally stopping altogether, less frequent bathing, and so on. Substitutes that were formerly impractical for these uses because they were expensive as compared to water now come to be used. The dog will be the beneficiary of dry shampoo, people will carpet or pave their lawn areas, the car will be left dirty, and we shall no doubt see a boom in the underarm deodorant industry. The point is, a substitute for one use of water is not necessarily appropriate as a replacement for other uses. Water usage will decline gradually in a sequence that reflects the availability of substitutes for the different uses at different prices. The more uses there are, the more finely stratified are the users, gradually dropping out as price rises. Perhaps, finally, when the price of water is extremely high and its availability extraordinarily low, only drinking will remain as a use and that under conditions of relative infrequency.

What role does income play with regard to price elasticity?

There are two possible ways that income can influence price elasticity of demand. Generally the relationship is that, all other things being equal, the lower the price of the item relative to a person's income, the lower the coefficient of price elasticity of demand will be. One reason is that the item may simply be so inexpensive that it is not worth the bother of looking for a substitute, assuming that one exists. If the price of penny bubble gum doubles to two cents, it may not be worth the bother for the typical "good Daddy" to search out a cheaper substitute. There is another technical point here. Even if there are some who do search out a substitute, it is doubtful that the percentage change in quantity will be as great as the percentage change in price. The penny increase is a 100 percent increase in price. Because elasticity involves percentage changes, elasticity will be low as long as the percentage change in quantity is less than 100. For higher-priced items, there is a need to pay attention. In the case of an automobile, a $400 increase may involve only a 10 percent increase in price. Statistical studies of auto demand suggest a 12 to 15 percent decline in the number of autos sold can be expected. Demand is said to be relatively elastic. Additionally, there is an income effect to consider. Even if the same number of cars were bought, the higher price would reduce the remaining real income available to purchase other commodities. This decline in real income will reduce the purchase of all normal goods, among which is cars, and therefore the quantity of cars will decline further. Income effect is a fairly technical subject that is discussed at some length in the next chapter. Here we should note how it contributes to elasticity of demand.

Is price elasticity of demand of much practical importance?

Many economic policies are formulated in terms of the anticipated price changes that they will induce. All excise taxes, tariffs, and subsidies involve price changes. The agricultural program influences the price of food. Establishment of public colleges involves the price of education. State-wide restrictions of pollution will effect prices charged by industries under the jurisdiction. Without considerations of elasticity of the products affected, it is impossible to predict the ultimate outcome of these actions. If excise taxes are levied to raise money for the state, levying them on highly elastic products will reduce the volume sold to such an extent that tax revenues will fall. Regardless of whether the policy makers consider the subtleties of the mathematics of elasticity, they certainly must reckon with its effects. Price elasticity of demand is indeed of much practical importance.

You specify price elasticity of demand. Are there other kinds of elasticity?

Conceivably there are as many types of elasticity possible as there are functional relationships. Elasticity, after all, refers to the responsive-

FIGURE 3–19. Other Elasticity Measurements

In addition to price elasticity of demand, we can develop coefficients showing percentage change of any dependent variable relative to percentage changes in some other independent variable. The formulas of several are shown here.

Elasticity of supply

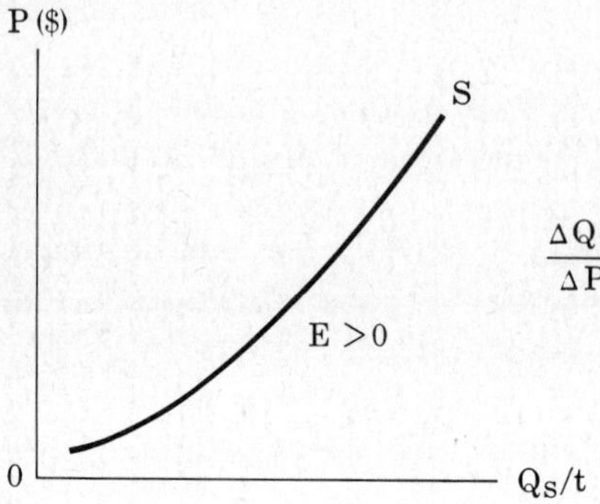

$$\frac{\Delta Q_S}{\Delta P} \times \frac{P}{Q}$$

Income elasticity

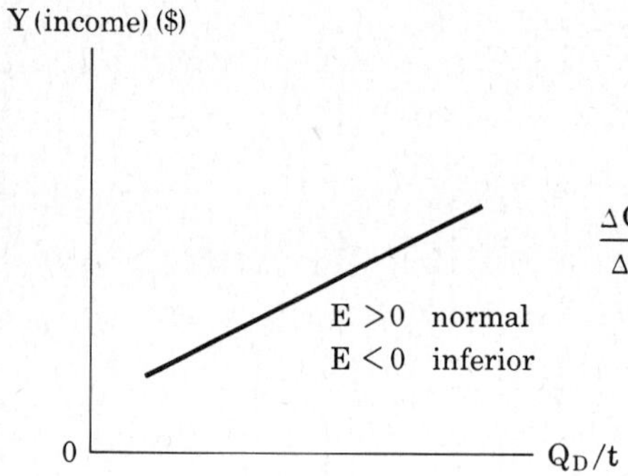

$$\frac{\Delta Q_D}{\Delta Y} \times \frac{Y}{Q_D}$$

Interest elasticity of investment

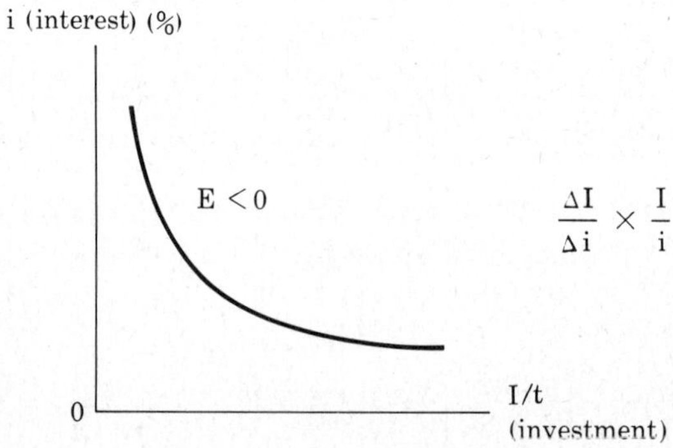

$$\frac{\Delta I}{\Delta i} \times \frac{I}{i}$$

Cross-elasticity of demand

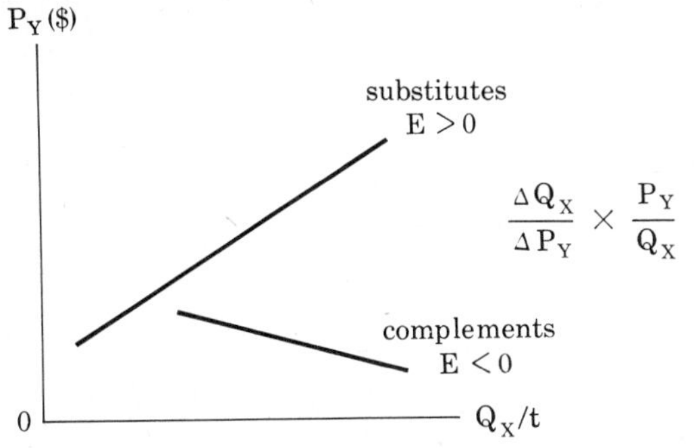

ness of a dependent variable to percentage changes in an independent variable. We have focused on changes in quantity *demanded* relative to price change. Why not have price elasticity of *supply?* This would measure the percentage change in the quantity a seller offers relative to a percentage change in price. Because the supply curve slopes upward, we would find that this coefficient always has a positive sign. Another commonly used elasticity is *income* elasticity. In Chapter 2 we referred to normal goods as those for which demand increases with an increase in income and inferior goods as those for which demand declines with an increase in income. It is sometimes stated that the income elasticity (percentage change in quantity taken relative to the percentage change in income) of normal goods is positive and the income elasticity of inferior goods is negative. Important studies have been made of the income elasticity of many consumer goods, because income fluctuates over the business cycle and producers like to have some means of forecasting what will happen to their sales. In another area, Federal Reserve System economists are interested in something they call the *interest elasticity of investment.* We shall see in Chapter 12 that investment fluctuates with the level of interest rates. Monetary authorities like to quantify the relationship, and they want to know the percentage change that will occur in investment relative to the percentage change in interest rates. Still another form of elasticity that we can mention is the *cross-elasticity of demand.* We have described the effect of substitutes and complements on a demand curve. An increase in the price of a substitute shifts the demand curve of a product to the right, whereas an increase in the price of a complement sends the demand curve to the left. Cross-elasticity measures the percentage change in the quantity demanded of one product relative to the percentage change of price in another. In 1975 the auto industry was having a terrible sales year due to the simultaneous inflation, recession, and petroleum crunch that were occurring. All companies experienced drastic reductions in their sales figures. In the face of this, Chrysler lowered the prices of its cars. You can bet that General Motors and Ford were interested in the coefficient of cross-elasticity between Chrysler's price change and sales of their own products. Apparently these coefficients looked too high. Ford, GM, and American motors quickly matched the price reduction.

No doubt you can think of other important economic relationships that can have elasticity measures. Those we have just discussed are among the most commonly used ones (Figure 3–19).

CHAPTER HIGHLIGHTS

1. *We identified elasticity as a measure of the responsiveness of a dependent variable to changes in an independent variable. Specifically, price elasticity of demand was defined as the percentage change in quantity demanded relative to the percentage change in price.*
2. *A formula for computing the coefficient of price elasticity of demand was developed:*

$$E = \frac{\Delta Q}{\Delta P} \times \frac{P}{Q}$$

3. *We saw that the absolute value of the coefficient ranges from zero to infinity. Values between zero and one were defined as connoting relative inelasticity. Values between one and infinity were defined as connoting demand that is relatively elastic.*
4. *Point elasticity was described, and we noted that we could not compute its coefficient by simply substituting into the formula. An alternative geometric measure was developed.*
5. *A relationship between total revenue and elasticity of demand was seen to exist. Total revenue varies inversely with price change if demand is relatively elastic. Total revenue varies directly with price change if demand is relatively inelastic.*
6. *Several product and market characteristics that determine the relative degree of elasticity were delineated. These include availability of substitutes, number of uses of the product, and price of the product relative to income.*
7. *Finally, a number of other elasticity concepts were noted. We reviewed the essentials of elasticity of supply, income elasticity, cross-elasticity of demand, and interest elasticity of investment.*

QUESTIONS

1. Late in the recession year 1974, sales of new automobiles in the United States fell far below expectations and inventories of auto dealers rose to record levels. Chrysler Corp. announced a plan whereby anyone buying a new automobile within 90 days would receive a rebate from the manufacturer of up to $500. What price and income elasticity assumptions did the management of Chrysler have to make to put this plan into action?
2. Would this plan work just as effectively whether or not the other manufacturers matched Chrysler with rebate plans of their own? What would happen if the other firms did match the Chrysler plan? What would happen if they did not?
3. As the rebate period drew to a close, Business Week described it as an "unmitigated disaster." Could this have been anticipated from measured automobile elasticity demand figures of approximately -1.4 for price and $+3.5$ for income?
4. Recognizing that an aggregate demand curve is found by taking the sum of the individual demand curves, a budding economist computed the elasticity for automobiles in general by adding together the elasticities of demand for the individual makes. Comment on both the validity of his assumption regarding demand curves and his actions on computing elasticity.
5. When the Organization of Petroleum Exporting Countries quadrupled the price of oil, what price elasticity assumptions did they make? Were they right?
6. President Ford pressed for a tax on petroleum to accomplish two goals. He hoped it would (1) produce tax revenues; and (2) curtail demand for petroleum products. To what extent are these two goals compatible? What elasticity considerations should be made?

4 Demand analysis: ordinal utility

Indifference curve analysis is an alternative way to study the theory of consumer behavior. When we examined the basis of the demand curve approach, we pointed out its dependence on *cardinal* utility. Even though the idea that each consumer could quantify utility and make first difference comparisons among all possible consumer goods seemed far-fetched, we nevertheless used it. It gave us useful results. However, we had our reservations, and wished we could formulate a theory on a less restrictive set of assumptions. Indifference analysis allows us to account for all of the behavioral phenomena explained by the cardinal utility theory and more, and it allows us to do it *without* resorting to the assumption of measurable utility. It is the next generation of consumer theory.

What does indifference analysis use in place of cardinal utility?
It assumes that although we cannot make cardinal measurements, we can make ordinal comparisons. You remember that ordinal utility involves ranking goods in terms of desirability. We state that *A* is better than *B*, but we are not required to say how much better. The basic tool for implementing this ordinal utility theory is the indifference map.

What is an indifference map?
Physically, it is a graph with an *x* (horizontal) and a *y* (vertical) axis. Unlike the demand diagram, where we measured price on one axis

FIGURE 4–1. The Indifference Map

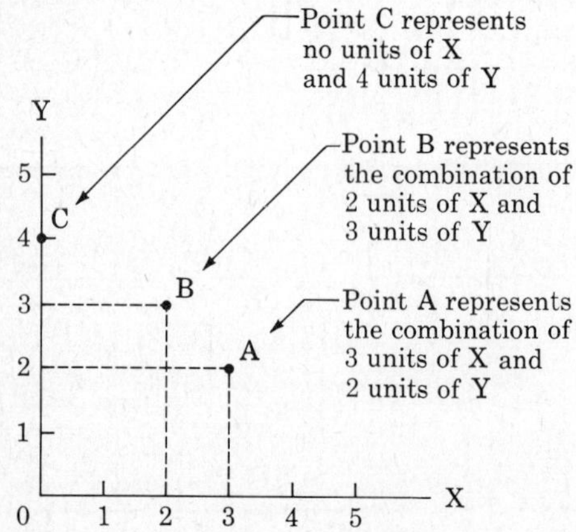

The indifference map can show only quantities of *X* and *Y*. Points of the map represent bundles of *X* and *Y*—so many units of *X* and so many units of *Y*.

FIGURE 4–2. Construction of an Indifference Curve—I

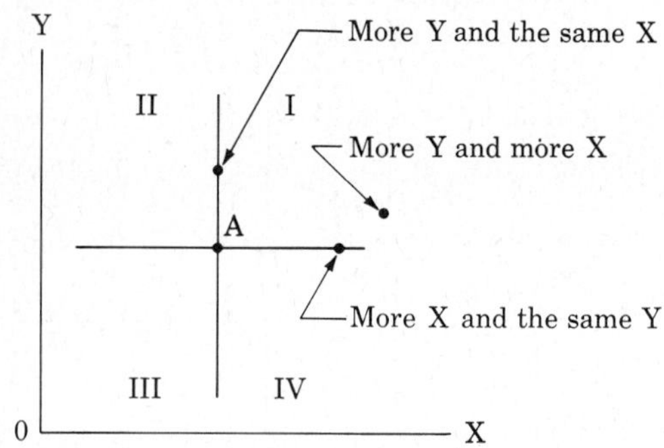

If we take point *A* as a reference point (say it contains 15 units of *X* and 10 units of *Y*) and propose to the consumer that he has a choice of having the combination represented by point *A* or any combination in quadrant I (including points along the axes of quadrant I), the consumer will prefer points in quadrant I. They have more of both *X* and *Y*. Points on the vertical axis of quadrant I have the same amount of *X* as Point *A* and more *Y*. Points on the horizontal axis have the same amount of *Y* and more X. The consumer, if rational, and if X and Y are not nuisances, will prefer more to less.

and quantity on another, the axes on an indifference map measure only quantities of goods. The *x* axis measures units of commodity *X*. The *y* axis measures units of commodity *Y*. It is important never to forget that the *x* and *y* axes measure quantities of goods, and that any other values described on an indifference map are expressed in terms of quantities and ratios of *X* and *Y* (Figure 4–1). Each point on the map represents a *combination* of goods *X* and *Y*. For example, point *A* in Figure 4–1 shows 3 units of good *X* and 2 units of good *Y*. Point *B* shows 2 units of *X* and 3 units of *Y*, and point *C* represents no *X* and 4 units of *Y*.

What are indifference curves?

Under ordinal utility we try to rank the different combinations of *X* and *Y* represented by the points on the map in order of their ability to satisfy. If we are able to rank *each* item as being either more or less desirable than each of the others, we have what is known as a *strong ordering*. There are none that are described as *equally desirable*. Our powers of discrimination are acute enough to sense the smallest difference and thus allow a strong ordering. If, however, our perceptions are more coarse or the criteria less refined, there will be some items that cannot be distinguished from others in terms of ordinal utility. They will be considered to have identical utility and will share a rank. An ordering that contains shared ranks is said to be a *weak ordering*. The evaluation used in indifference curve analysis involves a weak ordering. Some combinations of commodities *X* and *Y* are perceived to have the same utility as others. The subject is presumed to be *indifferent* with regard to which item he would rather possess. An indifference curve is a graph of all the combinations of goods *X* and *Y* that share a rank. A person will willingly swap any combination occurring on an indifference curve for any other combination occurring there.

Is it possible to determine an indifference curve?

Here is an experimental approach that will permit you to determine someone's indifference curve. Present a consumer with a combination of goods *X* and *Y*, such as that represented by point *A* in Figure 4–2.

FIGURE 4–3. Construction of an Indifference Curve—II

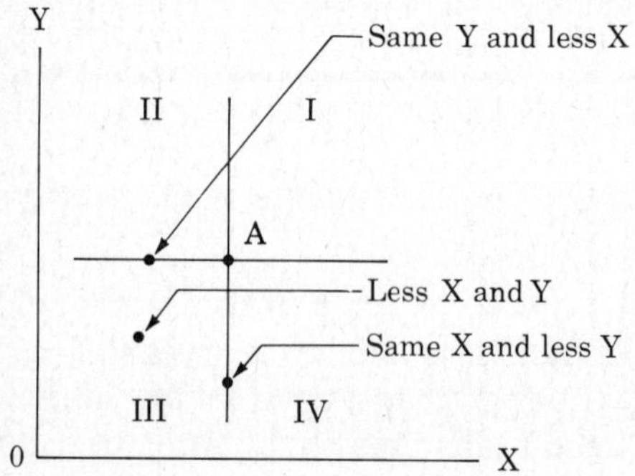

Given a choice between point *A* and points in quadrant III, the consumer will prefer point *A*. Compared to point *A*, combinations in quadrant III have the same *X* and less *Y*, the same *Y* and less *X*, or less of both *X* and *Y*. Again, the consumer prefers more to less.

FIGURE 4–4. Construction of an Indifference Curve—III

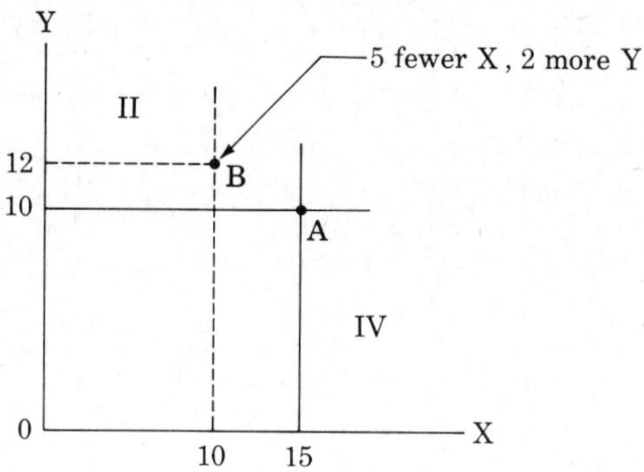

Points in quadrants II and IV represent a trade-off as compared to point *A*. In quadrant II they have more *Y* and less *X*. In quadrant IV they have less *Y* and more *X*. In effect, a price has been paid in terms of one commodity for the other. Point *B* represents 12 units of *Y* and 10 units of *X*. Compared to point *A*, the consumer has 5 fewer units of *X* and 2 more units of *Y*. If he is perfectly willing to give up 5 units of *X* for 2 units of *Y* but would not give up *any* more than 5 units of *X* for 2 units of *Y*, he should find himself with the same utility at point *B* as at point *A*. He is indifferent between the two alternatives. Any other combination with the same utility as *A* also lies on the indifference curve.

Now offer him an opportunity to trade that combination for each of a series of alternative combinations. For each alternative, ask if he prefers it or the original combination A. Some of the alternatives will be preferred to A; for others he will prefer A. Then there will be a group about which he cannot make up his mind. If forced to choose, he would choose each over A about as often as he would choose A over them. We can say that he is indifferent among this group as to which he has. Connecting all these combinations (including A) forms the indifference curve (Figures 4–2, 4–3, 4–4).

Are indifference curves sometimes called iso-utility curves?
Sometimes. The prefix *iso* means *same*, as in isometric exercises, which take place in the same place with no movement. Iso-utility lines are lines of same utility in the sense that the individual derives the same amount of pleasure, or utility, from any combination falling on the curve.

Do all points on the indifference map lie on some curve?
Yes. The indifference *map* has an infinite number of points on it, and each of these points lies on some indifference curve. Thus there are an infinite number of indifference curves as well, although it should be noted that the infinite number of curves is certainly smaller then the infinite number of points. A funny thing about infinity is that there are an infinite number of measures of it. It is subject to ordinal, but not cardinal measurement. Anyway, if we select any other point on the map not on the curve containing point *A*, we can repeat the experiment. Again, there will be some combinations preferred, some held inferior, and some about which the subject cannot make up his mind. All of these latter points will form another indifference curve (Figure 4–5). If the curve is to the right of or above point *A*, we say that all points on it are preferred to point *A*, and also to all points on point *A*'s indifference curve. If the new curve is to the left of or below point *A*, we say that point *A* and all points on its curve are preferred to all points on the new curve. In Figure 4–6 we can say that the combination of 15 units of *X* and 10 units of *Y* is preferred to 20 units of *X* and 3 units of *Y* and also to 1 unit of *X* and 17 units of *Y*.

FIGURE 4–5. Construction of an Indifference Map

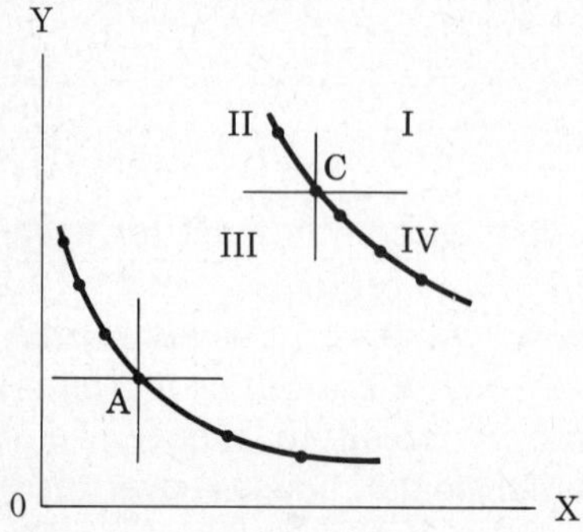

Having established the indifference curve for point *A*, we choose another point, *C*. Draw axes around *C* and repeat the procedure of testing. Note that there are new quadrants I, II, III, IV referring to the new point and the new axes. An indifference curve can be drawn through all points having the same utility as point *C*.

FIGURE 4–6. Indifference Maps

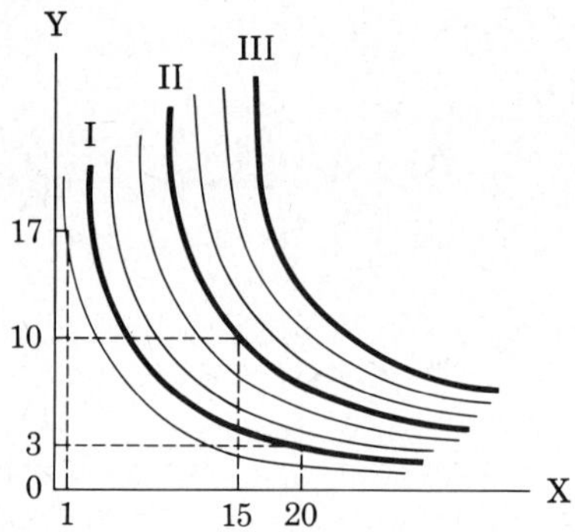

Curves I, II, and III are merely three of an infinite number of indifference curves. Every point between the sample curves is also on some curve. If *X* and *Y* are infinitely divisible, the curves are so close together that they form a continuum.

FIGURE 4–7. Combinations to the Right on the Indifference Curve are Preferred

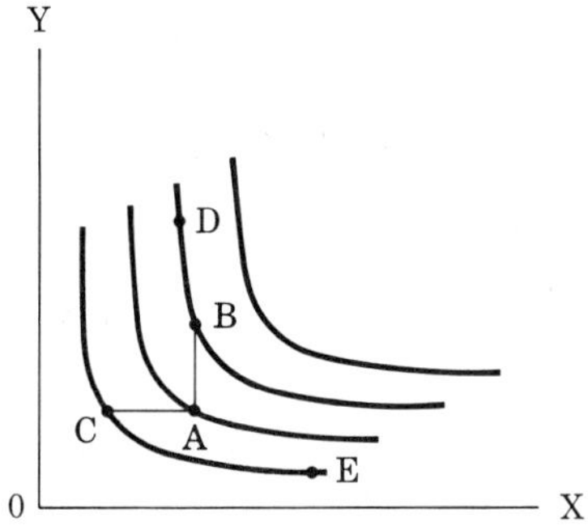

Because we know that *B* is preferred to *A* and *D* is equal in utility to *B*, it follows that *D* is also preferred to *A*. Because *A* is preferred to *C* and *E* is equal in utility to *C*, *A* is also preferred to *E*. Also, *D* is preferred to *E*. We can rank-order all combinations as either better, equal, or worse than all others.

How do you know that combinations to the right of, or above a given indifference curve are preferred to all points on the curve?

This is a little exercise in deductive logic that you should enjoy. Any point to the right of an indifference curve represents a combination of *X* and *Y* that contains at least as much *X* and more *Y* than some point on the curve, or at least as much *Y* and more *X* than some other point on the curve. Either way, the combination to the right of the curve will be preferred to the point on the curve because it represents more goods. Because all points on the curve have equal utility, the point to the right is preferred to all of them. If the utility of *B* is greater than the utility of *A*, it is also greater than all values that are equal to *A* (Figure 4–7). Once the indifference map is drawn completely, we can make at least a weak ordering statement about every combination of *X* and *Y*. The curves represent greater levels of utility as you get further away from the origin of the graph.

Suppose that two curves intersect? Won't the point of intersection have two levels of utility at the same time?

If two curves intersect, the point of intersection will lie on both of them at the same time and would indeed have two levels of utility. That

FIGURE 4–8. Indifference Curves Never Intersect

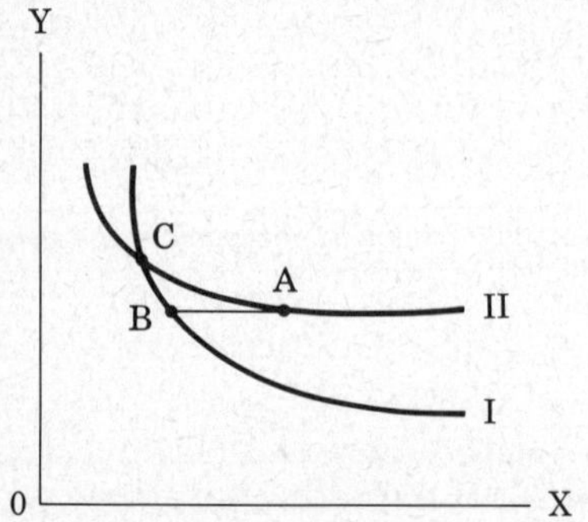

The logical inconsistency in intersecting indifference curves can be seen as follows. On curve I, utility of *B* equals utility of *C*. On curve II, utility of *A* equals utility of *C*. However, because *A* contains the same amount of commodity *Y* as *B* but more *X* than *B*, *A* should have higher utility than *B*. But if *A* equals *C* and *B* equals *C*, then *A* must equal *B*. Under our analysis it is apparent that *A* is preferred to *B*, so there must be something wrong. There is. The curves intersect and they cannot.

FIGURE 4–9. Indifference Curves are Neither Horizontal nor Vertical

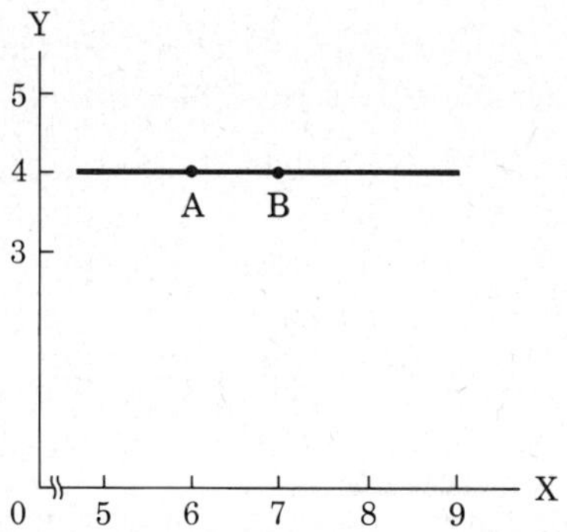

A horizontal indifference curve implies that the subject is equally happy with 4 units of *Y* and 6 units of *X* as with 4 units of *Y* and 7 units of *X*. If *X* is a normal good, 4 units of *Y* and 7 units of *X* should be on a higher indifference curve than 4 units of *Y* and 6 units of *X*. Hence horizontal indifference curves are unlikely. The same argument applies for vertical curves.

is precisely why indifference curves can never intersect within the assumptions of the analysis (Figure 4–8).

Is there some change in the assumptions of the analysis that would permit the curves to intersect?

Indifference analysis is a *static* analysis. This is a technical term that means we are looking at a snapshot of preferences rather than a motion picture. No allowance is made for the passage of time, and therefore there can be no change of tastes—because tastes may only change over time. The preferences are as of some *moment in time*. Suppose that tastes do change. If commodity Y becomes more attractive, a point could have two levels of utility and lie on two indifference curves on the same diagram. However, this is possible only because it does not have the two levels of utility at the same time. We have allowed time to pass in the analysis, and it was this violation of a basic assumption of the analysis that permitted the intersecting curves. To repeat, all indifference curves on an indifference map refer to some point in time and therefore refer to the same set of tastes, so they cannot intersect.

Why are indifference curves always drawn sloping down to the right?

The downward slope follows from the assumption that both goods X and Y are useful and able to provide satisfactions. If a consumer is to be indifferent among various combinations of useful goods, those combinations that contain more X must also contain less Y. If this were not so, he would not be indifferent, but would rather prefer the combination with the additional X and the same amount of Y. A perfectly horizontal indifference curve implies that the additional units of X are useless; a perfectly vertical curve implies that the additional units of Y are useless (Figure 4–9). The curve for perfect complements is often drawn as a right angle with the vertex pointing toward the origin of the x and y axes. The vertical portion of the curve shows that additional units of Y are useless unless there are additional units of X to go with them. Similarly, the horizontal portion implies that the additional units of X are useless unless there are extra units of Y to complement them (Figure 4–10).

Can the curve ever slope upward to the right?

If one of the commodities is a nuisance good, the curve can slope in this direction. A nuisance good is one that violates the assumption that additional quantities will bring additional satisfactions. In the case of a nuisance good, the more you have, the less satisfaction it gives. In

FIGURE 4–10. *Indifference Curve for Perfect Complements*

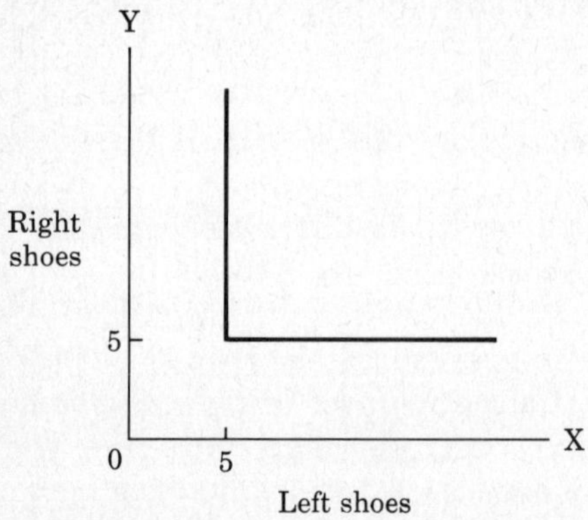

In this figure, suppose that *X* is left shoes and *Y* is right shoes. If the subject has 5 right shoes, he must have 5 left shoes also. He is no better off having 6, 7, 8, or more left shoes to go with them. This provides the horizontal leg. The vertical leg occurs by focusing on 5 left shoes and more right shoes. Utility can only improve by increasing quantities of both shoes together. The analysis, of course, presumes that there is no market for left shoes. If there is, redundant shoes can be traded for something else of value. In that case, the indifference curves will take on a normal, downward-sloping shape.

FIGURE 4–11. *Indifference Curve for Nuisance Goods*

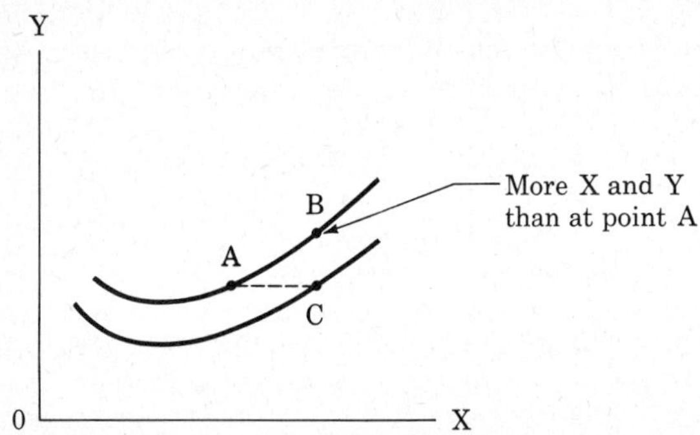

An upward-sloping indifference curve implies that point *B* has the same utility as point *A*, even though *B* has more of both commodities *X* and *Y*. This is inconsistent with the normal assumptions. Also, point C, with the same amount of Y and more X than point A, has a lower utility than A. This is explainable only if one commodity gives disutility, that is, it is a nuisance good.

terms of goods X and Y, rather than feel that you are willing to sacrifice some Y for additional units of X, you instead feel that you must be bribed to take the additional X. If you are given more X without the bribe, your level of satisfaction falls (Figure 4–11).

How does this lead to an upward-sloping indifference curve?
For your level of satisfaction to fall as additional units of X are added to a constant amount of Y, the map must be constructed so that, as you project horizontally across it, the successive combinations of a constant amount of Y and an increasing amount of X put you on lower and lower indifference curves. Similarly, as you get more of both X and Y, you remain on the same curve. The only way for both of these requirements to be met is for a family of curves to slope up to the right.

Why are the indifference curves usually drawn convex to the origin?
Points along the indifference curve represent different combinations of goods X and Y that give the same level of satisfaction. As you move along a curve, you are giving up some units of one good in return for additional units of the other. Because you remain on the same indifference curve, the units of X you acquire are just sufficient to replace the satisfactions lost by foregoing consumption of some Y (Figure 4–12). If X and Y are perfect substitutes, you can go on replacing Y with X in fixed proportions indefinitely. This is the case of the straight-line indifference curve. Whereas perfect complements are represented by a right-angle curve, perfect substitutes are generally shown by a straight line sloping downward at an angle that reflects the rate at which units of Y are substitutable for units of X (Figure 4–13). For most goods, however, substitutability is imperfect. Although the utility lost by sacrificing some Y can be replaced by adding more X, if you continue to give up Y until you are left with very little, it will become more and more difficult to replace the utility lost. Therefore it will take more and more units of X to replace loss of additional units of Y. This causes the curve to flatten out

FIGURE 4–12. Movement Along an Indifference Curve

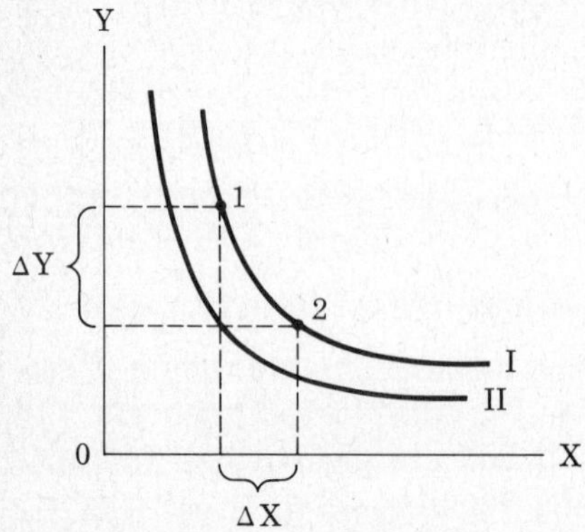

Point 2 has less Y and more X and the same utility as does point 1. Therefore the utility lost by giving up ΔY was exactly offset by getting ΔX. If you just gave up ΔY with no replacement of ΔX you would go to the lower utility curve II.

FIGURE 4–13. Straight-Line Indifference Curve

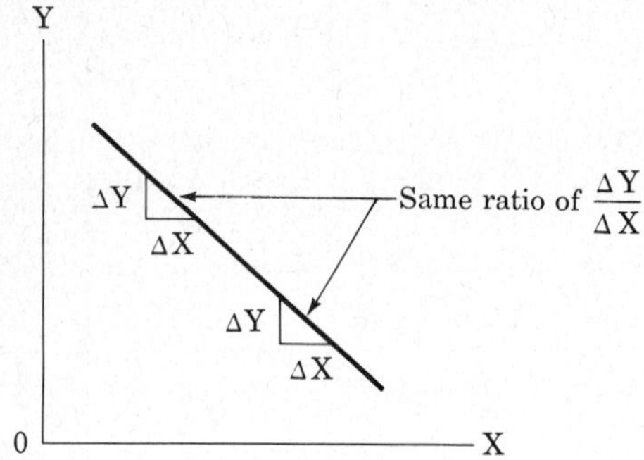

If indifference curves were straight lines, the amount of Y you would be willing to exchange for a unit of X would be the same, regardless of whether you have much Y and little X or little Y and much X. If the ratios do not change, the indifference curve will have no curvature.

as you move farther to the right on it. Finally, if Y becomes *absolutely* necessary at some minimum amount in order to maintain a level of utility, the curve becomes horizontal (Figures 4–14, 4–15).

It sounds as if the curvature of the indifference curve depends on the concept of diminishing marginal utility, an idea we were supposed to have gotten rid of.

Certainly the ideas suggested here are consistent with marginal utility. The less Y you have, the higher the utility of the marginal unit of Y. When you lose the marginal unit, you therefore lose a lot of utility. It is replaced with utility gained from X. However, the more X you have, the lower the marginal utility of additional X. It takes more units of low-marginal utility X to replace a unit of high-marginal utility Y. The difference between this idea and the cardinal marginal utility idea is that the actual *levels* of total and marginal utility need not be known in the indifference curve approach. The relative rates of exchange of X and Y are used as a means of inferring *relative* levels of marginal utility. If we give up 2 units of Y for 1 unit of X and remain on the same curve, we infer that the marginal utility of X is twice as great as that of Y. However, we do not know if the levels of utility are 2 to 1, or 4 to 2, or 200 to 100. What's more, we don't care. On the other hand, in the marginal utility analysis the rates of exchange are inferred *from* cardinal marginal utility levels, which are in turn found by subtracting successive total utilities. In the indifference analysis we use the concept of *marginal rate of substitution*.

What is the marginal rate of substitution?

Marginal rate of substitution refers to the ratio of exchange between the goods X and Y. The notation MRS_{XY} is used to denote the marginal rate of substitution of X for Y. This is defined as the amount of Y the subject is willing to give up for one additional unit of X. The important consideration, of course, is that in giving up Y and getting X, the individual remains on the same indifference curve, or level of utility (Figure 4–16).

What is the relationship between the marginal rate of substitution and marginal utility?

As mentioned before, these ideas play similar roles in dealing with rates of exchange, but they are different concepts. First, let us recognize that the slope of an indifference curve is equal to the marginal rate of substitution. The *MRS* is equal to the amount of Y you give up,

FIGURE 4–14. Convexity of the Indifference Curve

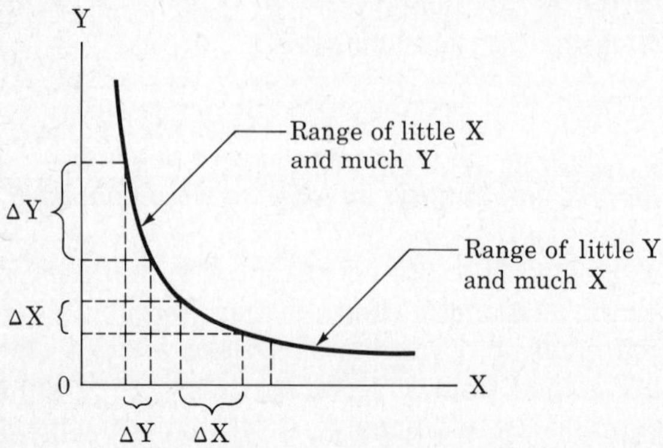

As you go from having much *Y* and little *X* to having little *Y* and much *X*, the relative values *to you* of *X* and *Y* change. Therefore the amount of one commodity that you are willing to exchange for the other will vary at different points along the curve. These changing ratios give the indifference curve its convexity.

FIGURE 4–15. Do Indifference Curves Touch at the Extremes?

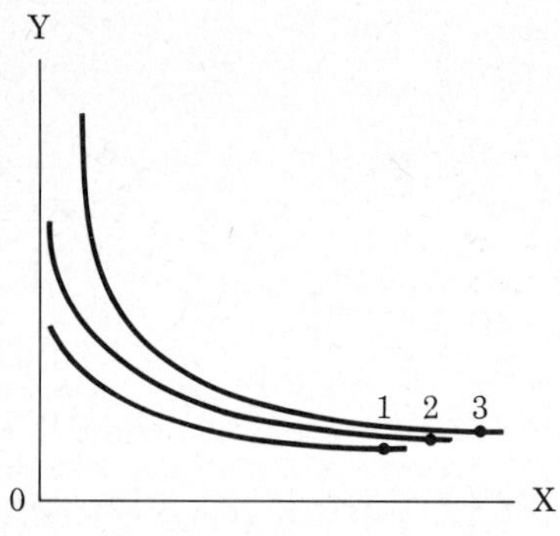

At the extreme ends of the maps, the curves appear to converge. Although they all approach the horizontal at the axes, their convergence is an illusion. Points 1, 2, and 3 are actually on different indifference curves.

FIGURE 4–16. Marginal Rate of Substitution

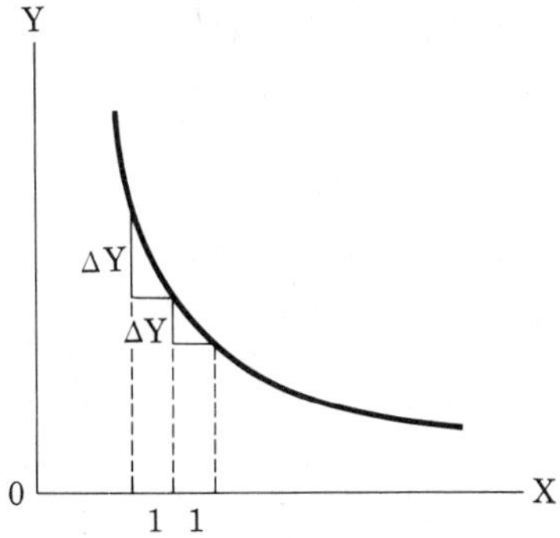

The marginal rate of substitution (*MRS*) is the ratio of $\Delta Y/\Delta X$, or the amount of Y you will give up for *one* unit of X. This is the slope of the indifference curve.

divided by the amount of X you get. That is the definition of the slope of the curve as well. This is a very important and basic definition (Figures 4–17 and 4–18).

$$\text{slope} = \frac{\Delta Y}{\Delta X} = MRS_{XY}$$

Marginal utility enters the discussion when you recognize that by giving up some amount of X for some other amount of Y while remaining on the same indifference curve, you are in effect replacing all the utility lost as a result of the loss of X with an equivalent amount of utility gained from Y. If each unit of X is worth MU_X utils and you give up ΔX units, you are giving up $\Delta X \times MU_X$ utils. You replace it with $\Delta Y \times MU_Y$ utils. Because you have remained on the same indifference curve, the total utility given up is exactly equal to the total utility gained. Therefore the following equation holds:

$$\Delta X \times MU_X = \Delta Y \times MU_Y$$

$$\frac{\Delta Y}{\Delta X} = \frac{MU_X}{MU_Y} (= MRS_{XY} = \text{slope})$$

Thus there is a way to state the marginal rate of substitution (slope) in terms of marginal utilities. The *MRS* is the inverse of the ratio of the marginal utilities (Figure 4–19).

FIGURE 4–17. Review of the Idea of Slope

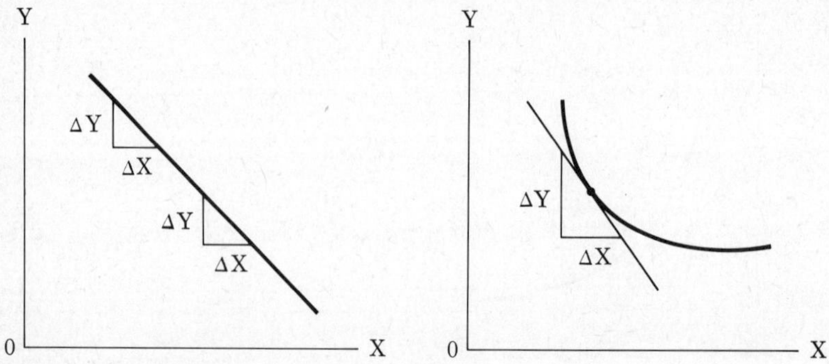

Slope is a graphical measure of rate of change of one variable relative to another. It is shown on a straight line as being constant over the entire length of the graph. For a curve, the usual way to show slope is to draw a tangent to the curve at the point of interest and measure the slope of the tangent line. This is interpreted to be the slope of the curve at the point of tangency. The slope will change as you move along the curve.

FIGURE 4–18. Relationship of Slope to Marginal Rate of Substitution

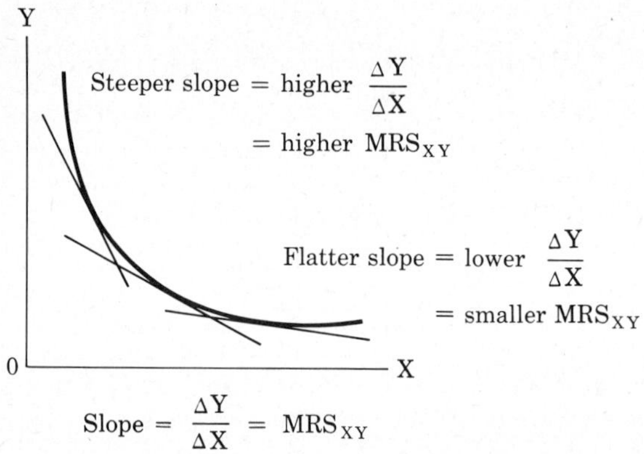

The slope of the indifference curve is the marginal rate of substitution. For normal curves, it is greater at the upper left end and smaller at the lower right end of the curve.

FIGURE 4–19. Movement Along Curve, Holding Utility Constant

In order to hold utility constant while moving along an indifference curve, you must replace the utility lost by giving up one commodity with utility gained from additional units of the other commodity.

Amount of Y given up	×	*Utility of each Y given up*	=	*Amount of X gained*	×	*Utility of each X gained*
ΔY	×	MU_Y	=	ΔX	×	MU_X

Therefore,

$$\frac{\Delta Y}{\Delta X} = \frac{MU_X}{MU_Y}$$ because we stay on same indifference curve

Is it logical that the marginal rate of substitution be equal to the inverse of the marginal utilities, or is it just algebra?

If you stop to think about it, it is perfectly logical. The higher the marginal utility of an item is, the less anxious you are to give it up. However, if you are induced to give it up, it will only be for a large amount of some *other* item. If $\Delta Y/\Delta X$ measures the minimum amount of Y you are willing to accept for the surrender of one unit of X, it follows that the higher MU_X is, the more Y you will want for it. This statement is consistent with the relationship:

$$\text{slope} = \frac{\Delta Y}{\Delta X} = \frac{MU_X}{MU_Y} = MRS_{XY}$$

The higher the marginal utility of X, or the smaller that of Y, the greater will be MRS_{XY}. Hence the indifference curve will be steeper.

Does this mean that the marginal utilities remain constant for perfect substitutes because the indifference curve has the same slope throughout its length?

As long as the purpose to which each product is to be put can be performed just as easily by the substitute, there is really no reason for marginal utility to change as you replace one with the other. For example, if X represents nickels and Y is quarters, the marginal utility of Y will remain five times that of X in the sense that 5 units of X and 1 unit of Y can be used interchangeably, no matter which end of the

FIGURE 4–20. Indifference Curves of Perfect Substitutes (Almost)

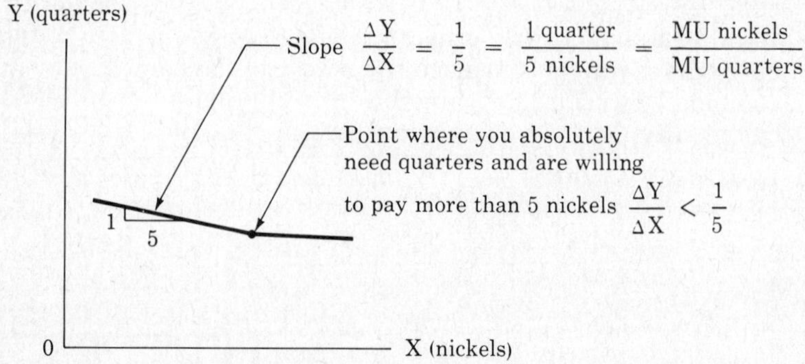

Note: MU nickels/*MU* quarters = 1/5 means quarters are five times as valued as nickels. We do not say that the marginal utility of quarters is 5 and of nickels 1, or 50 and 10. We do not know. All we know are relative measures as indicated by indifference curves and the subject's behavior.

FIGURE 4–21. Concave Indifference Curves

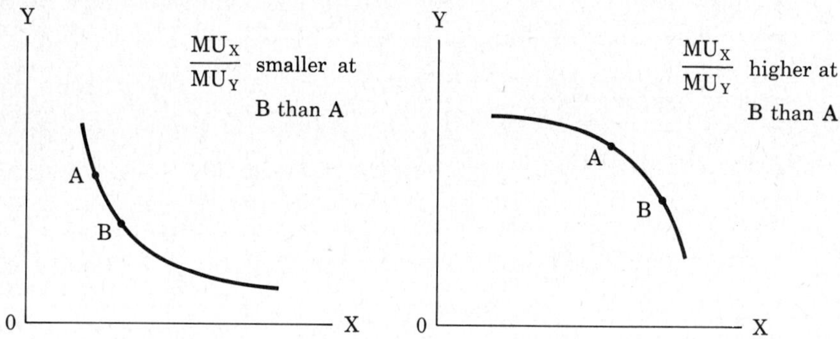

The normal curve is convex to the origin. With more X and less Y, $\Delta Y/\Delta X = MU_X/MU_Y$ becomes smaller.

The concave indifference curve sees $\Delta Y/\Delta X = MU_X/MU_Y$ getting larger as more X is acquired.

indifference curve is involved. Even though the quantity held of one coin may increase and that of the other decrease, the rate at which we are willing to convert one into the other does not alter. They will remain perfect substitutes unless some outside influence enters the picture.

What do you mean by outside influence?

They will remain perfect substitutes as long as there is no storage problem for nickels, or need that can be served by one form of currency but not the other. If you trade away all of the quarters for nickels and then find a cigarette vending machine that takes only quarters, they are no longer perfect substitutes. In this case, as you get fewer quarters, their marginal utility will rise. Because $MRS_{XY} = MU_X/MU_Y$, we are suggesting that MU_Y (quarters) is rising. The curve will be flatter (lower slope) as a result. This means that you will pay more than 5 nickels for a quarter. Gresham's law suggests that different money forms frequently become imperfect substitutes (Figure 4–20).

Suppose that an indifference curve were drawn concave to the origin?

Because the slope of the indifference curve is equal to the ratio MU_X/MU_Y, a concave indifference implies that the marginal utilities of X and Y become greater as more of these products are held, rather than smaller, as is the normal assumption in economic analysis. We make this assertion because the slope of a concave indifference curve is greatest at the point of most X and least Y and is smallest at the point of least X and most Y (Figure 4–21). An example of this situation might be the collector who feels that the more of an item he gets, the more he must have. The Gestalt psychologists employ the concept of *closure*, which says that a subject, upon perceiving a nearly perfect or complete figure, feels a tension to complete it. Applied behaviorally, this idea accounts for the tension we feel to complete a job that is nearly finished. If product X is, let us say, a particular set of stamps, the nearer one comes to having them all, the more one wants to complete the set. Hence, there will be a configuration of a concave indifference curve. More Y will be willingly traded, the closer the set of X is to completion.

How do prices and income enter the indifference analysis?

The indifference map is concerned with the individual's *subjective* valuations; it reflects personal tastes and judgments. Prices and income are *objective* facts of the market. They are data as far as the individual is concerned, and he has no control over them while deciding what to buy. The purpose of the analysis is to see how the individual behaves

FIGURE 4–22. Line of Attainable Combinations (Budget Line)

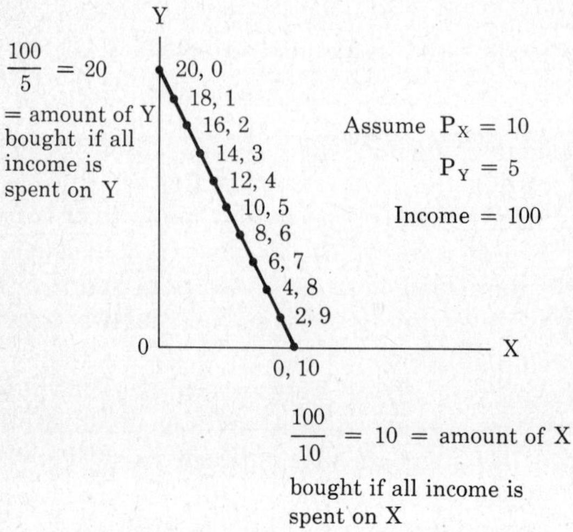

The budget line is a graph of the alternative combinations of X and Y that can be bought if all income is spent. Y can be exchanged for X at the ratio of P_X/P_Y. In this case, that is $10/5 = 2$. Two units of Y exchange for 1 unit of X.

to maximize subjective satisfaction while accommodating to the objective facts of the market, that is, given prices and limited income.

How are prices and income represented on the indifference map? The budget line, sometimes more descriptively called the line of attainable combinations, is used to show these two variables. Assume that the person has a given amount of income I, and the problem is to allocate it all among goods X and/or Y. If this total income is spent, the following relationship holds:

$$(P_X \times X) + (P_Y \times Y) = I$$

That is, the amount of money spent on goods X is the product of the number of units bought multiplied by the price of X. The amount spent on Y is the number of units of Y bought multiplied by the price of Y. The sum of these expenditures equals the total income. The budget line is the graph of this equation. It shows the combinations of X and Y that can be bought with all of the income available. Because the budget line shows all attainable combinations, its slope shows the amount of additional Y you can buy for each unit of X you forego. Since all income is spent, foregoing a unit of X frees P_X money, which you can then spend on as many units of Y as it will buy at the given price of Y. The slope equals P_X/P_Y (Figure 4–22).

What happens if the subject does not spend all of the income?
In that case we think of the budget line as representing the boundary of the set of all attainable combinations. These are all the points within the triangle bounded by the x and y axes and the budget line. Here we use the inequality:

$$(P_X \times X) + (P_Y \times Y) \leq I$$

This reads: The money spent on X and Y is equal to or less than the income available.

How do you draw this budget line on the indifference map?
All it takes to establish a straight line is the location of any two points on it, so we seek to locate two attainable combinations, given the income and prices. The formula for the budget line is

$$(P_X \times X) + (P_Y \times Y) = I$$

We can use any two points of the line to locate it, so let us look at the special case where we spend all of our money on only one of the products and none on the other. First, if the amount of X that is bought is zero, the formula for the budget line becomes

$$(P_X \times 0) + P_Y \times Y = I$$
$$0 + (P_Y \times Y) = I$$
$$Y = \frac{I}{P_Y}$$

Similarly, if all the money is spent on X and the amount of Y bought is zero, the formula becomes

$$(P_X \times X) + (P_Y \times 0) = I$$
$$(P_X \times X) + 0 = I$$
$$X = \frac{I}{P_X}$$

We now have the coordinates of two points on the budget line. The point involving purchase of zero units of X lies on the y axis, and its coordinates are $(0, I/P_Y)$. The point involving purchase of zero units of Y lies on the x axis, and its coordinates are $(I/P_X, 0)$. If we plot these two points and connect them, we have drawn the entire budget line. Any other values of X and Y, when substituted into the budget line equation

FIGURE 4–23. The Slope of the Budget Line

The slope of the budget line equals $\Delta Y/\Delta X$. By similar triangles,

$$\frac{\Delta Y}{\Delta X} = \frac{I/P_Y}{I/P_X}$$

Therefore, if

$I = 100$

$P_X = 10$

$P_Y = 5$

then

$$\frac{I}{P_Y} \times \frac{P_X}{I} = \frac{P_X}{P_Y}$$

$$\frac{\cancel{100}}{5} \times \frac{10}{\cancel{100}} = \frac{10}{5} = 2$$

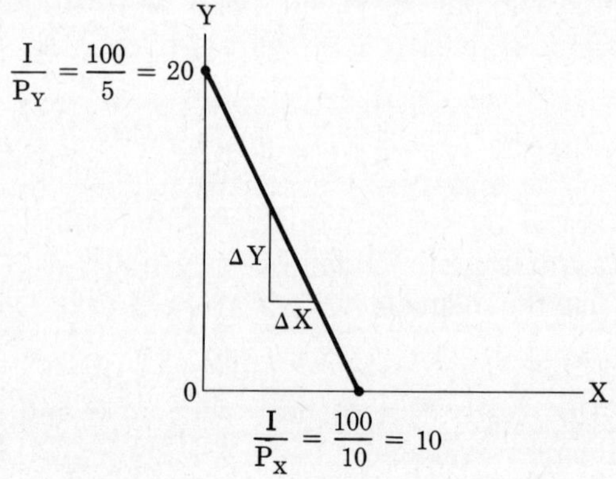

FIGURE 4–24. Consumer Equilibrium

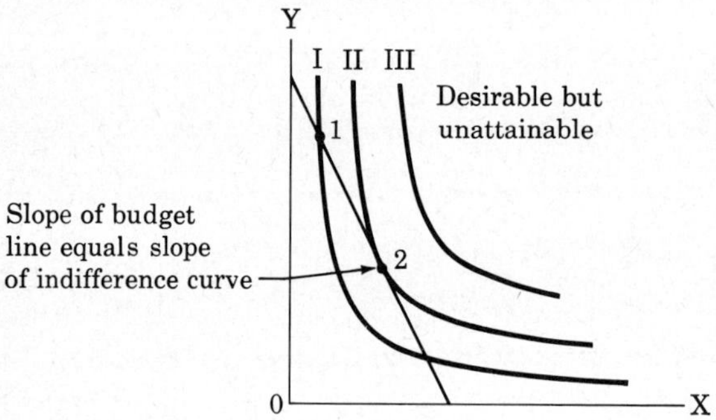

At point 1 all income is spent. However, higher utility is attainable by spending less on Y and more on X, thus moving to the right on the budget line. At point 2 all income is spent and no higher utility is attainable. This is equilibrium.

and plotted, will fall on the line just drawn. Note that the slope of this line equals the vertical intercept (I/P_Y) divided by the horizontal intercept (I/P_X). This ratio,

$$\frac{I/P_Y}{I/P_X}$$

is simplified by inverting the denominator and cancelling the I term. The result is P_X/P_Y, which is consistent with the common-sense value of slope that we figured out before (Figure 4–23).

Where do the prices come from?

We have said that the prices are market data that must be accepted as a fact of life by the individual. They are determined in the market place by the vast, impersonal forces of supply and demand. The individual must accommodate his own preferences, likes, and dislikes to the inescapable reality of the market-determined prices. He can vary the amounts of X and Y he buys under the circumstances, but he can do nothing about changing the circumstances.

How do we use the budget line and the indifference curve to analyze consumer behavior?

The consumer is presumed to be a utility maximizer who would like to use his income to purchase the particular combination of goods X and Y that gives him the most satisfaction. When he does this, he is said to be in equilibrium. He will have no incentive to change his purchase pattern as long as the conditions such as price, income, and taste remain the same. Another way of looking at this is to say that he wishes to obtain a combination of X and Y that lies on the highest indifference curve attainable with his limited income. Every point on the map lies on some indifference curve, so those that fall on the budget line all fall on different indifference curves as well. We are after that point which coincidentally lies on both the budget line and also on the highest (farthest to the right) indifference curve. Because it lies on the highest indifference curve, it gives the most utility. Because it lies on the budget line, it is attainable within the income constraint. As it turns out, if the curves are convex to the origin (the normal situation), the highest level of utility attainable from the limited income occurs on the curve that is just tangent to the budget line, and the combination that is bought is the one located on the map at the point of tangency (Figure 4–24). All other points on the map either lie on lower indifference curves or else are unattainable within the income constraint. The consumer should buy this combination for utility maximization.

FIGURE 4–25. At Equilibrium, Slopes of Budget Line and Indifference Curve Must Be Equal

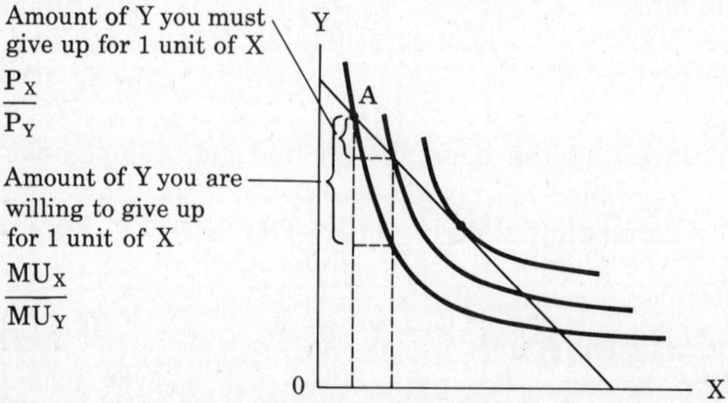

The key to understanding this diagram is to recognize that the slope of the indifference curve (MU_X/MU_Y) equals the subjective, personal amounts of Y we are *willing* to exchange for a unit X. The slope of the budget line (P_X/P_Y) equals the amount of Y the market says we *must* give up for a unit of X. These must be equal for us to be happy doing what we must do.

$\frac{MU_X}{MU_Y} > \frac{P_X}{P_Y}$ at point A

FIGURE 4–26.

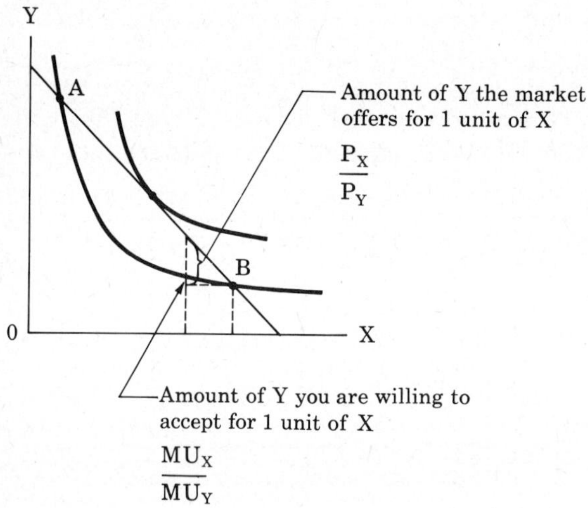

Figure 4–25 from another point of view

$\frac{MU_X}{MU_Y} < \frac{P_X}{P_Y}$ at point B

Are the slopes of the budget line and the indifference curve equal at this tangency point?

Obviously they are. Remember that the slope of a curve at any point along its length is equal to the slope of the tangent to the curve at that point. Applying this geometric principle to our situation, we recognize that, because the line and the curve are tangent, the slope of the line is also, by definition, the slope of the curve. This fact, that the slopes of the budget line and indifference curve are equal at the point of equilibrium, is quite important to the logic of our argument.

Why is the equality of the slopes of the budget line and the indifference curve so important?

For one thing, it means that the consumer is *willing* to exchange in the market at the same rate he is *required* to. We defined the slope of the indifference curve as the marginal rate of substitution and said that it represented the amount of Y the consumer is willing to give up for one additional unit of X. We also described the slope of the budget line as representing the amount of Y he must give up if he is to make available enough money with which to buy an extra unit of X. More formally, the slope of the budget line is equal to P_X/P_Y, and the slope of the indifference curve is equal to MU_X/MU_Y. At the point of equilibrium these slopes are equal:

$$\frac{P_X}{P_Y} = \frac{MU_X}{MU_Y}$$

$$\frac{MU_X}{P_X} = \frac{MU_Y}{P_Y}$$

We arrived at this identical conclusion through the cardinal utility analysis. It says that in order to maximize utility, the marginal utility per dollar spent on each of the goods bought must be equal. Under conditions of diminishing marginal utility, any reallocation of money between X and Y will diminish total utility (Figure 4–25).

Suppose that the consumer buys some other combination of goods?

If he does, he will obviously not be buying the quantity of each that we have just asserted maximizes utility. Let us see why not. At point *A* in Figure 4–25, the slope of the indifference curve is greater than that of the budget line. Thus $MU_X/MU_Y > P_X/P_Y$. This suggests that the consumer values X more highly relative to Y than does the market in general. At least he is willing to give up more Y for a unit of X than the market says he must. If he gives up Y for X at the rate he is willing to (marginal rate of substitution), he will remain at the same level of

FIGURE 4–27. A Common Error

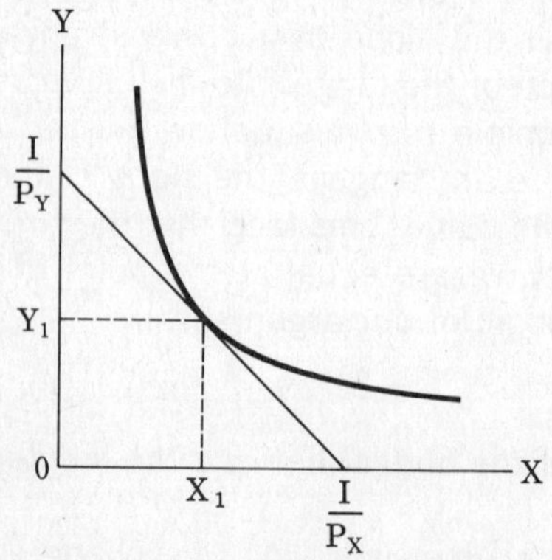

The answer to the question, How much X and Y will be bought in equilibrium? should be X_1 and Y_1. There is a tendency to say, in error, I/P_X and I/P_Y. It makes no sense to makes this error, and don't ask me why it occurs. It just does, and you should not make it.

utility, but he will now have some money income left because the new point on the indifference curve lies below the boundary formed by the budget line, and not on it. If, instead of sliding along the indifference curve, he exchanges Y for X at the rate the market demands, along the budget line, he will move to a higher level of utility. He can do this as long as the budget line intersects the indifference curve (Figure 4–26).

How does exchanging X for Y at the market rate eventually bring about an equilibrium?

If we proceed down the budget line from point A in Figure 4–25, we get more X and give up Y. As the amount of X we get increases, its marginal utility (MU_X) decreases. As the amount of Y we have decreases, its marginal utility (MU_Y) increases. All this time prices remain fixed, so the slope of the budget line (P_X/P_Y) remains the same while the ratio MU_X/MU_Y gets smaller. Because MU_X/MU_Y was *greater* than the slope of the budget line at point A, it must approach that value as it gets smaller. At the point where $MU_X/MU_Y = P_X/P_Y$, the consumer is in equilibrium. He is willing to exchange at the rate the market demands. If exchange continues along the budget line beyond the equilibrium point, we come to combinations such as in Figure 4–26, where the individual is back on the indifference curve from which he started. Obviously, B involves a lower level of utility than was attainable at equilibrium. Here MU_X/MU_Y is less than P_X/P_Y. At this point the market demands that the consumer give up more Y for a unit of X than he is willing to, or, alternatively, offers more Y for a unit of X than he really demands in order to be induced to give up a unit of X. By accepting the market's offer of units of Y for X, the consumer can move up the budget line to higher levels of utility and eventually reach equilibrium.

How long do you remain at equilibrium?

As long as the conditions prevailing—tastes, income, relative prices of X, Y, and all related goods—remain constant, the consumer will have no incentive to change from a utility-maximizing behavior. He continues to purchase the utility-maximizing quantities of X and Y. A good part of our subsequent analysis will be devoted to examination of the effects of changes in income and prices, because we are interested in behavior under different circumstances in the market. Incidentally, it is important to remember that, in reading the indifference map diagram, the quantities of X and Y are read by projecting from the equilibrium point out at right angles to the axes. Do not make the careless mistake of thinking of the X and Y intercepts of the budget line as the quantities taken (Figure 4–27).

What happens to equilibrium in the event the indifference curves are concave, rather than convex, to the origin?

A concave indifference curve reflects a condition akin to increasing marginal utility. Because the assumption of diminishing marginal utility was necessary to a stable equilibrium, we may expect something quite bizarre when that condition is violated. At point A in Figure 4–28 the marginal rate of substitution (slope of the indifference curve) is greater than the price ratio; that is,

$$\frac{MU_X}{MU_Y} > \frac{P_X}{P_Y}$$

or

$$\frac{MU_X}{P_X} > \frac{MU_Y}{P_Y}$$

Under these circumstances, logic says to increase consumption of X, because it gives a higher level of marginal utility per dollar than does Y. The price ratio P_X/P_Y determines the rate at which one can exchange Y for X. The consumer will move along the budget line, exchanging Y for X at the rate of P_X/P_Y. However, in the case of concave indifference curves, as he does so, he moves to successively higher indifference

FIGURE 4–28. Concave Indifference Curves Again

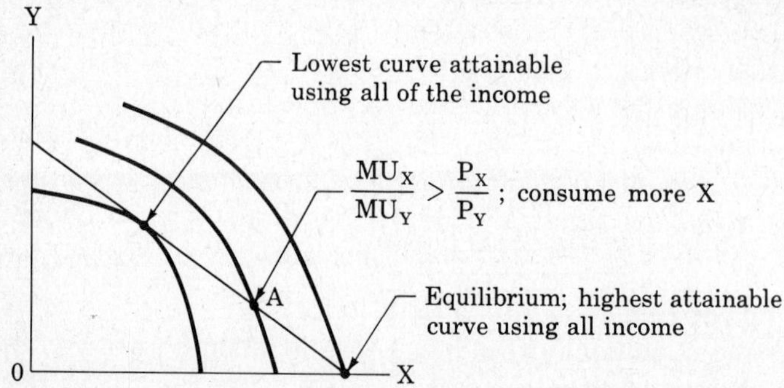

With concave indifference curves, the tangency between budget line and indifference curve does not put the consumer on the highest indifference curve attainable. The utility maximum occurs where a curve intersects one of the axes.

FIGURE 4–29. Formula for the Budget Line

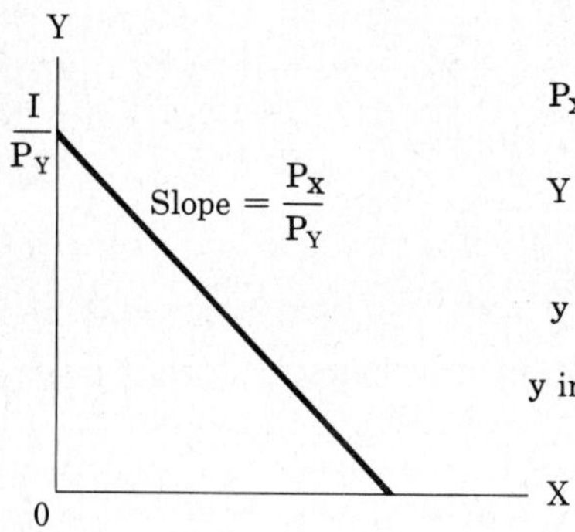

$$P_X \times X + P_Y \times Y = I$$

$$Y = \frac{I}{P_Y} - \frac{P_X}{P_Y} X$$

$$y = b + m x$$

y intercept   slope

The budget line is a linear function expressed implicitly in terms of X and Y. We can put it into the explicit linear format of $Y = b + mx$.

curves. What is more, the inequality $MU_X/P_X > MU_Y/P_Y$ increases as he gets farther away from the tangency point, thereby giving an incentive to move still further away. In fact, he will continue to trade Y for X until all of the Y is gone and he has only commodity X. This combination coincides with the highest attainable indifference curve. Thus, when the condition of diminishing marginal utility does not prevail, we do not get the nice interior equilibrium point for which we usually look. Without diminishing returns, none of the elaborate analysis of marginal economics holds. For a stable equilibrium to occur, total utility must increase with quantity, but the rate at which it increases must diminish.

Suppose that some conditions of the analysis change? Suppose that the price of X changes? How is this shown?

If the price changes, the effect shows up in the slope of the budget line. Remember that the budget line assumes that all income is spent on X and Y and that its equation is

$$(P_X \times X) + (P_Y \times Y) = I$$

If we make Y an explicit function of X, this expression becomes

$$Y = \frac{I - P_X(X)}{P_Y}$$

or

$$Y = \frac{I}{P_Y} - \frac{P_X}{P_Y}X$$

This is now in the more familiar form of a linear equation, $y = b + mx$, where b represents the y intercept and m represents the slope of the function. In our budget line equation, the term I/P_Y stands in the place of the y intercept, and the coefficient of x, that is, P_X/P_Y, represents the slope of the line. Notice that it is negative in sign, which means that it slopes down to the right (Figure 4–29). Now, if the price of X changes, we note that it will change the value of the slope because the expression for slope (P_X/P_Y) contains this variable. The y intercept does not have a P_X term in it and will be unaffected. If the price of X goes up, the slope becomes greater. Because the y intercept is unchanged, the line rotates inward around this point. Similarly, a decline in the price causes the line to rotate to the right, around the y intercept (Figure 4–30).

How can an increase in income be shown on an indifference map?

Indifference maps can show an increase in income very easily. There are three variables involved in the budget line, P_X, P_Y, and I. We are now talking about a change in I while P_X and P_Y remain unchanged.

FIGURE 4–30. Change in Price Changes the Slope of the Budget Line

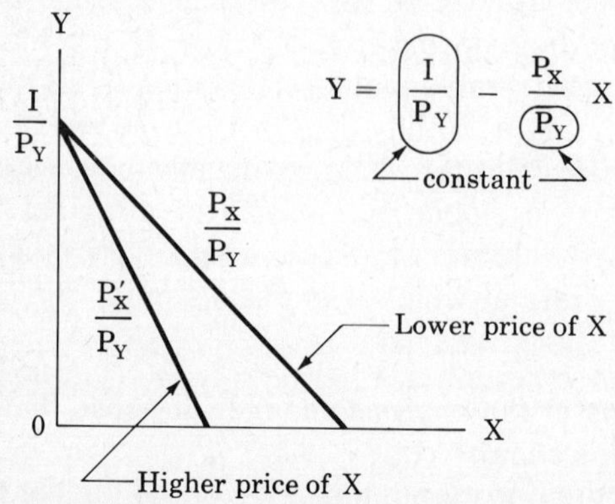

If P_X increases but I and P_Y remain the same, the formula for the budget line is affected in the following manner: I/P_Y (*y* intercept) is the same; P_X/P_Y is bigger; the slope is steeper.

FIGURE 4–31. Change in Income Only

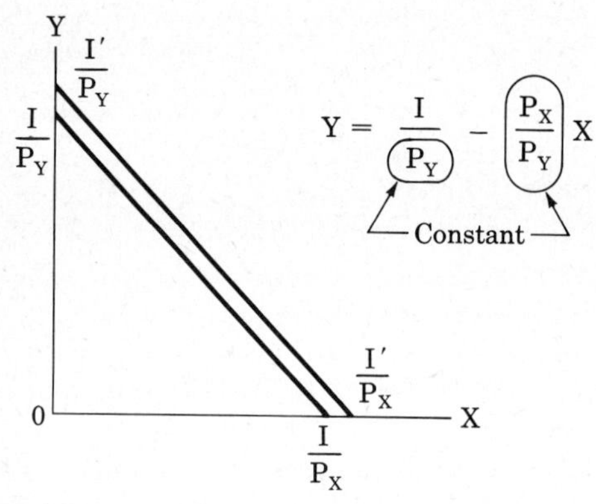

If I increases but P_X and P_Y remain the same, the slope is unchanged. Only the *y* intercept increases.

FIGURE 4–32. Change in Price of Y Only

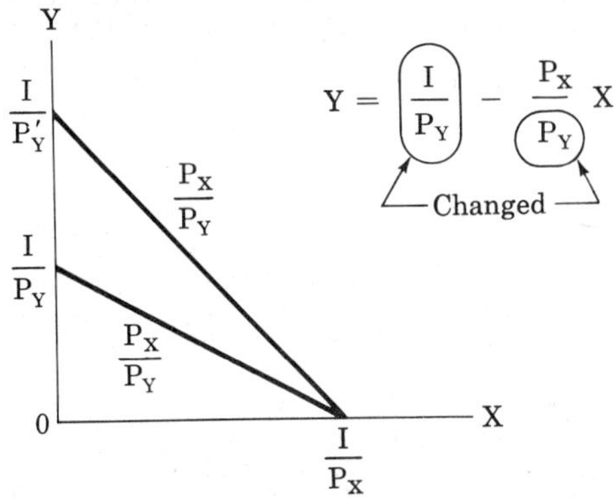

If the price of Y changes and income and the price of X remain unchanged, the y intercept changes and the slope of the budget line changes. The x intercept remains unchanged.

Therefore the slope of the budget line remains unchanged because it is determined by the ratio P_X/P_Y. Changing I shifts the y intercept, I/P_Y. If I increases, the y intercept gets greater and the budget line shifts to the right, remaining parallel to the old budget line. If income falls, the budget line makes a parallel shift to the left. Change in income alters the amounts of X and Y that are obtainable. It does not affect the rate at which they exchange one for the other (Figure 4–31).

What if the price of* Y *changes?

Usually the analysis is carried on in terms of X as a variable good. One favorite device is to treat Y as all other goods. Another is to treat Y as money (income). As long as income remains constant in either of these cases, the y intercept remains fixed and it is again P_X with which we are concerned. Of course, if Y is just another single good and P_Y changes, we must examine our formula to see how the elements of the apparatus are affected. Because the slope of the budget line equals P_X/P_Y, an increase in the price of Y would make the budget line flatter as the slope declined. If P_Y decreased, the slope would become steeper. Also, note that a change in P_Y will change the y intercept (I/P_Y). Thus the budget line pivots around the x intercept to reflect these changes in prices in Y, rotating clockwise to reflect decreases in P_Y and counterclockwise to show increases (Figure 4–32).

FIGURE 4–33. Budget Lines; Y Equals Money

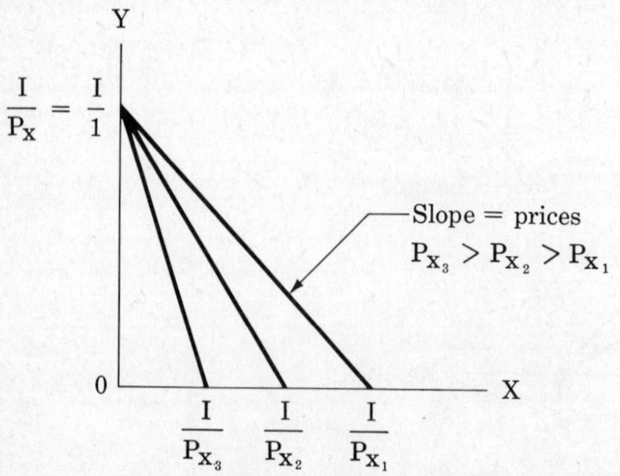

If *Y* equals money, we make the price of *Y* equal one. The slope of the budget line now equals $-P_X$.

FIGURE 4–34. Another Really Dumb Mistake

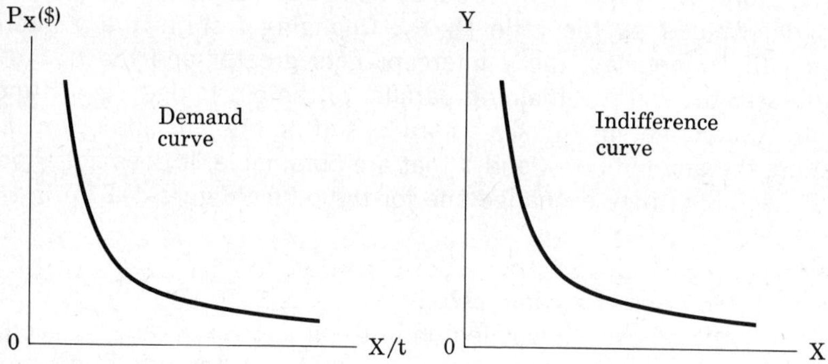

Sometimes a student less sharp than you are will mistake an indifference curve for a demand curve just because the *y* axis stands for money. Remember that an indifference map shows combinations of *X* and *Y* that are held. A demand curve shows prices you are willing to *give up* for *each* one of a number of units of *X*. They are clearly not the same.

If Y is assumed to be money, what is its price?

We discussed this briefly in Chapter 2. A better understanding requires some background in the Walrasian general equilibrium theory. Walras discussed the general case in which there were *n* commodities being studied. He was interested in seeing how a change in the price or quantity of any one of them would affect all of the others. He pointed out that any one of these commodities could serve as the monetary standard, and the prices of the other $n - 1$ commodities could be measured relative to it. Whichever commodity was chosen to be money was referred to as the *numeraire*. All other items were evaluated relative to numeraire, so it was easiest if the value of numeraire were placed at unity. It exchanges for itself in a one-to-one ratio. Because numeraire is what we generally call money when it acts in its role as a medium of exchange, we make its price also equal to unity.

What happens to the slope of the budget line when Y represents numeraire?

The slope of the budget line is P_X/P_Y and P_Y equals 1: therefore, the slope equals P_X. The higher the price of *X*, the steeper the budget line will be. The *y* intercept is I/P_Y. Again, because P_Y equals 1, the *y* intercept measures the level of income and remains fixed as long as income is unchanged. This makes sense because the budget line shows attainable combinations of commodity X and money (in this case Y). It should show that if you buy zero units of X you still have your entire income on hand. This point is the *y* intercept, where *x* equals zero and *y* equals income (Figure 4–33).

When Y represents money, is the indifference curve the same as the demand curve?

Absolutely not!! The indifference curve still shows quantities of *X* and *Y* (in this case, money) held. A demand curve can be developed from the indifference map, but it is not the same thing as an indifference curve under any circumstances (Figure 4–34).

How can the demand curve be developed from the indifference map?

A demand curve shows the utility-maximizing quantities of some commodity (*X*) that will be purchased at different alternative prices, all other things being equal. We can show different prices of *X* by varying the slope of the budget line, holding the *y* intercept constant at the given income. Then we examine the map to see what quantities of *X* are taken by the utility maximizer at the different prices. For each price

FIGURE 4–35. Drawing a Demand Curve from an Indifference Map

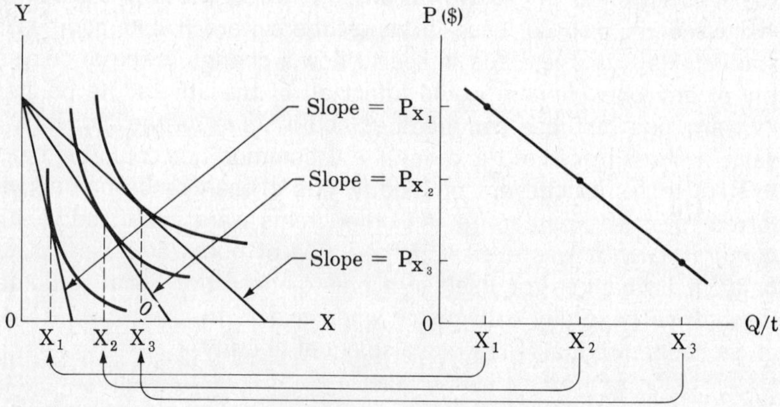

There is no way to do this simply by projecting line segments. However, value of price and quantity can be read from the indifference map and plotted on a separate set of axes.

FIGURE 4–36. Finding Total Revenue on an Indifference Map

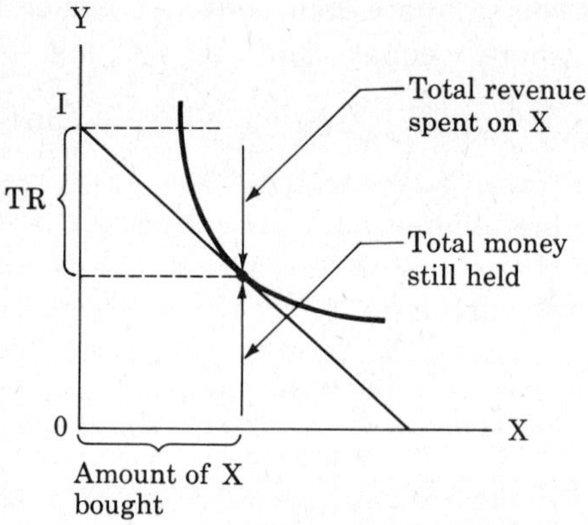

By reading *down* from the *y* intercept to the equilibrium quantity of *Y*, we read the total revenue spent. By reading *up* from the origin to the equilibrium quantity of *Y*, we read the money left on hand.

the quantity taken will be that coinciding with a tangency between the budget line and an indifference curve. Again, the indifference curve tangent to the budget line represents the highest level of utility attainable at the price, and the coordinates of *X* and *Y* at the point of tangency show the product combination that affords this highest attainable level of utility. We can read from the indifference map the data that we need to construct the demand curve. On a separate pair of axes, with the *y* axis representing price and the *x* axis representing quantity, we plot the different prices (taken from the slopes of the budget lines) and the quantities (taken by reading down from the point of tangency to the *x* axis on the indifference map). In so doing, we have constructed a demand curve (Figure 4–35).

Can you show elasticity of demand on an indifference map?

This is one of the more interesting applications of the analysis, in that it employs a trick that is quite useful in other indifference map applications. The trick is worth learning. First, recall the relationship between total revenue spent and price elasticity. If the price elasticity is greater than one, the total revenue spent varies inversely with the price level. A decline in price will increase quantity to such an extent that the total revenue rises. A rise in price will decrease quantity to such an extent that the total revenue falls. If we can measure the changes in total revenue spent at different prices on the indifference map, we can say something about the price elasticity of demand.

How can you measure changes in total revenue on an indifference map?

This is the trick. Again, think of quantities measured along the *y* axis as representing total income. When *x* is zero, *y* represents the total money income. Any point on the map represents, as usual, some quantity of *X* and some quantity of money held. If measuring *up* from the origin shows you how much money you have left when you buy a certain amount of *X*, the difference between this amount of money held and the total income with which you began shows how much you no longer have, or, in other words, the total revenue you spent on *X*. Thus, if you simply measure down from the *y* intercept to the *y* value at the equilibrium point, you will be accounting for what we have referred to as total revenue. If the equilibrium point associated with a lower price shows that the *y* value is less than it was with a higher price, we interpret this to show an elastic demand (Figure 4–36). The reasoning is that because the *y* value is less with the lower price, the amount of money spent must be more. Hence the inverse relationship between price and total revenue reflects a price elasticity greater than one (Figures 4–37 and 4–38).

FIGURE 4–37. Elasticity of Demand—I

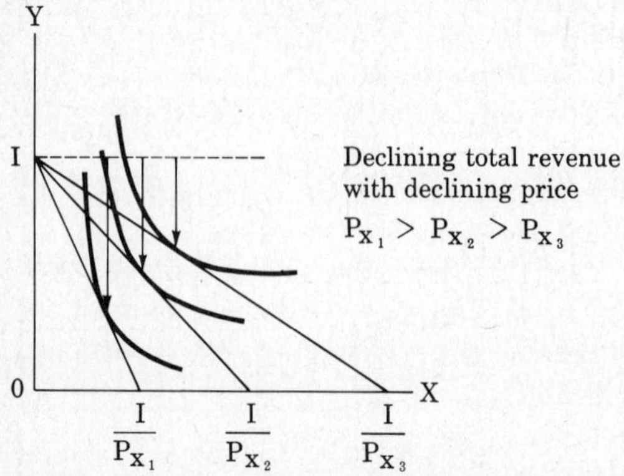

Employing the relationship between elasticity and total revenue, we note in this figure that the budget lines to the right represent lower prices and that, reading down from the income level, total revenue spent falls with these lower prices. Therefore demand is inelastic.

FIGURE 4–38. Elasticity of Demand—II

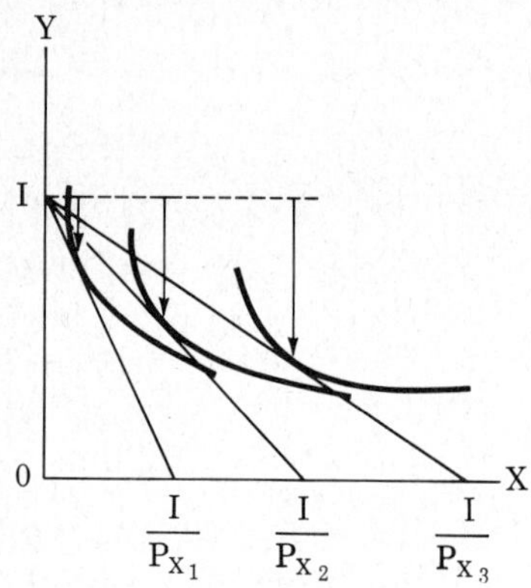

Rising total revenue with declining price

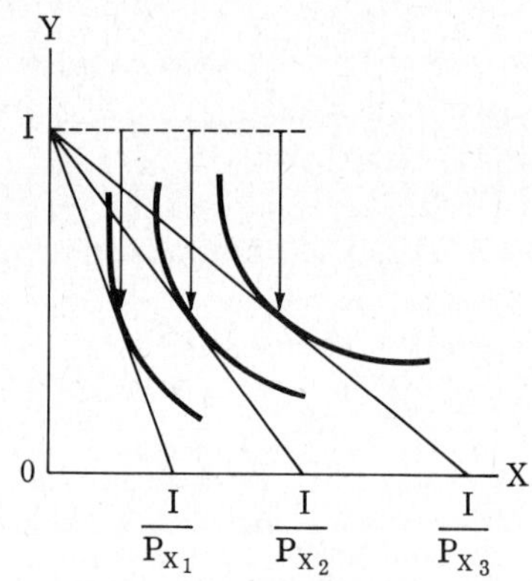

Constant total revenue with declining price

As price declines in the figure on the left, total revenue increases, thus indicating elastic demand. On the right, we see that total revenue remains constant while prices decline. Elasticity is unitary.

FIGURE 4–39. Linear Demand Curve

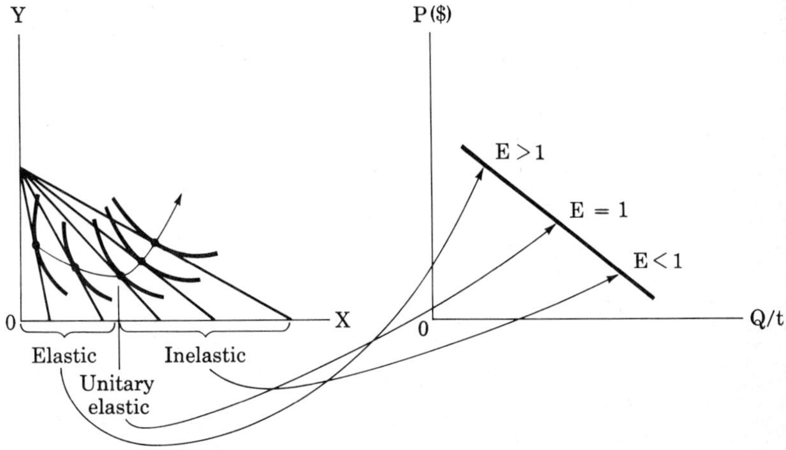

As price falls, total revenue rises, then is constant, then falls. Therefore demand is first relatively elastic, then unitary elastic, then relatively inelastic.

What would the indifference map for a linear demand curve look like?
A linear demand curve has a constant slope, but the coefficient of price elasticity of demand is not constant. Remember that it is greater than unity at high prices, equals unity at some point in the middle, and then falls below unity. Thus as price declines from high to low levels, we would expect total revenue spent first to rise, then to be constant, and then to fall. To show a series of declining prices, we construct a family of budget lines of lesser and lesser slope around a constant *y* intercept. We examine the equilibrium points of indifference curve tangency for each price. A line connecting the equilibrium points is sometimes called the *price-consumption* line. The price-consumption line for a linear demand curve should be a curve sloping downward during the elastic phase, running horizontal during the unitary elastic phase, and then sloping upward during the inelastic phase. A configuration such as this would be consistent with our generalizations about elasticity and total revenue (Figure 4–39).

What are income and substitution effects?
The law of demand, or the downward-sloping demand curve, states that,

FIGURE 4–40. Income and Substitution Effects—I

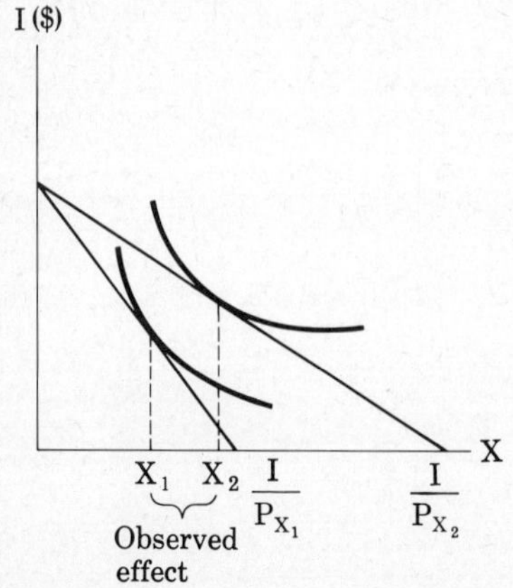

If the price falls from P_{X1} to P_{X2}, the amount of X taken rises from X_1 to X_2. The change in quantity $X_1 - X_2$ is referred to as the observed effect. It is the total quantity change resulting from a drop in price. Note, however, that purchase of X_2 involves a higher indifference curve than did X_1. This higher level of utility is thought of as an increase in real income.

all things being equal, the lower the price of a normal good, the greater will be the quantity of it demanded. The income and substitution effects are the reasons that this demand curve slopes downward. They are two behavioral tendencies that we expect to see manifested when price changes occur. The change in quantity that we observe accompanying a change in price is the sum of these two parts (Figure 4–40).

What exactly is the income effect?

Let us take the case of an individual who is in equilibrium at one price and then the price of *X* falls. If he were to continue to consume the same amount of *X* as before the fall in price, he would have some money left over. If we stick to the assumption that he spends all of his income, he will have to distribute this residual money by increasing his expenditures on the various things he buys. He buys a little more of each normal good in his budget, including item *X* (if it is normal). The additional amount of *X* that is bought because of the increase in real purchasing power that occurs as a result of a decrease in the price of

X is called the *income effect*. We have already observed that purchase of normal goods will increase with an increase in income. The additional wrinkle is that, in this instance, the increase in real income occurred as a result of a decrease in the price of a product, rather than, as is more usual, an increase in money income. Nevertheless, the effect is the same and the purchase of all goods (including *X*) is affected. Generally, since we spend our income on many commodities, *X* absorbs a very minor part of our total expenditure. A drop in its price will not free too much money, so the income effect is very small relative to the substitution effect. Most diagrams exaggerate its size.

What is the substitution effect?

The substitution effect is the part of the total change in the amount bought of commodity *X* that is not in any way related to the real income effect cited above. In other words, it is the rest of the observed effect, after accounting for the income effect. If we could hold real income constant while changing prices, the quantity change would reflect only the change in *relative* prices. You will notice that in our original statement of the law of demand we stipulated that all variables other than price should remain constant. We included money income among the variables we controlled. This was rather sloppy, because price changes also affect real income. A real effort to hold all other variables constant requires our controlling for the income effect also.

How can you hold real income constant while changing prices?

One theoretical way would be to subsidize (or tax) the consumer by an amount equal to his change in real income each time price changes. If the price of *X* were reduced, thereby giving rise to a positive income as well as to substitution effects, the technique would be to measure the increase in real income, and tax that income away. With real income reduced to its earlier level, the income effect would be zero, and the total observed effect would equal only the substitution effect. In the event the price of *X* went up, with an accompanying reduction in real income, this theoretical construction would call for a subsidy to replace real income lost from the price rise.

How would you measure the amount by which a change in the price of* X *changes real income?

There is some difference of opinion on this among economists. Let us examine the method suggested by Sir John Hicks. He won the Nobel Prize in Economics, so we can assume there is some merit to it. His

FIGURE 4–41. Income Substitution Effect—II

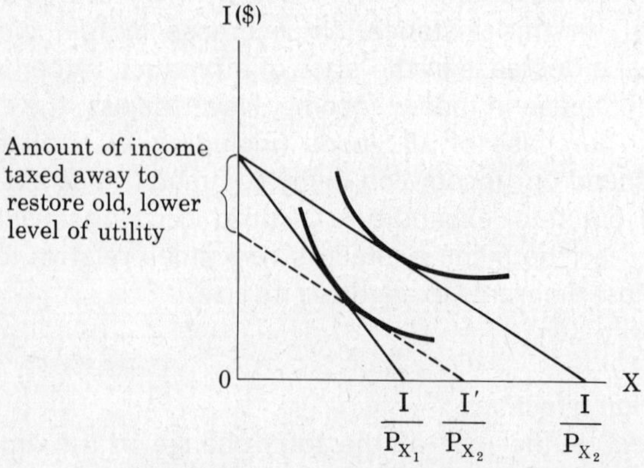

In order to remove the income effect, we must hypothetically tax away enough income to restore the old level of real income. This involves a reduction of income (shift of budget line) to a level where there is tangency with the old indifference curve. Note that the downward shift is parallel, because P_X/P_Y remains unchanged.

FIGURE 4–42. Income and Substitution Effect—III

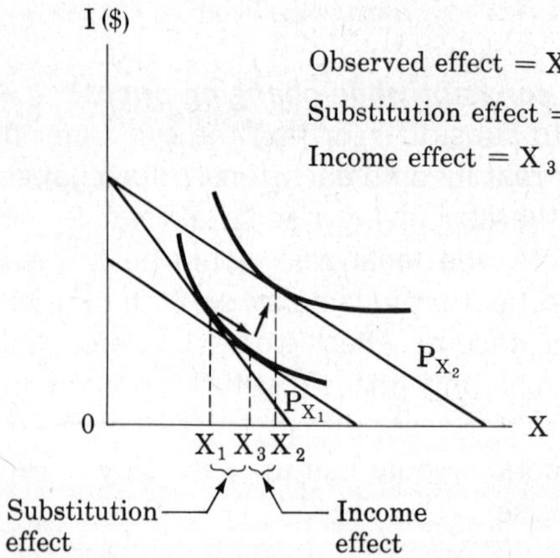

The observed effect is divided into an income and a substitution effect. The income effect is shown as the change in *X* resulting from a movement between curves. The substitution effect is the change in *X* resulting from a movement along an indifference curve following a price change.

method identifies real income with level of utility. If you look at any one of the indifference maps we have drawn, you will note that a fall in the price of *X* not only raises the amount of *X* bought, it also puts us on a higher indifference curve. If we could measure how much money income must be taxed away to restore the consumer to his original equilibrium level of utility, we would have a measure of the real income change resulting from the price reduction of *X*. If the price of *X* had risen, we would have fallen to a lower indifference curve as the budget line rotated to the left. Here, we would be interested in measuring how much money subsidy would be necessary to raise the subject back to his old level of utility (Figure 4–41).

How is this done diagrammatically on the indifference map?
Look at Figure 4–42. Assume that we are in equilibrium and the price is P_{X1}. The amount of *X* purchased is X_1. Now assume that price falls to P_{X2}. The new equilibrium quantity of *X* is X_2, and it can be seen that the consumer is on a higher indifference curve. As suggested above, to isolate the income and substitution effects, we want to tax away enough income to establish an equilibrium on the old indifference curve but at the new price level. This is done by constructing a line parallel to the new budget line and tangent to the old indifference curve. Obviously it will not be tangent at the same point as the old budget line because the prices are different. (If it were tangent at the same point, it would means that the curve had two different slopes at the same point.) Because the new price is lower and the slope of the constructed budget line is flatter, it will be tangent to the indifference curve at a flatter portion of the curve. This occurs farther to the right. The law of demand says that the lower the price of a commodity or service, the more you will substitute it for others. Hence, you would expect the amount of *X* taken at the new point, X_3, to be greater than X_1. The difference between X_1 and X_3 with the income effect removed is the substitution effect. The remainder, the difference between X_2 and X_3 that was associated with the increase in utility (real income), is the income effect. The vertical distance between the *y* intercepts is the amount that real income was changed by the change in price level.

Suppose that X is an inferior good?
An inferior good is a good for which the real income effect is negative. If real incomes rises for any reason, the quantity taken (as a result of the rise in income) will be less than before. Hence if a price reduction creates an increase in real income, the effect of the increase in income will be to reduce the quantity of this good taken (Figure 4–43).

FIGURE 4–43. Inferior Goods—Income Effect

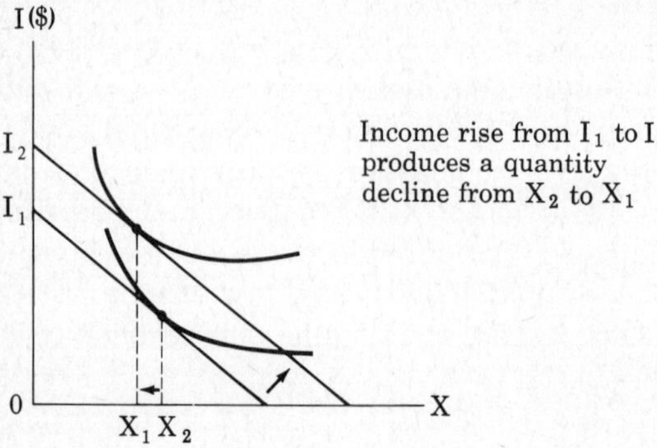

An inferior good is one that shows a quantity decline when income rises. Here prices are held constant and income is increased. The resultant decline in quantity taken indicates an inferior good.

FIGURE 4–44. Inferior Goods—Price Effect

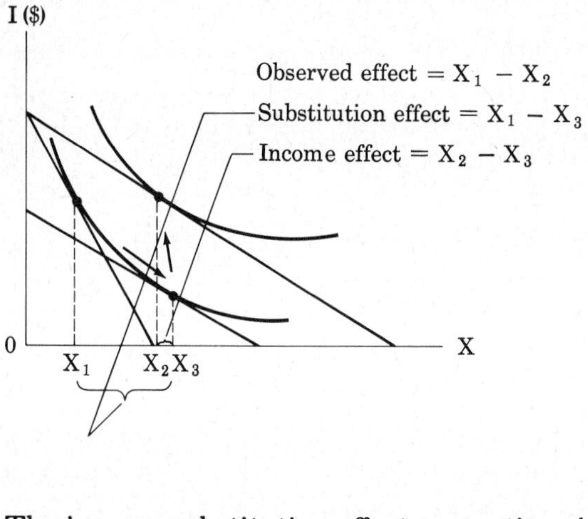

The income–substitution effect separation shows the normal substitution effect, but an opposite income effect. As price falls, quantity increases from the substitution effect, but tends to fall somewhat from the income effect. The observed effect is a netting out of these two opposite tendencies.

Does this mean that inferior goods defy the law of demand and increase in quantity taken as price falls?

Definitely not. Remember that the total observed effect is comprised of two parts—the income effect and the substitution effect, with the substitution effect generally the larger. Even though the income effect for an inferior good is opposite in sign to the substitution effect, the total effect will normally bear the sign of the substitution effect because it is the more important. Therefore, if the price of X falls, the quantity of X demanded as a substitute for the now *relatively* more expensive other items in the budget will rise. So too will real income. But the result of the rise in real income is to somewhat offset the increase induced by the substitution effect. They net out against one another. But to repeat, the total observed effect, even for an inferior good, is inverse to a price change (Figure 4–44).

Does the law of demand hold for all goods?

There is one classic case that is cited as an exception. This is the so-called *Giffen* good. Remember that the point was made that the change in real income resulting from a change in the price of X would be small because generally X occupies only a small part of the expenditure budget. However, if X is very important in the budget, any reduction in the price of X would produce a large change in real income because the same living standard can be bought for a great deal less money. For instance, if X takes up 10 percent of the budget and the price of X drops 50 percent, there is a 5 percent increase in purchasing power. On the other hand, if X involves 90 percent of the consumer budget, a 50 percent drop in the price of X means a 45 percent increase in purchasing power. In the event that X is strongly inferior, this increase of purchasing power will sharply reduce the amount of X bought. If this reduction is so great as to exceed the increase produced by the substitution effect, the total effect will be a reduction in quantity taken accompanying a reduction in price. This is contrary to the law of demand.

What do indifference curves look like for inferior and Giffen goods?

The characteristic that creates an inferior good is a reduction in the willingness of the individual to trade money for X as he gets more money. If we treat Y as money, MRS_{XY} must decline as income increases. Thus higher indifference curves are flatter at any given level of X. This being so, as income rises, any family of parallel budget lines for which the slope is P_X/P_Y will achieve tangencies to the indifference curves at points connoting smaller and smaller quantities of X (Figure 4–45).

FIGURE 4–45. Inferior Goods

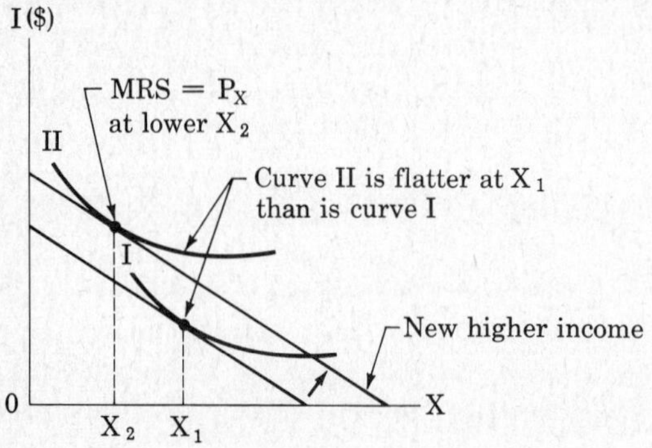

The slope of the indifference curves shows willingness to substitute money for *X*. If the curve is flatter at higher income, it means that the consumer is less willing to substitute *X* for money at the higher income. You must have a lower stock of *X* in order for it to be attractive to substitute at a given price.

FIGURE 4–46. Giffen Good

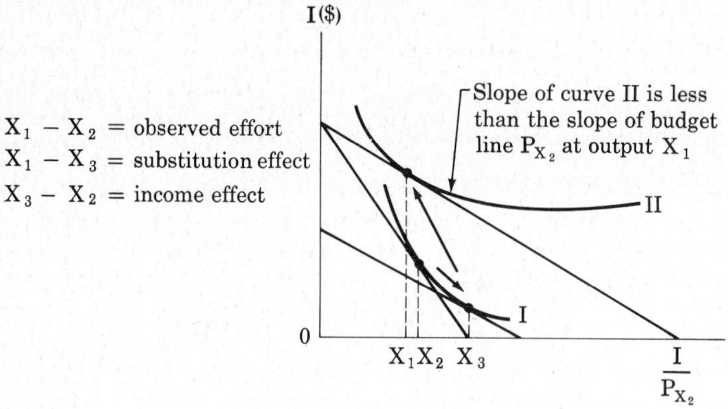

The very strong impact of a price change on real income causes the income effect actually to more than offset the substitution effect. This case contradicts the law of demand.

For a Giffen good, the same condition must prevail but, in this case, it must be carried to the extreme of having the MRS_{XY} for a given quantity of X decline faster on higher indifference curves than does the slope of the budget line as it rotates to the right about the y intercept. If this happens, the tangencies will occur closer to the y axis as prices fall, denoting lesser quantities of X being taken (Figure 4–46).

CHAPTER HIGHLIGHTS

1. *Indifference curve analysis was seen to involve ordinal not cardinal utility.*
2. *We defined an indifference curve as showing the different bundles of goods and services that give the subject identical utility. The indifference map is an ordinal ranking of indifference curves.*
3. *Characteristics of indifference curves were discussed: They slope downward, never intersect, and are normally convex to the origin.*
4. *The concept of marginal rate of substitution was developed, and we observed that it is equal to the slope of the indifference curve. An alternative way of stating its value is as the ratio* MU_X/MU_Y*. This ratio diminishes as you move along an indifference curve from left to right.*
5. *The income constraint was seen to take the form of a budget line in the analysis. This line, the slope of which is* P_X/P_Y*, is a boundary between the attainable and unattainable combinations of X and Y.*
6. *The consumer strives to maximize utility within the budget constraint. This is achieved at the point of tangency between the budget line and an indifference curve. Here* MU_X/MU_Y *equals* P_X/P_Y*.*
7. *We noted the effects of varying price and income on the utility-maximizing solution.*
8. *Finally, the income and substitution effects were defined, and we saw how to separate them from each other. We did this for normal, inferior, and Giffen goods.*

QUESTIONS

1. *Joan Robinson, a prominent economic theorist, has written, "It is idle to pretend that we could ever draw up indifference curves even for a single buyer, . . . for to find out what combinations he buys at different prices . . . we would have to observe his behavior at different times and there is no guarantee that his tastes and preferences have not changed meanwhile." If it is as Robinson says,*

why do economists bother to "pretend" to draw up indifference curves?

2. *Ruby Turner Norris, another economic theorist, has written, "If one is in the income class which is accustomed never to having at any one time more than six pairs of stockings, it would be exceedingly difficult to compose an indifference curve starting with forty pairs. One would be completely out of one's depth." What do you think of this criticism? Is it the same as Robinson's or different? Can indifference curve analysis survive it?*
3. *A question raised by George Stigler in his book,* Theory of Price, *is " 'I wouldn't eat olives if you paid me.' Draw the indifference curve that would be consistent with this statement." Can you draw this indifference curve? What point is the question trying to make for the student?*
4. *The term* money illusion *refers to a tendency on the part of people to pay more attention to the size of their money incomes than to their real incomes. How would the presence of money illusion affect the drawing of a budget line that showed a price rise in both products X and Y?*

5 Supply analysis: production

In economics the term *production* refers to the conversion of goods and services from one form into another. The goods and services to be converted are in the form of *inputs* or *factors of production*. They come out of the conversion process as *outputs* or, more simply, *products*. Presumably the outputs will contain more market value than the inputs did in their preproduction form. Otherwise, why bother?

We are surrounded by production processes wherein inputs are converted into more desired outputs. Sometimes the output is a good; sometimes it is a service. Bread production involves the combining of land and seed and fertilizer and machinery and labor and insecticides and sunshine and water to produce wheat, a good. The wheat is moved off the farm and stored through the application of labor effort working with trucks, tractors, trains, ships, conveyors, grain elevators, and warehouses. The movement and storage represent production of services. The wheat passes through a variety of refining, blending, and baking processes, each of which embodies the use of labor and machinery until finally, the bread, wrapped in a printed, waxed package, is offered on a brightly lighted shelf in an air-conditioned store to be picked up and put in a cart by a shopper and taken to the checkout counter where it will be paid for, bagged, and carried to the parking lot, placed in the trunk of a $5000 machine, and carried to the home of the consumer. Remember that retailing is the production of a marketing service. When you buy the bread you also buy the services that went to make it conveniently and attractively available. As in the growing and processing of wheat, retailing involves *combining factors of production* to create an output that is more highly valued then the sum of the inputs.

What are factors of production?

This term is used to make categorical distinctions among the inputs. The list most frequently used breaks inputs into four classes: land, labor, capital, and entrepreneurship. The emphasis on the differences among the factors of production is largely a holdover from the classical writers who stressed separate laws of economic behavior for each, stemming from what were seen as their unique, inherent qualities.

What economic qualities set land apart from the others?

Land's distinguishing characteristic is the fact that no one is making any more of it. The total supply is fixed (perfectly inelastic). As a result, the rental incomes received by landlords fluctuate entirely with the demand for land use. Because the economies of eighteenth- and nineteenth-century Europe were heavily agrarian, the price of farm land was a popular topic among the political economists of the day. Students of the history of economic thought will recall that the theories of Quesnay, Malthus, Ricardo, Von Thunen, and Henry George took the fixity of land as its distinguishing trait that isolated it as a factor of production for separate study and tax treatment.

What is unique about capital?

There are two types of real capital: variable capital and fixed capital. Variable capital is in the form of surpluses used to support labor during the production process. Fixed capital is in the form of tools and buildings that come into being well before the production of a good and that last well after the good is consumed. Both forms of capital must be available in abundance if a country is to make the jump from an agricultural and trading nation to a nation of manufacturers. In order to accumulate capital, a nation must divert resources away from immediate consumption and into tools and supplies that will be used for *future* production and *future* consumption. People must be forced or induced to abstain from immediate gratifications so resources can be available for roundabout but more fruitful production after capital accumulation. Whoever owns these surpluses controls capital and earns whatever share of the output it earns as a factor of production. Needless to add, this point has not gone unnoticed by those who would have a better world. The quality that sets capital apart as a factor, however, is its ability to bridge *time* by providing future production from past accumulations.

What is entrepreneurship, and why is it a factor of production?

Webster tells us that an entrepreneur is one who organizes and directs a business undertaking, assuming the risk for the sake of profit. In our framework, the entrepreneur is the one directing the activities of the factors of production. He makes it happen, perceiving the opportunities in the marketplace and attempting to exploit them. Actually, the entrepreneur's function could be included under the labor input, but it is so critical that it is frequently broken out and treated as a separate factor of production.

How does labor enter the factor-of-production picture?

Labor is the ultimate factor of production. We can get by with poor land, scarce capital, and even bumbling entrepreneurship, but without labor nothing happens. It supplies the eyes, the hands, the brains, the muscles that convert inputs into desired outputs. As a factor, it is the major contributor to production, and in return for its factor services, labor receives more than 70 percent of the total product produced in the United States as income.

Do economists still make these distinctions among factors of production?

The distinctions are not made quite so clearly or dogmatically as they once were. The classical writers were as concerned with moralizing as they were with explaining. They worried about "functional" distribution of income, trying to justify the different returns to landlords, businessmen (undertakers, as they were known then), capitalists, and workers. Social class was fairly rigid in those days, and there was interest in who got what. We are still interested in who gets what, but our focus is not so much in terms of returns to different factors of production but is more oriented toward income distribution among the percentiles, no matter how earned. There is enough overlap in the economic roles that any one individual may play and also in the characteristics of the factors themselves to make rigid distinctions difficult. Corporations employ their presidents, who therefore earn "wages" and are included under labor. Land is reclaimed from the oceans and is therefore not completely inelastic in supply; millions of workers own common stock representing capital; computers make decisions and perform entrepreneurial functions; labor is educated and therefore embodies human capital; unique human skills such as those of Kareem Abdul Jabbar are neither reproducible nor increasable in supply, and they therefore share this characteristic with land. The differences blur.

Why use the term factors of production *then?*

Although the differences blur, they do not disappear. We want to recognize that there are alternative ways of performing a productive task. The idea of factors of production retains currency because it suggests the possibility of substitution of one input for another in the production of a unit of output. There are many different ways of producing a particular object, and we must think in terms of alternative combinations of inputs: many hands and few tools or many tools and few hands.

Our food retailing example is a case in point of the variety of ways in which a service can be rendered. Grocery stores 30 years ago were small, limited-line family affairs run by Mom and Pop with a kid to sweep out on Saturday. In a typical transaction each item of food was taken from the shelf by the clerk, priced, and handed to the customer. Capital investment was primarily in inventory of food and a long pole with a claw on the end for reaching packages on the top shelf. In today's supermarket the scale of operation has grown mightily, and there has been a substitution of capital for labor in the form of covered floor space, refrigerated display cases, shopping carts, parking lots, conveyor belts, and so on. Where the clerk used to say, ". . . and what else?" as he wrapped the items in your order, today's supermarket relies on impulse buying stimulated by package design, lighting, placing of items at critical locations, and so on. Where the clerk used to say, ". . . we have a special on pickles today," contemporary markets rely on mass distribution of circulars and newspapers listing items that are promotionally priced. Plans call for substitution of capital for labor to go yet further. Automatic point-of-sale devices (POS) are about to be visited on us as the next great innovation in the world of marketing. At the checkout counter we shall find an electronic scanning device that reads the price on each item, adds up the bill, accepts a check in payment, makes a quick review of the customer's credit rating, keeps track of inventories by recording how many of each item are sold, and orders replacement stock. All this is now available. POS is certainly quite a substitution of capital for Mom and Pop.

Generalizing, we can say that the study of production deals not only with maximizing the total supply from given inputs but also with selecting the most efficient scale and combination of inputs to produce any given output. The basic analytical tool for considering this problem is the production function.

What is a production function?

A production function is a technical statement of the relationship between inputs and outputs. It reflects engineering knowledge of how things work and tells us the manner in which inputs may be combined to produce different outputs. Its form is mathematical, and like all mathematical functions it shows a relationship among variables. In this case, it is the relationship between quantities of different factor inputs and the quantity of output of the specified product. Total output is the dependent variable, and the quantities of the different factors of production are the independent variables. It is understood that all factors not specifically mentioned are considered to be held constant.

What form might a production function take?

They are as varied as are the products in our economy. Their most generalized form for discussion purposes is simply

output = *f*(land, labor, capital)

Several attempts have been made to find a typical production function for overall industry. The best known is that of Paul Douglas and Charles Cobb, published in 1927. Through statistical regression methods, they found that a function

$$Q = 1.10L^{.75}K^{.25}$$

where
Q = quantity of output
L = labor input
K = capital input
had good predictive powers for a variety of industries. The so-called Cobb-Douglas production function is used in many economic models in the form

$$Q = aL^{\alpha}K^{1-\alpha}$$

It has a number of convenient economic characteristics, which will emerge as we go on.

What about the variables not in the function? What's with them?

Everything that is not explicitly considered as a variable is treated as a constant. "Everything" is a pretty big concept. We are concerned mostly with controlling those things that might influence output but are not themselves inputs. One such variable is the *quality* of inputs. Another is the quality of the surrounding environment. Unless specified to the contrary, we hold technology constant over the range of the pro-

FIGURE 5–1. A Production Function with Two Variable Inputs and Variable Output

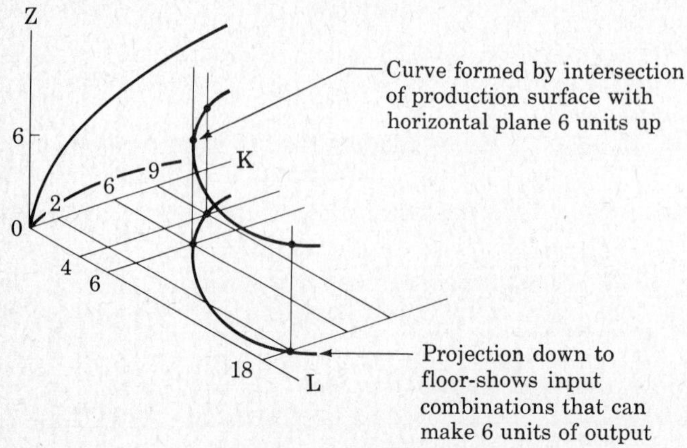

This three-dimensional drawing illustrates a production function in the form $Q = f(K, L)$. The function takes the form of a surface rising from the origin. Every point on the surface has three coordinates. The height of the point from the floor represents the quantity of output. The distance from the side axes represents the quantities of labor and capital inputs, repectively.

duction function. Also, we hold human capital constant. Human capital refers to the degree of training and education the workers have. Other considerations, such as weather, season, and location, are also held constant unless a variable is explicitly included in the function to represent them. If we wish to compare production functions, we must realize that these other, non-factor considerations are fixed.

What graphical treatment can be given to a production function?
Each production function can be handled by a number of different graphical representations. The common denominator they share is that they all, in one way or another, show the quantity of output depending on the quantity of factor inputs. The major considerations that influence which of the different forms of the production function to use are (1) how many independent variables are operative, that is, how many factors of production we consider able to vary simultaneously, remem-

bering that any factors not explicitly allowed to vary are considered held constant; and (2) whether we are interested in total output as a function of total input, or total product *per unit* of input. We shall examine five different forms that every production function can take in our economic analysis. Confusion will be lessened if you remember that they all deserve to be called production functions. The five are as follows:

1. Total product as a function of more than two inputs.
2. Total product as a function of two inputs.
3. Total product as a function of one input.
4. Marginal product as a function of one input.
5. Average product as a function of one input.

Take them one at a time. How can we show total product as a function of more than two inputs?

Our first embarrassment. We really cannot *conveniently* show this on a conventional graph. Graphical representation requires that a separate axis be drawn for each variable so that the coordinate values of all can be plotted. Because paper is a two-dimensional surface, we find that the most we can represent naturally are two variables. I say "naturally" because it is possible to add a third variable to a graph (as discussed below) by making a drawing in perspective and giving the illusion of depth. However, we have difficulty visualizing, let alone drawing, more than three dimensions. Economic problems involving many variables can be attacked algebraically, but the techniques needed to allow us to see what happens to outputs when three or more inputs are varied simultaneously go beyond the level of this book.

All right. How can we show total product as a function of two variable inputs?

There are two ways this is done. The first is to use an illustration such as shown in Figure 5–1. This is a three-dimensional perspective drawing giving the illusion of depth. Picture the lower corner of a room where the two walls and the floor come together (point 0). Where these three planes meet each other, three lines are determined ($0L$, $0K$ and $0Z$). From solid geometry we remember that the intersection of two planes is a line, and so we have three lines radiating out from an origin (the corner of the room) at right angles to each other (assuming that the house is properly built). These lines serve as axes on our graph. If quantity of labor is measured along one floor–wall line and quantity of capital is measured along the other, a combination of so much

FIGURE 5–2. Isoquant Map

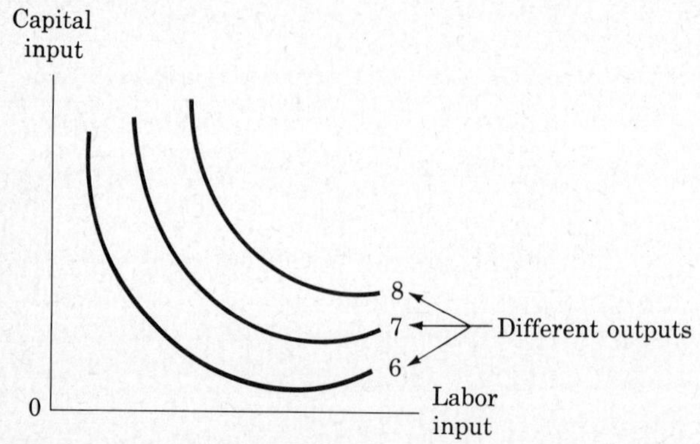

An isoquant map may be thought of as the floor of the diagram in Figure 5–1, with all the input combinations capable of producing a like quantity of output connected and labeled. There is an isoquant for each output.

capital *and* so much labor is represented by a point out on the floor. We measure the amount of capital along the capital axis and draw a line out at a right angle to the capital axis. The quantity of labor is measured along the labor axis and we draw a line at a right angle to it. The intersection of the two lines represents the combined quantity of labor and capital. We can do this for as many combinations of capital and labor as are possible to imagine. The floor will be covered with these points. Finally, we measure output vertically along the 0Z axis defined by the intersection of the two walls with one another. A production function is supposed to tell what output is produced by any given combination of labor and land. We can measure up from the point on the floor defining a given combination of inputs to the proper height as measured along the output axis. This will give us a point in space that is L units from the capital axis, K from the labor axis, and Z from the floor.

How about an example?

Suppose engineering data gives us a simple Cobb-Douglas function:

$$Q = \sqrt{LK}$$

If we have 4 units of labor and 9 units of capital, we shall produce the square root of 4 times 9, that is, the square root of 36, which equals 6 units of output. This will be represented by a point 4 units out from the capital line, 9 units out from the labor line, and 6 units above the floor. If we draw such points for different combinations of labor and capital inputs, we shall have a number of points, each located above their labor–capital coordinates and at a height equal to their output dimension. If there are enough of these points close enough together, they will form a smooth surface. This surface is the graphical representation of the production function. After all that, however, we should add that this is a cumbersome graphical technique and is usually used only for illustrative purposes. The production functions usually used in situations of two variable inputs and one output are called *isoquants*.

What are isoquants?

The first thing to note about isoquants is that they are very similar to indifference curves. In fact, they are often called production indifference curves. Following through on our discussion of the three-dimensional production surface, let us focus on the floor alone. This is a two-dimensional surface. One axis measures labor inputs. The other axis measures capital inputs. The points on the floor measure combinations of labor and capital inputs. An isoquant is a curve connecting the points on the floor (i.e., those combinations of labor and capital) that produce the *same* quantity. For instance, in the production function

$$Q = \sqrt{LK}$$

there are many ways to produce 6 units of output. A few are: $2K$ and $18L$; $3K$ and $12L$; $4K$ and $9L$; $6K$ and $6L$; $9K$ and $4L$; $18K$ and $2L$. An isoquant connects all these coordinates. We would then go on to consider other output quantities and draw separate isoquants through all the combinations of inputs that produce those outputs.

Another way to think about the construction of the 6-unit isoquant is to imagine that we cut the production surface itself with a horizontal plane parallel to the floor but at a height 6 units up from it. When the plane cuts the production surface the intersection is a curve outlining the shape of the surface at the height of the plane. Each point on this curve has three coordinates: L, labor; K, capital; 6, output. We can project the curve straight down from the surface to the floor. When we do this we have drawn an isoquant; we now have, on a two-dimensional figure, the combinations of labor and capital inputs that produce 6 units of output. If a series of horizontal planes intersects the surface at various levels of output and the curves thus created are projected to the floor, we have a family of curves called an isoquant *map*. The same information may be obtained from the map as from the surface, providing that each isoquant is labeled with the quantity information that would be read off the vertical axis in the three-dimensional diagram. The characteristics of the isoquants themselves will be taken up shortly (Figure 5–2).

FIGURE 5–3. The Conventional Total Product Curve

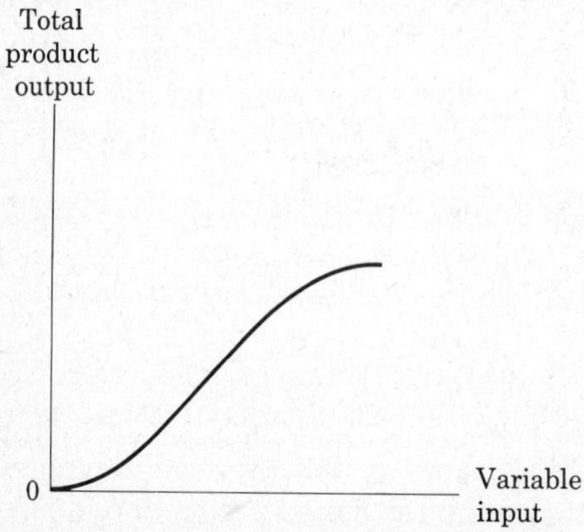

The total product curve is the graph of a production function in which there is one variable input (the others are fixed) and total output varies with the variable input. Its shape is the result of the law of variable proportions in operation.

Isoquants have two variable inputs. What does a production function with one variable input look like?

Most students think of this production function as the *total product* curve. First we dealt with the production function $Q = f(K, L)$, all other things being equal, and got a surface. Then we held Q constant and drew an isoquant. Now we are dealing with $Q = f(L)$, all other things (including K) being equal. Figure 5–3 shows a typical total product curve.

Why does it have the shape you show?

The reasons for its shape as shown have to do with a principle called *variable proportions*, or more popularly, *diminishing returns*. The two terms are frequently used interchangeably.

What is the law of diminishing returns?

The law of diminishing returns is one of the basic axioms in economic theory. In brief, it states that all other things being equal, the more of a thing you have, the less important it is to have still more. It is a general proposition that has been applied to both production and consumption. In the case of consumption we referred to it as the *law of diminishing marginal utility*. In production it is known as the *law of diminishing marginal productivity*.

What is the law of diminishing marginal productivity?

Formally stated, the law reads: As you combine increasing amounts of some inputs with a fixed quantity of at least one other input (all other things being equal), output will rise, but after a point the *rate* at which it rises will diminish. Because we are dealing with changing quantities of inputs, we should recognize that each time we add or subtract one unit of input, it is the marginal unit. Furthermore, if one input increases and the others do not, the proportions in which the inputs are mixed with one another obviously change. Hence the term *variable proportions*. As the proportion of labor to capital increases, the *rate of change* in output (marginal productivity) may rise, remain constant, or fall. If it rises, we say that we have increasing marginal productivity; if it falls, we say that we have diminishing marginal productivity; if it remains constant, we say that we have constant marginal productivity. The law of diminishing marginal productivity states that sooner or later (and it may be much later) the marginal unit of input will add less to the total output than did the prior unit. When this occurs diminishing marginal productivity is upon us.

Can you give an example of diminishing marginal productivity?

We have been dealing with agriculture, so let us take a look at the production of another staple, beef. Here, too, is an industry that has seen a lot of technological change. In this instance, it is a substitution of capital in the form of the feedlot for open land. Whereas cattle formerly would roam the romanticized range eating grass where they found it and feeling right at home until reaching a marketable weight, today they are confined to relatively small, fenced-in feedlots where they receive a carefully balanced diet of vitamin-enriched goodies until they are ready for slaughter. It took 2.5 years for a steer to grow from 600 lb to marketable size on the open range; it takes about 6 months on the feedlot. Because beef is a highly income-elastic commodity that has seen skyrocketing worldwide demand occur as a result of rising incomes, the speed with which cattle can be raised is extremely important in determining the supply available to meet that demand.

Let us imagine that a feedlot operator attempts to increase the beef output from his facility by placing additional cattle in a single pen. Through the additional cattle, he intends to increase the total weight of

FIGURE 5–4. *Variable Returns*

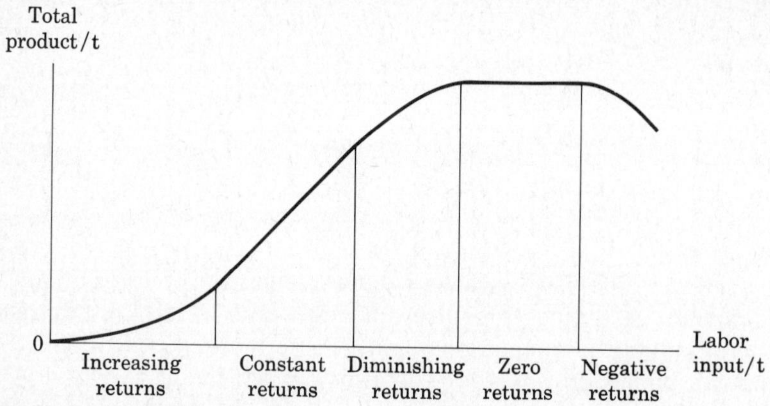

As the proportions of inputs vary, the marginal rate of returns varies. Here is a total product curve that goes through phases of increasing marginal returns, constant marginal returns, diminishing marginal returns, zero marginal returns, and negative marginal returns. The slope of the total product curve indicates the phase.

meat brought to market from his facility. We would certainly expect the total weight to rise, but would it rise indefinitely, and at a constant rate? The law of variable proportions suggests that after some point in the process, the time it takes the typical steer to reach marketable weight will increase. This occurs at the point of diminishing *average* product. As we shall see shortly, such a development implies that the *marginal* productivity began to turn down even earlier in the cattle-adding process.

What would cause the rate of increase to turn down?
You do not have to be an agricultural expert to picture the scene of increasing numbers of cattle milling in the same area and trying to get at the same number of feed trays. Even if the food input were increased commensurately with the number of cattle, it would become harder for each to get its proper ration. They would jostle each other

away; there would be more injuries, less rest. Carried to the extreme, with the lot jammed there is no room for those fed to move away so that those unfed can take their place at the feed bins. When that occurs, we are well past diminishing and into negative returns.

How can you be so sure that all this will happen?

We can be fairly sure that diminishing returns occurs as described because professional cattle feeders—men who devote their total energies to making a buck from a bull—build new facilities in order to increase output. Given a choice between adding cattle to the existing pen, thereby changing the proportions in which cattle and space are combined, or building additional facilities so the proportions can be held more or less constant, they opt, after a point, to build the new facilities. It must be because their experience has demonstrated that they cannot keep on adding cattle to a fixed land area and expect output to increase proportionately. Kenneth Boulding, past president of the American Economic Association, summarized the point most succinctly when he observed that it was necessary to believe in diminishing returns because, without it, you could grow the world's food supply in a flower pot!! Think about it.

How is diminishing returns related to the shape of the total product curve?

The total product curves we draw show the quantity of output produced by various amounts of labor input working with a fixed capital input. If successive rises in the proportion of labor to capital causes total output to grow at an ever-faster rate, we are in the increasing returns phase. Output accelerates. The slope of the total product curve becomes greater as you move from left to right (Figure 5–4). If each successive unit of labor input adds the same increment to total output as the one before, production is in a phase of constant returns and the slope of the total product curve remains constant—that is, it is a straight line. When diminishing returns sets in, the total product curve continues to rise, but the slope lessens as we go from left to right. Hence the curve takes on a "humpbacked" look. Eventually, it becomes horizontal (slope of zero) as additional workers do not contribute anything to total output, and then it turns down as additional labor inputs actually reduce total output. Inputs cost a firm money, so it is obviously not too practical to keep adding them if they reduce output. A rational producer will never operate under these circumstances. All of these phases are reflected more directly through the marginal product curve.

FIGURE 5–5. A Numerical Example of a Production Function

By substituting into the function

$Q = 15L^2 - L^3$

we can observe the phases of increasing and diminishing returns.

L	Q	MP		AP
1	14	14	increasing MP	14
2	52	38		26
3	108	56		36
4	176	68		44
5	250	74		50
6	324	74	diminishing MP	54
7	392	68		56
8	448	56		56
9	486	38		54
10	500	14		50
11	484	−16	negative MP	44
12	432	−52		36
13	338	−94		26

FIGURE 5–6. Graphical Relationship Between Marginal and Total Product Curves

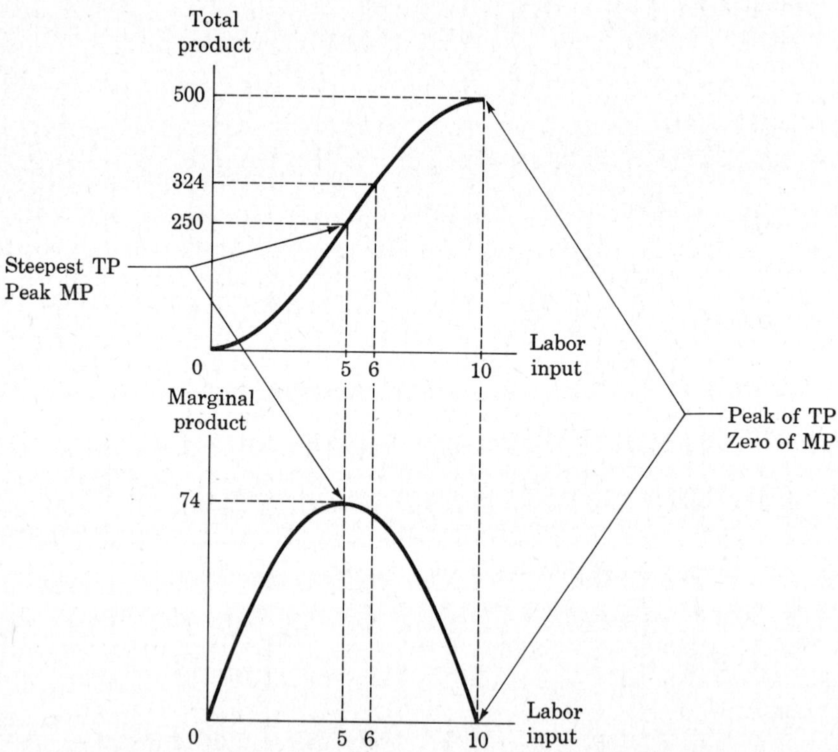

The marginal product curve is a graph of the slope of the total product curve at various labor inputs. When the total product curve is steepest, the marginal product hits a peak. When the total product curve is flat, the marginal product curve hits zero.

What is the marginal product curve?
This is a graph that shows the *rate of change* of the total output that occurs at different labor input levels. Just as marginal utility is the slope of the total utility curve, so too is marginal product the slope of the total product curve. To get the marginal product curve, measure the slope of the total product curve at different points and then plot these numerical values on a separate pair of axes.

What shape will the marginal product curve take?
The shape of the marginal product curve depends on the shape of the total product curve from which it is derived. If there is a range of labor input, with increasing marginal returns, the marginal product curve slopes upward over that range. If there is a range of constant returns, the marginal product curve is horizontal. If there is a range of diminishing returns (as the law of diminishing returns says there eventually will be), the marginal product curve slopes down. When negative returns sets in—that is, when total product actually falls with increased labor input—the marginal product curve will be below the x axis in the negative range. Figure 5–5 presents an example of a possible production function with the total product and derived marginal product *schedules*. These, in turn, are plotted in Figure 5–6 as *curves*. These schedules also show the relationship of marginal product to average product.

What is average product?
Whereas marginal product was defined as the change in total product divided by the change in labor input, average product is defined as total product divided by total labor input.

$$MP_L = \frac{\Delta TP}{\Delta L} \qquad AP_L = \frac{TP}{L}$$

It is the output produced by the *typical* worker. The average product curve is drawn by measuring the total product at different levels of labor

FIGURE 5–7. Relationship Between Marginal, Total, and Average Product Curves

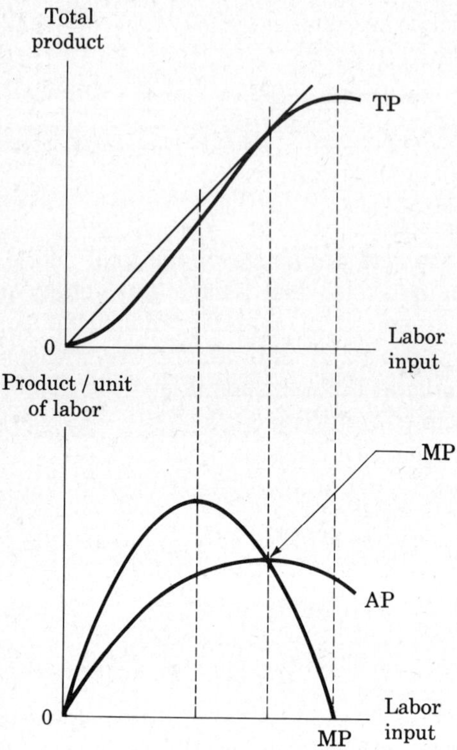

The marginal product and average product are equal at the maximum average product value. The marginal product curve is zero at the peak of total product.

FIGURE 5–8. Radius Vector (Gradient)

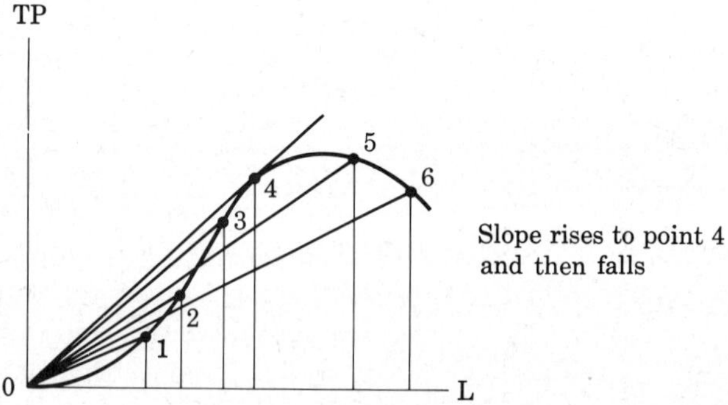

The terms *radius vector*, or *gradient*, refer to a line drawn from the origin to a point on a curve. The slope of the radius vector drawn to the total product curve equals the average product because the horizontal distance it strikes off is the labor input and the vertical distance is the total product. Average product is defined as total product/labor; so too is slope.

input and then dividing the total product by that amount of labor. These values are plotted at their respective labor quantities. The average product curve is frequently plotted on the same axes as the marginal product curve (Figure 5–7).

How are marginal and average product related?
Figures 5–5, 5–6, and 5–7 show typical total, average, and marginal product curves derived from a production function that varies labor input while other variables are held fixed. Relationships to note are the following: (1) Marginal product and average product are equal to each other at the point where average product is maximum, and (2) marginal product is zero at the point where total product is maximum.

Why are marginal and average product equal to each other at the labor input where average product is a maximum?
There are two ways to see this: through a straightforward geometric explanation or a logical, arithmetic explanation. Let us look at the geometric explanation first. A line drawn from the origin of a graph to a point on the graph is called a *radius vector*, or sometimes a *gradient*. We can draw such gradients to any point on the total product curve (Figure 5–8). The *slope* of a gradient can be interpreted as being equal to the average product of the labor quantity at which the gradient intersects the curve.

Why is the slope of the gradient equal to the average product?
Remember that the slope is equal to the ratio of the vertical change to the horizontal. Draw a gradient intersecting the total product curve. Measure the vertical distance from the point of intersection down to the x axis. Measure the horizontal distance along the x axis from the

FIGURE 5–9. Comparison of Slope of Gradient and Slope of Curve

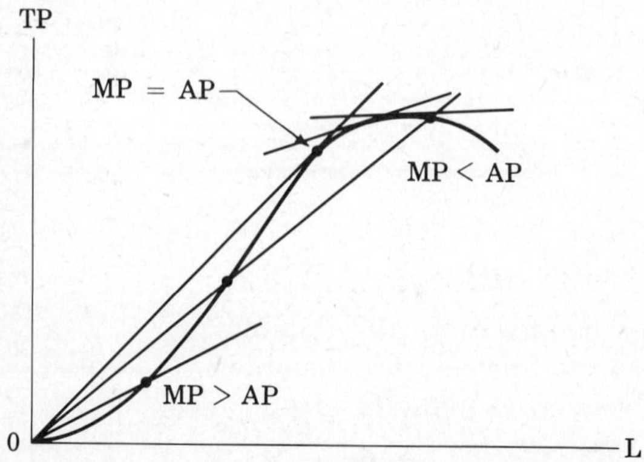

The gradient has maximum slope at the point where it is tangent to the total product curve. Here its slope is equal to the slope of the curve, so average product equals marginal product. Beyond this point, the curve has flatter slope than gradient. Average product is greater than marginal product.

origin to the value at the point of intersection. Now take their ratio. This equals the slope of the gradient. Note that on this particular graph, the vertical distance represents total product and the horizontal distance represents amount of labor. Thus, we have the ratio TP/L, which is, of course, the definition of average product. If the gradient is steep, it is interpretable as representing a relatively large average product. If the gradient is flatter, the average product is smaller.

How does this relate to average product equaling marginal product at the maximum of average product?

Notice in Figure 5–8 that as we draw gradients to points successively farther out on the total product curve, they grow steeper up to a point and then they get flatter. This means that average product gets larger up to a point and then gets smaller. Now, by logic, the point where average product stops rising and starts falling is the maximum value that average product will take on. You will see that this maximum occurs where the gradient is just tangent to the total product curve. Therefore, the slope of the gradient to this point is the same as the slope of the curve at this point. (The slope of a curve at a point is measured by the slope of a tangent to the curve at that point.) Now, the final element in the argument is to recall that the slope of the curve is equal to the marginal product at the different points along its length. If the slope of the gradient is equal to the slope of the curve at the point where the slope of the gradient is highest, it also follows that the average product (equal to the slope of the gradient) equals the marginal product (equal to the slope of the curve) at the point where average product is greatest (where the slope of the gradient is greatest). This is illustrated in Figure 5–9.

That seems pretty confusing. Is there another way to look at it?
Would it help if we call attention to the fact that in Figure 5–9 the slope of the curve is greater than the slope of the gradient at all labor quantities to the left of the maximum gradient and less at all values to the right of the maximum. Therefore, the slopes must be equal at the labor input where the gradient is of maximum slope.

Let's try the logical, arithmetic explanation that you promised.
This involves an arithmetic relationship that is inherent in all average–marginal numerical series. We shall see it again when dealing with marginal costs and average costs. However, it also comes up with such familiar ideas as baseball batting averages. It is simply the observation that if a baseball player has a day in which he hits above his batting average, that day's performance will raise his average. Every day that is better than the average will increase the average. The procedure here is to keep a running total of times at bat and number of hits and to divide times at bat into hits to compute the batting average. In our problem, total product is analogous to hits and labor input is analogous to times at bat. Marginal product is comparable to the incremental number of hits achieved during the most recent game. Now, as long as performance is improving—that is, as long as successive units of labor input have increasing marginal product—the average product will rise, just as batting average will rise if there are successive days of steadily improving performance (Figure 5–10). If the marginal is above the average, it will continue to pull the average product up. The only time that the average will fall is if the marginal is *less* than the average. In the batting example, if the player has a particularly bad day, the different increments to hits and at-bats will be such as to reduce his batting average. If he has a day in which he hits exactly his average, his average will not change. This is comparable to having a marginal value equal to the average value. The average value does not change.

FIGURE 5–10. Baseball Example

Suppose that you play in seven games and go 1 for 5, 2 for 5, 3 for 5, 4 for 5, 3 for 5, 2 for 5, and 1 for 5. Your daily and cumulative average would be as shown here. Note the relationship between daily and cumulative average.

Game	*AB*	*Hits*	*Daily percentage*	*Cumulative percentage*
1	5	1	.200	.200
2	5	2	.400	.300
3	5	3	.600	.400
4	5	4	.800	.500
5	5	3	.600	.520
6	5	2	.400	.500
7	5	1	.200	.457

FIGURE 5–11. Relationship of Marginal to Average Values

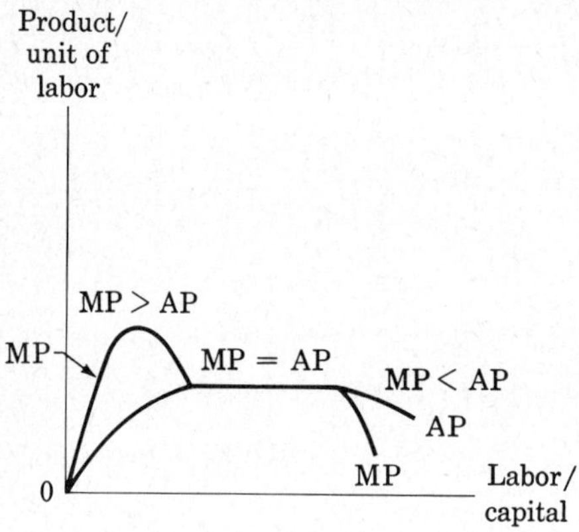

As long as marginal values are higher than average values, the average value will rise. If the marginal equals the average over some range, it means that the average stays the same over that range. When marginal drops, the average will fall too, but not as quickly as the marginal. The average embodies a legacy of earlier values. The marginal value has no history. It depends on the immediate observation at hand.

How does all this pertain to production functions?
The law of variable proportions suggests that certain output patterns occur. As long as the proportion of labor relative to capital is small, increasing marginal productivity of labor occurs. Each successive worker adds more to total product than the one before. This increasing marginal product will pull the average product up. While both marginal and average products are climbing, the marginal product is greater than the average. After a point, the ratio of L/K rises enough for diminishing returns to appear. Thereafter marginal product declines with further increases of labor. However, as long as the marginal product remains higher than the average, the average continues to rise. As marginal falls and the average rises with increased labor inputs, they inevitably head toward a point where they intersect. At the point of intersection, marginal and average product are equal. This is the maximum point for average product; at still greater levels of labor input, marginal product falls still lower (still under diminishing returns), and with a marginal value lower than average, the average is pulled down. Thus, we find that the marginal product curve intersects the average product curve at the maximum value of the average product (Figure 5–11). Marginals always intersect averages at their extreme values, be they maximums or minimums. It depends on whether the marginal has gone from high to low or from low to high. We shall take up this latter case in the discussion of marginal and average costs.

What is the economic significance of this point?
The maximizing of average product of labor means that labor is being used as efficiently as possible, given the amount of capital available. A firm should employ this much labor if it wishes to get the most from the average worker.

Does that mean that a firm should produce at that point?
Probably not. Usually a firm's goal is to maximize total profits. Profits involve revenues minus cost. We may find that costs are higher than need be, even if labor is maximizing its productivity. Suppose that labor is very inexpensive and capital very dear. Do we want to economize on labor? Managers of multinational corporations tend to make the error of *over*capitalizing a production process in plants located in relatively underdeveloped nations. Because the managers are frequently trained in the Western nations and gain their job experience working in plants in the United States or Europe, they have a bias toward trying to hold down labor inputs to achieve high marginal productivity of labor. Engineers take pride in using the most advanced technology available, and

FIGURE 5–12. The Stages of Production

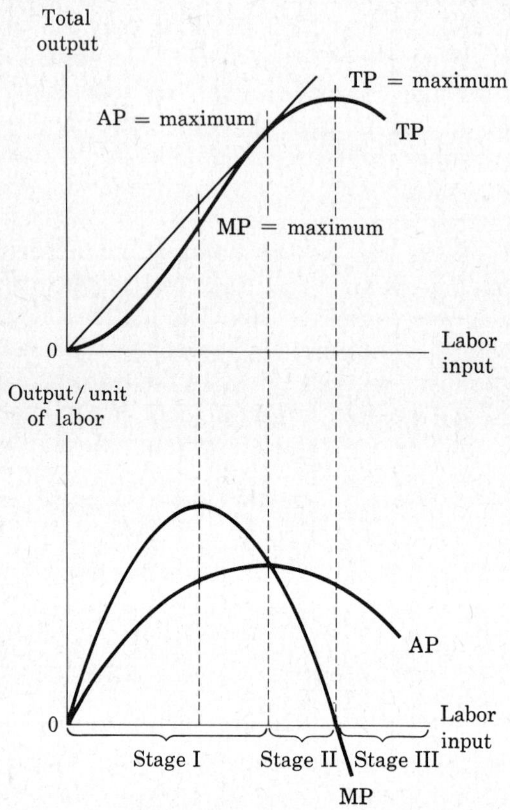

The three stages of production are defined by the range of increasing average product (stage I) and the range of negative marginal product (stage III). Between them is stage II.

this is generally a technology that substitutes capital for labor. The trouble is that manual labor is abundant and cheap in these nations, whereas technical skill to run and maintain the sophisticated equipment is scarce. Management may be well advised to pass mechanization by, even to the point of foregoing the use of materials-handling equipment, and instead employ sheer human brawn. Under the circumstances, it represents proper production technique.

How does a firm know at what point it should produce?

Until a firm knows the prices of the various factors of production it will employ, it cannot come to a definite answer. We can give, however, a range in which the actual labor-capital ratio should fall. In order to understand this range, we must first introduce the idea of the *stages of production*.

What are the stages of production?

Economists identify three conditions that can prevail with regard to the ratio of labor to capital input. They refer to these three conditions (not too imaginatively) as stage I, stage II, and stage III. The stages are usually illustrated along the average-product-of-labor curve. Reading from left to right, we define all points between the origin and the labor value where average product is maximized as being in stage I; points between the maximum average product and zero marginal product lie in stage II; and all points to the right of zero marginal product are in stage III. A rational producer will produce somewhere within stage II. Stages I and III are held to represent irrational conditions under which to produce (Figure 5–12).

Why is stage II the only rational stage within which to produce?

We show this by demonstrating that it is *irrational* to produce in either of the *other* stages. Let us consider stage III first. That is the easy one. Stage III is the range in which there is negative marginal product of labor. The more labor a firm employs (with fixed amounts of other variables), the less total product it produces. Because labor must be paid with revenues that come from the sale of the output it produces, it would appear that stage III sees the firm increasing its costs by hiring labor at the same time that this labor works to reduce revenue. This is irrational. No employer would intentionally carry on production under stage III conditions.

That is believable. Why is production in stage I irrational?

The irrationality of stage I is just as ironclad as that of stage III, even though at first it appears that the increasing returns accruing to labor in stage I would make it an attractive range within which to produce. Before we can answer the stage I question, we must take up a fairly confusing, albeit interesting topic called the *symmetry of the stages of production*. Once you understand the symmetry of the stages, you will understand why production in stage I is no better than production in stage III. Getting the symmetry of the stages clear in your mind is quite another matter.

FIGURE 5–13.   L/K and K/L Ratios

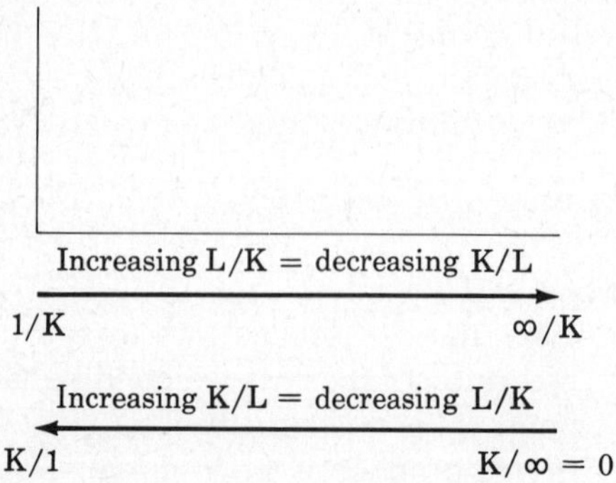

As you read from left to right on the conventional average product diagram, the proportion L/K increases. The proportion K/L therefore increases as you read from right to left.

FIGURE 5–14.   Dual Roles for Total Product and Average Product Curves

In part (*a*), we see the conventional fixed capital (K) and variable labor (L) inputs, resulting in the AP_L and TP_L schedules shown, which are taken from the production function in Figure 5–5. In part (*b*), labor is treated as the fixed input and an appropriate amount of capital is used to keep the same ratios of inputs as used in part (*a*). The result is a reduction in the *scale* of inputs. We can observe that under conditions of constant returns to scale the TP_K schedule equals the AP_L and the AP_K schedule equals the TP_L.

(*a*) *Capital*	*Labor*	*L/K ratio*	AP_L	TP_L
1	1	1/1	14	14
1	2	2/1	26	52
1	3	3/1	36	108
1	4	4/1	44	176
1	5	5/1	50	250
1	6	6/1	54	324

(*b*) *Capital*	*Labor*	*K/L ratio*	TP_K	AP_K
1	1	1/1	14	14
½	1	½/1	26	52
⅓	1	⅓/1	36	108
¼	1	¼/1	44	176
⅕	1	⅕/1	50	250
⅙	1	⅙/1	54	324
		same L to K ratio	$AP_L = TP_K$	$TP_L = AP_K$

I shall have to take a chance. What is the symmetry of the stages of production all about?

In our discussion we have used the terms total product, marginal product, and average product. For precision, we should add the suffix ". . . of labor" to each term. That is, total product of labor, marginal product of labor, average product of labor. In our examples we have held the capital input constant. Any increase that occurred in output came about because more labor was working with each unit of capital. We note that as labor input increases while capital remains constant, the proportion of labor to capital increases. The ratio L/K gets larger. Notice that in stage I, the ratio L/K is smaller than in stage III. Let us now turn the proportion upside down and consider the ratio K/L (Figure 5–13). For any stage III mix of labor and capital, we find that where L/K is big, K/L is small. We can interpret stage III for labor as involving either a large amount of labor working with each unit of capital input or a small amount of capital working with each labor input. Similarly, where L/K is small (stage I for labor), we find that K/L is very large. There is either a little labor with each unit of capital or a lot of capital working with each unit of labor. In other words, the labor-capital mix that puts us in stage I for labor (small L/K) also puts us in a stage III-type situation for capital (big K/L), and that which puts us in stage III for labor (big L/K) also puts us in a stage I situation for capital (small K/L). This is what is meant by symmetry. We can talk about the average product per unit of labor or, alternatively, we can discuss the average product per unit of capital. If we could show that the stage I-stage II boundary for labor is exactly the same factor mix as the stage II-stage III boundary for capital, we would demonstrate that it is not rational to produce in stage I (for labor) because this is also stage III for capital and this has a negative marginal product of capital. If we had such a K/L ratio, we would abandon some of the capital and thereby increase output. Thus stage II is the only rational area in which to produce because it is the only area that is not stage III for one variable or the other. Understand?

I think so. How can you demonstrate that the boundaries are the same?

We must draw the total, average, and marginal product curves for capital (holding labor constant). When we do this, we find a most interesting phenomenon. The average product curve for labor is the same as the total product curve for capital, and the average product curve for capital is the same as the total product curve for labor.

How do you know that?

Look at the data in Figure 5–14. In production schedule (*a*) the amount of capital is held at a constant value of 1 and the total product varies

FIGURE 5–15. Relationship of Total Product and Average Product

TP_L = output using 1 unit of capital
AP_K = output using 1 unit of capital
TP_K = output using 1 unit of labor
AP_L = output using 1 unit of labor

FIGURE 5–16. Symmetry of the Stages

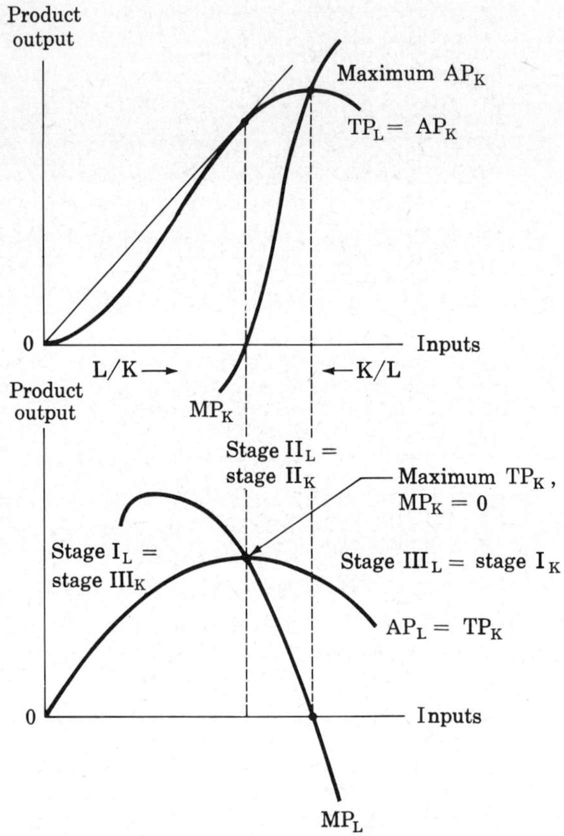

The boundary between stages I and II for labor is the same as the boundary between stages II and III for capital. The boundary between stages II and III for labor is the same as the boundary between stages I and II for capital. Under constant returns to scale the stages are symmetrical.

as labor input is increased. The L/K ratios are $1/1$, $2/1$, $3/1$, $4/1$, $5/1$, . . . , and so on. Now we want to develop total and average product curves with capital as a variable input and holding labor constant. Let us hold labor at 1 unit. In order to keep the same L/K ratios as before, we must *reduce* capital by an appropriate factor. Because $2L/1K$ means twice as much labor as capital, the appropriate K/L ratio is $\frac{1}{2}K/1L$. $4L/1K$ should be altered to $\frac{1}{4}K/1L$. This holds the ratios constant. We must reduce the scale of inputs by factors of ½, ⅓, ¼, and so on. If there are constant returns to scale, the outputs will also be reduced by ½, ⅓, ¼, and so on. Figure 5–14(*b*) shows these total-product-of-capital figures. Notice that we are now holding labor constant and varying capital to see what impact there is on total product. If you look carefully, you will see that these total-product-for-capital figures are also the same output figures as we had under average product for labor.

I see!! Is it a coincidence?

Not really. Remember that average product for labor is defined as TP/L. That is, it is the product produced by 1 unit of labor under various conditions of input proportions. Well, total product of capital also involves producing with 1 unit of labor under various input conditions. Thus its formula is also TP/L. In order to compute average product of capital, we must divide TP_K by K. This gives us the output produced by 1 unit of capital with various labor quantities. But this is the same condition under which we computed total product of labor. Here the capital amounts in the denominators are fractions, so AP_K (which equals TP_K/K) turns out to be bigger than just TP_K (Figure 5–15).

How does this identity of the curves lead to symmetry of the stages?

Once we have the total and average product curves drawn, we must recognize that each one has two identities. The boundary between stage I and II for labor occurred where average product for labor was a maximum. However, the dual identity means that total product for capital is also a maximum at this point. When total product is a maximum, we know that marginal product is zero. But this is the boundary condition between stages II and III. What is more, at points to the left of this maximum, the proportion of capital to labor is even higher than at the point of zero marginal product. In this range marginal product is negative. This means that we are in stage III for capital. It is the same range as stage I for labor. We long ago concluded that we should not produce in this range of L/K combinations. An identical argument can be made for the boundary between stages II and III for capital being

FIGURE 5–17. Isoquant Map

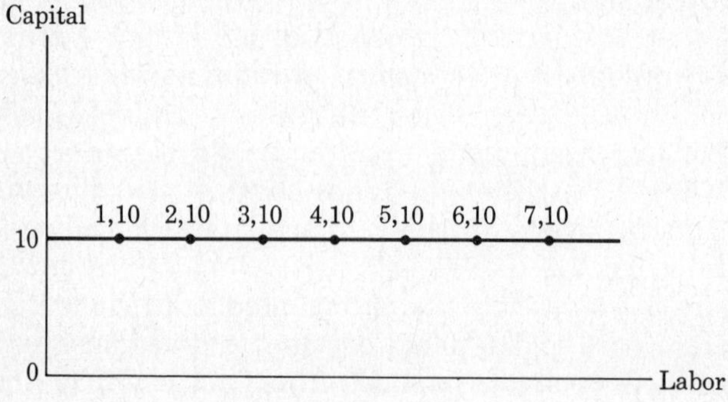

To hold capital constant on the isoquant map and vary labor, we measure up to the amount of capital on the vertical axis. Then, reading across, we read the coordinates of that fixed capital with variable amounts of labor.

FIGURE 5–18. Isoquant Map

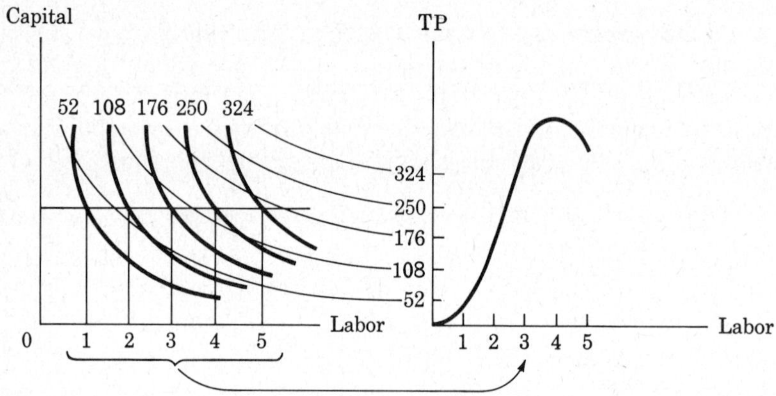

To read the output associated with different amounts of labor and a fixed capital, we read the numerical values of the isoquants intersected by the horizontal line described in Figure 5–17. We could plot these values against the different labor inputs to get a total product curve.

at the same point as the boundary between stages I and II for labor. This occurs where the total product curve for labor is at a maximum. The dual identity means that the average product curve for capital is also maximum and therefore this is the boundary between stage I and stage II for capital. To the right, there is even less capital relative to labor then at the boundary, and it is irrational to use this little capital with so much labor. Hence these stages really are symmetrical (Figure 5–16).

I'll go back and look at that again later!! Let's get back to isoquants. What did you say an isoquant is?
An isoquant is a form of a production function, $Q = f(L, K)$, where we know the Q and want all the L's and K's that satisfy it. The isoquant shows all the alternative quantities of labor and capital that can produce the *given* output. An isoquant map shows the alternative inputs for all outputs.

Is there any relationship between isoquants and the total product curve, or are they separate topics?
Logically, they must be closely related because both can be forms of the same production function. Remember that the total product of labor curve holds capital constant and varies labor as well as output. In order to show this idea on an isoquant map, it is necessary to note the different outputs that can be produced by a fixed capital and different quantities of labor. We do this on the isoquant map by measuring up on the vertical axis to whatever amount of capital is being used and reading horizontally across the map along a line from that capital input point (Figure 5–17). The coordinates of points along such a horizontal line show different quantities of labor combined with that given level of capital. Each isoquant intersected by the line has a different quantity of output associated with it (Figure 5–18). These are the total product values that we plotted before. Thus, we can read from the isoquant curve the same values that we read on the total product curve. What is more, we can draw total product curves for various capital input levels.

Can the stages of production also be shown on the isoquant map?
Yes, but before getting into that, we should point out some of the basic characteristics of isoquants. The easiest generality to keep in mind is that the isoquant is basically a *production indifference curve*. We shall want to make statements about its slope and shape, and also bring

FIGURE 5–19. Marginal Rate of Technical Substitution

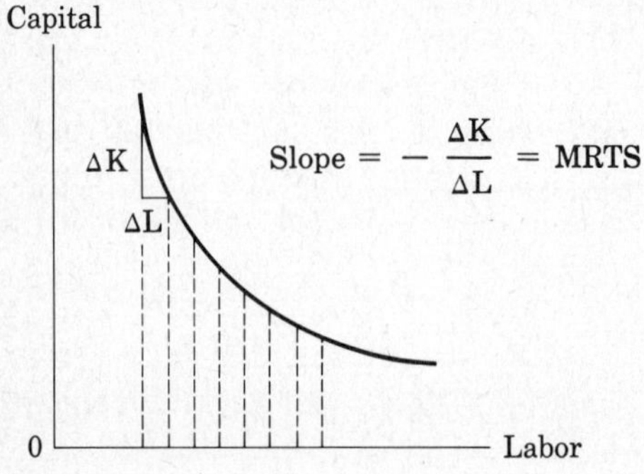

The *MRTS* shows the amount of capital that will replace 1 unit of labor in the production process. It is measured as the slope of the isoquant.

FIGURE 5–20. The Marginal Rate of Technical Substitution

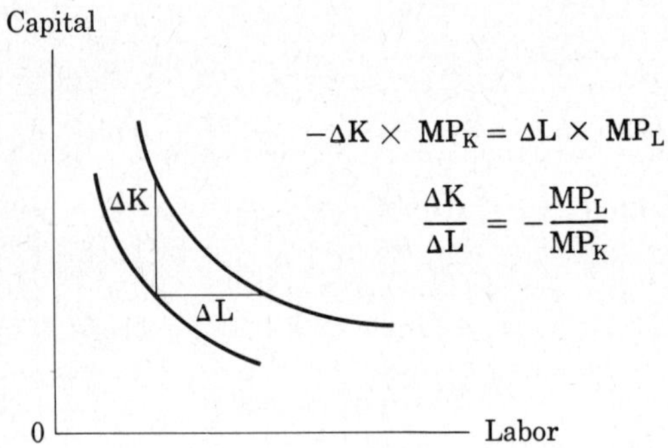

The *MRTS* can be shown to be equal numerically to the ratio of marginal product of labor to marginal product of capital. The minus sign occurs because ΔL and ΔK go in opposite directions.

into the analysis a function similar to the budget line with which we worked in consumer analysis.

In the indifference analysis, the slope represented the marginal rate of substitution. What is its meaning in the isoquant analysis?
Not too different. Here it is called the *marginal rate of technical substitution* (*MRTS*). As we read along an isoquant, we are holding output constant and substituting one input for another (Figure 5–19). Reading down from left to right, we substitute labor for capital. The slope of $\Delta K/\Delta L$ shows the amount of capital given up in order to add 1 unit of labor and still keep the level of output constant.

What is the relationship of marginal rate of technical substitution to the marginal product?
Remember that marginal product equals the change in total product resulting from a one-unit change of an input, everything else remaining constant. Well, in this instance, we have a one-unit increase in labor that is obviously going to add the marginal product of labor to total output if everything else remains equal. However, everything else does not remain equal. Capital is reduced so we can remain on the isoquant and hold the total output constant. Therefore the number of units that capital is reduced, multiplied by the marginal product of capital, must be equal to the marginal product of labor multiplied by the number of units of increase in labor. We had an analogous situation in the indifference analysis when we said that marginal utility of Y times ΔY must equal marginal utility of X times ΔX in order to stay on the indifference curve. Here

$$MP_K \times -\Delta K = MP_L \times \Delta L$$

Performance of a little algebraic magic gives us the following:

$$MRTS = \frac{\Delta K}{\Delta L} = -\frac{MP_L}{MP_K}$$

This tells us that the slope of the isoquant is equal to the ratio of the marginal products of the inputs (Figure 5–20).

Is the curvature of the isoquant related to diminishing returns?
Yes, it is. We know that when one input is relatively scarce, its marginal product is high. When it is relatively abundant, its marginal product is low. At different points along the isoquant, the relative quantities of capital and labor vary. At the upper end, labor is scarce and capital

FIGURE 5–21. The Isoquant Is Convex to the Origin

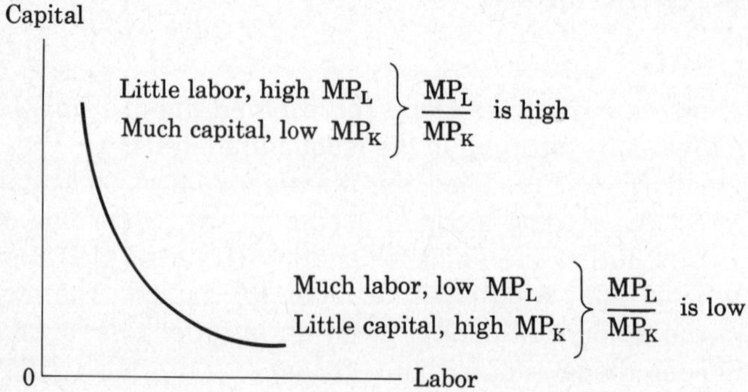

Because at different points along the isoquant the relative amounts of capital and labor vary, so too do their marginal products. Remember that we are operating under conditions of diminishing returns, so MP_L will be high when there is relatively little labor and low when there is a lot, and MP_K will be high when there is little capital and low when there is a lot. Thus the slope MP_L/MP_K will also vary

FIGURE 5–22. Stage I and Stage III

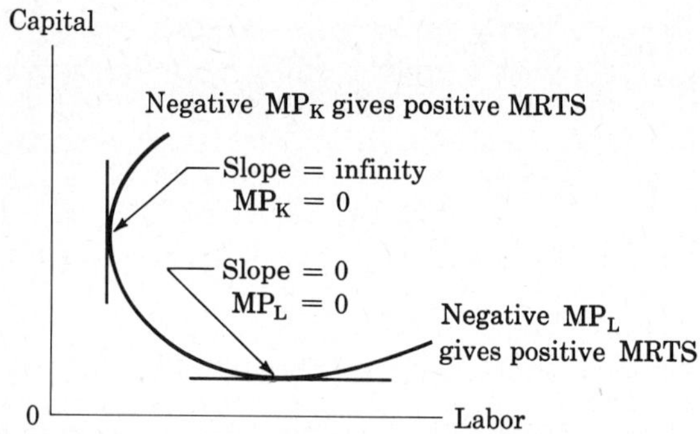

Isoquants can slope up to the right in different areas. This represents stages I and III. Note that if the direction of the curve is reversed, it means there is a negative marginal product for one of the factors. Hence it is stage III for one or the other.

abundant. Therefore marginal product of labor is high, marginal product of capital is low, and their ratio gives a high value. The curve is steep. At the other end, you can see that the opposite conditions prevail and the curve is relatively flat (Figure 5–21).

It appears that the isoquants not only become vertical and horizontal at the extremes, but they seem to continue and eventually slope upward.
Yes, that is true, and it is this observation that finally brings us back to the question about the stages of production. If the isoquant is vertical, the slope MP_L/MP_K is infinite. This will happen if the marginal product of capital approaches zero. Adding more capital beyond this vertical point, the slope goes the other way. This implies that marginal product of one of the inputs is negative. It is obviously capital, whose marginal product has gotten progressively smaller with the addition of capital, that has reached zero and now is moving into negative territory. You may recognize the condition of negative marginal product as characteristic of stage III. Zero marginal product occurs at the boundary between stage II and stage III. Hence this range where the isoquant bends the "wrong" way is stage III for capital (also stage I for labor). At the opposite extreme where the curve goes the wrong way, we have stage III for labor (stage I for capital). Again, the area of general economic interest is that over which the isoquant is downward sloping, that is, stage II (Figure 5–22). Notice that the slope of the isoquant is negative in stage II (downward sloping). In stages I and III, when one of the marginal products turns negative, the expression for *MRTS* is positive (quotient of two negatives). Hence the isoquant slopes up to the right here.

What is the significance of the different shapes of isoquant in stage II?
Capital and labor can be freely substituted for one another over a broad range in some productive activities, but in others there is only a small number of capital-labor combinations that will work. In the first case the ratio MP_L/MP_K remains fairly constant, and the isoquant approximates a straight line. In the second case it changes rapidly; the isoquant is sharply curved. In the first instance labor and capital are considered good substitutes for one another; in the second they have a complementary relationship.

Please elaborate on the substitute and complement nature of labor and capital.
Labor and capital work together. However, the flexibility with which they work together varies, and this is where the complementarity and substitutability come in. The best way to see this is through an example.

FIGURE 5–23. Complementary Factors of Production

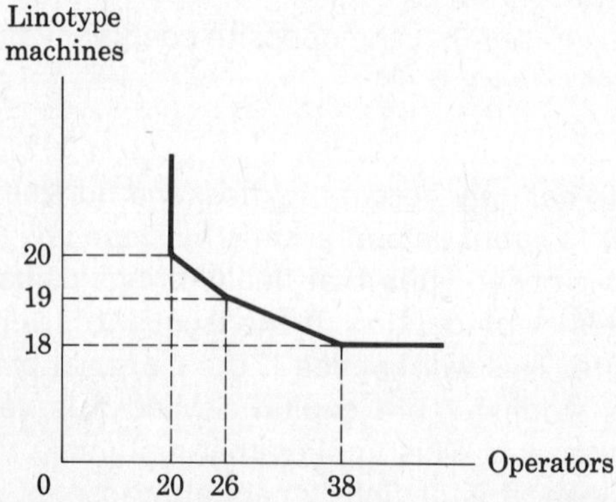

An isoquant with sharp curvature implies complementarity between labor and capital. In the linotype example discussed in the text, the curve goes rapidly from vertical to horizontal, indicating sharp changes in the marginal rate of technical substitution.

Let us examine some of the process that went into the production of this book. Book manufacture involves a wide variety of crafts, perhaps the least demanding of which is writing. Focus on typesetting for a moment. A fairly simple approach to typesetting is through use of the linotype machine, a Rube Goldberg-type contraption that has a typewriter keyboard on the front and a thousand levers, arms, and wheels in the back controlling a trayful of type. Typically, the operator sits in front of one machine and "types" the material out on the keyboard. The arms, levers, and wheels release tiny molds of each letter typed, bring them together, pour molten lead into the molds, and cast a lead line of type from which the printing will be done. It is highly skilled and demanding work. Each machine requires an operator, and the obvious proportion of labor to capital is 1/1. Let us assume a plant of 20 machines and 20 operators that between them set 200 pages of book type in a single day. Now, let us see what the possibilities are for substitution. Can we remove one machine and hold output fixed at 200 pages per day? Removal of the machine reduces output by 10 pages and frees one operator. How can we replace the output of the missing machine? Under the L/K ratio of 1 labor to 1 capital, there is quite a bit of time lost due to operator fatigue as well as the need for him to leave the machine to perform other auxiliary tasks. The machine must be cleaned. Different type faces must be put on and taken off. New lead must be added from time to time. The finished type must be taken away and stored until it is ready for use. By bringing in additional labor to perform some of these auxiliary tasks for the workers at the 19 operating machines, the productivity of each can be increased enough for the total output to remain at the same 200 pages. Assume that it takes six additional men to do this. The *MRTS* is 1/6. This means that the marginal productivity of capital is six times that of labor.

Now remove one more machine. This also might reduce output by 10 pages per day. How many men will it take to pick up the additional slack? Because most of the obvious areas were filled by the six men who came on the job to replace the first machine, it will be more difficult to keep output at 200 pages now. Perhaps it can be done with twice as many additional workers. Let us say that it takes 12 men to replace the marginal machine. Now *MRTS* is 1/12; the marginal product of capital is 12 times that of labor.

Now let us try to remove a third machine. We are likely to find that there is no way we can restore the output to 200 pages per day if this is done. Even if we add 50 additional workers, we cannot restore production to its earlier level. We simply need another machine. At this point, men and machines are perfect complements. The only way to improve output by adding a man is to simultaneously add a machine for him to work on. The isoquant is perfectly horizontal, because the same 190 pages will be produced with 17 machines and 38 men or 17 machines and 58 men. The marginal productivity of labor is zero.

Go back to the other end of the isoquant at the 1/1 ratio at which we began. Suppose, then, that we ask how many machines we must add if we wish to reduce the labor force by one operator and retain the output at 200 pages per day. Here, the answer must be, "No way!" Unless there is an operator, an additional machine is of no use. Nineteen operators will simply not produce what 20 operators can do, regardless of how many machines they have. Here the isoquant is vertical (Figure 5–23).

The linotype operation is a highly complementary production process between capital and labor. The isoquant goes from vertical to horizontal over a range of 3 units of capital. The ratio of MP_L/MP_K went from infinity to 1/1 to 1/6 to 1/12 to 0 very rapidly. That is complementarity.

What kind of production process shows high substitutability?

We can look at another operation within the printing plant. Rolls of paper must be moved from place to place. Let us assume that 1000 lb

FIGURE 5–24. Substitute Factors of Production

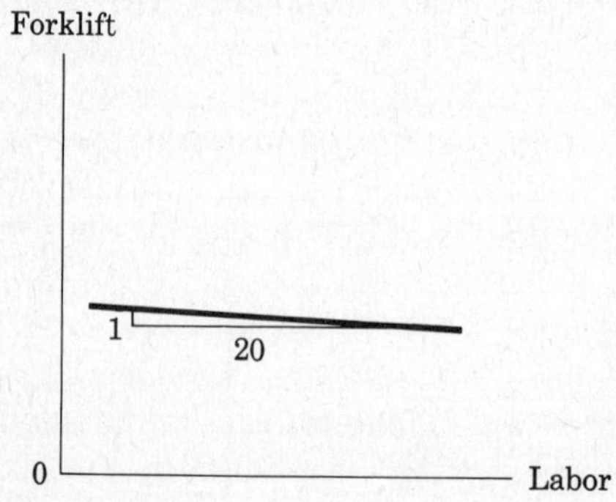

A straight-line isoquant implies high substitutability of factors. Each factor can do what the other can do if substituted in some given ratio, regardless of the relative amounts of each working. The paper-moving example used in the text involves a task with minimal changes in the marginal rate of technical substitution.

of paper can be moved by one forklift truck and one operator, or alternatively, that the work can be done by no forklift trucks and 20 strong men. This type of work can be done by truck or by men, and they can be substituted indefinitely at a ratio of 1/20. If a day's work involves moving 200,000 lb of paper, it can be done by 10 trucks and 10 men, 9 trucks and 30 men, 8 trucks and 50 men, and so on down to the point of zero trucks and 200 men. After all, they built the Pyramids that way.

This isoquant has no curvature. It is a straight line at the constant slope of 1/20. The marginal product of capital remains 20 times that of labor throughout the range of the isoquant (Figure 5–24).

We shall want to retain this idea of substitutes and complements when we deal with the effects of price changes of the factors, and try to decide which combination of factors to use at different factor prices.

How do we show factor prices in the isoquant analysis?

At this point we are ready to introduce the *isocost* into the analysis. The isocost is analogous to the budget line that we used in the indifference curve analysis. It, too, is a line of attainable combinations. It shows the different combinations of the two inputs, capital and labor, that can be bought with a fixed total dollar outlay. If we think of a production manager as having a total budget within which he must operate, the isocost shows the different combinations of factor inputs he can buy. Naturally, in order to compute this, we must first know the prices of the different factors of production.

Where do these prices come from?

They come from that great source of all prices in economic theory: out there in the market. The supply and demand forces for the different factors of production interact to form a price at which the supply will just be cleared from the market. If we assume that these are competitive markets, no one buyer or seller of factor inputs can affect price, and thus they arise externally to the firm. In a word, they are *given*.

How do we use the isocost in the analysis?

We plot the isocost in a manner similar to that used in plotting the budget line. Let us assume that the total money available to spend on factors of production is T. If the price of capital is P_K and the price of labor is P_L, then the equation for the isocost is

$$(P_K \times K) + (P_L \times L) = T$$

That is, total money available equals the number of units of capital bought times their price per unit, plus the number of units of labor bought times their price per unit. There are different ways to plot this. The simplest is to locate the y intercept and the x intercept on the graph and connect them. The y intercept indicates that there are zero units of labor employed and all the money is spent on capital. In this case you can buy T/P_K units of capital. We find this by substituting 0 into the formula for L and solving for K. The x intercept has a similar interpretation. If we buy zero units of capital, we can afford T/P_L units of labor. Again we substitute zero into the formula for K and solve for L (Figure 5–25).

Are we interested in the slope of the isocost?

Yes. The slope measures the rate of substitution possible in the marketplace at the given prices. The slope is found by taking the ratio of the y intercept to the x intercept:

$$-\frac{T/P_K}{T/P_L} = \frac{T}{P_K} \times \frac{P_L}{T}$$

FIGURE 5–25. Isocost

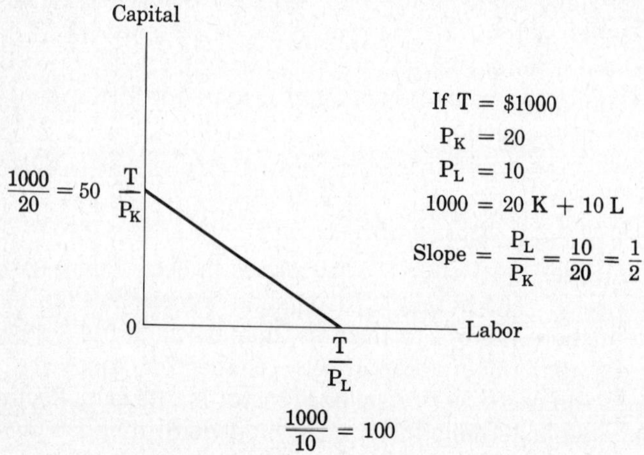

The isocost shows the different quantities of labor and capital that can be bought at some given outlay. Each isocost shows a different total outlay. The slope of the isocost depends on the relative prices of the inputs.

FIGURE 5–26. Maximizing Output from a Fixed Outlay

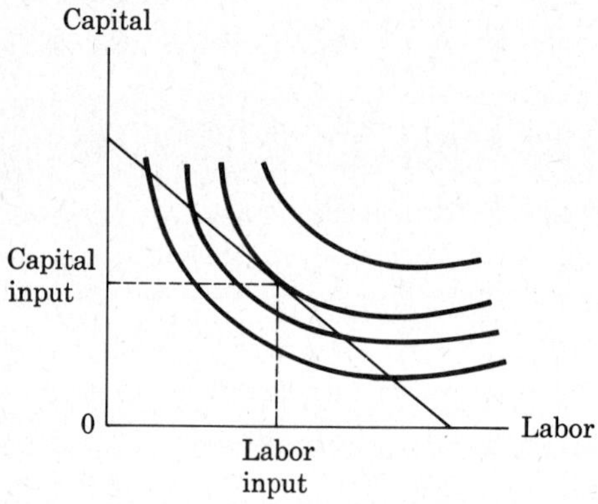

The isocost shows the maximum amount of money available for purchase of factor inputs. We wish to produce the largest quantity possible in light of that constraint. This is represented by the isoquant that is tangent to the isocost. The factor inputs to use are represented by the coordinates of the point of tangency.

This may be stated as

$$-\frac{P_L}{P_K} = \text{slope of isocost}$$

Are we now ready to find the proper input combination to use?
Just about. First we must define what we mean by *proper*. On the one hand, we may seek to maximize the output from a given total dollar value of inputs. On the other hand, we may try to minimize the dollar input required to produce a given output. Although similar, the problems are by no means identical.

How do you go about maximizing the output from a given input?
The diagram for this problem (Figure 5–26) consists of a single isocost determined by the total funds available for inputs as well as the respective factor prices, and a family of isoquants determined by the production function. We seek the highest isoquant attainable. You will not be surprised to learn that this is the one that is just tangent to the isocost. The coordinates of the point of tangency tell us how much capital and how much labor must be bought in order to produce this quantity. A firm that uses this combination of inputs operates in the most efficient manner in light of the budgetary constraints on it.

How do you go about minimizing the cost of producing a given output?
In this instance the diagram consists of a single isoquant and a family of isocosts. The isoquant shows the different capital-labor combinations that are technically able to produce the desired output. The least-cost combination is again found at the point of tangency between the lowest isocost and the isoquant. Any other point on the isoquant involves higher cost in order to produce the same output. Any lower isocost will not buy enough inputs to allow production of the desired output (Figure 5–27).

It looks as if the slopes of the isocost and isoquant are equal at the point of tangency.
You are certainly catching on. The slopes are equal because the isocost and isoquant are tangent to each other and therefore have the same slope at the point of tangency. The isocost's tangency to the isoquant leads us to an extremely important conclusion about the conditions necessary for maximizing efficiency. Remember that the slope of the isoquant equals $-MP_L/MP_K$ and the slope of the isocost equals $-P_L/P_K$.

FIGURE 5–27. Minimizing Cost of a Fixed Output

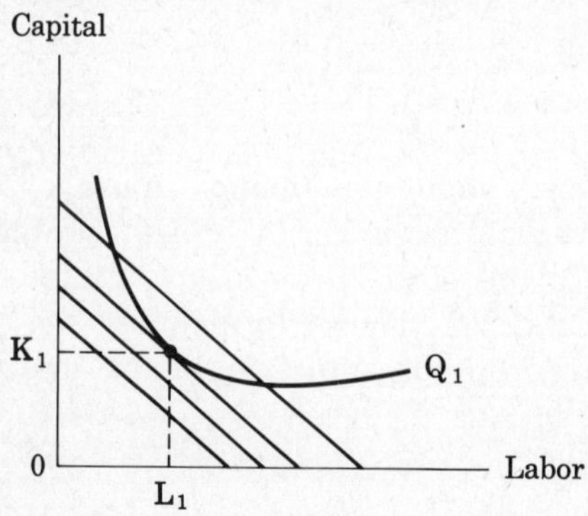

The family of isocosts represents various total outlays. If a firm decides that it wishes to produce Q_1 units of output at the lowest cost possible, it should seek that isocost that is just tangent to the given isoquant. The coordinates of the point of tangency give the amounts of capital (K_1) and labor (L_1) inputs to use.

FIGURE 5–28. Changes in Factor Prices—I

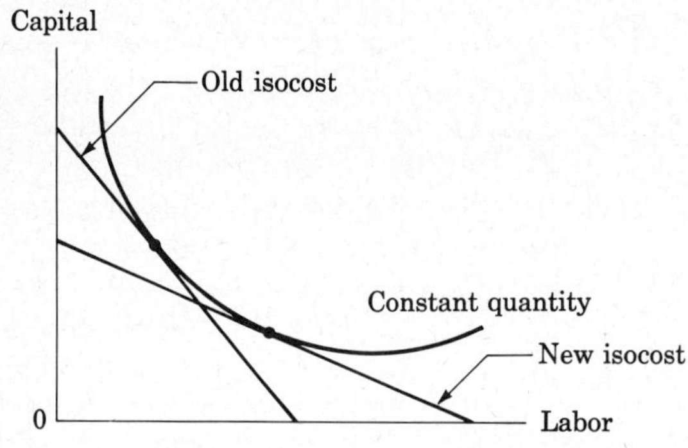

If output is kept the same, a change in the relative prices of the inputs causes the new isocost to shift to a new position where it is tangent to the isoquant. The diagram shown represents a reduction in labor price, or an increase in capital price. The total outlay (T) is changed in either case.

At the point of tangency they are equal to each other:

$$-\frac{MP_L}{MP_K} = -\frac{P_L}{P_K}$$

A little algebra gives us:

$$\frac{MP_L}{P_L} = \frac{MP_K}{P_K}$$

This relationship says that in order to maximize economic efficiency, funds should be allocated among factor inputs so that the marginal products per dollar spent on each input are equal. You can see why this is so. Under the conditions of diminishing marginal productivity that hold in stage II for both inputs, any deviation from this condition will lower total output. If we take a dollar's worth of labor away, and instead add another dollar's worth of capital, we shall be getting a lower marginal product per dollar from the capital than we lost from the labor. If a firm is in equilibrium at one set of prices, any change in prices will force it to change its mix of inputs if it is to reestablish the $MP_L/P_L = MP_K/P_K$ relationship.

How does the firm adjust to changes in factor prices?

Again, it depends on what problem it is facing. We recognize that the slope of the isocost is determined by the relative prices of the inputs. If the price of labor falls or the price of capital rises, the isocost gets flatter. If the price of labor rises or the price of capital falls, the isocost gets steeper. If the problem is to produce a given output in the least expensive way, we shall want to see the new point of tangency between the isoquant and the lowest of the new isocosts (Figure 5–28). The change in factor prices will lead the firm toward employing more of the relatively lower-priced factor and less of the higher-priced one. If the problem is to maximize output attainable with a fixed dollar outlay, we shall draw the new isocost and observe its point of tangency with the highest attainable isoquant. Here too there is substitution in favor of employing more of the relatively cheaper input. However, there will not necessarily be a reduction in the quantity used of the other input. It too may rise, as seen in Figure 5–29. It depends on the extent to which the inputs are complements or substitutes for one another.

That again!! How do complementarity and substitutability enter?

It is obvious in the first case, where we hold output fixed, that a reduction in the price of labor relative to capital causes a producer to sub-

FIGURE 5–29. Change in Factor Prices—II

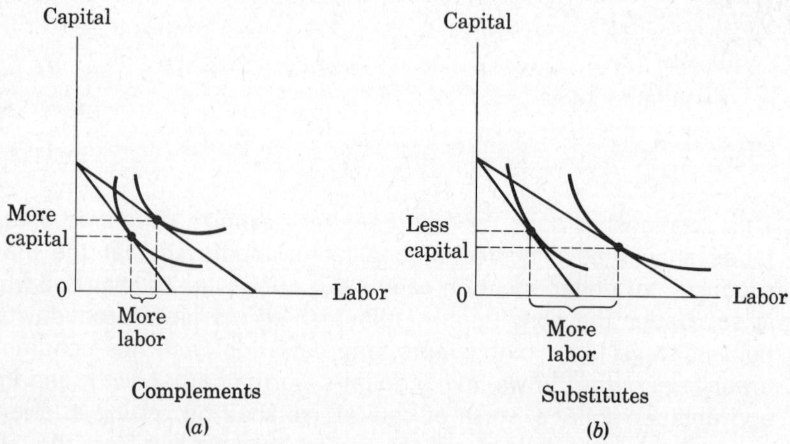

If the price of labor falls while the price of capital remains constant along with the total outlay (T), you employ more labor. Whether you also employ more capital depends on whether capital and labor are complements or substitutes. Here part (a) shows a complementary relationship; part (b) shows a substitute relationship.

stitute in the direction of the cheaper input and away from the more expensive one. The degree to which substitution occurs depends on the curvature of the isoquant, and we have just seen that isoquants with sharp curvature involve complementary inputs. The change in input prices changes the slope of the isocost. The question is, How much must the quantities of inputs used change before the ratio of MP_L/MP_K is again equal to P_L/P_K? If, as in the case of the linotype operation, the ratio of MP_L/MP_K changes very rapidly along an isoquant, there will be slight substitution. On the other hand, if the ratio of marginal products changes very slowly, or not at all, as in the case of the forklift truck, a lot of substitution will take place in response to comparatively small price changes. In effect, we are dealing with the elasticity of demand for factor inputs, and as we saw in the case of goods and services, elasticity is high when there are easy substitutes available. We shall pursue this question of elasticity further in Chapters 11 and 12 when we examine demand and supply for factors of production.

Is there a possibility of increasing the quantity bought of the input whose price is relatively higher?
Again it is a question of complementarity versus substitutability. Suppose that only the price of labor fell. The isocost rotates around the y intercept to a point of tangency with a higher isoquant. The movement to a higher isoquant is similar to the income effect found in the theory of consumer behavior. Reduction of the price of one input permits purchase of more of all inputs; therefore, more product can be produced. Now, the question is, Will all the freed funds be used to purchase additional (cheaper) labor, or will some of it go into the purchase of additional capital as well? If the inputs are complements, the purchase of additional labor will increase the marginal product of capital, because the K/L ratio will be reduced. This rise in marginal product of capital will encourage greater purchases of capital. On the other hand, if labor and capital are good substitutes, increasing labor input merely adds to the total number of functionally identical resources available to perform a particular task. This reduces the marginal productivity of all factors involved, capital as well as labor.

It sounds like a lot to keep in mind.
The complementarity and substitutability business is a bit sticky. The nice thing about the isoquant analysis is that it is all worked through for you by the tangency condition of the isocost with the isoquant. The shape of the isoquant contains the elements of the relationship among the factor inputs.

Are we finished discussing production now?
No, not quite. We have spent this chapter developing the theory of how to produce a given quantity. Unfortunately, there is nothing in the theory so far to tell us that the quantity we select is the profit-maximizing quantity. In order to determine profit, it is necessary to learn a little more about cost determination than we have so far. The next chapter will take this up in considerable detail.

CHAPTER HIGHLIGHTS

1. *We learned what a production function is, and how to develop total, average, and marginal product schedules.*
2. *We discussed the relationship between the average and marginal product schedules and saw why* MP *passes through the maximum* AP *and equals zero when* TP *is maximum.*

3. We reviewed the laws of variable proportions and diminishing returns and saw how they applied to production problems.
4. We went over the stages of production and examined the principles of symmetry. We analyzed why stage II is the only rational stage in which to produce.
5. We considered isoquants and isocosts as tools for dealing with production problems.
6. Finally, we touched on how to handle price changes among the factors of production, considering the role played by complementarity and substitutability of factors.

QUESTIONS

1. A wise man once said, "There is only one resource in the world: the mind of man." Do you agree? What about the other factors we have discussed?
2. The production function holds technology and weather constant. They are, of course, never that constant. How would you show a particularly good agricultural growing season's effects on the total product of labor curve? How would it affect the isoquant map?
3. Many production analyses work for a production function in which there are constant returns to scale. When we double all inputs, the output will double. What complications for constant returns to scale (homogeneous) production functions for agriculture are created by the possibility of good growing weather occurring one year but not the next?
4. Suppose that two factor inputs are perfect substitutes. What will their isoquant map look like? Can you demonstrate that as long as two inputs are perfect substitutes, only the cheaper one will be used?
5. Input-output analysis uses right-angle isoquants. These show only a single ratio of labor to capital is possible for producing each output. How would changing factor costs affect the factor combination used under these circumstances?
6. A "focused" factory is a plant that produces only a single product. Most plants are not focused but are instead used to produce a varied assortment of products. Proponents of the focused factory argue that they get the advantage of specialization. Proponents of the varied output argue for economies of scale. Which do you think is likely to be the most economical?
7. J. M. Clark wrote of the different factors of production, "The fundamental trait of the human laborer is an elastic sort of stability

without complete uniformity. He builds on a foundation of habit and custom yet he never does things twice exactly alike. Contrast this with the machine. . . . Uniformity is his passion, continuous operation his religion. He is tireless, his capacity limited only by the hours of the day." Are labor and captal really substitutes for one another? How can they be? Do Clark's remarks contribute anything to your thinking about Question 6?

6 Supply analysis: costs

Costs sounds like a simple enough topic, but by now you should know that there are no simple topics. Even if there were, economists wouldn't let them remain that way. When viewed from the point of view of the accountant of a firm, costs are simply what a company pays out to produce what it sells. However, our point of view is not that of the accountant, whose purpose is to measure flows of money through a firm, but rather that of the economist, whose purpose is to consider the allocation of scarce resources for the society as a whole.

The accountant is concerned with *explicit* costs. Since actual cash payments were made, he can compute these by looking at his checkbook and adding up the amounts on the stubs. The economist is concerned with a somewhat more subtle type of cost called *opportunity*, or *alternative*, cost.

What is opportunity cost?

Think of a firm with a number of products. Suppose that it hires a worker, pays him $10 per hour, and puts him to work in its production department. There he produces at least $10 worth of product per hour. Suppose, however, that he might have worked in the sales department, where with his skills he could have produced $20 worth of value per hour. The accountant would say that the cost of the worker is $10 per hour. The economist would say that his cost is $20 per hour.

FIGURE 6–1. Difference Between Economic and Accounting Cost

Suppose that the firm has an income statement:

Sales Revenue		$100,000
Materials	$40,000	
Labor	30,000	
Overhead	10,000	80,000
Net profit		$ 20,000

The $20,000 represents accounting profit. Economic costs are understated. Assume that the owner's implicit wage is $10,000; normal profit on sales of $100,000 is $5000; implicit interest on capital investment is $10,000; and implicit rent is $5000. When these are treated as costs there is a $10,000 loss rather than a $20,000 gain.

How can his cost be more than you paid him?

The economist is interested in minimizing the use of scarce resources in the economy. As far as he is concerned, the community might have gained $20 worth of value had the employee spent his time in sales. The cost of an hour spent in production is $20 regardless of what he was paid. If he were paid $2 per hour, the cost would still be $20. The important thing is the opportunities lost by committing a resource to a given activity.

Why didn't the company put the employee to work in the sales department?

They should have. This is a case of misallocating the services of their employee and thereby reducing their total revenues. However, the worker made a mistake too. He should not have accepted $10 for his services. In a competitive market he should "theoretically" be able to command a wage close to the value of his own marginal product. Assuming that he could do this, we would say that his opportunity cost was $20. However, just because the company and the worker made mistakes in employing their resources, this does not mean the economist must misstate his accounts.

Then how do you define opportunity cost?

Opportunity cost is the value of a resource employed in its best alternative role. If it is already in its best role, opportunity cost is equal to the accounting cost. Regardless of whether money exchanges or not, there is opportunity cost involved in everything we do. The opportunity cost of going to college is the earnings you might have gained by working during those years. The opportunity cost of sleeping an extra hour is the satisfaction you might have gained from reading, or watching TV, or whatever else gives you the next most pleasure. Nothing in this world is without opportunity cost.

Is this what they mean when they say, "There is no such thing as a free lunch"?
Exactly.

How are opportunity and accounting costs generally related?
Accounting costs for a total enterprise are generally less than opportunity costs because all resources are not perfectly allocated. Even if they were, accounting costs would omit *implicit costs*.

What in the world are implicit costs?
Implicit costs are a form of opportunity cost. They are the value of certain services that are consumed in the production process, but for which no bill is ever tendered and no payment ever made. Usually, these reflect the input of the entrepreneur's time and use of his property. If a storekeeper works 60 hours a week in his store, he should figure as an implicit cost the value of his labor were he to offer it in the labor market. If he owns the store, he should figure as an implicit cost the rent he foregoes by occupying it himself and not renting it out. If he has capital tied up in inventory and fixtures, he should figure the interest he could earn on that capital as an implicit cost. All of these additional costs might turn an ostensibly profitable accounting situation into an unprofitable economic situation (Figure 6–1).

Are there any other opportunity costs?
There is one more that may seem a bit subtle at first but that is important for our theory. This is the concept of a "normal" profit. If the entrepreneur assumes risk and offers his entrepreneurial services to his own business, he should figure as a cost the normal profit he might make in another business. Adding in this final element has the bizarre effect of making the economic profit of the normal firm under conditions of pure competition come out to zero.

Why is the normal economic profit equal to zero?

If we take all costs, explicit and implicit, and add *normal* profits to them, we get a value we can call total economic cost. In a "normal" situation costs plus profit should equal total revenue, thereby leaving economic profit (i.e., profit in excess of normal) equal to zero.

Suppose that an entrepreneur is abnormally good and earns abnormally high total revenues. Won't there be an abnormal profit greater than zero?

If a manager is good enough to earn abnormally high total revenues for the firm, his opportunity cost as a manager should be higher than normal. He is worth more working for somebody else if he is able to perform that well. The market would raise his income so he would receive as wages whatever extra profit he generates. Thus, what we were tempted to account for as abnormal profit becomes instead higher opportunity cost. The economic profit (i.e., profit in excess of all costs and normal profits) remains zero. A highly analogous situation arises when we see food prices rise and produce high farm profits. Land values keep right abreast of food prices, however. Economic reasoning suggests that the higher land value is an opportunity cost that should be added into the farmer's cost. It is quite likely that this calculation will reduce his economic profit to zero. Potential use of the land for a building site raises its economic cost still more. It appears that some farmers make this calculation and come up with a less-than-normal profit computation. One farmer who decided to sell his land to a developer was quoted recently as saying, "I would have to farm a thousand years to make as much money off of the land as I was paid for it." Who says the opportunity cost concept has no practical application?

Can there never be more than zero economic profit?

Yes, but this will generally occur as a result of some kind of intervention in the market that creates a monopoly-like situation for a seller. An entrepreneur reaping abnormal profits is not necessarily a superior manager with high opportunity cost. He may simply own the only game in town and charge accordingly. We shall take this up when we deal with monopoly in Chapter 9.

Okay. After all this we have defined cost. What next?

Next we want to make a distinction between costs that vary directly with volume of output and those that do not. Those that vary with output are called variable costs. Those that do not vary at all with ouput are called fixed costs. To be perfectly fair, we should note that all costs cannot be classified as being either wholly variable or wholly fixed. There are some that can best be called *semivariable*. They vary somewhat, but not strictly with output.

Can you give some examples of these different kinds of costs?
If labor were paid strictly on a piece rate, it would represent a cost that varies directly with output. If seamstresses get $.15 for every collar they sew onto a shirt, labor cost is variable. Union pressure has made straight piece rates largely a thing of the past, however. Instead, most shops have an hourly wage rate. Labor cost varies fairly directly with output. Assuming a fixed hourly rate of production, we can figure that the more hours worked, the higher the output will be. If, on the other hand, a worker has an annual contract that stipulates salary for the year regardless of whatever output the plant produces, he is an element of fixed cost. Labor is more likely to fall into the variable category, however.

What are some examples of fixed costs?
In addition to the possibility of the annual labor contract just suggested, a firm can have other fixed obligations. Interest cost on business indebtedness is an obligation that must be paid. Rental payments on leased property are also fixed costs, as are minimal maintenance costs. Besides all these, there is one other that, believe it or not, is the biggest of all and is frequently overlooked entirely. That is depreciation. Once a plant has invested in capital, it charges it off over the life of the asset. This charge is usually calculated as a function of time rather than output. Once the asset is purchased, there is no escape from having to meet this periodic charge.

It would seem that you could sell the machine.
Yes you can—eventually. This brings us to the recognition that there should be a time-period distinction made in the discussion. Economists refer to the *short run* and the *long run*. During the short run, the capital input is considered to be fixed and output can be increased only by varying the quantity of labor employed. In the long run, however, capital inputs can be varied. Plant can be sold off, or allowed to deteriorate, or burned down if things really get desperate. In the long run there are no fixed costs.

FIGURE 6–2. Semivariable Costs as a Step Function

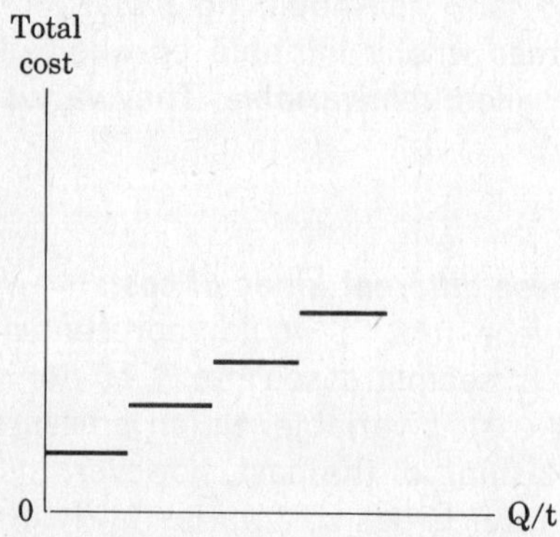

A step function takes on discrete values over some range of the independent variable. The graph appears as a series of steps; that is, it is not continuous.

Please elaborate on that.

Fixed costs remain obligations of the firm regardless of output. Even if the firm stops producing altogether, it still must meet payments on contracts, leases, indebtedness, depreciation, and so on. In the short run, these costs go on even at zero output. In the long run, leases can expire or be renewed. Plant can be totally depreciated or expanded, contracts can be terminated or extended, indebtedness can be retired or increased. These fixed-cost elements take on a quality of variability. Should the firm decide to shut down, in the long run it is possible to reduce the fixed costs, along with the variable cost, to zero. Should the plant expand or automate, it is possible to raise the level of fixed costs. Hence economists say that in the long run there really are no costs that are fixed.

Would it be accurate to say that the short run is a year and the long run is longer?

Not only is it inaccurate—it is incorrect. There is no chronological time associated with long and short run. This is not accounting, with its long- and short-term liabilities and assets (meaning one year). Long and short run are functional concepts—not chronological.

What are semi-variable costs?

These are costs that remain fixed over a range of output and then suddenly increase substantially—remain fixed for a while and then take another leap. Supervisory labor is like this. A foreman can supervise ten workers effectively. As long as the number of workers fluctuates but remains below ten, supervisory costs are fixed. Then when another foreman comes on because of an increase in work force beyond ten, there is a jump in supervisory costs. The same principle applies to some kinds of machinery. A machine has a range of output. If demand requires output beyond its range, an additional machine must be bought. Costs take a jump up. In mathematics, this is called a step function, constant over a range and then varying, and then constant over another range (Figure 6–2).

Describe the graphs of fixed and variable costs.

Remember that we are dealing with *functional* relationships. Cost is the dependent variable, and quantity of output is the independent variable. Of course, lurking behind quantity of output is the number of units of factor inputs being used. Costs are incurred because factor inputs are bought. Thus the production function is intimately related to the cost function. When inputs get larger in value, so too do costs.

How does this relate to fixed costs?

Very simply. The inputs related to fixed costs do not get larger as output increases. These remain constant. Therefore the graph of fixed costs as a function of output takes on the appearance of a horizontal line at whatever height represents the fixed costs. At the moment we are talking about *total* fixed cost. Shortly we shall deal with *average* fixed cost, which is different in nature. However, to repeat one more time, total fixed cost is graphed as a horizontal line (Figure 6–3).

How are variable costs graphed?

Total variable cost slopes up to the right. In the simplest case we ignore variable proportions: no increasing or diminishing returns. Here the variable cost graph is a straight line coming up from the origin with slope equal to the rate of variable cost. For example, if it takes $2 worth of labor and material to produce a pair of cheap jeans, variable costs are $2 for one pair, $4 for two pair, $6 for three pair, and so on. The slope of the line from the origin is 2 (Figure 6–4).

FIGURE 6–3. Total Fixed Cost

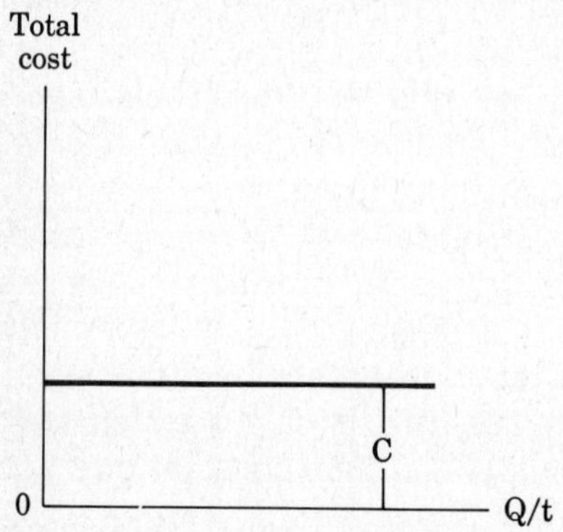

Total fixed cost does not vary over the range of possible outputs. Therefore its graph is a horizontal line. Its equation is

TFC = constant

FIGURE 6–4. Total Variable Cost, No Variable Returns Case

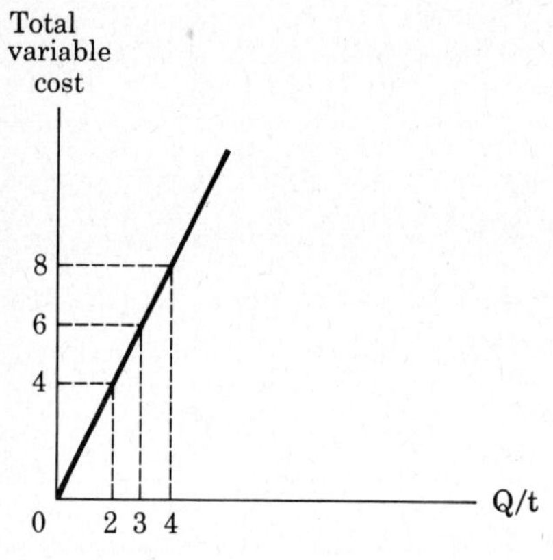

If there are no increasing or decreasing returns, but only constant, per-unit variable costs, the total variable cost function is a straight line from the origin, the slope of which equals the rate of variable cost. Thus, if materials and labor cost \$2 per unit, the equation is

$TVC = 2Q$

FIGURE 6–5. Total Variable Cost—Variable Returns Case

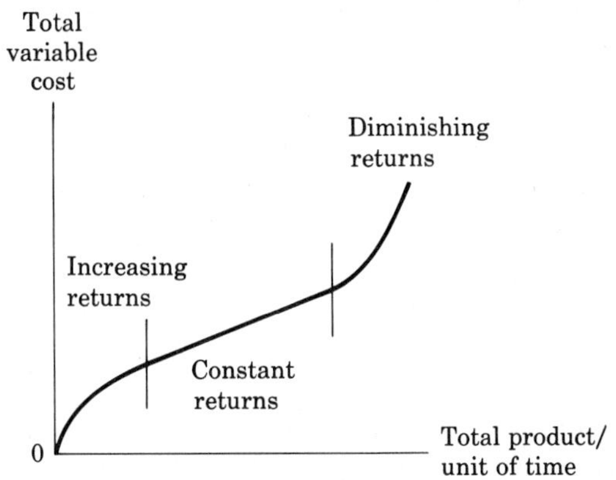

During the phase of increasing returns, the output rises faster than costs. The curve is hump shaped. During the phase of diminishing returns, costs rise faster than output. The curve is concave. Over any range of constant returns, the curve is a straight line.

How does variable returns affect this graph?

We have suggested that, rather than being constant over the entire range of inputs, output relative to labor input will increase for a time disproportionately rapidly (increasing returns), and then after a point will increase at a decreasing rate (diminishing returns). It stands to reason that if output rises faster than inputs during the phase of increasing returns, output must rise faster than costs as well. This is shown on the total cost curve by a humped portion of the graph near the origin. During the diminishing returns phase, output increases less rapidly than inputs. It thus increases less rapidly than costs. We find costs mounting disproportionately rapidly, as shown on the concave-shaped portion of the curve (Figure 6–5).

If costs exactly mirror inputs, why don't the cost and product curves look alike?

They would, except that in this instance the total product, which was the dependent variable in the production function, has become the independent variable in the total variable cost function. Total product

FIGURE 6–6. Relationship of Variable Cost Function to the Production Function

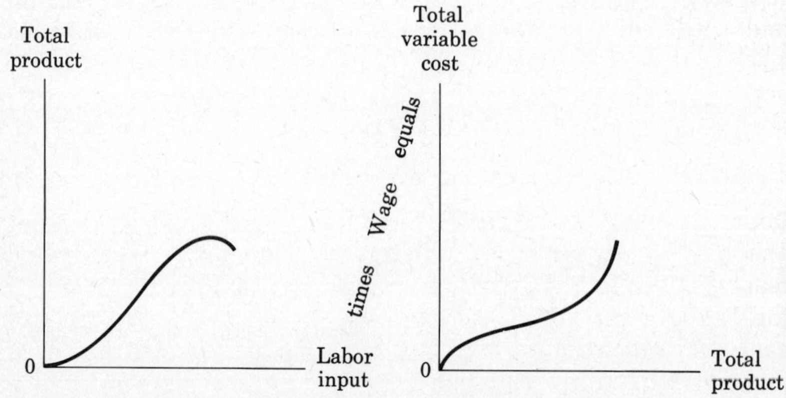

The two functions appear as mirror images of each other. This results from moving the total product variable from the vertical axis on the production function to the horizontal axis on the cost function. Quantity of labor was on the horizontal axis on the production function. Multiplied by the wage rate, this now becomes part of variable costs and moves to the vertical axis of the cost function, where it is labeled *total variable cost.*

FIGURE 6–7. Variable Cost Curve, Range of Zero, and Negative Returns

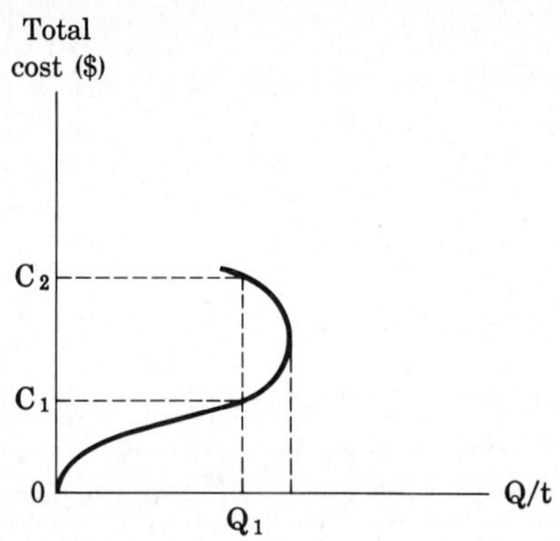

Stage III on the production function corresponds to the vertical and backward-bending part of the total variable cost curve. As you add more labor and increase costs, the output declines.

has moved from the vertical to the horizontal axis. This has the effect of turning the curve inside out, as it were. Where the product curve is convex, the cost curve is concave. Or, logically, during the diminishing returns phase, labor is less productive. This means that it takes more labor to produce a unit of output. Therefore it costs more to produce a unit of ouput. As output rises one unit, variable cost will rise disproportionately steeply (Figure 6–6).

Does the variable cost curve become vertical?
The curve becomes vertical once the limit to total output capacity is reached. You can keep adding labor inputs, and as you do, you drive the cost up, but the output does not increase at all. In fact, the curve can become backward-bending if you consider the possibility of getting into stage III (Figure 6–7).

How does stage III make the variable cost curve bend backward?
Stage III is a condition that sees the addition of variable inputs actually reducing total output. On the cost curve, this shows up as greater costs associated with less output. The backward-bending portion of the variable cost curve accents the irrationality of producing in stage III. In Figure 6–7 we see that output Q_1 can be produced either at variable cost C_1 or at the higher C_2. It makes little sense to do the latter.

Having plotted total fixed cost and total variable cost, how do we plot total cost?
We simply add them together vertically on the graph. The basic definition is

$$TC = TFC + TVC$$

Total cost equals total fixed cost plus total variable cost. We therefore get a curve that is exactly parallel to the total variable cost curve, but separated from it vertically by the constant interval of fixed costs. At every output, the slopes are identical. Remember this, because it will give you an insight into what goes on with marginal cost (Figure 6–8).

What is marginal cost?
As you may have guessed, marginal cost refers to the change in total cost resulting from a one-unit increment in output. Just as in the case of utility and production, marginal involves a rate of change—the slope of the total cost curve. As in those instances, the magnitudes involved

FIGURE 6–8. Total Cost

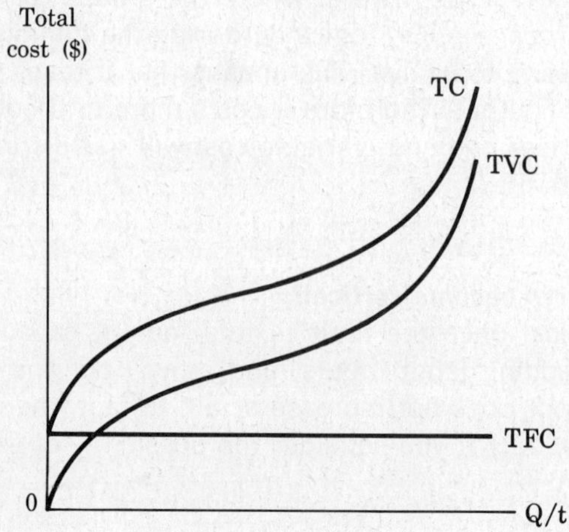

Total cost equals total fixed cost plus total variable cost. This gives a total cost curve parallel to the total variable cost curve line, separated by the constant total fixed cost.

FIGURE 6–9. Relationship of Marginal to Total Cost

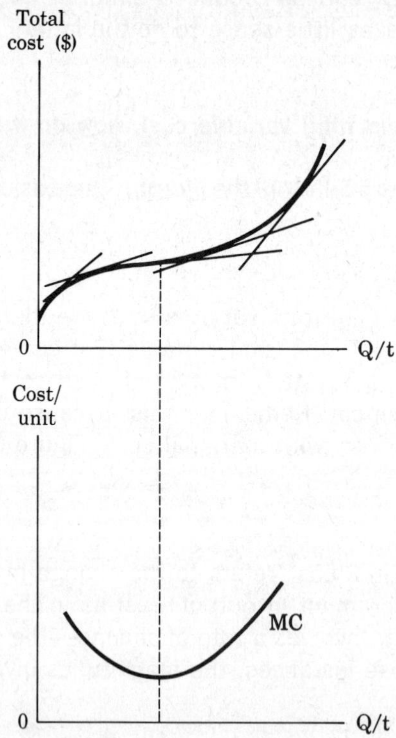

Marginal cost equals the slope of the total cost curve. Under the usual assumptions of variable proportions, marginal cost falls, hits a minimum value at the point of inflection of the total cost curve, and then rises.

are going to be much smaller because they are on a per-unit basis rather than a *total* cost basis. They must be plotted on a separate pair of axes scaled to per-unit magnitudes (Figure 6–9).

Are there other per-unit variables to plot in cost analysis?
Yes. We concern ourselves with the same types of variables as we were interested in when discussing the production function: average and marginal. In the case of costs, however, we add a flourish by dealing with *average fixed cost* and *average variable cost*, and then adding them together to get *average cost*.

Take them one at a time. What's the story on average fixed cost?
Remember that fixed costs do not vary with increases in output. They are the same at zero output as at capacity and beyond. Therefore *average* fixed cost (*AFC*) equals nothing more than this constant total divided by the different possible quantities of output. The higher the output, the bigger the denominator and the smaller the average fixed cost. The graph is what the geometricians call a rectangular hyperbola (Figure 6–10). As output approaches zero, average fixed cost approaches infinity. As output approaches infinity, average fixed cost approaches zero. In business, fixed costs are thought of as overhead, and the process of averaging by the output is called "spreading" the overhead, or assigning to each unit of output its share of the total fixed cost of the entire operation. The bigger the output, the less burden each unit produced must bear.

What are the characteristics of a rectangular hyperbola?
The algebraic form is

$$y = \frac{\text{constant}}{x}$$

Multiplying by *x* gives

$$xy = \text{constant}$$

FIGURE 6–10. Average Fixed Cost

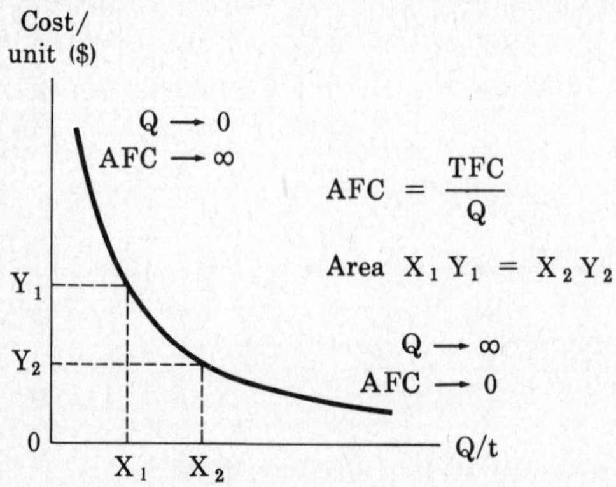

Average fixed cost plots as a rectangular hyperbola. It equals constant total fixed cost divided by quantity. As quantity rises, *AFC* falls.

FIGURE 6–11. Average Variable Cost—No Variable Returns Case

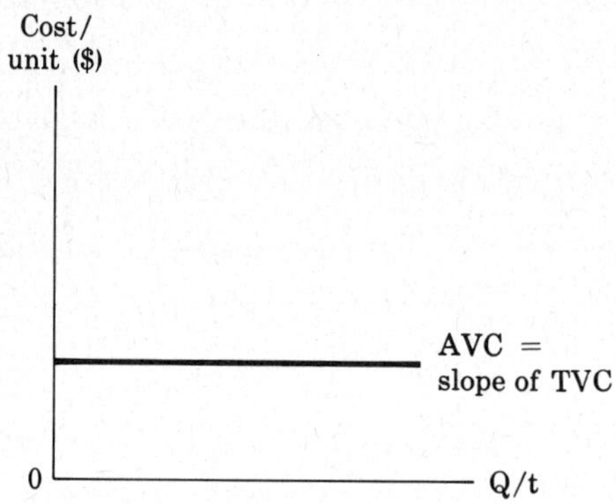

If the total variable cost curve rises as a straight line (see Figure 6–4) with slope equal to the rate of variable cost, this rate plots as a constant, that is, a horizontal line with value equal to the slope of the total variable cost line.

That is, output times average fixed cost equals total fixed cost. On the graph this means that the rectangle with quantity as one side and average fixed cost as the other has a constant area. All rectangles under the *AFC* curve, regardless of relative length and width, have the same area (Figure 6–10).

What about average variable cost? How does that behave?
Average variable cost (*AVC*) is found by dividing the total variable cost by the quantity of output. If there were no returns to variable proportions involved, that is, if the total variable cost curve were a straight line going up to the right at a constant slope, average variable cost would be constant and the curve a horizontal line at a height numerically equal to the slope of the total variable cost curve. It would, incidentally, be equal to marginal cost through its length. For example, if each unit costs $2 to produce (apart from fixed cost), the slope of the total variable cost curve is 2. Hence the marginal cost is 2. Finally, the variable cost of each unit is 2, so the average variable cost is also 2, regardless of output (Figure 6–11).

Suppose that there are variable returns?
This is the more normal case for economic theory. Numerically, average variable cost equals TVC/Q. By doing the division and plotting the numbers, we would find that the total variable cost curves described earlier in this chapter have average variable cost curves that are ∪, or saucer-shaped. However, it is more interesting to try to apply some of the generalities we learned about marginals and averages. During the increasing returns phase of the total variable cost curve, we observed that it took on a humped, convex shape. As you go from left to right, the slope is diminishing—the curve is getting flatter. This means that the marginal cost is falling. Because average and marginal started out equal at one unit of output, a falling marginal cost implies that it is also lower than the average cost value and is pulling the average down with it. When output is high enough to put production into diminishing returns, the marginal cost curve will turn up. However, as long as marginal cost is less than average variable cost, the latter will continue to fall. As average variable cost falls and marginal cost rises from below, sooner or later they will be equal; at outputs beyond the point of intersection, marginal cost will exceed average variable cost. At the point of equality, there is a minimum in average variable cost. After that, average variable cost rises. Hence the ∪-shape has its low point at the intersection of average variable and marginal cost (Figure 6–12).

FIGURE 6–12. Relationship of Marginal to Average Cost Curves

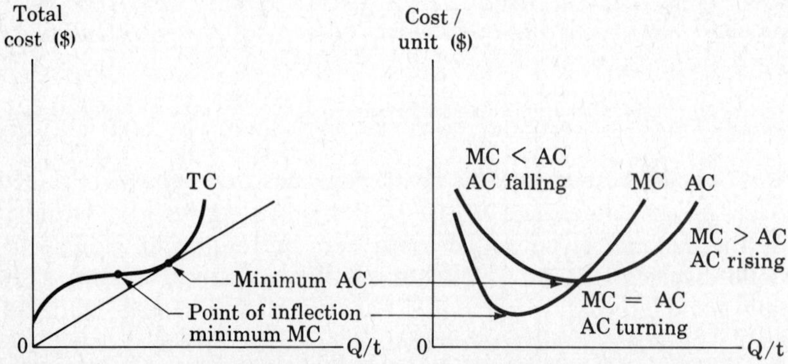

As long as marginal lies below average cost, the average is falling. If marginal lies above the average, the average is rising. Where marginal equals the average, the average is at a minimum. Because the *MC* curve has been described as U-shaped, the basic shape of the average cost curve is determined.

FIGURE 6–13. Use of Radius Vector to Find Average Variable Cost

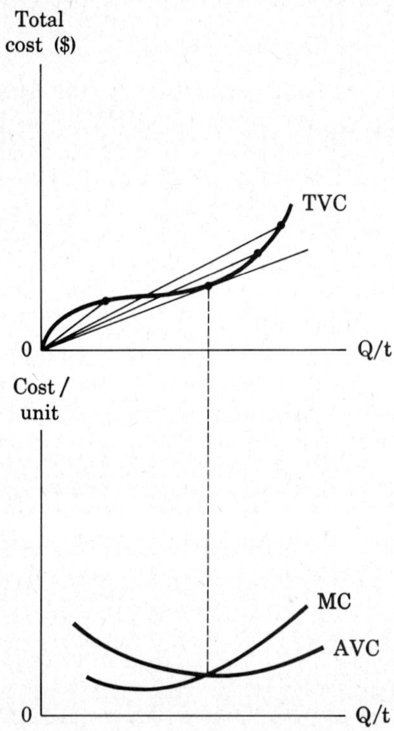

Radius vectors drawn to the total variable cost curve have slopes that decline to a minimum at the quantity where the radius vector is tangent. Then they rise again. This gives U-shaped average variable cost curves, with values equal to marginal cost at the minimum point.

Is there any geometric construction we can use that is analogous to the radius vector that denoted average product?

Yes, there is an exactly parallel construction. By drawing a radius vector (gradient) to a point on the total variable cost curve and measuring its slope, we get a value for average variable cost. The vertical distance to the point is total variable cost and the horizontal distance is quantity. The slope is their ratio, which is also our definition for average variable cost (TVC/Q) (Figure 6–13).

As in the analysis for average product, we compare the slope of the gradient with that of the curve itself. In this instance we see that the gradient is steeper than the curve during the increasing returns phase. Thus, average cost is greater than marginal cost. As output increases, the slope of the gradient falls until the gradient reaches a point where it is just tangent to the curve. Here the curve and gradient have the same slope; that is, average variable cost equals marginal cost. Then, at higher outputs, the slope of the curve is greater than that of the gradient, even though the slope of the gradient is increasing. Here the average variable cost is increasing but is less than the marginal cost.

Now that we have discussed the average variable and average fixed cost curves, is there anything new to say about the average cost curve?

Not much other than to note that $AC = AVC + AFC$. We add vertically the average variable cost and the average fixed cost to get the average cost curve. The space between the average variable and average cost curves is the average fixed cost, and we know that this gets smaller as output gets greater. Therefore these two curves will tend to converge. The U-shape of the average cost curve can be thought of as the outcome of a contest between the tendency for average fixed cost to fall with increases in output and average variable cost to rise. We have seen that both fall while output is small. Beyond some level of output, diminishing returns cause average variable cost to increase, and eventually diminishing returns becomes strong enough to overcome the falling

FIGURE 6–14. Relationship of Average Cost, Average Variable Cost, and Average Fixed Cost

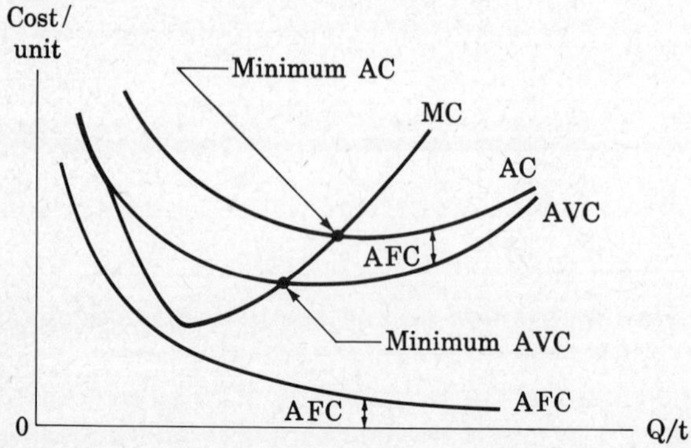

The average cost is the vertical summation of the *AVC* and the *AFC*. Because the *AFC* falls with higher volume, the *AC* and *AVC* tend to converge.

overhead cost and pull average cost up. It is interesting to note that at its minimum, average cost is equal to marginal cost (Figure 6–14).

Why does average cost equal marginal cost at the low point of the average cost curve?

They are equal for basically the same reasons that pertained to marginal cost and average variable cost. The marginal cost curve is just as relevant to the average cost curve as it is to the average variable cost curve. As long as marginal is below average, the average falls; when they are equal, the average turns; and when marginal exceeds the average, the average rises.

Isn't there a marginal variable cost curve?

No. There is only one marginal cost curve. The change in total costs resulting from a one-unit increase in output is due entirely to increases in variable costs. Fixed cost was determined at zero units of output. Any change in total cost occurs because of variable cost increments. Thus there is only one marginal cost curve. It measures change in total variable cost, but this is also the change in total cost because the change in fixed cost is zero.

Let's see. We have described seven cost functions. Do we need to use all of them?

The seven cost functions we have discussed are as follows: (1) total fixed cost, (2) total variable cost, (3) total cost, (4) average fixed cost, (5) average variable cost, (6) average cost, and (7) marginal cost. All serve a purpose in the discussion. However, we shall find that the two most frequently used are the average cost and marginal cost curves. These form the basis of most of the analysis of the theory of the firm.

Have we been discussing the long run, the short run, or both?

We have been discussing the short run. Remember that in the long run there are no fixed costs. In the short run capital remains fixed and output is increased by increments in variable inputs such as labor, raw materials, energy, and so on.

What's the big deal if capital is fixed?

By fixing one input, we set the stage for variable returns to proportions. The whole discussion of increasing and decreasing returns, U-shaped cost curves, and so on, depends on varying the proportions of inputs while output grows. If we were free to vary *all* inputs, we could hold the proportions of the inputs constant while output was increased by increasing the *scale* of the operation.

What do you mean by scale?

Scale refers to the *size* of the production operation. If we increase every input by a multiple of 2, we shall have constant proportions but a scale that is twice as great. You can get a good idea of scale by considering two maps of a given area drawn to different scales. The distance from Cleveland to Akron, Ohio, is 3 inches on a map at a scale of 1 inch to 10 miles. The distance from Akron to Columbus is 9 inches. If the scale were changed to 1 inch equals 30 miles, the Cleveland-to-Akron distance would measure 1 inch and the Akron-to-Columbus distance would be 3 inches. Columbus is still three times as far away from Akron as Cleveland. However, the scale is reduced. The same applies to production. There may still be three times as many units of labor as capital, but the scale will be permitted to vary through 1 capital–3 labor, 3 capital–9 labor, 400 capital–1200 labor. If we hold proportions fixed and vary scale, there is no cause for variable returns to proportions. Our cherished returns goes out the window. Any variable returns that do occur under this circumstance must be ascribed to *variable returns to scale*, as distinguished from *short-run variable returns to proportion*.

Please elaborate on returns to scale.

We may find that the average cost of producing a product differs depending on whether output is taking place in a large- or small-scale effort. If we find average cost lower for large-scale firms, we say there is increasing returns to scale. When average cost is higher for larger firms, we refer to decreasing returns to scale. When the average cost is the same for different scale operations, we label it constant returns to scale.

What factors might cause variable returns to scale?

The key word in this context is *specialization*. When the volume of output to which a firm is geared is high enough, it can put each worker to work performing an extremely narrow and repetitious task, and be assured that there is enough volume of work of that sort to keep him occupied for a full day, every day. With big output a firm can avail itself of all of the blessings and curses of assembly-line production. There is no time lost as workers move from task to task, picking up and putting down tools. The tools can remain in their hands. Their feet can remain rooted to the spot where they perform their small but vital role in a production process. Specialization is efficient, but it can be deadly dull. Much has been written about the tedium of the assembly line. While boredom may cut into worker productivity, we usually find that in industrial processes, high specialization of labor leads to lower average costs of production.

Why must there be big volume of output in order to have specialization?

A long time ago, Adam Smith observed that specialization was the key to high productivity. However, the degree to which specialization could be undertaken was limited by "the extent of the market." There was no use producing the high volumes of output that specialization made possible unless the market was large enough to absorb them. Smith described an assembly-line operation in a pin factory where the men, each working at one or two specialized tasks, could produce 48,000 pins per day, whereas if each of the ten men attempted to make the complete pin by himself without the interaction of specialized tasks, they could not make 20 pins. However, unless there was a market for 48,000 pins rolling off the assembly line daily, there would be no justification for the plant and the great output would represent just so much exercise and economic loss.

The same principles hold in present-day industry. When there is a limited market, a factory is limited to using general-purpose machinery that can be converted to make a variety of products. A large market permits highly specialized machinery designed to perform a very narrow purpose and able to operate continuously at that purpose with speed and precision. The same principle applies to personnel. Firms require the performance of accounting, legal, advertising, shipping, and personnel relations functions. But to justify hiring a staff person to perform each task, there must be enough work to do in each area. In a small business one man may perform all the tasks. He is frequently good at all but excellent at none. A loss of productivity must accompany this loss of expertise at the staff level.

Are there any sources of increasing returns to scale other than those that come with specialization?

There are two other major categories of opportunities to economize: First, there are the purely technical sources of increasing returns to scale. Second, there are financial opportunities that benefit a large firm but are unavailable to a small one. Technical sources of increasing returns are the purely mechanical efficiencies that accrue to larger-scale machines and processes. The simple geometric fact that the volume of a container increases more rapidly than the surface area of the materials from which it is made accounts for one large group of technical efficiencies. Because output of a container relates to its volume but the cost of building it relates to its surface area, there are average cost economies inherent in large- over small-volume containers. Many manufacturing activities involve holding and processing materials, and hence this volume economy pervades industry. Another all-pervasive source of economies of scale comes from the technology of electrical motors. These too are found throughout industry, and these too have very definite average cost advantages accruing to large scale. Professor George Stigler, in discussing this point, compares costs of various horsepower electrical motors. In 1950 (the year of his data), a 2 hp motor cost \$80, or \$40 per hpw; a 10 hp motor cost \$176 or \$17.60 per hpw; a 500 hp motor cost \$5819, or \$6.41 per hpw; and a 1000 hp motor cost \$5819, or \$5.82 per hpw. Technical factors therefore permitted a considerable economy of scale, providing the firm had need for such high-capacity equipment.

What are the financial economies of scale?

The financial or *pecuniary* economies derive from the fact that sellers and lenders will often charge differential rates according to the size of the firm with which they are dealing. Large firms have access to capital through the bond markets, offering their promises to repay loans 20 and 30 years later. Small firms are seldom able to issue debenture

FIGURE 6–15. Sources of Economies of Scale

1. Specialization—Machinery and personnel designed to run all day at a limited task.
2. Technical—Engineering phenomena whereby the inputs required to build a bigger machine are not as great as the resulting increase in output.
3. Financial—Better credit terms, quantity discounts.

bonds to the general public, and when they do, the interest terms are never so favorable as those accorded a "blue-chip" firm. Hence capital availability is a significant economy of scale. Another such economy is the saving that comes to a firm that is able to buy its supplies in large quantities. Suppliers realize significant unit savings when they can ship large quantities to a single buyer, and they frequently share these savings in the form of quantity discounts to high-volume purchasers. Back in the bad old days of the trusts, big buyers would exact quantity discounts that went beyond the cost savings to the sellers, thereby enhancing their competitive advantage to an even greater extent because the reductions in the prices paid by these big buyers represented still further reductions in their average cost of production (Figure 6–15).

It appears that the bigger the firm, the more efficient it is. Is this always the case?

Naturally the extent to which increased scale of operation brings economies varies with the industry and the type of product being produced. In the case of personal service, with its one-to-one relationship between seller and consumer, it is difficult to envision specialization, technological factors, or financial advantages playing too great a role. The average time spent giving a haircut is the same, whether in a 2- or 20-chair barbershop. No tonsorial assembly line appears likely as a result of greater volume. On the other hand, manufacturing operations where a standardized product with a relatively high ratio of value to weight is made and shipped in bulk lend themselves to economies of scale. These industries—chemicals, petroleum, glass, and aluminum, to name a few—have high degrees of concentration of total industry output in a comparatively small number of firms. They have also waged an unending battle with the Justice Department over antitrust matters (a diseconomy of scale), and the literature and casework have grown large in this area.

What about industries where economies of scale do apply? Do these economies continue indefinitely with growth of the company?

Most economists feel they will not. Regardless of the technical nature of the industry and the economies that come with increased scale, sooner or later the cost of producing a unit of output will increase as a firm gets larger. The rationale for this has to do with the problems of management inherent in coordinating the activities of a giant firm. As a multi-plant, multi-product, highly integrated company expands across market as well as national boundaries, the difficulties of coordinating its myriad arms and functions multiply. Communications become an insuperable problem. Memoranda must be sent both horizontally and vertically to keep the various strata of management aware and informed of the business' activities. Despite efforts at control, mistakes increasingly cause inventories to get lost and shipments to go astray. On another level, management may lose touch with the tastes of its diverse markets. We find that the industries in which fashion plays a dominant role tend to involve small-scale firms. A long chain of command between those in the market and those charged with making meaningful decisions in response to market shifts will inevitably reduce the ability of a firm to react swiftly. The committee system frequently used by giant corporations as a means of coordinating activities is a notoriously sluggish mechanism for decision making.

To sum up, most long-run average cost curves are presumed to be saucer-shaped. The curve slopes downward as output (and scale) rises, reaches a minimum range, which may be quite broad, then is believed to slope upward with still further increases of output (Figure 6–16).

Why do firms permit themselves to grow too big?

Usually they don't. The upturn in the long-run average cost (*LAC*) merely says that producers incur diseconomies if they keep on growing. Under pure competition a firm cannot afford to grow too big, because it will not survive if its costs are higher than those of its smaller peers. We should recognize, however, that these cost phenomena are not as cut-and-dried as the curves seem to imply. The benefits of specialization are not lost with giantism. They continue to accrue, but they become more and more offset by the diseconomies that crop up. The upturn in the cost curve is in effect a *net* result, balancing the continuing gains from specialization and the gradually mounting difficulties of management. The difficulties in management increase from the very beginning of the firm's expansion. However, after relatively little growth, they are more than compensated for by technical, financial, and specialization economies of scale. After some point, the trade-off becomes disadvantageous. It is not always easy for a management to be aware of

FIGURE 6–16. Shape of the Long-Run Average Cost Curve

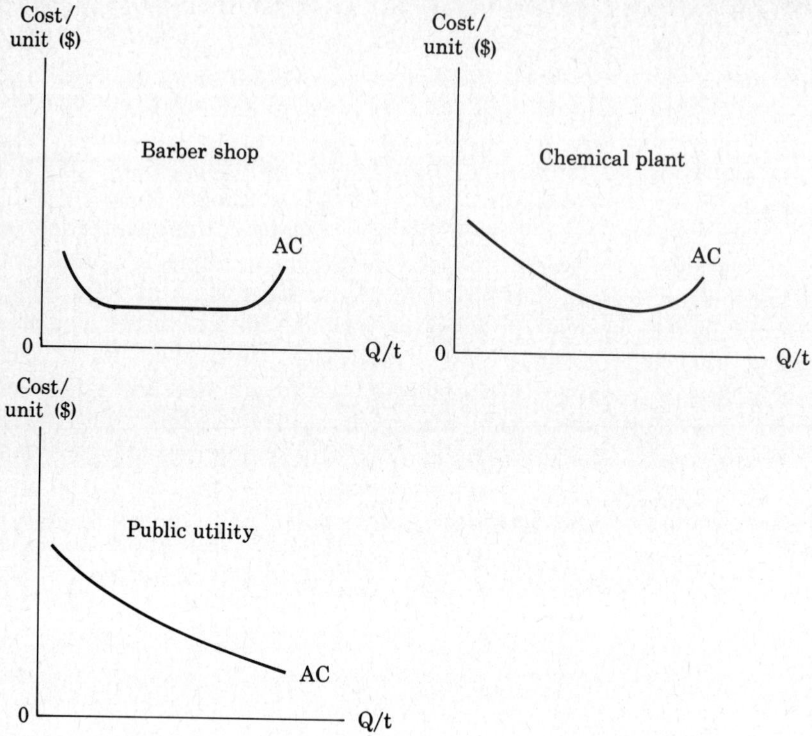

Different industries will have differently shaped curves. Increasing economies of scale lead to the downward-sloping segment. Constant returns produce a horizontal segment. Decreasing returns gives an upward-sloping segment. All three combine to give a U-shaped, or saucer-shaped curve.

FIGURE 6–17. Long-Run Economies and Diseconomies of Scale

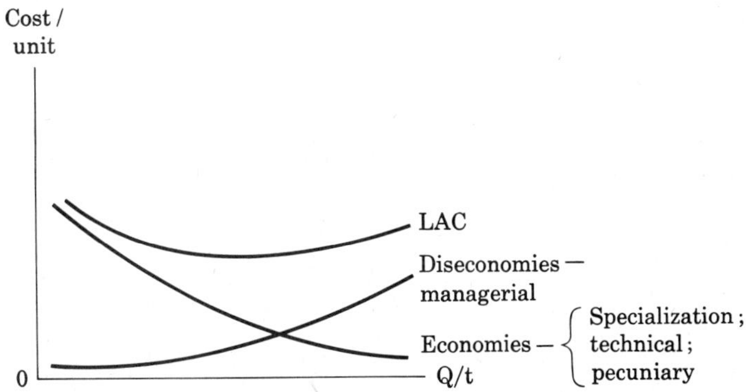

The long-run U-shape results from a netting out of economies and diseconomies of scale. The factors making for increasing economies continue throughout. The factors making for decreasing economies are also present. The overall effect is what is seen as occurring. When the diseconomies overwhelm the economies, the curve turns up.

precisely where the point is. Often it is seen only in retrospect during the bankruptcy proceedings (Figure 6–17).

Are economists sure that diseconomies of scale set in sooner or later? The existence of diseconomies of scale has general acceptance in the theory of the firm for one major reason. Unless costs behave this way, economic theory predicts an outcome that simply does not occur in the real world. If continuously increasing scale led to continuously greater efficiency, each industry would be dominated by a single giant monopoly firm. Once a firm became bigger than its competitors, it could produce at lower average cost and undersell them in the market. As the competitors were driven out of business, the large scale firm would absorb their assets and customers and grow more efficient yet, ultimately coming to a position of monopolist, meeting the entire market's needs. The fact that this does not inevitably occur leads economists to believe that there must be some source of diseconomy that eventually causes a firm's cost curves to turn up (Figure 6–18).

FIGURE 6–18. Long-Run Average Cost Curve Must Turn Up

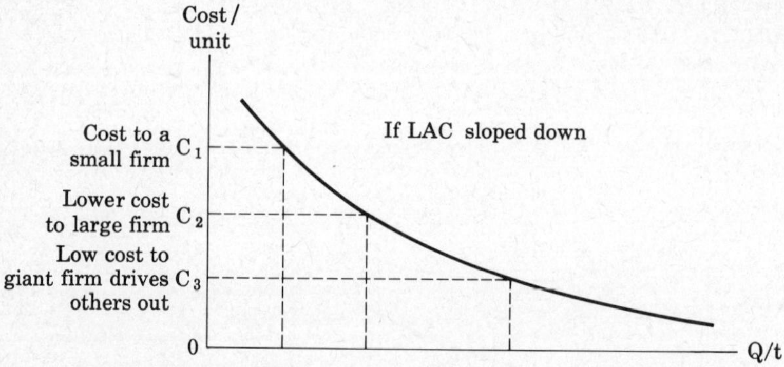

If the *LAC* did not turn up, each industry would be organized as a monopoly. Small firms would have higher costs than big firms and would be driven out of business. Upturn in costs limits the potential size of a firm.

I thought it was the antitrust laws that prevented monopoly.
The antitrust laws do prohibit firms from becoming monopolies or attempting to monopolize. We must recognize that firms can become monopolies for reasons other than efficiency. Exclusive ownership of raw materials and energy may prevent would-be competitors from entering an industry. Alcoa gained its monopoly position in the aluminum industry from just such an advantage. Patent protection can also permit at least a temporary monopoly, with the result that a Xerox or a Polaroid gets an insurmountable head start on the competition. We shall discuss the analysis of monopoly at some length in Chapter 9. We should observe in the present context that the vast majority of industries in the American economy in no way approach monopoly, nor is this so because they are prevented from doing so by the antitrust laws. It is not, after all, the bigamy laws that prevent most men from taking on two wives. There are simply diseconomies of scale operating here, just as they do in the monopoly instance. Seriously, you should recognize that social and economic pressures are far more effective in shaping behavior than is legislation.

What about public utilities? Aren't they monopolies?
The case of the public utilities does provide us with an instance of indefinitely increasing returns to scale. Industries such as electrical generation, gas, telephone, and water supply have technologies that

offer such great *technical* economies of scale that the long-run average cost curves continue to fall over any forseeable level of output. Economists call these situations *natural monopolies*. Market forces would lead to monopoly conditions in these industries. Recognizing this, the government has exempted a handful of firms in each area from the antitrust laws and permitted them to develop all of the economies of scale possible. In this way, a single company serving the entire market can do so more cheaply than if the market were divided among two or more competitors. In return for the monopoly privilege, the company agrees to be regulated by a public utilities commission and have its rates set by the agency rather than market forces. The firm, in effect, is the industry as well.

What is the difference between the* industry *and the* firm*?

An industry consists of different firms competing to sell similar products. Under conditions of perfect competition there are a great number of small firms in an industry. Under monopoly, as mentioned, the industry consists of only one firm. The greater the tendency there is for economies of scale to occur, the fewer the number of firms there will be in the industry. After all, if firms keep on growing, the rules of long division tell us that it takes fewer of them to serve the total market. However, there is a good possibility that as economies of scale cause a particular product to be offered more inexpensively, the entire industry will grow in size. We should keep separate the consequences of industry growth from growth of a firm within the industry.

What is the difference between growth of an industry and growth of a firm within the industry?

When discussing changes in costs of production that resulted from an increase in the scale of operation of a single firm, we described how technical, financial, or organizational benefits became available to high-volume producers. These benefits resulted from events *internal* to the firm. In dealing with industry growth, we really do not need to consider that the single firm grows at all. We can simply have an increase in the number of firms producing a product. The effects of this industry growth are particularly pronounced when the proliferation of firms has a regional character. The garment industry is concentrated in one geographic region of New York City, the advertising industry in another, the financial industry in another, the printing industry in still another. Growth of the electronics industry occurred in the Boston–Cambridge, Mass., area; 50 years before, the auto industry located in Michigan. This growth of industries in concentrated areas sets up economic forces that are external to the individual firms but that affect their internal costs of production. Some of these external forces work to lower costs; others work to increase them. Whether or not the net effect of external economies and diseconomies is to raise or lower average cost of production depends on their relative strength. If the external economies of industry scale are greater than the external diseconomies, the long-run average cost of each firm will shift down with industry growth. If the external diseconomies are greater, the long-run average cost of each firm will shift up.

How does growth in an industry lead to reduction of costs for each firm?
External economies to firms in one industry come as a result of internal economies to firms operating in some other industry. There are firms all along the channels of production and distribution with which the public never deals. They are strictly industrial suppliers and service organizations. If their markets grow, it permits them to enjoy the economies that come with increased specialization, technical factors, and financial advantages of large-scale operation. Their markets grow when the industries they service expand operation. The internal economies these industrial suppliers enjoy get passed along to their customers in the form of lower prices. This, in turn, reduces the costs of the latter and shifts their long-run average cost curves down.

It may even come to pass that growth of one industry will present an opportunity for another industry actually to come into being. As long as an outsider can sell a service to a firm at a price below its own cost of producing that service for itself, it will find a place in the marketplace. As the number of potential customers grows, the viability of specialized suppliers increases. Their survival indicates that the function is being performed more economically than before, when it was but one activity among many being carried on within the buying firms. As a result the long-run average cost curves for all of them shift downward.

Can you give some examples of these external economies?
There are many. Take the restaurant business as a simple case. Along with everything else, a restaurant owner has to get up and go to the meat and produce markets each morning at 4:00 A.M. to buy the food he will serve that day. Each operator takes time away from his primary activity to do this, and in addition to the pain of seeing the sun come up amidst the boxcars and banana peels, he has the opportunity cost of time missed from the restaurant. If the number of restaurants in an area grows large enough, a middleman will emerge. He will go to the market, buy the meat and produce, and resell it to the restaurants on a regular route basis. Each saves the cost of going himself. It would not be possible for any one of them to get this benefit if the others did not comprise a sufficiently large market to support the middleman.

There are numerous other common examples of specialized service industries finding niches in the economy once the size of their markets grows large enough to permit a specialized producer to charge less than the cost would be to perform the task internally. As computer usage grew, it provided opportunities for separate companies that did nothing but train operators, write programs, or punch and tabulate cards. If there were only a few small computer users, each of these activities would have to be performed internally at higher cost. Bookkeeping companies will handle billing chores when there are enough small businesses wanting billing services to keep them busy. Rag companies will rent and launder wiping rags when there are enough machine shops to keep them busy. There are even bankruptcy auctioneers who can put a company out of business more efficiently than it can do itself—but only if there are enough companies going bust to keep them busy. The point is that specialized service industries need a sufficiently large client industry for which to perform their services, and the larger the client industry, the more efficiently these services can be performed.

What would cause external diseconomies of scale?

No one living through the late twentieth century need wonder about this one. As industries grow and use specialized and scarce forms of raw materials and labor, they bid up the prices of these inputs. Bottlenecks appear in the production process as strategic materials go into short supply. Higher prices of materials means higher costs for all firms, regardless of what output they produce. This causes the long-run average cost curve to shift upward, both as a result of higher prices paid and the necessity to interrupt the smooth flow of production, due to delay in getting needed materials. The same considerations apply to specialized forms of labor. With lengthy training and apprenticeship periods necessary for many industrial skills, such as machinists and electricians, the elasticity of supply of workers in these areas is quite small. Industry expansion bids their prices up, with a consequent rise in cost of production. Once again, whether industry growth ultimately produces economies or diseconomies depends on the *relative* size of these two offsetting forces and how they net out (Figure 6–9).

Can you summarize the difference between industry effects and firm effects?

The returns to scale for the firm are called *internal* economies and diseconomies. They cause the long-run average cost curve to have its characteristic U-shape. The returns to scale for the industry are called *external* economies and diseconomies. They cause the long-run average cost curve (whatever its shape) to shift up or down.

FIGURE 6–19. Industry Economies and Diseconomies

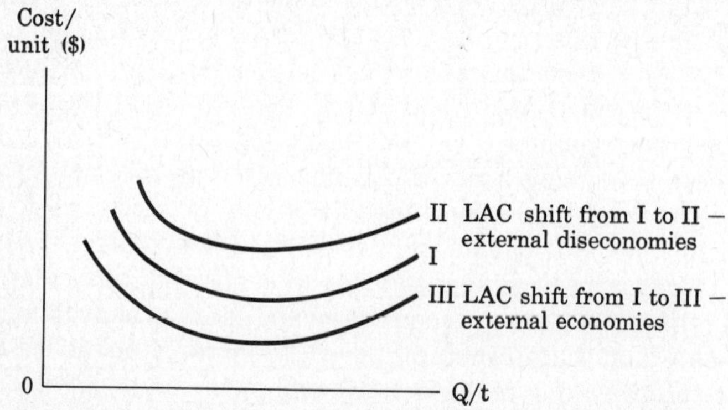

External economies and diseconomies arise as an industry grows. Every firm, regardless of whether it is large or small, is affected. It will find its costs reduced or raised, depending on whether there are economies or diseconomies. It appears on the graph as a shift up (diseconomies) or down (economies) of the long-run average cost curve.

FIGURE 6–20. Use of the Isoquant Map to Plot Long-Run Costs

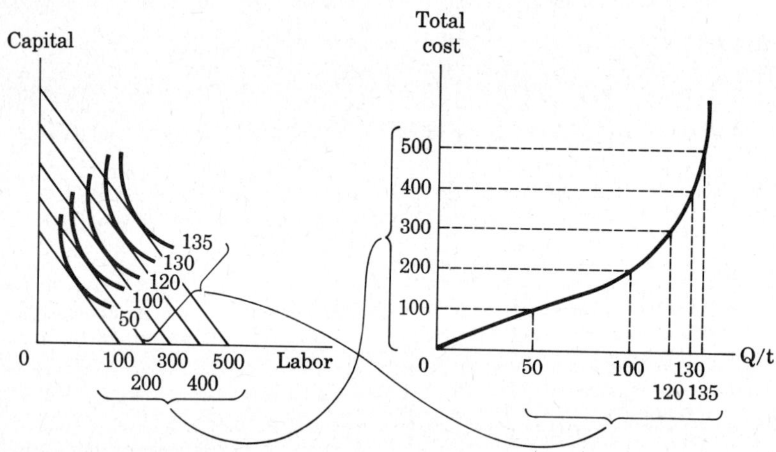

Each isocost represents a long-run total cost. The isoquant to which it is tangent represents a level of output that can be produced at that total cost. Plotting these data gives the long-run total cost curve.

There were seven short-run cost curves. Are there as many long-run curves?
Here we come upon the interesting business of the relationships between long- and short-run cost curves. First, we should recognize that there is no long-run fixed cost curve, either total or average, because, as we have seen, in the long run all costs are variable. Thus, there is no need to distinguish between long-run average variable cost and average cost. They are one and the same. We need concern ourselves only with long-run total cost, long-run average cost and long-run marginal cost in our analysis. Isoquants provide the best tool for examining long-run cost.

How do isoquants picture the long-run cost situation?
The isoquant map is basically a long-run production and cost function because all inputs are free to vary. Remember that the vertical axis shows capital inputs and the horizontal axis shows labor. As we move in a general upward and rightward direction, we increase output by adding to both capital and labor inputs. This is certainly the long run. If we assume the price of labor and capital are fixed at P_L and P_K, respectively, we can draw a series of isocost lines. The tangency of the isocosts with the isoquants gives the cost and quantity data necessary to plot the long-run total cost curve: the cheapest cost at which different quantities can be produced (Figure 6–20).

How can we determine the long-run average cost curve?
There are two ways to think of this curve. One is to treat it as a plotting of the quotients of total cost divided by quantity. Recall that the slope of a gradient to the total cost curve shows this quotient because the vertical leg is total cost and the horizontal is quantity. We draw a series of gradients, measure their slopes, and plot these values on a separate axis. This gives the long-run average cost curve. We have assumed stages of increasing, constant, and decreasing returns to scale in the long-run total cost curve (*LTC*), which give us the saucer-shaped average cost curve shown in Figure 6–21.

What is the other way to think of the long-run average cost curve?
This involves a notion of the long-run average cost curve as an *envelope*, enveloping the family of short-run average cost curves.

What do you mean by envelope curve?
In the planning stage, while trying to decide how best to proceed with its building program, a firm has a wide selection of options open. Until

FIGURE 6–21. The Long-Run Average Cost Curve Drawn from Slopes of Gradients

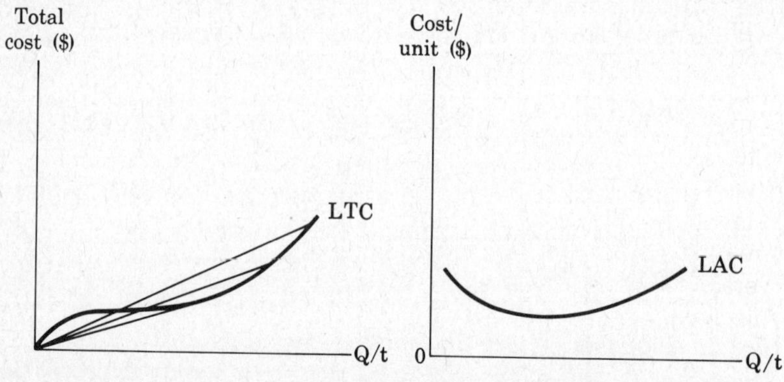

Just as with the short-run average cost curves, we can construct gradients from the origin to different points on the total cost curve. The slopes of these gradients are equal to average cost. By plotting them we get the familiar U-shaped average cost curve.

FIGURE 6–22. Long-Run Average Cost as an Envelope Curve

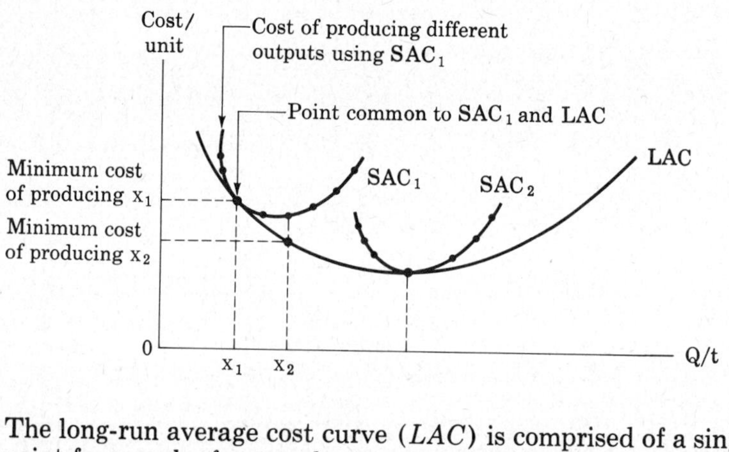

The long-run average cost curve (*LAC*) is comprised of a single point from each of many short-run average cost curves (*SAC*). This point shows the least cost of producing the output at which the point occurs. The other points on each *SAC* curve show short-run costs that are incurred if the particular plant is used with other quantities of labor to produce other levels of output.

it commits itself to a particular scale of operation, it is in the economist's long run. As we can see from the isoquant diagram, the decision regarding the amounts of capital and labor to employ depends on the volume of output the firm intends to produce. Once a decision is made about the intended level of output, isoquant and cost considerations dictate the scale plant to build. Having built the plant, the firm moves from the long-run to the short-run analysis. Furthermore, you should note that no production takes place in the long run. It is necessary to have a plant of *some* scale on the ground in order to produce, and once it is in place, the pertinent period is the short run. Now if you will stretch your imagination, you will see that a point on the long-run average cost curve shows the cheapest way to produce some output. This point on the long-run average cost curve is also on a short-run average cost curve. This curve shows the average cost of producing other outputs while holding plant size fixed. Moreover, every point on the long-run average cost curve is also on a short-run average cost curve that shows the cost of producing different levels of output using fixed capital and variable labor. There is a family consisting of one long- and many short-run average cost curves. The long-run average cost curve has one point of tangency with each of the short-run curves. In fact, the long-run curve is made up of these points of tangency. The short-run curves lie entirely above the long-run curve. That is, they are enveloped by it (Figure 6–22).

How do you know for sure that the short-run curves are enveloped by the long-run curve? They might merely intersect.

A point on the long-run average cost curve occurs when the ideal combination of factors for producing an output is used. It shows the *lowest* possible average cost for producing at that rate (Figure 6–23). Production of this quantity with some input combination other than the ideal must mean a higher average cost. The short-run average cost curves show production with input combinations other than the ideal, except for the output where the *SAC* and the *LAC* are tangent. Therefore all other costs on the short-run curves must be higher than those on the *LAC*.

Is the point that the long- and short-run average cost curves share the low point on the short-run average cost curve?

It would be if there were no variable returns to scale Remember that if two curves are tangent to each other, they have the same slope at the point of tangency. If there were constant returns to scale, the long-run average cost curve would be horizontal throughout its length, and

FIGURE 6–23. Meaning of the Long-Run Average Cost Curve

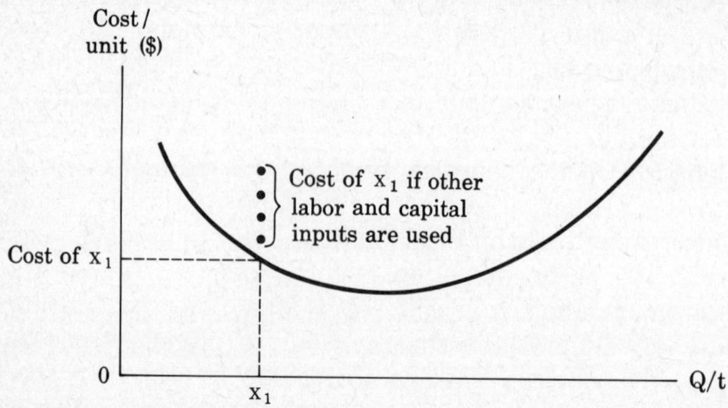

Every point on the *LAC* curve shows the least cost for which an output can be produced. To do this, the ideal combinations of capital and labor must be used. If some other combination is used, the cost is higher and the point lies above the *LAC* curve.

FIGURE 6–24. SAC *and* LAC *Tangency*

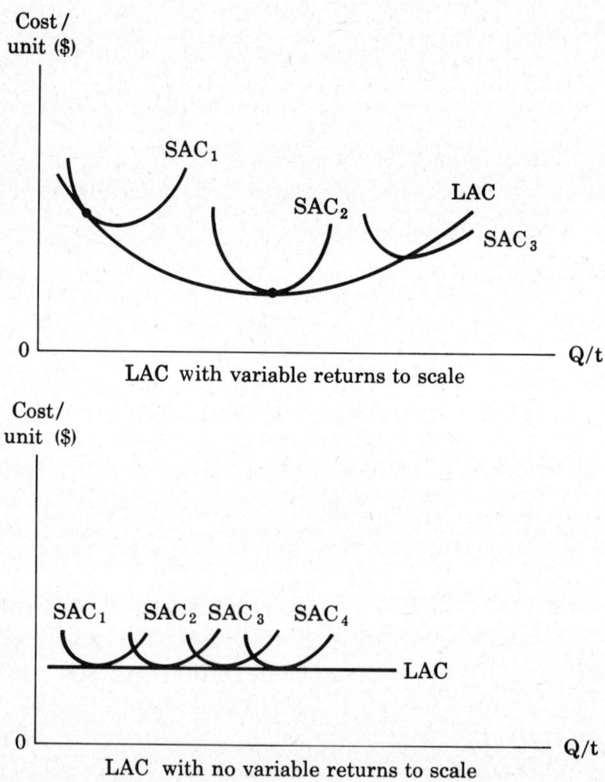

SAC and *LAC* are not usually tangent at the low point on *SAC* if there are variable returns to scale. This will only occur at the output coinciding with the minimum *LAC* (SAC_2). For other outputs *SAC* is either tangent at a point to the left or to the right of the minimum. If we attempt to show the common point as the low *SAC*, we shall have the curves intersecting rather than being tangent to one another (SAC_3).

the short-run average cost curves would also be horizontal at the point at which they were tangent to the *LAC*. This would occur at the minimum point of the U-shaped *SAC* curve, because the slope here is also zero. However, we assume that there are variable returns to scale and a U-shaped *LAC* curve as well. The only point at which both the *SAC* and the *LAC* can have a common slope of zero is where they are tangent at the output that corresponds to the low point on the *LAC* curve. At other points along the long-run curve, tangency will occur either to the left or right of the low point of the *SAC*. When output in less than optimal, the tangency will be to the left; at larger outputs, to the right (Figure 6–24).

What is the economic significance of this observation?
It means simply that whenever a product is produced under conditions of optimum long-run efficiency, it is probably not being produced under conditions of optimum short-run efficiency (unless the quantity being produced happens to be that which occurs at the low point of the long-run average cost curve). For smaller quantities the plant will be underutilized, and for larger quantities the plant will be used too intensively. That is, production will take place along the downward-sloping section of the short-run average cost curve for smaller outputs and on the upward-sloping section for larger outputs (Figure 6–25).

That seems strange. How can you be efficient in the long run, but not in the short run?
Look at Figure 6–25. Remember that the long-run average cost curve shows the cheapest per-unit cost of producing any *given* output. You cannot produce 100 units for less than $.60 apiece. It turns out, however, that the plant that produces 100 units most cheaply produces 120 units even more cheaply. The fly in the ointment is that there is still another plant size that can produce 120 units even more cheaply. This is the one tangent to the *LAC* curve at 120 units.

FIGURE 6–25. Relationship of SAC *and* LAC *Curves*

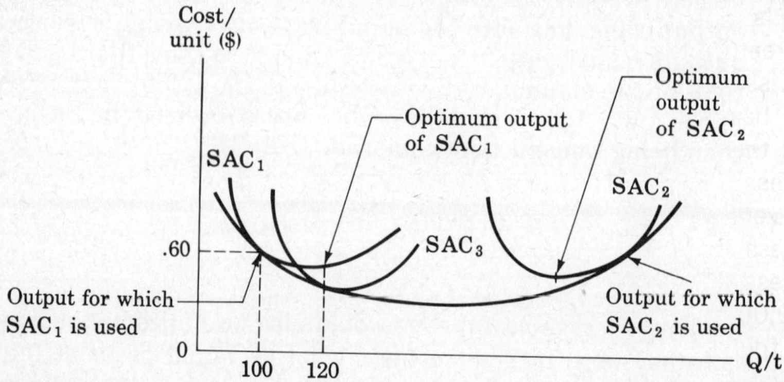

During the increasing-returns-to-scale phase, the plant is used at less than its ideal capacity. During the decreasing-returns phase, the plant is used at more than its ideal capacity. Only during constant returns is the plant used at ideal level.

FIGURE 6–26. Relationship of LAC *and Long-Run Marginal Cost Curves*

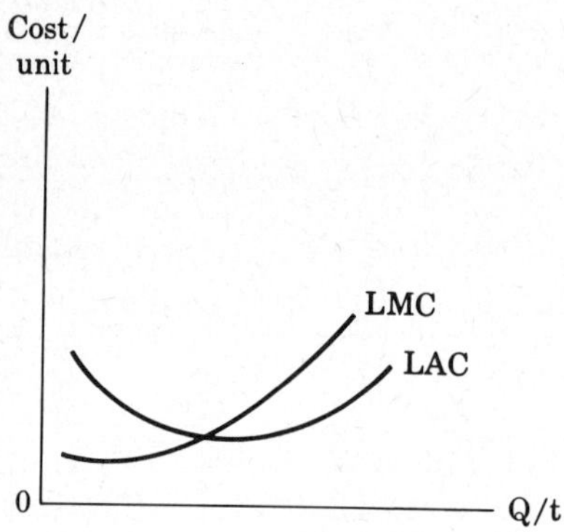

The long-run marginal cost curve (*LMC*) functions like the short-run curve. It passes through the low point of *LAC*, lying below as *LAC* falls and above as *LAC* rises.

Can you give an example?

Let's go back to our friend with the printing plant. Suppose that he has three printing presses: a small hand-operated press, a larger automatic press, and a still larger, fully automated press. Suppose further that he has to print 500 sheets. It would turn out that the cheapest way to do this is to use the hand-operated press. However, the hand-operated press is most efficient when printing quantities of 5000. Yet he would never use the hand press for outputs of 5000, because the automatic press does that quantity more cheaply. Nevertheless, the automatic press has 20,000 as its most efficient quantity. Alas, for a quantity of 20,000 the fully automated press is cheaper, even though its optimum output is 100,000, and so on. The point is that the most efficient output level of each is different than the volume for which it is used.

So what?

There are social implications in this situation. If a plant is used at a volume that is below its optimum, it is in effect wasting capital. If a plant is used at a level beyond its optimum, labor is being wasted. The only output at which no resources are wasted is at the low point on the *LAC* curve. Then production involves the low point on the *SAC* curve as well. Economists look for situations that will lead producers to want to or be forced to produce at this output. When we discuss purely competitive markets in Chapter 8, we shall see that such a market structure leads firms to produce at this most efficient level.

Is there a long-run marginal cost curve?

Yes. It is defined simply as the change in total cost incurred from producing one extra unit of output with all inputs free to vary. As we might expect by now, it is geometrically equal to the slope of the long-run total cost curve. From our knowledge of the relationship between average and marginal values, we would expect it to lie below the long-run average cost curve while that curve is falling and above it while the average cost curve is rising, passing through the low point of the long-run average cost curve (Figure 6–26).

It appears that at the low point of the* LAC *curve there is an intersection of four cost curves.

That is correct. At the low point of the *LAC* curve, *LAC* and *SAC* are tangent to each other. Because this is the low point of both, their respective marginal cost curves also intersect them at this output. Thus all four values—*LAC*, *SAC*, *LMC*, and *SMC*—are equal at this point

FIGURE 6–27. The Low Point on the LAC *Curve*

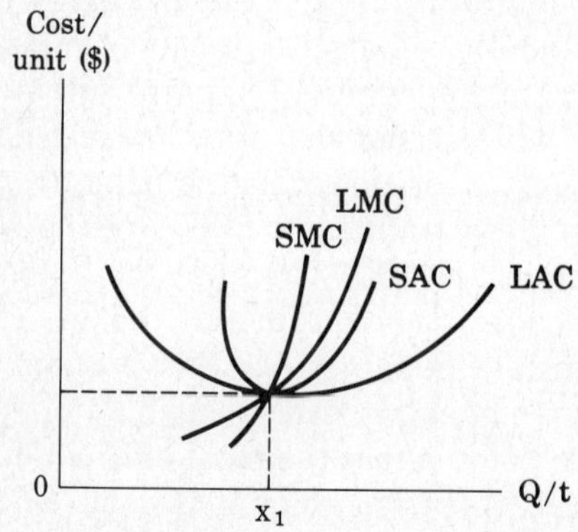

At the low point on the *LAC* curve, four cost curves intersect and therefore have identical values: *LAC* = *LMC* = *SAC* = *SMC* at output x_1.

FIGURE 6–28. Relationship of the Four Curves at Outputs Other Than the Long-Run Optimum

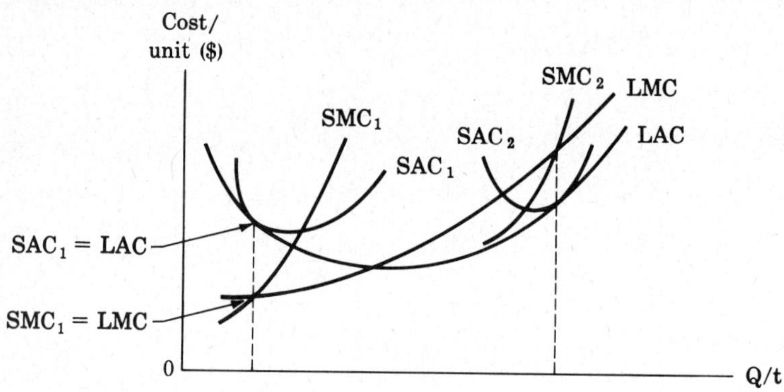

The short-run marginal cost equals the long-run marginal cost at the same output that the short-run average cost equals the long-run average cost.

FIGURE 6–29. Long- and Short-Run Cost Curve Relationships

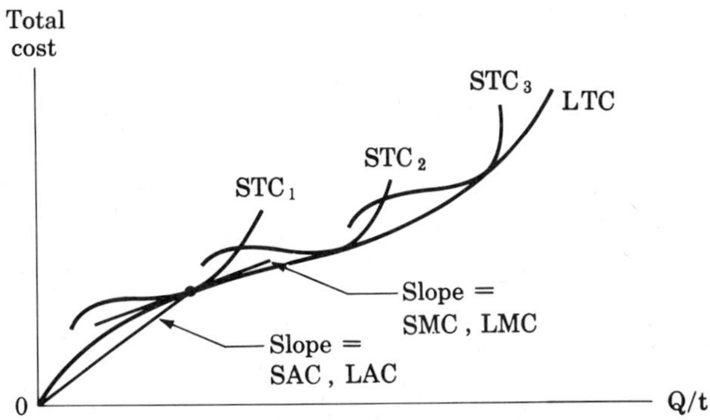

A long-run average cost curve and its family of short-run average cost curves have their counterpart in the form of long- and short-run total cost curves. These are constructed by multiplying the average cost values by the appropriate quantity. The slope of a gradient drawn to an *LTC* curve is equal to both the long-run average cost and the short-run average cost of the tangent *SAC* curve. The slope of both curves at the point of tangency is the same, so *LMC* equals *SMC*.

(Figure 6–27). There is one other relationship that is important to note, and we shall mention it here. If we take *any* output and draw the appropriate *SAC* curve tangent to *LAC* at this output, we shall find that the short-run marginal cost curve intersects the long-run marginal cost curve at this output also. Thus, at the output where SAC_1 equals *LAC*, so too will SMC_1 equal *LMC*. Where SAC_2 equals *LAC*, SMC_2 equals *LMC*. There is only one *LMC* curve, but there are as many *SMC* curves as there are points on the long-run average cost curve. Each *SMC* cuts the *LMC* at the output where its *SAC* is tangent to the envelope (Figure 6–28).

Is this just a coincidence?

You know better than that. We work primarily with short- and long-run *average* cost curves. Let us multiply each of these average costs through by quantity and plot the appropriate short- and long-run *total* cost curves as in Figure 6–29. At the output where each short-run total cost curve is tangent to the long-run total cost curve, the respective average cost curves are also tangent. The slope of a gradient to a point of tangency measures the average cost (both long and short run). Also, we notice that because the curves are tangent to each other, they both have the same slope at the point of tangency. This slope, of course, measures marginal cost. Short-run marginal cost equals long-run marginal cost at the point of tangency of short-run and long-run average cost. It is not coincidence.

What do we do with all this stuff?

We now have a basic understanding of the tools with which price theorists work. Our problem is to explain the behavior of the firm under different market conditions. We shall see if we can use these tools to explain the behavior of economic markets.

CHAPTER HIGHLIGHTS

1. *We discussed the difference between opportunity costs and accounting costs, and why economists prefer the former to the latter concept.*
2. *We learned the difference between explicit and implicit costs and that normal profit is part of implicit cost.*
3. *We considered the differences in the behavior of fixed and variable costs, recognizing the difference between the long- and short-run periods.*
4. *A sizable number of unit cost curves were considered, with principal emphasis on marginal and average cost.*
5. *In dealing with the long run, we introduced variable returns to scale, distinguishing between internal forces that pertain to the firm and external forces that relate to industry events.*
6. *There was a discussion of the relationship between the LAC and SAC curves, pointing out that the LAC serves as an envelope for the SAC's.*

QUESTIONS

1. *Microeconomic theory calls for increasing unit cost as volume of output increases. Yet businessmen always maintain that their costs fall with increasing volume. Indeed, during a recession, the drop in volume leads to high unit costs and severe losses. How do you reconcile these apparent differences?*

2. *In 1973 Congress enacted the Comprehensive Employment and Training Act (CETA), designed to give public employment to the chronically unemployed. One economist said, "I would be willing to bet that if we compare the costs of a $4000-a-year broom pusher with a $15,000-a-year sanitation man operating a $30,000 street sweeper, we would find the second combination cheaper." What does he mean? Draw the cost curves.*
3. *In 1933 the U.S. government set the price of gold at $35 per ounce. In 1975 gold sold in the neighborhood of $180 per ounce. Do you think it would have been a good speculation to buy gold in 1933 at $35 per ounce and hold it until 1975? What role does opportunity cost play in your consideration?*
4. *An "efficient" entrepreneur prides himself on having no employees. He boasts, "I do all my own typing, lick my own stamps, pack my own orders. That way, I have no costs." Evaluate this statement. How efficient is the entrepreneur? Does he really have no costs?*
5. *In a study of economies of scale, economist Joe Bain observed that the optimum size plant in the auto industry would be big enough to produce only 7½ percent of the industry output (in 1951). Yet the average share of market held by each of the first four firms was 23.5 percent. Indeed, General Motors held about 50 percent. What might account for firms reaching a size that is far in excess of their minimal long-run cost point?*
6. *In the original article describing LAC and SAC curves, Jacob Viner instructed his draftsman to draw the LAC curve passing through the low point on each SAC curve and also to lie entirely below the SAC curves. The draftsman replied that this was impossible. Do you understand why?*

7 Theory of the firm: profit maximization

Buyers and sellers who trade in the market do so with the intent of improving their well-being. We have used total utility as a measure of well-being for the household. Well-being of the firm is often measured in terms of *total profit*. Since a firm is defined as an economic unit within which a central management directs the efforts of the factors of production to produce marketable goods and services, the theory of the firm deals with the way in which management accomplishes this while, at the same time, striving to maximize total profit.

In the chapter on cost and production we dealt with some of the internal considerations that are of importance to a manager—namely, how productivity and costs vary with output. However, we did not deal with the manner in which a manager can use this information, along with the other data he has on market considerations and customer behavior, to maximize profit. Although we suggested how costs could be minimized and output maximized, we did not point out that it is perfectly possible to do so and nevertheless go bankrupt. Along with producing efficiently, a firm must price its product properly and market it effectively. If there is no demand for a product, there is no way a producer can make money from it. It is extremely difficult to thrive as a manufacturer of trolley cars or stagecoaches in today's market. Although the supply side may be handled beautifully, lack of demand at a price that will cover costs makes it all for naught (Figure 7–1).

The theory of the firm considers how management copes with different market conditions in its efforts to maximize profit.

FIGURE 7–1. Efficient Production of an Unprofitable Product

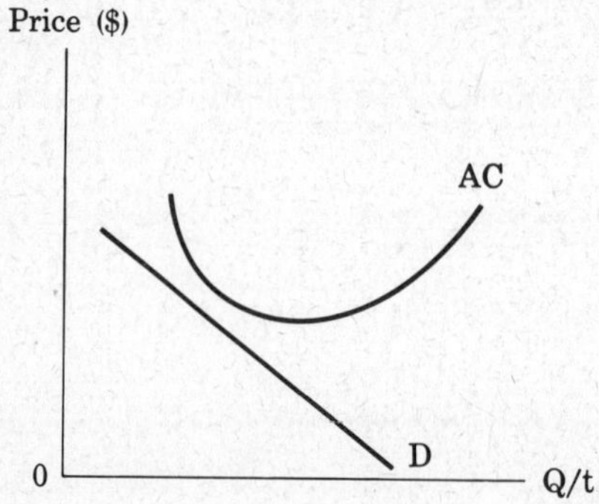

Profitability depends on the price at which a product is sold as well as on the cost of producing it. In this case, there is no level of production at which price is higher than average cost. Such a condition may exist in an obsolete industry such as trolley cars or stagecoaches. Indeed, it may well exist in passenger rail traffic.

FIGURE 7–2. Market Classification Depends on the Number of Firms in the Industry and on Product Characteristics

The major classifications as seen from the seller's point of view are shown in this chart.

	Number of sellers		
Type of product	*One*	*Few*	*Many*
Homogeneous	Pure monopoly	Homogeneous oligopoly	Pure competition
Differentiated		Differentiated oligopoly	Monopolistic competition

What different types of market conditions are there?

It has already been pointed out that all firms participate in two major markets simultaneously: They are in the factor-of-production market as demanders and in the goods-and-service market as suppliers. Management has complete control over some parameters in both these markets, slight control over others, and virtually no control over others. For example, it is able to select the products it wishes to produce. However, it must accommodate itself to the product characteristics preferred by the market. It can select the manner in which it produces and its marketing approach. It cannot be assured that the personnel and materials it requires will be available. Most important, it cannot control the activities of its competitors, either in the selling of products or the buying of factors. It must anticipate their actions and accommodate itself as well as possible to the market environment they create. In the language of microeconomic theory, these competitive considerations determine the shape and position of the demand curve a firm faces for its output, as well as the supply curve of its factor inputs. If there are large numbers of direct competitors, a firm's product demand and factor supply will be relatively low. If competition is less vigorous, demand and supply will be relatively greater. The competitive situation can range all the way from local markets, in which there are no competitors at all (monopoly), to worldwide markets with literally thousands of firms (pure competition). The product involved may be one that is unique and protected by airtight patents (Polaroid, Xerox, Valium), or it may be one that is exactly like everyone else's up to the point of being graded and sorted by a government agency (Macintosh apples, red winter wheat). The labor market may comprise unlimited numbers of workers available at meager wages, as is encountered in agriculture with its floating supply of migrant workers, or it may be a tightly organized, limited-supply market, as is encountered with airline pilots or electricians.

A generalized theory of the firm must deal with all these situations, because it is possible for any combination of them to occur. By the same token, any line of analysis that can handle such a diversity of situations is clearly valuable.

Is there a line of analysis that can handle all these situations?

In a broad sense there is. The chapters that follow deal with the behavior of the firm under conditions of pure competition, pure monopoly, oligopoly, and monopolistic competition in the product markets and pure competition, pure monopsony, oligopsony, and monopsonistic competition in the factor markets. Each term connotes different conditions with regard to the number of competitors and the nature of the product they offer. Pure competition means that there are many many sellers (buyers) and a perfectly homogeneous product. Monopoly means that there is a single seller; monopsony a single buyer. Oligopoly means that there are a small number of sellers. In standardized oligopoly the products offered by the different firms are alike; in differentiated oligopoly each firm offers a fairly unique product. Monopolistic competition is a market condition in which there are a large number of sellers with each offering a slightly differentiated product, thus combining the large number of firms characteristic of pure competition with the unique product found in monopoly (Figure 7–2).

Each market condition imparts a different quality to the demand and supply curves. However, the criteria used to analyze any decision by the firms is always the same: How will profits be affected? We are therefore always working with a single basic line of analysis. In each case we try to predict how a firm will behave under the circumstances present in order to maximize its profits.

How do you know that the goal of a firm is to maximize profits?
Frankly, we don't know. It is an assumption that follows upon the heels of our selection of *economic man* as our principal character. Within that context we assume that rational and pleasure-maximizing behavior leads to profit maximization.

Actually, the first goal of the firm is to survive. We shall see in the next two chapters that under market conditions of pure and monopolistic competition, long-run economic profits get squeezed down to zero. Therefore, if a firm is to make it at all, it must maximize its profit. Any less would mean losses. There is no doubt that easy entry of competitors into an industry produces profit-maximizing behavior.

Oligopoly and monopoly leave some room for discretion on the part of management. Firms with these market organizations can survive on less than maximum profit. Because ownership and management are separated in the giant corporation, it is quite possible that the managers will not be motivated to earn the maximum profits possible for the shareholders. They may find some other goals that suit their personal needs more directly. Some economists believe that sales-revenue maximization rather than profit maximization is a more realistic goal for a management intent on job security. Others theorize that a management will strive for a "satisfactory" profit, that is, just enough to keep the board of directors happy without taking on too many risks. There is a major school of thought that stresses planning and stability rather than profitability as the most important goal of today's corporate giants.

Research into the field continues, as does the conflict over whether or not corporate managers behave as profit maximizers. Again, we shall take the pragmatic view used in Chapter 1. An assumption should be accepted or rejected on the basis of its *usefulness* as a predictor of behavior rather than on its strict compliance with the details of the "real world." Profit maximization passes muster on that count to a greater extent then any alternative assumption. You cannot throw an assumption out of a theory until you have something to replace it, and until something is demonstrated to be a more consistent predictor of behavior, profit maximization will retain an important place in the theory of the firm.

How does a firm go about maximizing its profit?
The theory of the firm treats profit maximization as one more application of marginal analysis. Remember that marginal analysis is a *trial-and-error* process in which we ask ourselves: Why not one more or why not one less? In demand analysis we found that a buyer takes a particular quantity at a given price because taking one more would mean giving up more than was received in return, and taking one less would mean holding money that could provide more satisfaction if it were converted into an additional unit of goods at the given price. In production, marginal analysis led us to select a particular combination of inputs because any dollar shifted from one factor to another at the margin would reduce total output from a given outlay.

The quest for profit maximization proceeds along the same trial-and-error line. Management wants to make decisions that will maximize the *total* profit of the firm. It recognizes that total profit is equal to the difference between total revenue and total cost. Therefore it wishes to take any step that will *increase total revenue more than total cost* or *decrease total cost more than total revenue*. With this as a yardstick, many seemingly diverse problems reduce themselves to a common approach. Let us see how marginal analysis helps in considering four questions with which managers must cope: (1) what to produce; (2) how much to produce; (3) what to charge for it; and (4) how to sell and advertise it.

Start with number one. How does a firm decide what products to make?
By our criteria, a firm will produce any product that will generate more total revenue then cost. This is a fairly straightforward statement. You must be careful, however, to be sure that you understand the full meaning of *cost*. If, in order to add a new product to an existing line of merchandise, a firm must drop one of its old items, the lost profit from the old product must be included as part of the cost of introducing the new one. If there is idle capacity in the firm, the cost of introducing a new product will be lower. As long as the revenues derived from the new product cover their variable costs, the firm may well decide to go ahead, because the fixed costs will be the same whether the new product is introduced or not. If, on the other hand, it is necessary to add plant capacity in order to offer a new product, the firm must recognize its outlay on capital as part of the cost, as well as the managerial time diverted away from other activities and toward the new project. You can see that opportunity cost comes to play an important role in the deliberations over what products to make and sell.

Once all costs are recognized, the answer to what products a firm will produce resolves itself to those that it *thinks* will be profitable. Capital and resources flow out of the relatively less and into the relatively more promising areas.

Saying that a firm will produce whatever appears profitable seems a bit glib. The market isn't that perfect.

That's true. In outlining the assumptions of microeconomic theory, we stipulated that resources were *mobile* and *divisible*. This assumption implies that labor, capital, and raw materials are free to move in search of the greatest return. But it often turns out that although profits in an industry are high, there is no opportunity for new capital to flow in. In fact, profits may be high *because* entry by competitors has been effectively blocked and the existing firms keep their monopoly-like advantage.

How can entry to an industry be blocked?

There are several means of blocking entry into an industry. Industries with increasing economies of scale are likely to have oligopolistic structures, with a few giants producing at the relatively low cost that comes with big volume. Any firm that attempts to enter the industry on a smaller scale will find that it cannot produce as cheaply as the big companies. If the existing firms set their prices just below the low point on the average cost curve for a fledgling, entering firm, there is no way the new firm can compete. At its most efficient, it can only produce at a higher cost than the competition is charging in the market. Economists refer to this as *limit pricing* by established firms to block others from entering.

If the potential competitor attempts to enter the industry on a large scale, the problem is compounded. In this circumstance the new company would at least have the potential to produce as cheaply as the others. It would, however, drastically increase the total supply offered on the market and drive the price below that prevailing before entry. It is possible that the added supply and the consequently lower price will cause one or more firms in the industry to fail. In this event, the established firms have other advantages that would make them the probable survivors. One major advantage is customer goodwill built up over the years. Brand-name advertising has made names like Coca-Cola, Buick, Jello, and Maxwell House into household words. Although the balance sheets of the companies making them may carry "goodwill" at $1, this goodwill represents millions of dollars worth of advertising investment that should pay off in terms of consumer loyalty.

Other means of blocking entry include patent protection, which gives the inventor of a product a legal monopoly for seventeen years; raw material control, which as practiced by Alcoa gave that corporation a virtual monopoly in aluminum until 1945 when the courts established two competing firms; and preferential tariff treatment, for which countless industries have successfully lobbied in the corridors of the national Capitol building. Government can set up more formidable barriers to entry than tariffs, however. Charters and licenses are required to operate any number of businesses, and without them, entry is legally impossible. The New York City taxi medallion is a frequently cited case in point. In order to operate legally as a cruising taxicab in New York City, it is necessary to display a city-granted medallion. However, the city no longer issues them. To enter the industry, one must negotiate purchase of a medallion from a cab owner who is leaving the industry. In effect, city licensing places a ceiling on the number of participants in the legitimate taxicab business in New York. Trade associations, too, are frequently sanctioned by government to place limits on entry into industries and professions. The legal, medical, accounting, and engineering professions all have entry requirements that are set and enforced by those already in the practice. So, too, according to one student of the subject, do egg graders, guide-dog trainers, pest controllers, yacht salesmen, tree surgeons, well diggers, tile layers, and potato growers. It is estimated that 75 percent of all occupational licensing boards are made up exclusively of practitioners of the trade being regulated. One need not be too cynical to think of this as a means of blocking entry of other would-be suppliers.

In brief, the number and variety of barriers to entry is quite large and, to the extent that they are effective, people and firms are unable to offer goods and services that marginal analysis would normally call for.

Interesting! Let's return to the use of marginal analysis to solve different business problems. How do firms make their price and quantity decisions?

In this context we must distinguish between price takers and price givers. They behave differently. A price taker is a firm that has the price it can charge determined by its competitors, and there is nothing it can do about it. Its price-and-quantity decision is really one of quantity alone. Such a situation arises when the firm is very small in relation to the market as a whole. We deal with this case in detail in the next chapter, on pure competition. As a price taker, a small firm knows that it can sell as many units of output as it can produce at a fixed, given price. The more units it sells, the higher will be the total revenue it takes in by the simple arithmetic of price times quantity. In the event that average cost remains constant, and as long as it is less then the price,

FIGURE 7–3. Breakeven Chart

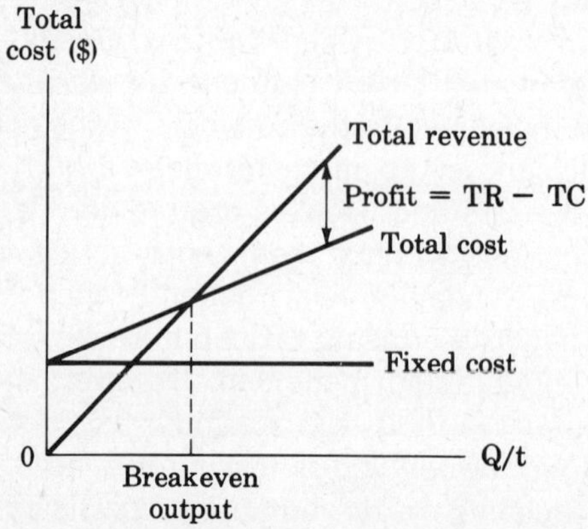

The breakeven chart is a favorite management tool. It compares total costs and revenues at different levels of output. Businessmen use the comparison to estimate what level of production is needed to break even and to estimate profit that will be earned at different levels of production. The breakeven chart assumes that both prices and average costs are constant over the entire range of output. This leads to straight-line total cost and total revenue functions. One result of these linear functions is that, once breakeven output is reached, profit will increase indefinitely with growth in output. There is no one profit-maximizing output. The higher the output, the higher the total profit.

FIGURE 7–4. Breakeven Chart Under Imperfect Competition

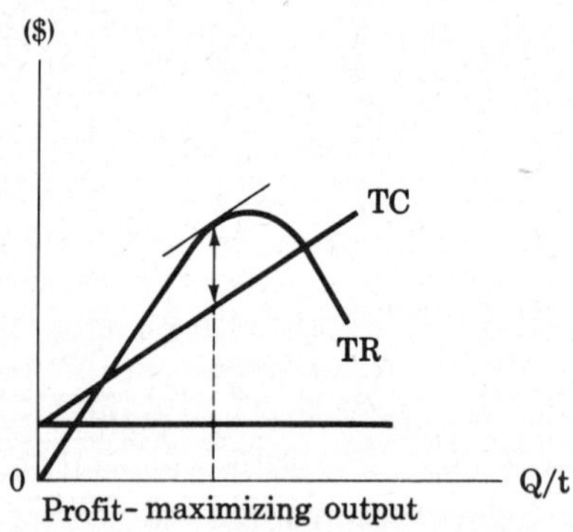

Even if costs remain constant, the downward-sloping demand curve causes total revenue first to rise and then to fall. Because of this, profit does not expand indefinitely with output, but rather we find that there is a determinate profit-maximizing output.

each additional unit produced adds to total profit, and a firm has an incentive to increase total output indefinitely. Such a case is the one we find represented through the use of the *breakeven chart* (Figure 7–3). We should note, however, that there is an internal inconsistency here. If a firm were to increase its count indefinitely, it would no longer be a small firm operating in an environment of pure competition. Instead, its high rate of output would affect the market price and its situation would edge over toward that of the price giver. Before discussing the price giver, we should note that variable returns causes the average cost curve to turn up rather than remain constant, so in no event would there be a temptation to increase output indefinitely.

The price giver's situation is a bit more complicated. This is a firm that can set the price in the market, recognizing that the quantity of output it can sell in the market is a function of the price it sets. Situations like this arise in the imperfectly competitive markets of monopoly, oligopoly, and monopolistic competition. Whereas a price taker can sell whatever quantity it produces at a constant price, a price giver recognizes that in order to sell greater quantities of output, it must lower price, and, alternatively, it can increase price only if it is willing to sell fewer items. Rather than simply increasing with output, the price giver's total revenue behaves according to our rules for price elasticity of demand. In the range where demand is relatively elastic, lower prices bring higher total revenue, and in the range where demand is relatively inelastic, lower prices produce lower total revenue (Figure 7–4). The price giver must work this out to select a price level at which the relationship of total revenue to total cost gives maximum profit, and any trial-and-error change in output at the margin will reduce earnings. Cases of this sort will come up in our various discussions of imperfect competition.

What about the area of sales promotion? How does marginal analysis contribute to our thinking here?

Price givers recognize that there is a limit to their ability to increase profits through manipulation of price. Because they may generate retaliatory actions by competitors, and due to the effects of price elasticity of demand on total revenue, management frequently chooses

FIGURE 7–5. Role of Marginal Cost and Marginal Revenue

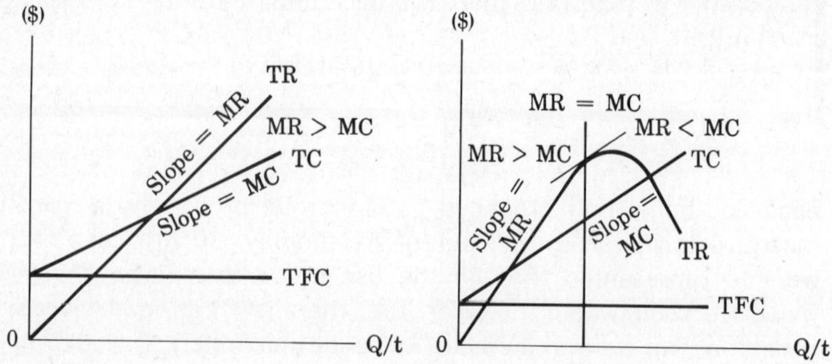

Because marginal revenue equals the slope of the total revenue curve and marginal cost equals the slope of the total cost curve, the rule that says produce anything that adds more to total revenue than it does to total cost also says produce more if the total revenue curve is steeper than the total cost curve, and less if the total cost curve is steeper than the total revenue curve. This means that you stop increasing output at the quantity at which marginal cost equals marginal revenue. In the purely competitive breakeven chart, this never happens. In the break-even chart representing imperfect competition, it does.

non-price competition as its means of increasing profitability. This competition takes the form of merchandising, advertising, product improvement, personal selling, public relations, and so on through the marketing man's bag of promotional tricks. The decision facing the firm is, How much non-price competition should it engage in, and what "marketing mix" should it employ? There is no doubt that selling effort will increase sales revenues realized by a firm. The question is, To what extent will it increase total cost as well?

Now expenditures on selling efforts suffer from diminishing returns just as do expenditures on production. Salesmen will visit the biggest and most probable customers first and leave the less likely, smaller-order people for later. The most difficult, least profitable accounts are likely to require the most effort, so naturally they will only be undertaken if there is a large selling force. Similarly, advertising will easily influence brand-switchers. The first advertising dollars spent will be more productive than subsequent outlays aimed at consumers with a strong loyalty to a competitor's brand. Management must decide at what point to stabilize its marketing effort and settle for its share of the market. Presumably it will be the point where any further total expenditure, as well as any redirection of money out of one selling means into another, will only reduce total profit.

Is there some overriding, general principle that enters into all these decisions?

There is. Profit-maximization analysis revolves around the *equating of marginal cost* with *marginal revenue*. Marginal cost has already been defined as the change in total cost that results from a one-unit change in output. Marginal revenue is the change that occurs in total revenue when output is changed by one unit. Because a rational producer should take any action that increases total revenue more than total cost, it follows that he should do anything that generates revenues that are greater than marginal costs, and should avoid actions that produce marginal costs higher than marginal revenues. The point where you stop doing and start avoiding is the point where marginal revenue equals marginal cost (Figure 7–5).

Is it really as simple as that?

In principle it is. However, problems begin to arise when you try to estimate just how high marginal cost and revenue will be in the event an action is undertaken. Revenue is particularly difficult, because there are many uncontrollable market forces—especially competitor reaction. The job of the businessman is to live with, and cope as well as possible with, these uncertainties of the marketplace. They are what keeps business management an art and successful business managers a rare breed. During the 1960s the conglomerate corporation became a popular form of business organization. These were firms that considered themselves to be essentially a bundle of assets that could be employed in any field where profits were promising. The conglomerates raced to diversify into new areas through waves of corporate acquisition. Companies were bought up eagerly by managers who understood corporate finance but had little familiarity with the businesses they were entering. The subsequent selling off or failure of many of these divisions at enormous financial losses reflected the ease with which managements can overestimate revenues and underestimate costs.

In all of the analyses that come up in the succeeding chapters, we must remember that, in practice, the result is only as good as the accuracy of the data that go into the considerations. And much of the data, unfortunately, is simply guesswork. However, let us look at the body of theory that has been developed over the years and see how the marginal decisions should be made by a firm intent on maximizing its profit.

CHAPTER HIGHLIGHTS

1. *We defined a firm as an economic unit within which a central management directs the efforts of factors of production to produce marketable goods and services. The goal of the firm is to maximize its profits in the process.*
2. *Profit maximization was seen to be another application in decision making at the margin. A firm maximizes profit by equating its marginal cost and marginal revenue.*
3. *We defined different market structures in which firms operate. These are distinguished by the nature of the product they produce and by the number of firms competing in the market.*
4. *Then we discussed the application of marginal analysis to different managerial problems: what to produce, how to produce it, what to charge for it, and how to sell and advertise it.*
5. *The assumption of mobile and divisible factors of production was examined. We described some of the barriers to entry that exist in different industries and considered how these affect profits.*
6. *Finally, we considered the pitfalls in attempting to forecast revenues and costs amid the uncertainty of a real business situation.*

QUESTIONS

1. *Do you believe that business firms attempt to maximize their profits? Milton Friedman has written, "Few trends could so thoroughly undermine the very foundations of our free society as the acceptance by corporate officials of a social responsibility other than to make as much money for their stockholders as possible." Do you agree?*
2. *Frank Knight, considered by many to be the founder of the Chicago school of economic thought, has written on the role of the business manager: "With uncertainty entirely absent . . . there would be no occasion for anything of the nature of responsible management or control of productive activity. . . . With the introduction of uncertainty, the actual execution of activity becomes in a real sense a secondary part of life; the primary problem of function is deciding what to do and how to do it." Does our treatment of the business firm incorporate conditions of certainty or uncertainty?*

3. Some firms spend as much as 25 percent of their total sales revenue on advertising. Others spend 1 to 2 percent on advertising. Can both be profit-maximizing?
4. Professor of Management William H. Newman has written with regard to decision making: "In choosing between several alternative courses of action, those factors that remain the same in all instances may be disregarded and attention focused on those that vary. The procedure sharpens the real issues and avoids those that are irrelevant." How does this advice relate to marginal analysis? Do you agree with it?
5. Bowmar Industries was an early producer of mini-calculators as a consumer good. They assembled the calculator from electronic parts manufactured by Texas Instruments. Texas Instruments subsequently entered the mini-calculator field itself. It was a short time before Bowmar was in financial difficulty. Is there anything in our chapter that might have saved Bowmar some anguish?
6. Suppose that you invest $100,000 in drilling an oil well. Operating costs are $2 per barrel. If oil sells for $12 per barrel, you will recover your investment in 10 years. Suppose, however, that after making the investment, the price of oil falls to $3 per barrel. If you knew the price would be $3 per barrel you would never have invested. Does this mean that you should shut down operations? Draw the respective breakeven charts.

8 Pure competition

Pure competition is a set of assumptions about markets. It is a construct that exists in the economist's mind to permit him to gain insight into economic behavior. We should understand at the outset that there are no actual markets that have all the qualities economists require in their definition of pure competition. Nevertheless, the model of market behavior under conditions of pure competition is one of the best developed and minutely analyzed in the body of economic theory. It deserves our careful attention because it is used as a reference point against which we measure the performance of other market structures. In a sense it is an *ideal*, just as the notion of a perfect vacuum is an ideal in physics, and a line that takes up no area is an ideal in geometry. They are useful for reasoning purposes and derive their acceptance from how well they serve us, rather than from whether they exist.

Pure competition assumes the following market conditions prevail:

1. There are an infinite number of buyers and sellers in the market. Operationally, the number must be great enough so that no one buyer or seller can affect the price, no matter how much he increases or decreases his supply or demand.
2. The product being traded in the market is perfectly standardized and homogeneous. The product any one supplier puts out is identical to that of all other suppliers. They are perfect substitutes.
3. Resources are perfectly mobile and divisible and will flow to the most profitable or satisfying use.
4. Information regarding present and future alternative uses and opportunities is available to all at no cost.

That certainly is a restrictive set of assumptions. Are there any markets that contain all these characteristics?

In theory, this should be true for the worldwide markets for agricultural products such as wheat and corn. There are millions of small farmers and hundreds of millions of buyers of wheat and corn products. At the wholesale level organized commodity exchanges provide instantaneous information and prices are determined by the impersonal interplay of supply and demand. Farmers can allocate their land and labor to crops promising the highest profit. Products are perfectly standardized and the output of one farmer is readily substitutable for another.

When we contemplate the reality of the agricultural markets, however, we find a number of critical departures from the competitive model. For one thing, we discovered in 1973 that the Soviet government, acting as a single buyer, was certainly able to demand enough grain to affect the price. Furthermore, our own department of agriculture enters the market with its subsidies and support programs, which influence the products into which farmers direct their resources. National import quotas and tariffs protect inefficient small-scale farming in each of the Common Market nations. Governments have for years been committed to protecting agriculture from the volatility of food price fluctuation, with the result that prices and quantities are more responsive to the forces of bureaucracy than to the market.

How does a purely competitive market work in theory?

In a purely competitive market every individual is a price taker. No one buyer or seller has the power to set the market price by himself. Rather, each must accommodate himself to the equilibrium price that clears the total market. We described in Chapter 2 the manner in which individual demand curves are aggregated to form the market demand curve. We shall see shortly the manner in which individual supply curves are determined, and these too are aggregated to form the market supply curve. The demand curve shows the number of units of product that will be taken from the market at alternative prices (or less), and the supply curve shows the number of units that will be placed on sale in the market at alternative prices (or more). Through the process of buyers seeking out the lowest prices available and sellers hoping to get the highest, an equilibrium price and quantity are determined. At prices below equilibrium, the quantity demanded will exceed the quantity supplied, and those buyers unable to satisfy their demand will increase their bids, thereby coaxing more supply out and reducing the market demand of others. At prices above equilibrium, willing suppliers will not find demanders, and some will reduce the price they ask, thereby coaxing out more demanders and causing other suppliers to leave the market. The essence of the equilibrium price is its stability. As long as there is no change in the parameters that determine supply and demand—that is, income, price of substitutes and complements, tastes, technology, price of factor inputs, weather, number of participants, and so on—the equilibrium price will remain unchanged. This means that each seller sees the market price as a constant. In effect the demand curve facing him is horizontal.

How can the demand curve facing the individual supplier be horizontal?
Consider a market in which a large number of individual demand and supply curves are aggregated to form a *market* demand and supply curve. Suppose that in this market, commodity X turns over at an equilibrium rate of 1 million units per day and each unit sells for $3. Assume that the competitive market comprises 10,000 firms each of which is selling 100 units at the equilibrium price of $3. Let us imagine now that *one* firm *doubles* its output to 200 units. What effect would this 100 percent increase in output have on the market price? In terms of the overall market, this doubling constitutes an increase of only .01 percent in total product supplied. The effect that an increase in quantity supplied has on price depends on the coefficients of price elasticity of demand and supply. The lower the price elasticity of demand and supply, the greater the effect on price. Let us assume that supply is *perfectly* inelastic and that price elasticity of demand is $-1/4$. The doubling of output of one supplier would decrease market price by .04 percent. The $3 price would drop by approximately $.0012 to a level of $2.9988. We thus find the slope of the demand curve facing the individual seller to be .0012/100. For all intents and purposes this curve is treated as being horizontal (Figure 8–1). This means that the quantity offered by the individual seller can be increased or decreased with virtually no effect on the market price. He literally is a price taker (or refuser) but not a price giver (Figure 8–2).

Suppose one firm withdraws from the market entirely?
If one firm withdraws from the market entirely, its supply curve is removed from the aggregate with a resultant shift to the left of the market supply. However, in the case of our industry of 10,000 firms, this is a shift of only .01 percent. In effect, we treat this shift as if it were less than the width of the line drawn to represent the demand curve Figure 8–3. Therefore equilibrium price is unchanged because to all intents and purposes, supply still intersects demand at the same level. Under a magnifying glass we could see a shift in supply against demand (Figure 8–4). However, without an optical instrument the price remains

FIGURE 8–1. Horizontal Demand Curve

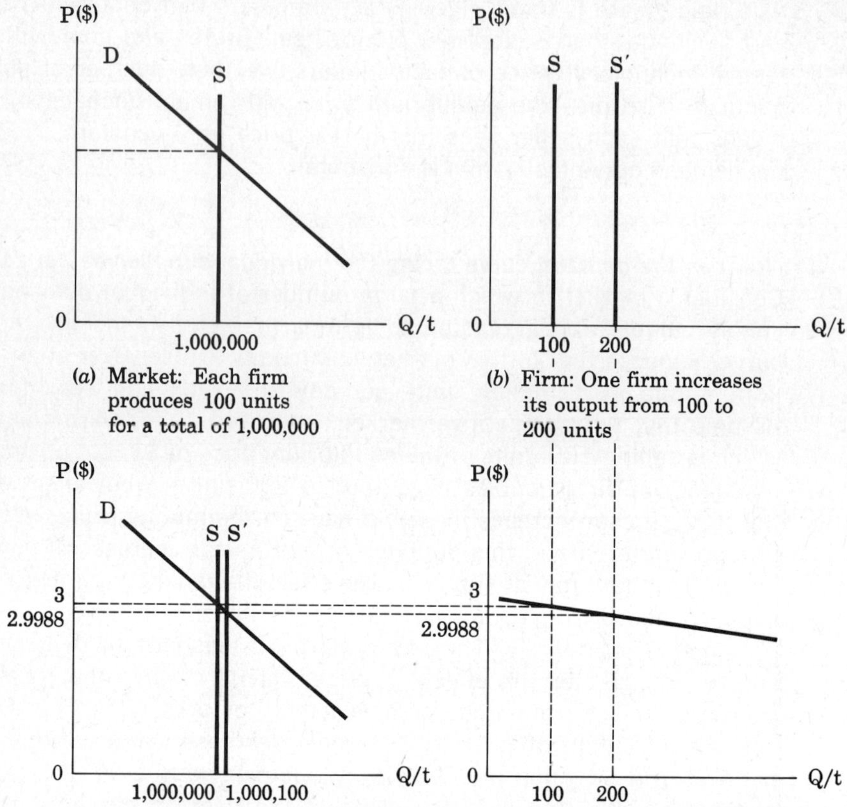

(*a*) Market: Each firm produces 100 units for a total of 1,000,000

(*b*) Firm: One firm increases its output from 100 to 200 units

(*c*) Market: The market supply curve shifts .01% to the right. If demand elasticity is $-\frac{1}{4}$, the price falls .04 percent

(*d*) Firm: Because the slope of the demand curve facing the single firm is −.0012/100, it is treated as horizontal

Assume a market in which 10,000 sellers each offer 100 units at the equilibrium price of $3, thereby giving an equilibrium quantity of 1 million units. If one of these sellers increases his individual output by 100 percent to 200 units, the change in total market quantity is .01 percent. The exact effect on equilibrium price depends on the coefficients of price elasticity of demand and supply. Here supply is assumed to be perfectly inelastic and price elasticity of demand is assumed to be $-1/4$.

FIGURE 8–2. *Demand Curve Facing the Individual Seller*

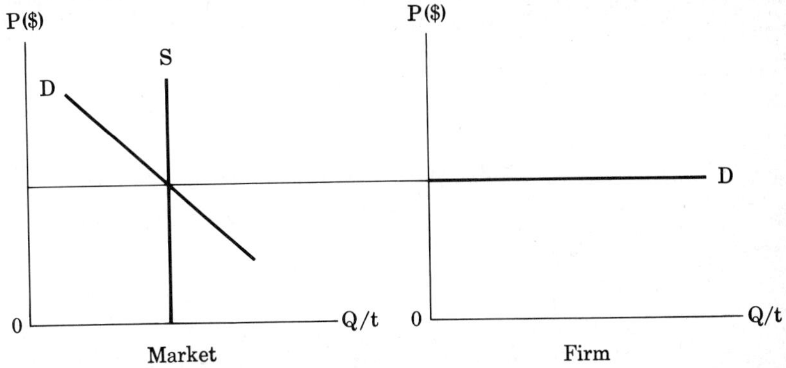

Because each seller is so small in relation to the total market, he is in effect a price taker. No matter how much he increases or decreases his output, he will not signicantly affect the market price. Therefore his demand curve shows a constant price prevailing for all outputs within his productive capacity.

FIGURE 8–3. *Exit and Entry of Firms from Industry*

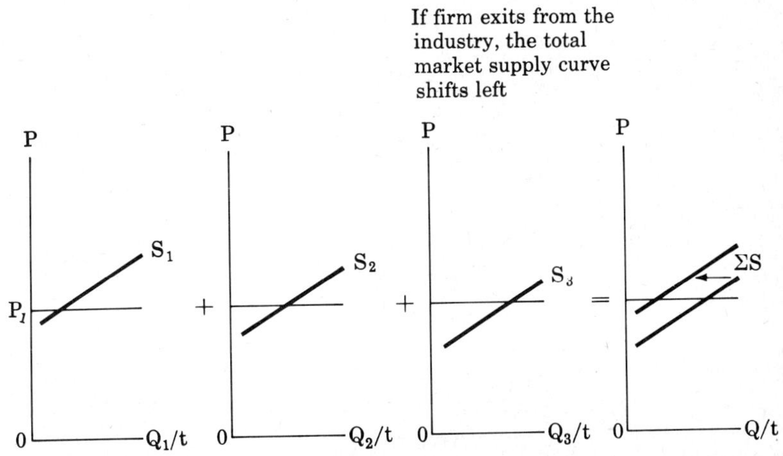

Exit of a firm from the market normally shifts the market supply curve to the left. Entry shifts the market supply curve to the right. Because the market supply is comprised of the supplies of the many individual firms, entry and exit will change the quantities offered at each price.

FIGURE 8–4. Exit and Entry of Firms from Industry: Pure Competition

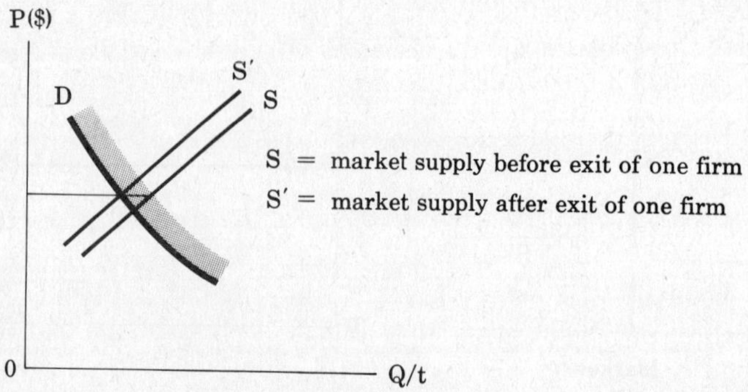

Under pure competition the shift in the market supply curve that occurs with the entry or exit of a single firm is so slight that it goes unnoticed. This is illustrated by drawing the market demand as a thick line and recognizing that the shift in supply is less than the width of the demand curve.

FIGURE 8–5. Supply of Factors of Production

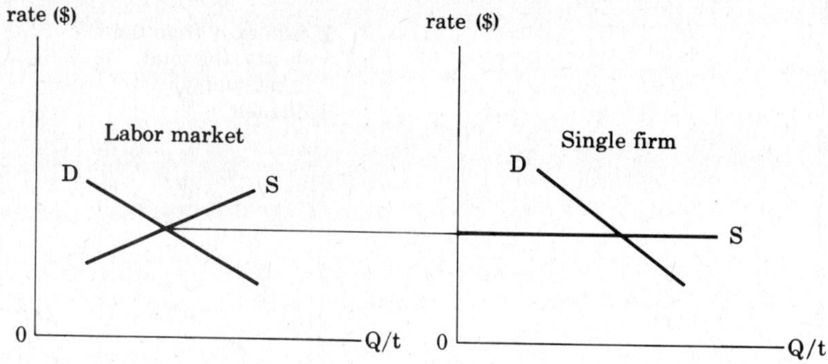

Just as the demand curve appears perfectly horizontal to a seller in a perfectly competitive market, so too does the supply of factors of production appear perfectly horizontal to a competitive buyer. Because the firm's labor demands are so small relative to the total market, it can hire as many or as few workers as it wants without affecting the market place. The supply curve of labor to the firm is in effect horizontal, even though aggregate labor supply is upward-sloping.

essentially unchanged. Each supplier faces a demand curve that cannot be changed by his own actions. If all suppliers were to act in concert, they would produce significant shifts in the curves. But it is not in the nature of pure competition that they all act in concert.

If each firm has a horizontal demand curve, why is not the aggregate demand curve also a horizontal curve? You said earlier that the aggregate demand curve is the summation of individual demand curves.

This seems like a confusing point. However, if this is bothering you, it may just reflect a misunderstanding on your part. The horizontal demand curve is the demand curve as seen from the individual seller's point of view. The downward-sloping curve is the demand curve for the product from the individual buyer's vantage point. Each buyer is unwilling to take in additional units of a product unless its price is reduced. The aggregate downward-sloping demand curve shows what the total number of *buyers* are *willing* to do. The horizontal demand curve, on the other hand, reflects what each *seller* sees himself as *able* to do. Each can sell as much or as little as he wishes at a certain price. These horizontal demand curves cannot be aggregated because their very nature requires that all other sellers maintain *ceteris paribus* while the one seller adds to or substracts from the quantity he offers at the fixed price. If the others also change their quantities, the total supply in the market will alter and price will change as well. The downward-sloping demand curves do not have this interdependence. Adding them together is simply arithmetic. But if you attempt to add together the horizontal demand curves, you alter them qualitatively because each one requires that the others remain completely unchanged.

It sounds as if it makes a big difference whether we deal with the overall picture as against the picture from the individual's point of view.

It does. We must continuously distinguish between analyses pertaining to the firm and those pertaining to the industry. Here we have dealt, on the one hand, with the horizontal demand curve as seen by the individual firm, and on the other with the downward-sloping curve reflecting the industry point of view. Supply curves also differ in this manner. If a firm is a tiny purchaser of factor inputs, it can have as many units as it wishes at a constant price (Figure 8–5). Still, from the industry point of view, supply will be upward sloping with increased quantities available only at higher prices. A dominant buyer, such as an oligopsonist, must face an upward-sloping supply curve because, by increasing or decreasing the quanity it takes it affects total demand enough to change the market price. However, the pure competitor faces only a

FIGURE 8–6. Horizontal Curves Imply Infinite Elasticity

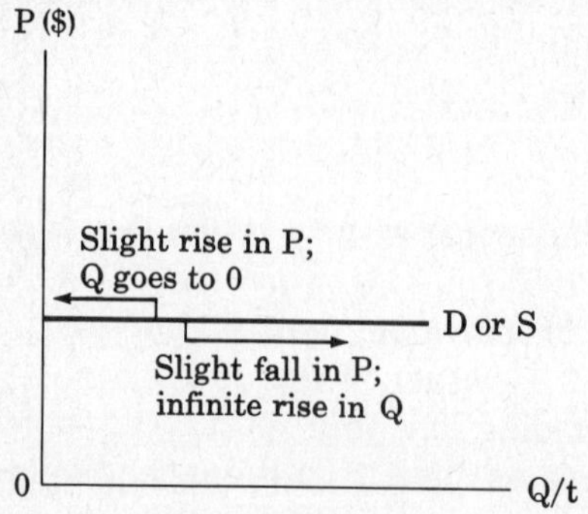

When a curve is horizontal, it not only means that all quantities can be bought or sold at the same price, it also means that (in the case of demand) none can be sold at a higher price and an infinitely great amount can be sold at a lower price. In the case of supply, it means that none will be offered at a lower price and an infinitely great amount will be forthcoming at a higher price. These great jumps in quantity associated with slight price changes produce the infinitely great elasticity.

horizontal supply curve. When we deal with a firm that is a monopolist or monopsonist in a particular market, its point of view is exactly the same as the industry's because it *is* the industry. The demand curve the monopolist faces is downward sloping and the supply curve upward sloping because they show the disposition of the entire market to buy or sell different quantities at different prices. Put another way, the industry demand and supply curves have some finite measure of elasticity, but the curves facing the pure competitor are infinitely elastic.

Why is a horizontal demand curve called infinitely elastic?
We discussed this in Chapter 3. When the demand curve is horizontal at a certain price level, it means that everyone else is selling at that price. If a seller attempts to increase the price he asks, he will sell nothing. If he reduces his price ever so slightly, he can theoretically increase his sales infinitely. These tiny price changes, which can produce great quantity changes because of the perfect substitutability of each seller's products, give us infinite elasticity (Figure 8–6).

So much for demand curves. What do the cost curves look like under pure competition?

Short-run cost curves tend to look pretty much alike under all market conditions. After all, the laws of engineering and physics do not know how many competitors there are in the market where the goods are being sold. The difference between competitive and monopolistic cost curves lies more in the range of output than in the form of the function. Firms under competition will be producing a very small percentage of the industry output, whereas firms under oligopoly will produce a significant percentage of the industry output and a monopolist, of course, produces the entire industry output. However, all have U-shaped short-run average cost curves with marginal cost curves that intersect them at their low points. The problem of the firm is to maximize demand curve and U-shaped average cost curve.

How does a firm under pure competition maximize profits?

When we discussed profit maximization, we said that a firm will add to its output as long as in doing so it increases its total revenue more than its total cost. The increase in total revenue is found by measuring the marginal revenue, and the increase in total cost is found by measuring marginal cost.

I see marginal cost on the diagram. Where is marginal revenue?

In the case of pure competition, the marginal revenue curve of the single firm is the same as the demand curve. The demand curve shows the price per unit at which the various quantities are sold. Because it is horizontal, all quantities sell at the same unit price. If the quantity sold increases by one unit, the total revenue increases by the price of that one unit. Thus the marginal revenue is equal to the price, which is shown on the demand curve. Additionally, from our average–marginal relationships, we can observe that when the marginal revenue is constant, so too is average revenue. In fact, under pure competition this very same horizontal demand curve shows price, marginal revenue, and average revenue simultaneously (Figure 8–7).

How do you make the comparison between marginal revenue and marginal cost so as to maximize profit?

In stage II of the production function under diminishing returns the marginal cost curve slopes upward with increases in output. If it is below price at some relatively low output and increases as output rises, sooner or later it will equal the constant price (marginal revenue) and

FIGURE 8–7. Relationship of Demand Curve to Marginal Revenue

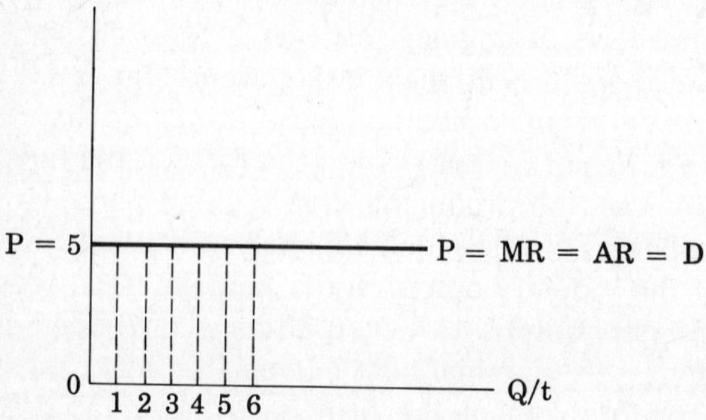

Under pure competition, the demand curve facing the firm is also its marginal revenue curve, as well as its average revenue curve.

Quantity *n*	*Price*	*Total revenue* *P × Q*	*Average revenue* *(P × Q)/Q*	*Marginal revenue* $PQ_n - PQ_{n-1}$
1	5	5	5	
2	5	10	5	10 − 5 = 5
3	5	15	5	15 − 10 = 5
4	5	20	5	20 − 15 = 5
5	5	25	5	25 − 15 = 5
6	5	30	5	30 − 25 = 5

FIGURE 8–8. Profit-Maximizing Output

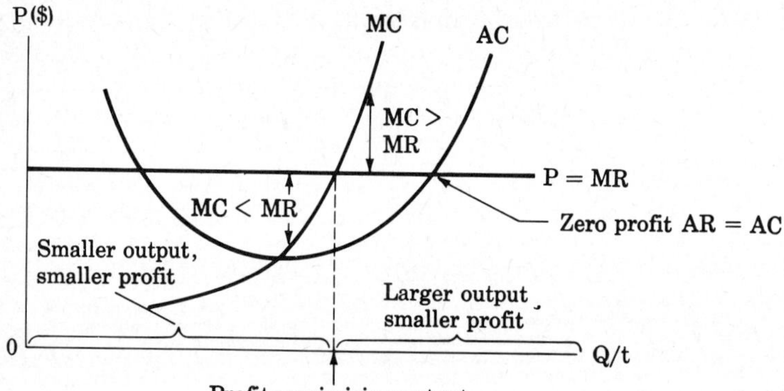

The classical solution to problems in profit maximization is to produce at that output at which marginal cost equals marginal revenue. At larger outputs, the increase in cost is greater than the increase in revenue. At smaller outputs, there is a potential to increase revenue more than cost with each increment in output.

then surpass it at higher rates of production. We are looking for the point of intersection between the marginal cost and marginal revenue curves, for it is at this output that profit is maximized (Figure 8–8). At all lower rates of production, marginal revenue is greater than marginal cost. If we were to depart from the MC = MR rate of production and make *fewer* units, the loss in revenue would exceed the reduction in cost and total profit would be reduced. On the other hand, if we were to attempt to produce *more* units of output than that at which marginal cost equals marginal revenue, we would find that we add more to total cost than total revenue with another resultant drop in total profit. By a process of elimination, *the point at which the marginal cost curve intersects the marginal revenue curve from below marks profit-maximizing output.*

Why isn't total profit maximized at the output corresponding to the low point on the average cost curve?

You're not paying attention. *Total profit is maximized at the output where marginal cost equals marginal revenue.* If this happens to occur at the low point on the average cost curve, then that is the profit-maximizing output (Figure 8–9). However, if marginal cost does not equal marginal revenue at that output, we must assume that despite the efficiency of production, profits are not as high as they could be at some other rate of output. Look at the data in Figure 8–10. Here the minimum average cost is \$6. The horizontal demand curve is at price \$10. While the low \$6 average cost occurs at 5 units of output, the intersection of marginal cost and marginal revenue does not occur until output of 8 units. At 8 units the average cost is \$6⅞, which is clearly less efficient than \$6 average cost at 5 units. Nevertheless, total profit is \$25 versus the \$20 found at 5 units. Let us see what happens as output is increased from 5 to 8 units, one at a time. The sixth unit raised average cost to \$6⅙ (Figure 8–12). The marginal cost of the sixth unit was \$7, but the marginal revenue was \$10, thereby increasing total profit by \$3. Six units is clearly more profitable than 5 units. If we add another, and then another, unit of output we increase total profit each time, because marginal revenue exceeds marginal cost.

FIGURE 8–9. Low Point of the Average Cost Curve

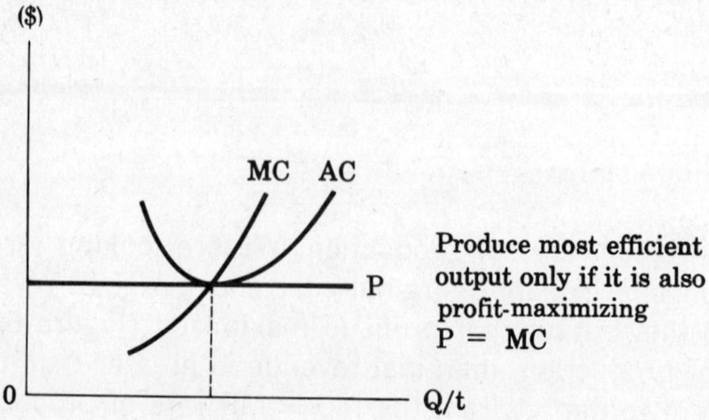

The low point on the average cost curve shows the output at which average cost is lowest, that is, production is most efficient. A firm will operate at this output, however, only if its price is also at this level, and then it will operate there because it is profit-maximizing, not because it is most efficient.

FIGURE 8–10. A Numerical Example of Profit Maximization

Quantity	*Price (MR)*	*Total cost*	*Average cost*	*Marginal cost*	*Total revenue*	*Profit*
0	10	10			0	−10
1	10	14	14	4	10	−4
2	10	16	8	2	20	4
3	10	19	$6\frac{1}{3}$	3	30	11
4	10	24	6	5	40	16
5	10	30	6	6	50	20
6	10	37	$6\frac{1}{6}$	7	60	23
7	10	45	$6\frac{3}{7}$	8	70	25
8	10	55	$6\frac{7}{8}$	10	80	25
9	10	67	$7\frac{4}{9}$	12	90	23
10	10	85	$8\frac{1}{2}$	18	100	15

In this numerical example, the maximum profit attained is 25. It occurs at an output of 8 units, where marginal cost equals marginal revenue. You may be troubled as to why total profit of 25 occurs at 7 units of output as well as at 8. Arithmetically it must because, if marginal revenue and marginal cost of the eighth unit are both equal to 10, total revenue for 7 units equals total revenue for 8 units minus 10 (MR), and total cost for 7 units equals total cost for 8 units minus 10 (MC). Profit at 8 units is $TR_8 - TC_8$, that is, $80 - 55 = 25$, and profit at 7 units is $(80 - 10) - (55 - 10) = 25$. They are the same. The difficulty arises because the example uses discrete unit changes rather than continuous smooth functions (see Figure 8–11).

FIGURE 8–11. *Discrete vs. Continuous Functions*

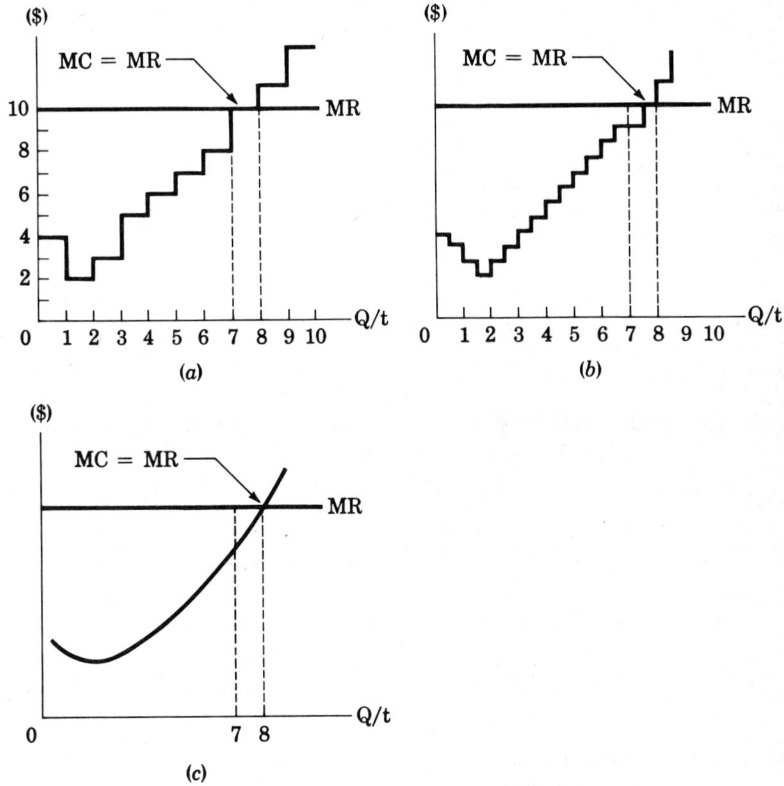

Most of the diagrams in the text show smooth, continuous curves. Yet the numerical examples are in terms of discrete quantities. The difference is illustrated here. In part (*a*) we plot the numerical data from Figure 8–10. Profit is maximized over the range between outputs 7 and 8. As the size of the units is reduced, as in part (*b*), the profit-maximizing range is reduced. Finally, in part (*c*) the units are made infinitessimally small, which is the assumption behind smooth curves. Here the profit-maximizing output is the unique one where *MC* equals *MR* at 8 units of output.

FIGURE 8–12. A Numerical Example

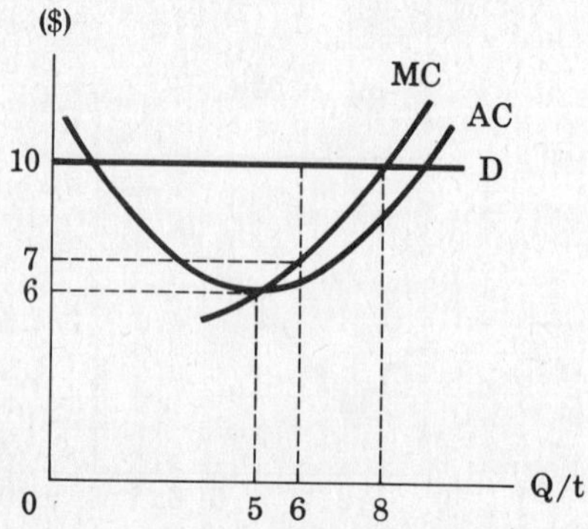

From the data in Figure 8–10 we find that efficiency is maximized at 5 units of output. Here average cost is minimum and equal to marginal cost. At this point

Total revenue	= 50	$(P \times Q)$
Total cost	= 30	$(AC \times Q)$
Total profit	= 20	

If output is raised to 6 units

Total revenue	= 50 + 10	= 60
Total cost	= 30 + 7	= 37
Total profit	=	23

So 6 is better than 5 units. We can continue up to 8, where profit is maximized.

FIGURE 8–13. Profit Maximization—Price Change

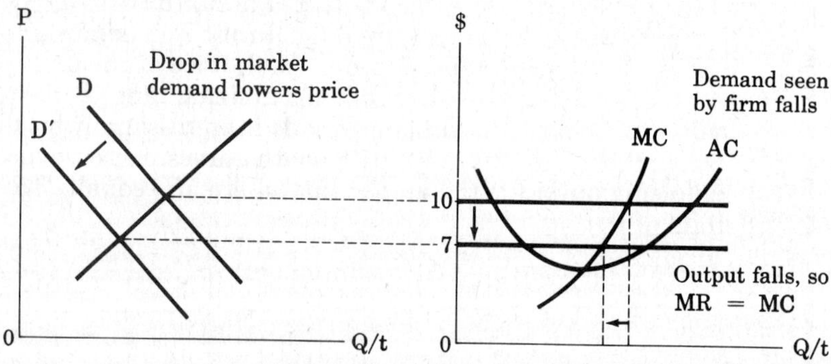

If price falls, it means that the $MR = MC$ condition is met at a lower output. Adjustment involves sliding down the marginal cost curve until price again equals marginal cost.

FIGURE 8–14. Price Below Average Cost

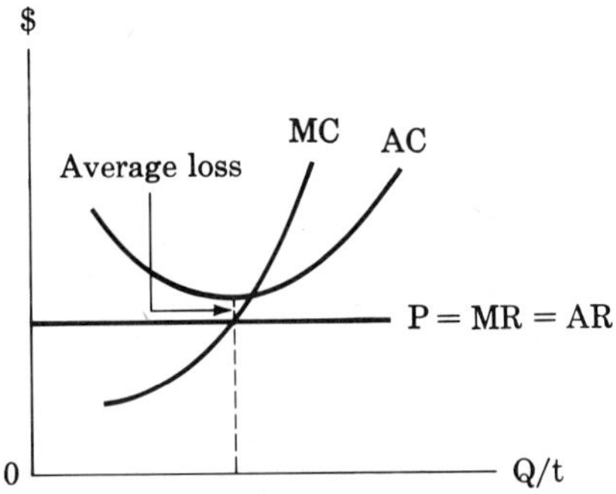

If the price is less than the short-run average cost curve at all points, the *loss-minimizing* output is that at which marginal revenue equals marginal cost. Here too, any other output adds more to cost than revenue, or takes more from revenue than cost.

Finally, we see that if we add a ninth unit of output to our production rate, average cost rises to $\$7\frac{4}{9}$, and the marginal cost is \$12 versus a marginal revenue of \$10. In this instance the extra unit reduces total profit by \$2, from \$25 to \$23. Obviously, the ninth unit is *not* a good idea. Of course if the price should rise, the ninth unit would become desirable because marginal revenue would again exceed marginal cost. On the other hand, if the price fell, even the eighth unit would be better left unproduced, because under the lower price circumstance the marginal cost of \$10 would exceed the marginal revenue and reduce profit (Figure 8–13).

Suppose that the profit-maximizing level of output is less then the output at which the average cost curve is minimum?
In that case, the firm operates at a loss. If the marginal revenue-marginal cost intersection is to the left of the low point on the average cost curve, it means that price is less than this minimum average cost. No matter what level of output the firm chooses to produce, there is no way for it to cover its costs. Its task becomes minimization of losses. It achieves this by following the marginal cost–marginal revenue rule (Figure 8–14).

FIGUE 8–15. Shut-Down Decision

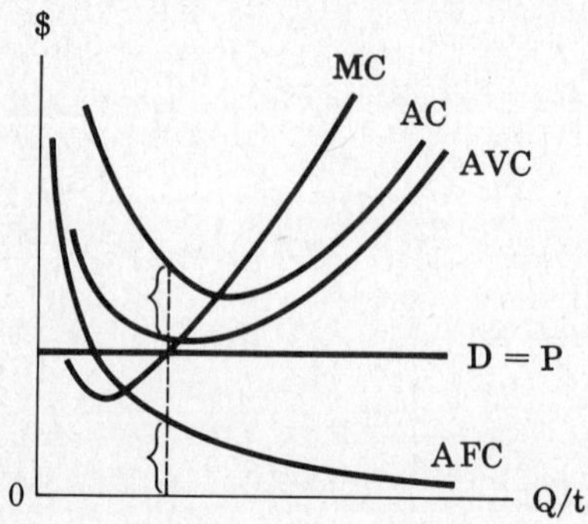

In deciding whether to keep operating at a loss or to shut down at a loss, you should compare the losses. Average fixed cost is the difference between the *AC* and *AVC* curves. Average operating loss (or profit) is the difference between the demand and *AC* curves. You should accept whichever is smaller.

FIGURE 8–16. Two Cases of Loss

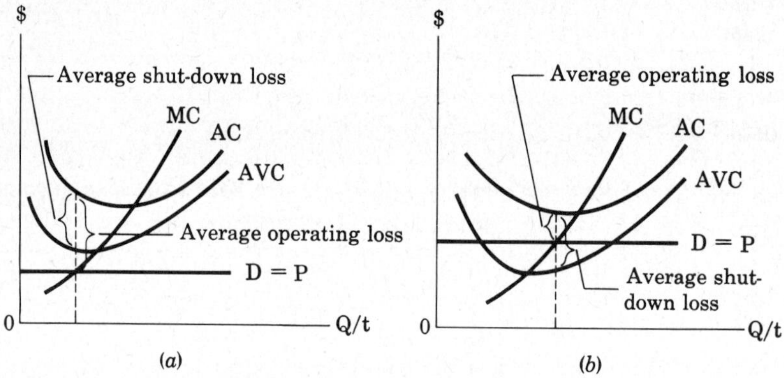

In part (*a*) you should elect to shut down, because operating loss is greater than average fixed cost. In part (*b*) you should continue to operate at a short-run loss, because it is less than would be lost if the plant were shut down.

Why not simply shut down the plant? Losing nothing is better than losing something.
The problem is that if you shut down the plant, you do lose something. Over the short run the fixed costs are lost. Remember that these go on even at zero output. They include items such as basic maintenance, rent, taxes, insurance, interest, and depreciation, and in the short run, at least, they are inescapable. However, shutting down the plant may be the loss-minimizing thing to do. It requires marginal analysis to decide.

What do you mean? How do you decide when to shut down the plant?
Remember that marginal analysis always involves making choices. If you lose money by keeping the plant open and lose money by closing it down, you want to do whichever loses the least money. If operating the plant causes a loss that is greater than fixed costs, the better choice is to shut down the plant. On the other hand, if losses from operation are less than fixed costs, you should continue operating in the short run. The losses will be less than the fixed costs if the price for which the item sells at least covers the variable costs. If it does, wages and materials will be paid for and something will be left over to contribute to paying the overhead. Although the surplus may not be enough to cover all of the overhead charges that cost accountants want to assign to each unit of sales, the firm is still better off than if it did not have this surplus at all, and still had *all* of the overhead.

The analytical approach to this problem is illustrated in Figures 8–15 and 8–16. In Figure 8–16(*a*) the price is below average variable cost. In Figure 8–16(*b*) the price, although below average cost, is still above average variable cost. Money will be lost in both situations, but the firm wants to lose as little as possible. The place to look is the output where marginal cost equals marginal revenue. This is the level of production that minimizes the loss if the firm continues to operate. The interval between the demand curve and the average cost curve at this output shows the loss on each item produced. This interval must be compared with the distance between the average cost and average variable cost curves. You will recall that this interval measures average fixed cost. If the fixed cost exceeds the operating loss, then the firm should continue to operate and take the operating loss, as preferable to the greater deficit that would have to be suffered by shutting down. If, however, fixed cost is less than the loss incurred by operating, our logic says to shut down and accept fixed costs as the limit on the losses. Of course, this reasoning refers only to the short run. In the long run there are no fixed costs, and a firm losing money will go out of business. To sum up another way, if the price is less than average variable cost, the firm will shut down. If the price is more than average variable cost

FIGURE 8–17. Total Revenue

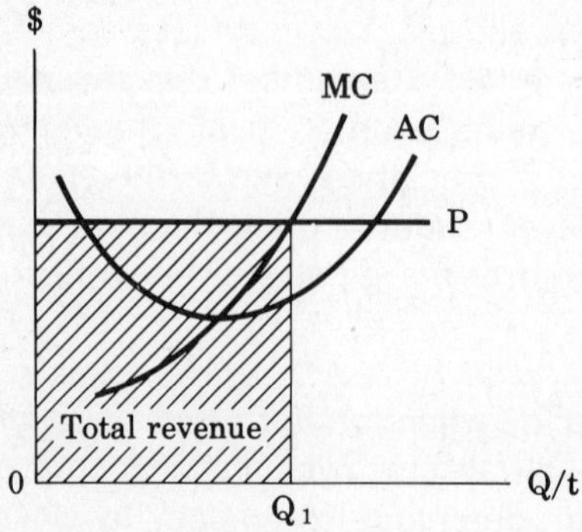

Total revenue is shown by the area under the demand curve at the quantity produced. This is equal, geometrically, to $P \times Q$.

FIGURE 8–18. Total Cost

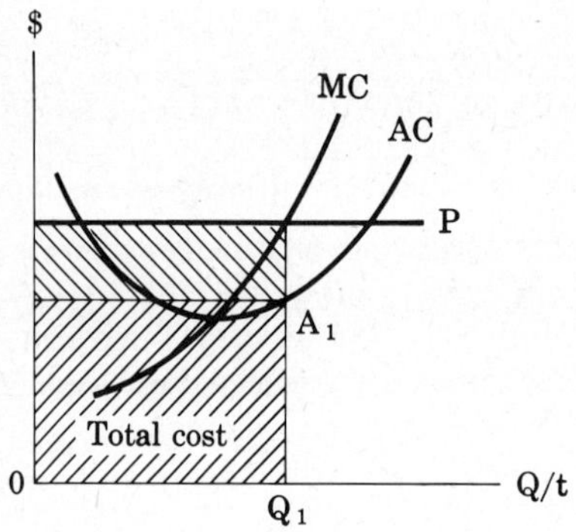

Total cost is shown by the area of a rectangle whose height is the average cost and whose length is quantity.

but less than average cost, the firm minimizes losses by operating where marginal cost equals marginal revenue.

The whole point of the analysis appears to be to maximize total profit. Then how can you show total profit on the diagram?
Total profit equals total revenue minus total cost. The vertical difference between the demand curve (average revenue) and the average cost curve is the average unit profit. By mutiplying this unit profit by quantity we get total profit. This is visualized on the diagrams through a group of rectangles that we can construct. The rectangle bordered by the price level on one side and the quantity produced on the other may be thought of as representing total revenue (Figure 8–17). Remember that this rectangle's area is equal to length times width, and in this case length is quantity and width is price. Now draw another rectangle, bordered this time on one side by a line drawn up to the average cost curve at the quantity produced and on the other by the quantity. This rectangle shows average cost times quantity and equals total cost (Figure 8–18). The rectangle that represents the distance between these two shows total profit; since it is unit profit (difference between average revenue and average cost) multiplied by quantity. The rectangle constructed in this manner, at the quantity where marginal cost equals marginal revenue, has the largest area among the profit rectangles because it is here that profit is maximized (Figures 8–19, 8–20, and 8–21).

Now are we ready to discuss the supply curve? How does the supply curve for the firm enter into this discussion?
The supply curve for the firm is shown by the marginal cost curve over the range of output at which marginal cost exceeds average variable cost. Think of it this way. A supply curve is supposed to show the different quantities that would be offered at different prices. We know that at any given price a firm will offer that quantity at which its marginal cost equals the price. Why? The price is also the marginal revenue as far as a perfect competitor is concerned. By producing the quantity at which marginal cost equals marginal revenue, a supplier maximizes profit. If we consider a number of different prices and recognize that for each one the quantity that will be produced is found by reading across the price to the marginal cost curve and then down, we conclude that the marginal cost curve shows the data we expect from a supply curve: the different quantities a profit-maximizing producer will offer at different prices. Of course, we have just seen that at prices below

FIGURE 8–19. Total Profit

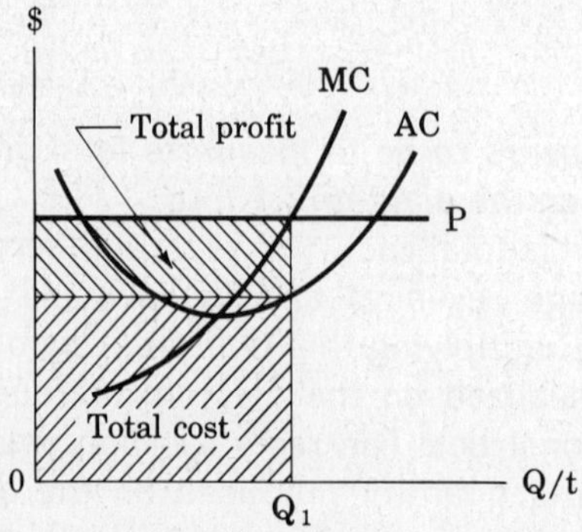

Combining the visualization of total revenue and total cost permits us to show total profit. The combined rectangles equal total revenue.

FIGURE 8–20. Total Loss

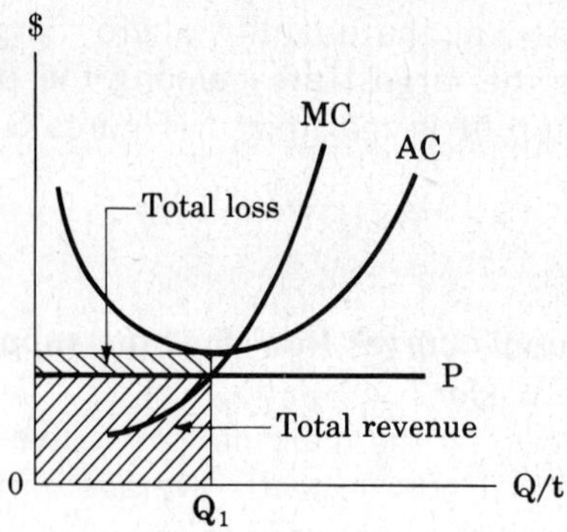

In this case the combined rectangles equal total cost. The total revenue is smaller than the total cost and the difference is total loss.

FIGURE 8–21. Shut Down Again

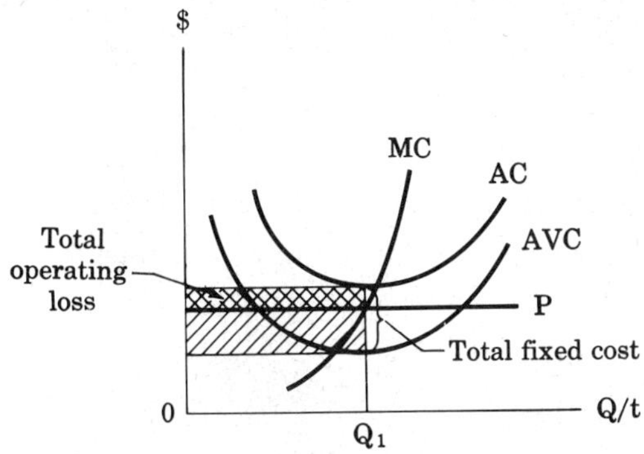

Using the rectangle construction, we can compare total fixed cost with total operating loss. In this case the combined rectangles equal the total fixed cost. Because this is larger than the operating loss, the decision should be to continue operations.

the minimum average *variable* cost, the profit maximizer will offer zero output, choosing to shut down the plant instead. Therefore the marginal cost curve is the supply curve only for prices and marginal costs in excess of average variable cost. At prices and marginal costs below this level, the supply curve is found along the *y* axis, meaning that output is zero (Figure 8–22).

You have described how a profit-maximizing firm selects the quantity of output it will produce. How does it go about deciding how to produce that output?

Naturally, if a management is going to all this trouble to produce the profit-maximizing level of output, it also wants to produce it in the most efficient manner possible. In Chapter 6 we pointed out that this requires the marginal product per dollar spent on each factor of production to be equal. To achieve this, a firm must be free to vary the quantities of all factor inputs (Figure 8–23). In the short run, however, the firm operates within the constraint of having a plant of fixed size. It can adjust its output only by adding or deleting variable factors (labor).

FIGURE 8–22. Marginal Cost as Supply Curve

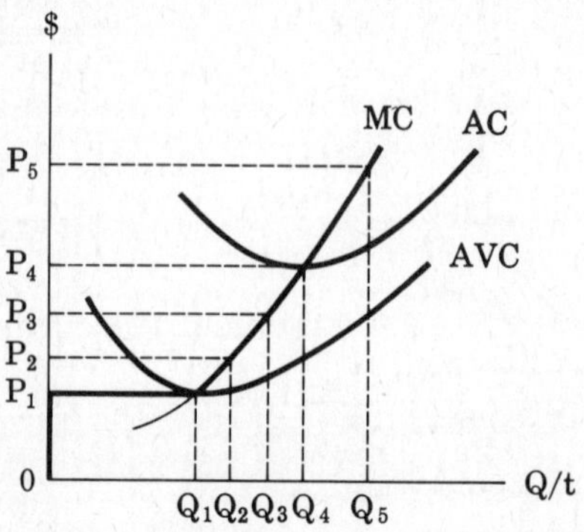

The supply curve for a firm should show the different quantities it will offer at different prices. If a firm is a profit maximizer, it should offer the quantity that equates its marginal cost with price. This is shown by the marginal cost curve from *AVC* up. Below *AVC*, the firm shuts down and supply is zero.

FIGURE 8–23. Most Efficient Production—Long-Run

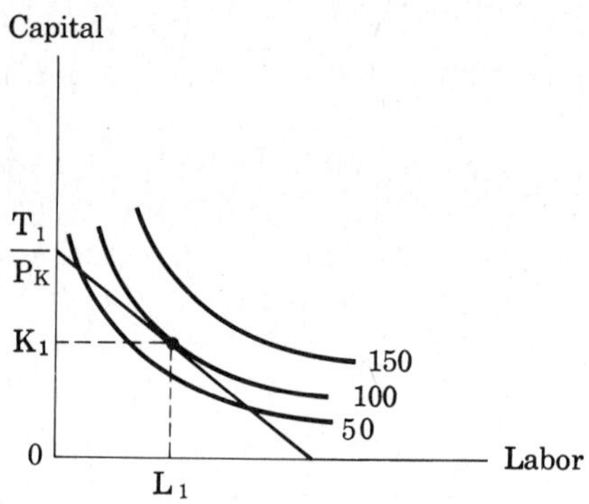

Whatever output is produced, the firm ideally wants to produce it at the least cost. This is accomplished by combining factors of production in such a manner that the marginal products per dollar spent on each is equal, that is, $MP_L/P_L = MP_K/P_K$. If 100 units is the profit-maximizing output, the firm should produce it by using the factor combination indicated by the point of tangency between an isocost and the 100 isoquant. In the figure the total cost of producing 100 units is T_1. There is no way to do it cheaper as long as the factor prices remain unchanged. This is considered a long-run solution, because it involves freedom to adjust the quantity of all inputs.

FIGURE 8–24. Most Efficient Production—Short Run

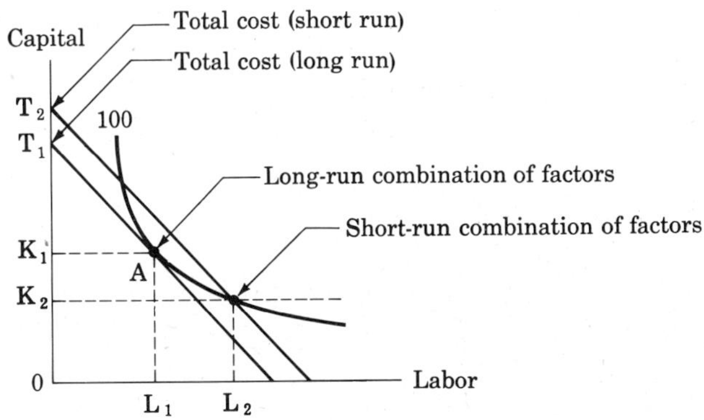

If the quantity to be produced is 100, the long-run solution is to use the quantities of labor and capital indicated by tangency point A at a cost of T_1. However, in the short run the plant already exists. If its scale corresponds to the amount of capital shown by K_2, the only adjustment that can be made is through varying the labor input. Hence it is necessary to use this comparatively undersized plant (smaller than K_1) with relatively high labor inputs to produce 100 units of output. The cost is T_2, which is more than the T_1 that is achievable through the long-run solution.

There is a good chance, therefore, that in the short run a firm will be unable to make the optimum adjustment.

You can see this problem on the isoquant map. Fixed capital permits only those labor–capital combinations that are found along a horizontal line drawn across the map at the fixed capital level. This line intersects the various isoquants, one of which is the profit-maximizing quantity. The labor input is found by reading down from the point of intersection to the x axis (Figure 8–24). Notice, however, that there is no guarantee that the isocost reflecting total cost will be *tangent* to the isoquant of the profit-maximizing output at this point of intersection. It is quite likely that there is a cheaper way to produce this output by employing the factor quantities indicated by a point of tangency between the isoquant and a lower isocost. The only way to attain this combination, however, is through a long-run adjustment in the plant size.

It would be best for a firm to select this plant size before production begins. While still in the planning stage a producer should estimate the range of output at which he is most likely to operate and design his plant to run at that rate. Unfortunately for our theory, prices and market conditions change, and the output a manager plans on as the profit-maximizing rate of production may turn out to be inappropriate. Theoretically, every time output changes, the scale of the plant should change also in order to keep costs at a minimum. This is obviously impractical. Different levels of output are attained through changes in labor input; that is, short-run adjustments. As a result, much output is produced in a less than optimally efficient manner. The wrong-sized plant is used in the sense that there is some other plant size that can theoretically produce the quantity in question more cheaply with a different amount of labor. Although this may seem trivial, we should recognize that it opens the way for a competitor with a plant closer to optimal size to sell at a lower price, because he can produce more cheaply. Such competitive pressures force long-run adjustments to be made in the direction of more efficient production. We wish now to turn attention to the theory of long-run adjustment of plant scale.

Will you discuss this in terms of the long- and short-run average cost curves?

It was pointed out in Chapter 6 that actual production costs are found on the firm's *short-run* average cost curve (*SAC*). This shows the cost of producing various quantities of output with *given* capital and *variable* amounts of labor. Also, there are a large number of other, hypothetical short-run average cost curves that would pertain if plants of other scales were built. There are many ways to produce each output, but there is one scale plant for each output at which cost of production is least. An envelope curve comprised of all these least-cost points serves as the long-run average cost curve (*LAC*). It is the *LAC* in that it shows the minimum cost of producing each output, if all inputs are free to vary. Of course, each plant can produce other outputs as well, and the cost of producing these other outputs is measured on the *SAC* curves. But for each of these "other" outputs there is another plant that can do it better, and these lower costs are shown on the *LAC* curve. As long as the adjustments in output are achieved through short-run means, we shall have a situation in which cost of production is higher than that shown on the long-run average cost curve. Only through long-run adjustments can the values shown on the *LAC* curve be attained

(Figures 8–25 and 8–26). Competitive pressures within the market drive the individual firms to make these long-run adjustments.

How are firms driven to make the long-run adjustments in production technique?

We have stressed the importance of mobility of resources in the competitive model. Individual firms readily enter and leave the market and can go from one industry to another. Capital resources are fluid and seek the highest profits attainable. We can therefore expect firms to leave industries in which profit opportunities are less than normal and enter those with greater-than-normal returns. The entry of firms into industries with greater-than-normal profits increases the supply of goods offered. This shows up on our diagrams as a shift to the right in the industry supply curve with a resultant drop in the equilibrium price. Similarly, by exiting from comparatively unprofitable industries, firms reduce supplies, shifting the industry supply curve to the left and increasing the market price (Figure 8–27). This diversion of resources from one industry to another works to raise the prices, and hence profits to be earned, in the industry losing resources, and to lower prices and profits to be earned in the gaining industry. As long as there is easy entry and exit of capital and none of the barriers discussed in Chapter 7 are operative, economic forces will push all industries in the direction of having the same rate of profit. In the long-run equilibrium, under pure competition all firms will earn a "normal" profit.

How much will the normal profit be?

We can't give it a number. The idea of normal profit must be considered in terms of opportunity cost. A normal profit is whatever can be made elsewhere. Entrepreneurship entails investing one's own capital in one's own business rather than lending it to someone else, and what is more, doing it at a risk rather than lending it backed by a collateralizing asset, so normal profit must at least cover what could be earned elsewhere, discounted for risk. Normal profit is whatever it takes to attract and keep capital in a given situation. It has been called *the supply price of entrepreneurship.* It is some percentage return on invested capital. It may be 10 percent, it may be 20 percent, it may be 100 percent. It depends on how the entrepreneur perceives the risk and uncertainty inherent in the business situation.

The important thing to realize is that normal profit is another opportunity cost. For this reason, the average cost curve includes not only explicit costs, implicit costs, and opportunity costs, but also normal profit. Therefore, if a firm earns normal profit on an item, our analysis

FIGURE 8–25. Comparison of Long- and Short-Run Cost of Production

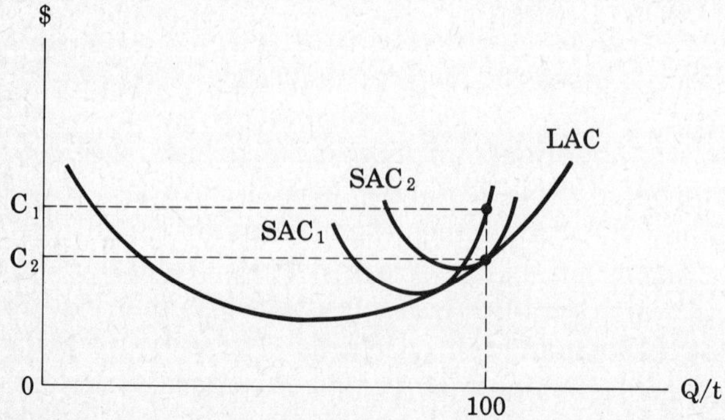

Output of 100 units can best be produced using a plant marked SAC_2 with an average cost of C_2. If, however, the plant whose short-run average cost curve is SAC_1 already exists, the only way to produce the 100 units is through more labor with this relatively small plant. However, the short-run average cost C_1 is higher than the optimum C_2. If a competitor were to enter and build the optimum plant for producing at a rate of 100 units of output, he could price his product lower because his average costs are lower.

FIGURE 8–26. Relationship of Isoquants to Average Cost Diagrams

Here we see that the long-run average cost of 100 units is equal to the total cost represented by the isocost that is tangent to the 100 isoquant, divided by 100.

$$LAC = \frac{T_1}{100}$$

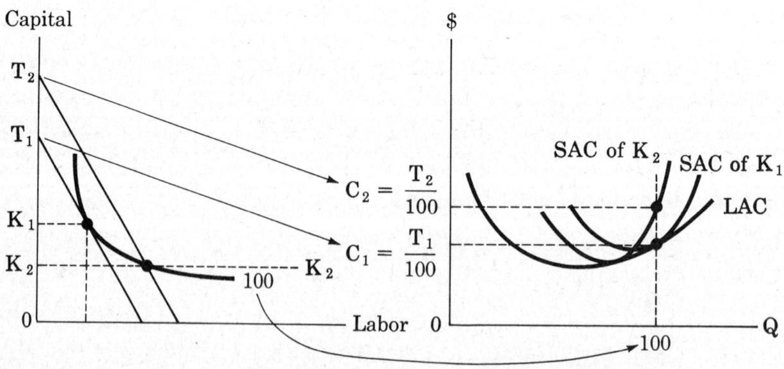

The short-run average cost is equal to the total cost represented by the isocost that intersects the 100 isoquant at the existing capital level, K_2, divided by 100.

$$SAC = \frac{T_2}{100}$$

FIGURE 8–27. Firms Entering and Leaving the Industry

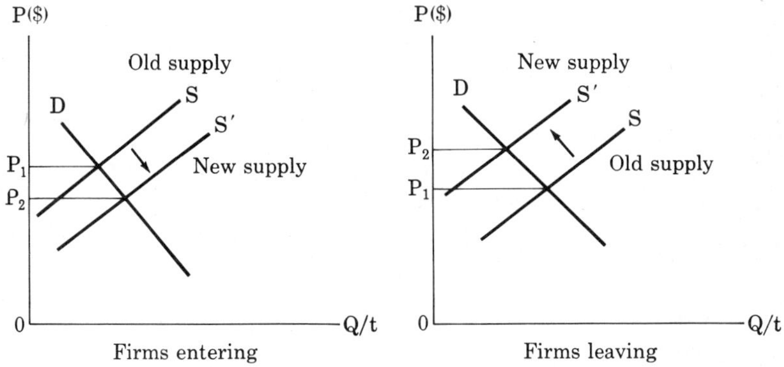

Firms attracted to an industry by high profit opportunities increase the supply of goods offered in the industry, and if demand remains steady, this will reduce the price. These firms must have left other industries, thereby reducing the supply of goods in those industries. If demand is steady, price will rise in those industries.

shows *average cost equal to price with zero economic profit.* The term economic profit is reserved for surplus earned beyond the normal return. You will remember, as discussed in Chapter 5, that we make the distinction between economic and accounting profit.

Please repeat again the difference between economic and accounting profit.

Again, economic profit equals total revenue minus economic cost. Economic cost includes normal profit. Therefore, when economic profit is zero, there is still an actual accounting profit being earned, equal in

FIGURE 8–28. Economic vs. Accounting Profit

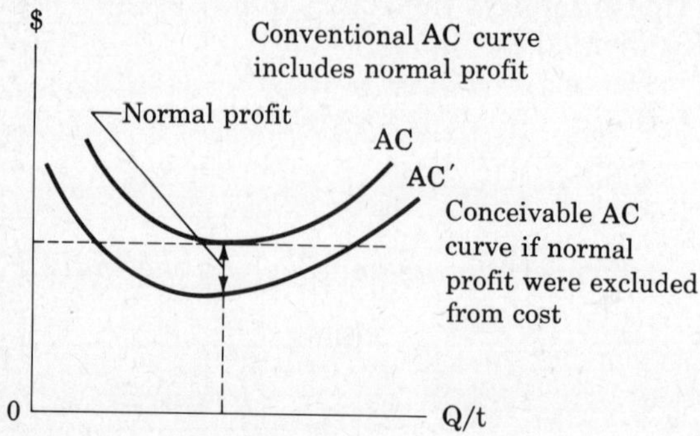

Is there any profit being earned here? Although there is no *economic* profit using curve *AC*, there is some accounting profit equal in amount to the normal profit. If it were excluded, the average cost curve would fall to *AC′*.

FIGURE 8–29. Profit Maximization—Long Run

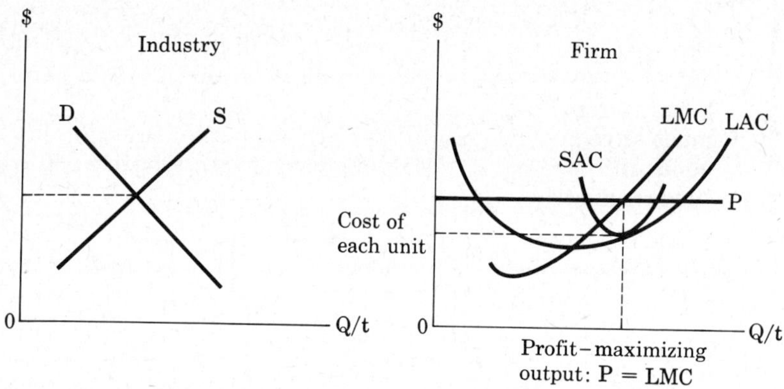

In order to maximize profits in the long run, the firm will produce that quantity at which long-run marginal cost equals the market-determined price. It uses the plant that is tangent to the long-run average cost curve at the profit-maximizing output.

size to normal profit. You will frequently see the equilibrium condition referred to as a zero profit condition, and may well ask: Why bother to knock yourself out if there is zero profit? The answer is that although there is zero economic profit in equilibrium, there is still a normal accounting profit, and this is equal to what could be earned elsewhere. If price exceeds average cost, then there is an economic profit and, of course, an accounting profit, that exceeds economic profit by an amount equal to normal profit (Figure 8–28).

Are you ready now to discuss the long-run equilibrium adjustments made by the firm?

We seem to have all of the pieces in place now. We can use the analysis of the long-run equilibrium of the firm to draw the many separate strands of our theory together. This is quite an important element of our theory, and deserves close attention.

First, let us one more time make the distinction between the market and the individual firm. Under pure competition the overall market comprises an infinite number of buyers and sellers. Diagrammatically, we represent the market (industry) by the conventional demand and supply curves, recognizing that the quantities are very large relative to those produced by the firm. The intersection of the industry supply and demand curves determines the equilibrium price that prevails until some force comes along to shift the demand or supply curve. As far as the individual competitor is concerned, this equilibrium price is a fact of life. It appears to him as a horizontal demand curve, denoting that he can sell as much or as little as he wants to at a constant price. We do well to look at the two diagrams side by side: the market curve on the left where the price is determined, and on the right the firm diagram where the price is perceived and reacted to by the individual firm (Figure 8–29).

How does the firm react to the market price?

Let us assume first that the firm does not yet have a plant built, but is in the planning stage. It knows that it will want to maximize its profit by producing the output at which marginal cost equals marginal revenue. No plant has been built yet, so it can vary all inputs and will want to produce the output at which *long-run* marginal cost equals price. In order to produce this output, a plant must be built and the plant size that is selected should be the one at which the profit-maximizing output can be most efficiently produced. This is the plant that has an *SAC* curve tangent to the *LAC* curve at the profit-maximizing output (Figure 8–29). Once the plant is built, we are in the short run. The plant should be run at the short-run profit-maximizing level.

FIGURE 8–30. Long-Run and Short-Run Profit-Maximizing Output are the Same

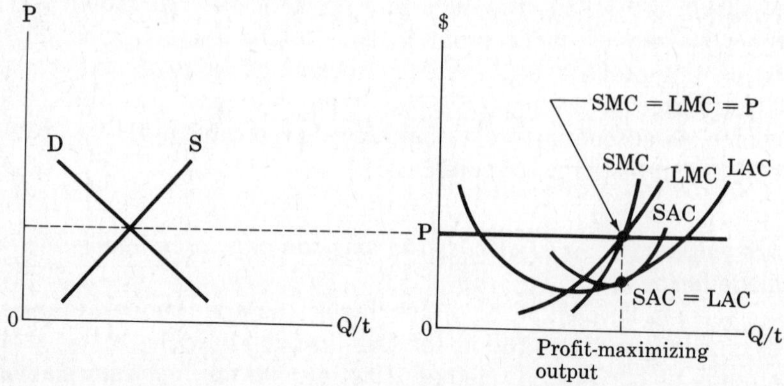

If the proper-size plant is used as far as long-run considerations are concerned, the level at which it operates to maximize short-run profits is the same as it is to maximize long-run profits. This occurs because the long- and short-run marginal costs are equal at the point at which the long- and short-run average cost curves touch.

But you have already fixed the quantity to be produced by equating price and long-run marginal costs. How can you now say that you must run the plant at the short-run profit-maximizing output?

We can say this because the scale of the plant we selected is the most efficient at producing the long-run profit-maximizing output. It so happens that this is also the short-run profit-maximizing output. To see this, you must turn back to Chapter 5, where we observed that the long-run marginal cost was equal to the short-run marginal cost at the same output at which long-run average cost equals short-run average cost. Look at what we have done here. First we equated price to long-run marginal cost. Then we built the plant that was designed for this output. The *SAC* curve for this plant is tangent to the *LAC* curve at this quantity. If *SAC* equals *LAC* at this output, the *SMC* must also equal the *LMC*. But *LMC* already equals price, so we therefore must conclude that short-run marginal cost will also equal price at this output. We are maximizing profits by both long- and short-run criteria, and shall continue to produce at this rate until something comes along to change the supply-demand market environment (Figure 8–30).

What happens then?
That depends on what changes. We have drawn Figure 8–30 to show an economic profit being earned. The demand curve is higher than the average cost curve at the profit-maximizing output. It was suggested earlier that an economic profit in excess of the normal profit that can be earned elsewhere is looked on with greed and envy. Producers working in less profitable areas are tempted to leave their current industries and enter into this one, and in fact a certain number will. They will enter the industry and build the same profit-maximizing-size plant geared to the market price, and begin to produce. The only problem is that when enough competitors enter the industry, they will increase the supply of goods flowing into the market, and the effect will be to shift the market supply curve to the right. Notice what happens. The shifting supply lowers the equilibrium price. As a result, the individual firms face a different horizontal demand curve. It is still horizontal, but it is lower on the diagram. What is more, marginal cost now intersects it at a different point. Profit-maximizing output is smaller. Firms already in existence using the first-size plant will want to reduce their output to equate the short-run marginal cost with the new price. They must do this through *short-run* means of labor cutback, and will find themselves producing in a comparatively inefficient manner. However, new firms, which continue to be attracted as long as there are economic profits to be made, will tend to build the smaller plants that maximize profits, shown by the intersection of the long-run marginal cost curve and the demand curve. The process continues, with new plants, drawn by profits, entering and, as they do, shifting the supply curve to the right. As the supply curve shifts to the right, equilibrium price gets lower and lower (Figure 8–31).

How far can price fall?
Price will continue to fall as long as new firms are attracted to the industry and add their output to the total supply. New firms will be attracted to the industry as long as there are economic profits to be made. It would appear that price can fall no lower than the low point on the long-run average cost curve, because at any lower level the firm would be incurring economic losses. Should this happen, firms would leave the industry. Normal profits could be earned elsewhere, and profits are better than losses. Because producers come in when prices are above the low point on the *LAC* curve and leave when prices are below this level, the low point represents the *long-run* equilibrium price. Price cannot permanently exceed this level, because entrance of other firms would drive it down. Price cannot remain below it, because exit of firms would reduce supply and raise price. Therefore the long-run equi-

FIGURE 8–31. *A Sequence of Adjustments*

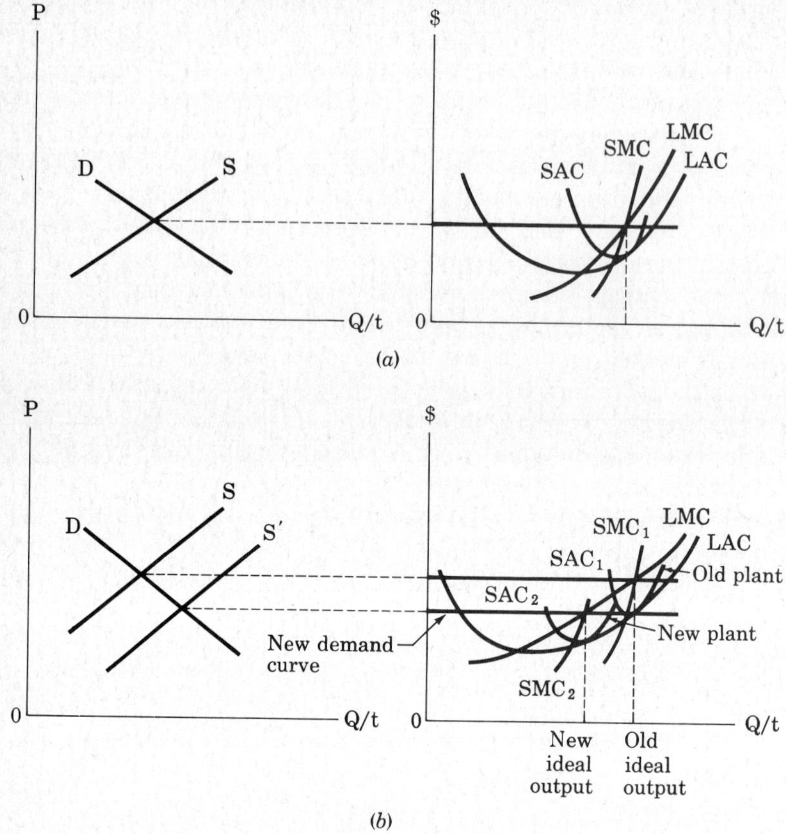

If firms produce at profit-maximizing levels as shown in part (*a*), there are abnormal profits generated. These attract entry and this shifts the supply curve, as shown in part (*b*). The shift in the supply curve produces a lower price, and the result is a reduction in the size of the optimal plant (because *P* equals *LMC* at a lower level of output) and also a lower rate at which the plant should operate (because *P* equals *SMC* at a lower output). This continues as long as there are abnormal profits earned in the industry.

FIGURE 8–32. Long-Run Equilibrium

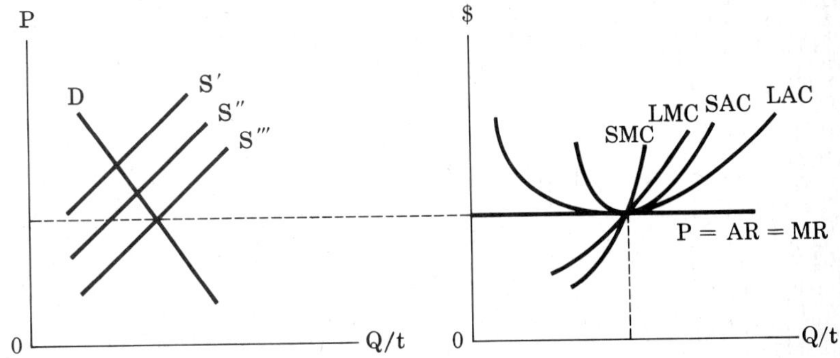

In long-run equilibrium price gets driven down as far as it can go without producing abnormally low profits or losses. This is the point of zero economic profits and is seen as the low point on the long-run average cost curve. Here the demand curve intersects the *LMC* and *SMC* and is tangent to both *SAC* and *LAC*; that is, all are equal in value. This low point represents the most efficient production. However, we should recognize that production occurs at this rate, not because production is efficient but because it is profit-maximizing.

librium price is one that generates zero economic profit for all firms in the industry.

Do firms profit-maximize at this equilibrium price level?
Yes, the long-run equilibrium output is an interesting one in that $LAC = SAC = LMC = SMC = P$ at this point. The demand curve will just be tangent to the *LAC* curve at its low point. At this point the *SAC* curve is also tangent, and both are intersected by their respective marginal cost curves. Thus the profit-maximizing condition is met. Price equals both short-run and long-run marginal cost (Figure 8–32).

It looks as if the firms are producing at a pretty efficient rate even while they are profit-maximizing.
One of the characteristics of pure competition that delights economists is this observation that the profit-maximizing output is also the most

FIGURE 8–33. External Diseconomies—Increasing Cost

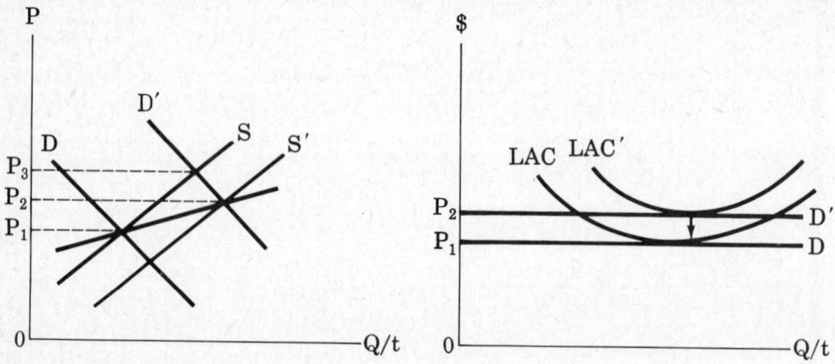

Assume that we are in equilibrium with price P_1. If demand now increases, price is bid up to P_3. This attracts new firms into the industry. If, upon entering, they bid up the cost of labor and other factors of production, the long-run average cost curves of all firms in the industry will be raised. This in turn will raise the minimum price at which normal profits can be earned, and so the equilibrium market price of the product will rise as industry output goes up. This is shown by a rising industry supply curve.

efficient in the long-run. If these firms are producing at the lowest point on their average cost curves, they are producing in the most efficient manner possible. This represents the ideal to the economist: saving of resources; getting prices as low as they can go and still attract suppliers; maximum efficiency. To the micro theorist, perfect competition is beautiful. Adam Smith's invisible hand is working, God's in his heaven and all's right with the world.

How long will it last?

As we said, equilibrium lasts until something comes along to disturb it. Equilibrium means that everyone is satisfied under the circumstances. If we vary the circumstances, we may engender some dissatisfaction someplace in the market and set off another chain of events. Let us suppose, for example, that after achieving equilibrium, the market was suddenly jolted by an increase in total demand. Something akin to this happened in the bicycle industry, which for years was a fairly stable producer of recreation for children in the United States and of basic transportation for adults in Europe. Then the combined effects of the ecologists' damning auto exhaust pollution and the energy crisis leapfrogging the price of gasoline produced a fairly sudden awakening to the transportation possibilities of the bicycle among adult Americans. The result was rightward shift in the market demand curve. As you can see, this raises the equilibrium price and shifts the demand curves facing the individual firms upward. Economic profits appeared in the industry and new firms were drawn toward it. The process discussed earlier again unfolded as the industry sought a new equilibrium price level.

Why won't the new price level be the same as the old, only with more firms in the industry now?
It may be. Then again it may not. It depends on whether growth of the industry creates external economies or diseconomies of scale.

What are external economies and diseconomies of scale?
We considered these in Chapter 5. The terms refer to the effects that changes in the size of an industry may have on the cost functions of its constituent firms. We pointed out that as the industry grows, some forces tend to push costs up. Other forces work in the opposite direction, depressing costs. Both tendencies occur simultaneously, and the dominant effect is to cause a net shift upward or downward in the long-run average cost curve. A shift upward implies net external diseconomies of scale, whereas a shift down indicates net economies of scale.

How do external economies and diseconomies affect the equilibrium?
Remember that the market price will continue to change as long as there are abnormal profits or losses in an industry. If the *LAC* curve shifts down due to external economies, the market price could fall to even lower levels than earlier before squeezing out all the profits. On the other hand, if there are external diseconomies, the new equilibrium price will be higher than before. These external economies and diseconomies add a dynamic element to the analysis. By connecting the intersections of the supply and demand curves on the industry half of Figures 8–33, 8–34, and 8–35, we can create what is called a *long-run industry supply curve*. Industries with external diseconomies of scale are called *increasing-cost industries*, and the long-run industry supply curve slopes up to the right. If, on the other hand, the industry has increasing external economies of scale, it is called a *decreasing-cost*

FIGURE 8–34. External Economies—Decreasing Cost

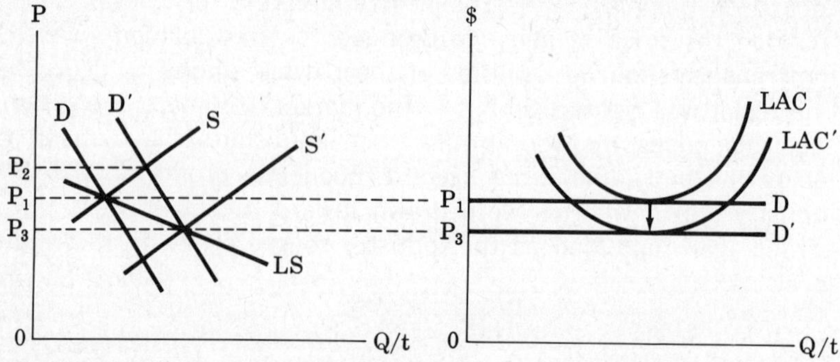

If entry of new firms to the industry encourages the creation of specialized ancillary service industries that make production more efficient, the long-run average cost curve shifts down. This permits increased industry output to be sold at lower prices.

FIGURE 8–35. No External Economies—Constant Cost

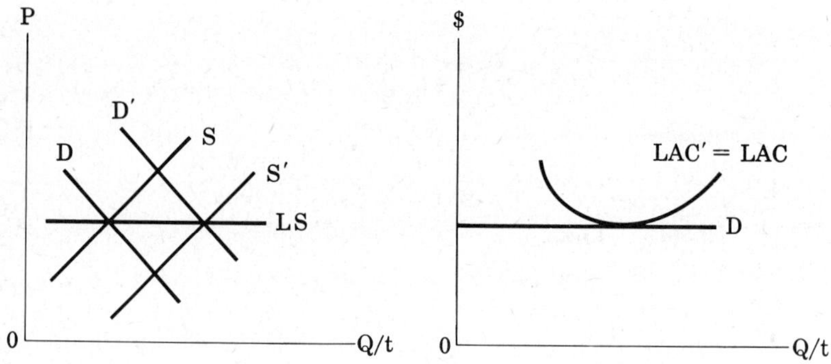

If the factors making for external economies of scale are exactly offset by those making for external diseconomies, the long-run average cost curve will remain at a steady level and the industry will supply increased output at a constant price.

industry, and the long-run industry supply curve slopes down. The simplest assumption is for a horizontal long-run industry supply curve, implying a *constant-cost industry.*

CHAPTER HIGHLIGHTS

1. *We defined pure competition and recognized that it is an ideal, rather than a description of a market condition that actually exists.*
2. *Within the competitive market, the impersonal forces of supply and demand interact to determine an equilibrium price that will clear the market.*
3. *We recognized that this price is seen by each individual firm in the competitive industry as an inescapable fact of life over which it can exert no control. The demand curve representing such a fact was seen to be a horizontal line.*
4. *We saw that a profit-maximizing firm under pure competition attempts to produce the output at which its short- and long-run marginal cost curves intersect the horizontal demand curve from below.*
5. *The possibility of loss came up, and we decided that in the short run a firm should continue to produce as long as price is greater than average variable cost.*
6. *We noted that over the long run firms losing money will leave the industry. We saw that this will reduce the supply offered in the market and will tend to increase the market price. When there are firms making a more-than-normal profit in an industry, new firms will be attracted to it. The entry of these new firms will increase supply and tend to reduce price.*
7. *We found that over the long run the equilibrium price will stabilize at a level that just equals the minimum long-run cost of production, thereby creating zero economic profits in equilibrium.*
8. *We discussed external economies and diseconomies and the manner in which they affect long-run equilibrium.*

QUESTIONS

1. *One author has written, "This is the day of the supermarket. . . . The most potent weapon of competition is price . . . and supermarkets can undersell smaller food outlets whenever they need to or want to because of the economies inherent in mass buying, mass distribution and mass management." Do you think this author is an economist?*
2. *"The New York Stock Exchange is a perfectly competitive market for stocks but not for brokers." Evaluate this statement. It has been said that if you want the Exchange to be a competitive market for stock, it cannot be a competitive market for brokers. Evaluate.*
3. *"A business firm tries to minimize the cost of whatever output it*

produces, but it does not attempt to produce the output at which it minimizes its cost." Think this statement through if you can, and explain if it is true or false.

4. *Two types of tax that may be levied on a business firm are an excise (per-unit) tax that varies with output and a franchise (lump-sum) tax that is paid once each year in a fixed amount. The excise tax is said to affect the profit-maximizing output a producer will make, but the lump-sum tax does not. Can you explain why?*
5. *The classical economists believe that the price of a thing was determined by its cost of production. The neoclassical economists stressed marginal utility. In light of what you known about the long-run equilibrium position of the firm, can you find some support for the classical position?*
6. *Fishermen lobby to have their coastal waters protected up to a distance of 200 miles. They claim that allowing foreign competition into the area drives up their costs. Is this a case of external diseconomies of scale? Explain.*
7. *When Adam Smith described how the "invisible hand" worked to maximize the social welfare, he did so without the benefit of marginal analysis or any of the tools employed in this chapter. The key elements of the invisible hand were profit incentive on the part of each producer and competition among producers. Explain how these ingredients work to produce the result Smith described, using the analysis employed in this chapter.*
8. *Adam Smith did not specifically mention external economies of scale. Do you think he would have agreed with the idea?*

9 Imperfect competion: monopoly and monopolistic competion

Imperfect competition is the term used to refer to markets in which any of the conditions required for perfect competition are violated. Since our purpose here is to develop a theory of economic behavior and our approach is heavily deductive, we have proceeded by making certain assumptions. Through deductive reasoning we have drawn conclusions about the behavior of economic units and the consequences of that behavior. The assumptions for pure competition are: (1) homogeneous products, (2) many small buyers and sellers, (3) perfectly mobile resources, and (4) free flow of information. A thumbnail sketch of the long-run equilibrium conclusions shows that (1) firms produce where price equals marginal cost, (2) in the long-run production is carried on in the most efficient-sized plant, (3) in the short run plants run at their most efficient rates of output, and (4) in the long run prices just cover costs and economic profits are zero. We now ask what happens to these conclusions when we omit, or violate, one or more of the assumptions of perfect competition.

What types of departures can we have from the assumptions of pure competition?

Any or all of the four assumptions cited above may be violated. The extent of the departure can range from very slight shadings to great and dramatic leaps. Curiously enough, the analytical differences do not shade off in such a smooth and continuous manner. The analysis for pure competition is *qualitatively* different from that of *any* form of imperfect competition. Under perfect competition each firm faces a horizontal demand curve. We shall see that this demand curve is instrumental in producing the optimum degree of efficiency gained under pure competition. As soon as the analysis departs from pure competition in any manner, we lose the horizontal demand curve facing the firm. Instead, each firm faces a more conventional, downward-sloping demand curve. Although a wide constellation of conditions share the name imperfect competition, and they differ from one another in many important ways, they all embody the common-element of a downward-sloping demand curve facing the firm. This common denominator makes the analyses of the various cases very similar to each other despite the difference in underlying conditions. We shall consider now the different divergences from the competitive model that can occur. They involve homogeneity of product, number of buyers and sellers, mobility of resources, and flow of information.

What different assumptions can we make about product homogeneity? Under pure competition we insisted that the products of all producers were homogeneous down to the point of being standardized and certified as such by a governmental agency. Examples were drawn from the agricultural industries, although basic industrial products also serve. Cement, steel, burlap—all of these can be thought of as homogeneous. However, let us look a little more deeply into this. When you buy a standardized product, from whom do you buy it? Do you buy it from an impersonal market, or do you buy it from a particular person, working for a particular firm for a particular number of years and with whom you may have had lunch, or played golf, or from whom you may have received a case of whiskey at Christmas time. Obviously, most business transactions involve personal relationships among human beings, and to the extent that a buyer thinks of a salesman from one firm as being different from that of another, the products they sell are no longer homogeneous. Standardization can be an illusion.

To take another example, consider the proposal to reduce medical costs by having physicians prescribe generic drug products rather than brand-name products. The reasoning put forth is that the drugs are all standardized according to the U.S. Pharmacopoeia requirements and are therefore interchangeably homogeneous. The industry argues in rebuttal (as do some but not all physicians) that although the active agents in a drug product are standardized, quality control, compounding techniques, and materials and general reliability of the manufacturers differ. They claim that once again homogeneity is an illusion. Service, reliability, and reputation are all just as important in product differentiation as are the physical traits of the product itself.

Branding is an extremely strong force for product differentiation, particularly in the consumer goods area. When a trade name is backed up by years of supportive advertising, very strong loyalties can be engendered. "As similar as peas in a pod" takes on a different meaning when one pea is a Del Monte brand and another is Green Giant. These peas are in no way identical, thanks to millions of dollars spent in promotional effort.

Location, too, is an obvious force for differentiation. Although all company-owned Exxon stations are pretty much alike, and certainly all franchised McDonald hamburger stands are designed to appear interchangeable, the fact that one in particular happens to be located close by gives it a unique advantage over its more remote competitors.

It should be obvious from these observations that perfect substitutability turns out to be an even stricter requirement than we would have suspected. Differentiation is the norm, not standardization. And as long as there is differentiation, the market is imperfectly competitive.

What variations can occur in the model in terms of numbers of buyers and sellers?

The number of buyers and sellers can range from zero to infinity. If there are zero participants in the market, it is because there is general agreement that the product cannot be made and sold at a profit. One of the fascinating things about the market economy is that if there is any way in which a good can be made and exchanged profitably, it will be.

If there is one seller in the market, we have a unique situation, qualitatively different from markets with two or more sellers. This situation is known as *monopoly*, and we shall deal with it extensively in this chapter. Obviously, if we consider that there is only one seller of a product, the product he offers must be unique on the basis of some criterion. If it is Alcoa during the 1930s, the product is unique to the extent that aluminum's qualities of stain resistance, light weight, conductivity, and strength may be needed on a job. However, where these qualities are not important, aluminum is just another metal competing alongside steel and copper and, in some cases, wood and concrete. There is a monopoly in the case where the product is wanted for airplanes, but a highly competitive market if it is wanted for construction. The particular market—not the product—determines whether or not we are dealing with a monopoly.

When the number of sellers exceeds one, but not by too many, we go from monopoly to oligopoly. There are a series of analyses that have been developed for the two-seller case of duopoly that most dramatically illustrate the problems of oligopoly. These problems are so different from those of monopoly that we shall split them out for discussion purposes and take them up in the next chapter.

Going from the case of a few to that of very many suppliers of differentiated products brings us to another set of circumstances that is like perfect competition on the basis of number of firms, but like imperfect competition in terms of the homogeneity of the product. This is the case of monopolistic competition, and we shall take it up shortly in this chapter.

What happens when the mobility of resources is blocked?

We saw in Chapter 6 that resources may not move into a profitable industry because of "barriers to entry." This term implies that the resources *would be mobile* if they were not somehow impeded. There are many institutions in our society that block the mobility of resources. Students ask why the miners of the Appalachian region of the United States didn't leave their homes to seek employment in the cities even though they could not eke out an adequate living from the mines. The truth seems to be that they like it where they are. The barriers are self-imposed. Similarly, in the good old days when our agricultural problems involved too much rather than too little food being produced, we used to describe it as a case of too many farmers rather than too much food. "Why don't they go to the city?" we would ask. Of course, millions of farmers did pull up stakes and go to work in industry. However, others stayed to live on less money, but in familiar and comfortable surroundings. Again, resources were not as mobile as economic models presume.

In addition to these self-imposed barriers, there are, of course, cases of intentional blocking of entry to profitable areas. We discussed this in Chapter 6. The high profits found in oligopolistic or monopolistic industries would certainly invite entry. However, we have seen that free entry eventually reduces economic profits to zero. There is obviously an incentive for producers to try to keep competition out of a profitable area. The monopoly model presumes the most success in this endeavor.

The consequences of barring competition are inevitably that higher prices are charged and fewer goods are offered in the market by the monopolized industries. Furthermore, the resources that might have gone into the barred industry remain unemployed, or are instead allocated to other markets where entry is easier. This acts to lower factor costs, increase supplies, and depress equilibrium price below the levels that would prevail otherwise.

Suppose that free flow of information is blocked?

One of the characteristics of a market-clearing equilibrium price is that all transactions occur at that price. We were able to draw the *horizontal* demand curve in pure competition because of this. In order for a single price to prevail in a market, it is necessary that everyone know the opportunities available in the market and the location and characteristics of other participants, as well as the prices at which they are doing business. If there were no free flow of information, the markets would become much more imperfect. In effect, small clusters of traders would deal with each other without awareness of opportunities elsewhere. The prices at which exchange takes place would differ from transaction to transaction.

Information is not free in the marketplace. It is acquired through the effort of search and comparison by the buyer and disseminated in the form of advertising and public relations by the seller. Because information is *not* a free good, it is frequently found to be inadequate for perfect market activity. Once again, the principle of opportunity cost will determine whether buyer and seller consider the benefits derived from information to be worth its cost. If not, they simply will not make the effort. We have all had the experience of shopping and comparing prices of automobiles for weeks before buying one, but simply picking a can of beans off the shelf without ever bothering to read the ads or to shop in different stores to see if beans are available for less elsewhere.

Although a perfect flow of information is necessary for a one-price market to exist, it is not sufficient to guarantee that such a market *will* exist. We shall deal at some length with the nature of price discrimination, whereby sellers with monopoly power are able to sell to different buyers at different prices, *despite* good information flows. However, although price discrimination is possible even with full information, it would become the rule without it.

Now that we have outlined some of the possible deviations from the pure competition model, we shall go on in this chapter to examine the monopoly and monopolistic competition models, and to look at the theory of oligopoly in the next.

What are the major characteristics of the pure monopoly model?

The first thing one notes in all models of imperfectly competitive markets is that the demand curve facing the individual firm always slopes downward to the right. This means that a supplier must accept a lower price if he wishes to increase the number of units sold and, of course, if he raises the price, he can expect to sell fewer units. This is in con-

FIGURE 9–1. Imperfect Competition Involves Downward-Sloping Demand Curves

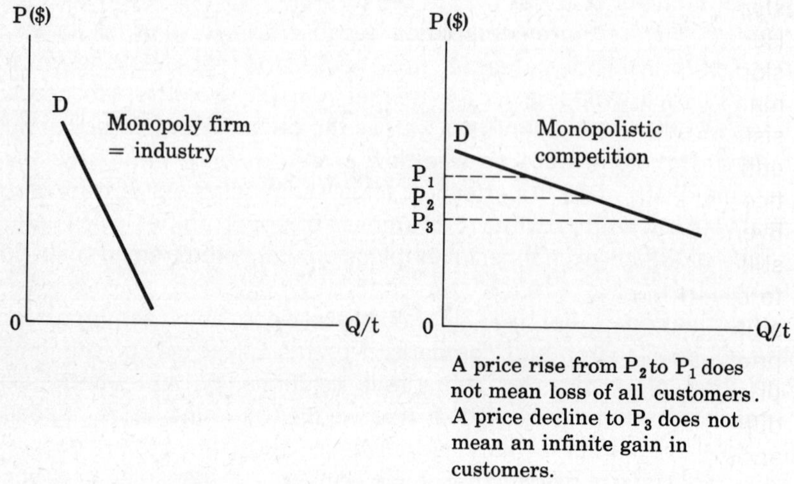

Under all forms of imperfect competition, the demand curve facing the individual firm slopes down to the right. Under pure monopoly the firm curve is the same as the industry curve and hence has the price elasticity characteristic of the generic product. Under monopolistic competition demand is highly elastic, because there are other, similar products available. However, they are not perceived by everyone to be *perfect* substitutes. Hence the downward tilt to the demand curve.

trast to the pure competitor, who is able to sell as many units as he can produce at a fixed price, but can expect to see his sales disappear completely in the event that he raises price at all. The reason the monopolist faces a downward-sloping curve is that he, by definition, is the only supplier in the industry. If the industry demand curve for the product is downward sloping (for reasons discussed in Chapter 2), then so too is the monopolist's. If the market will take more units at lower prices, this single seller provides them. If the market will accept less at higher prices, then it is this single seller who suffers the loss in volume.

I can see why the monopolist faces a downward-sloping demand curve. Why is the demand curve under monopolistic competition downward sloping?

Here the situation is different. Whereas the demand curve of a firm slopes down, its elasticity of demand is higher than that of the full market. Remember that in monopolistic competition the industry consists of a large group of firms offering similar, but nevertheless differentiated versions of a good or service. The marketing of soap or dentrifice provides an example of the world of monopolistic competition. Everyone knows that soap is soap and toothpaste is toothpaste, but still in all, advertising, shape, scent, packaging, color, and taste work to differentiate one brand from another. Consumers develop brand loyalties because they come to believe that these qualities matter. If the price of one brand is increased while the others remain unchanged, the price raiser will not lose *all* his customers. There are some to whom the differentiating qualities are more important than the price differential, and they will remain loyal. To others, however, the price differential is more important, and they will switch to competing brands. This reduction, but not complete annihilation, of sales gives the demand curve its slope. By the same token, lowering price will not increase quantity sold infinitely, because the competition also has brand-loyal purchasers who will remain with their favorites even though another is available at a lower price. If a firm plans to lower price, its advertising task is to convince the public that all soap is alike. If it is going to raise price, the message must be that differentiation is important. Note that the elasticity of demand of the individual product is considerably higher than that of the industry. We do not expect a few cents down on the price of soap in general to bring great new numbers of unwashed customers to the soap industry. We do expect, however, a few cents down on one brand to win a large number of users away from the competition (Figure 9–1).

How does the fact that the demand curve facing the firm slopes down affect the equilibrium analysis?

When the demand curve slopes downward, rather than running horizontally as in pure competition, the profit-maximizing decision becomes more difficult. Remember that profit is the difference between total revenue and total cost. Under pure competition increasing output always increases total revenue, because price is constant. However, under imperfect competition increasing output may cause a reduction in total revenue received. Because price must go down for quantity to go up, it all depends on the price elasticity of demand. Where demand is relatively inelastic, increases in quantity reduce total revenue. Where de-

FIGURE 9–2. Relationship of Marginal Revenue to Demand Curve

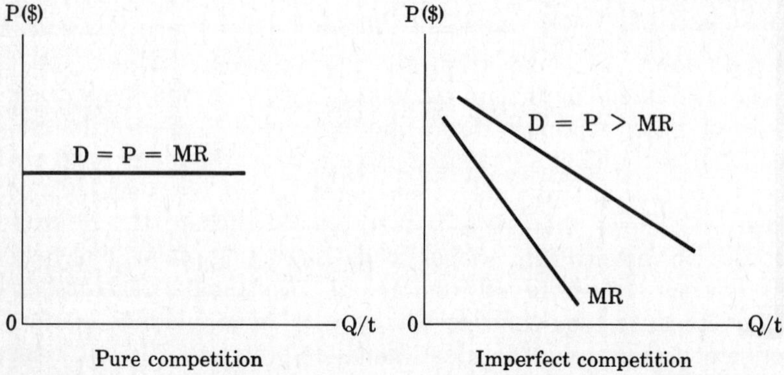

Under pure competition the demand curve and marginal revenue curve are the same horizontal line. Under imperfect competition marginal revenue lies below the downward-sloping demand curve. Thus, for any output, $P > MR$.

FIGURE 9–3. A Hypothetical Demand Shedule

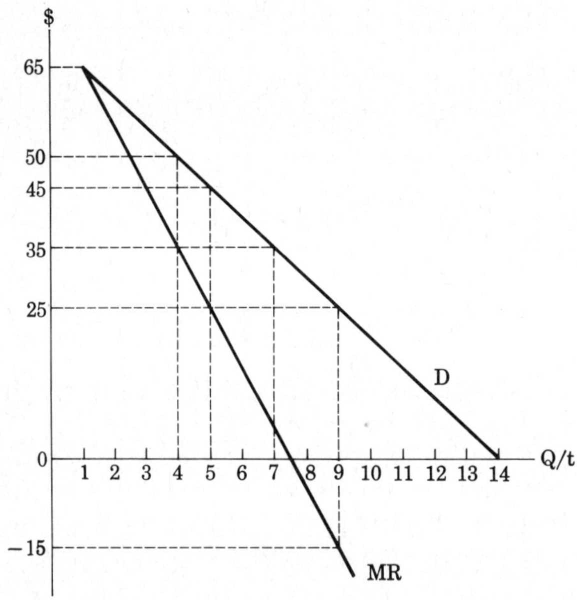

Quantity	Price ($)	Total revenue $P \times Q$	Marginal revenue $PQ_n - PQ_{n-1}$
1	65	65	65
2	60	120	55
3	55	165	45
4	50	200	35
5	45	225	25
6	40	240	15
7	35	245	5
8	30	240	−5
9	25	225	−15
10	20	200	−25
11	15	165	−35
12	10	120	−45

mand is relatively elastic, increases in quantity raise total revenue. And, of course, when we deal with increases or decreases in total revenue occurring with changes in quantity, we are dealing with marginal revenue. Marginal revenue behaves quite differently when the demand curve slopes downward than when it is horizontal.

How does the marginal revenue curve behave when the demand curve slopes downward?

If you remember, under pure competition marginal revenue equals the price (average revenue), and the demand curve and marginal revenue curve are represented by the same horizontal line. Under imperfect competition the marginal revenue curve always lies below the demand curve. For any given quantity, marginal revenue is less than average revenue (Figure 9–2). When we examined costs, we pointed out that as long as average cost was falling, marginal cost was below it, and when average cost increased, marginal cost was above it. We discussed the relationship between marginal and average values. Well, here we have another pair of average and marginal curves. If the average revenue curve slopes downward, the marginal revenue curve must lie beneath it, simply because it requires lower-than-average values to pull the average down. Although this arithmetic rationalization is sound, there is another line of thought that can give us greater insight into the nature of markets, and we shall discuss it now.

Why does the marginal revenue curve lie below the downward-sloping demand curve?

A demand curve, by definition, shows the different quantities that can be sold at different prices. We see in Figure 9–3 that 4 units can be

FIGURE 9–4. Profit-Maximizing Price and Output Under Monopoly Conditions

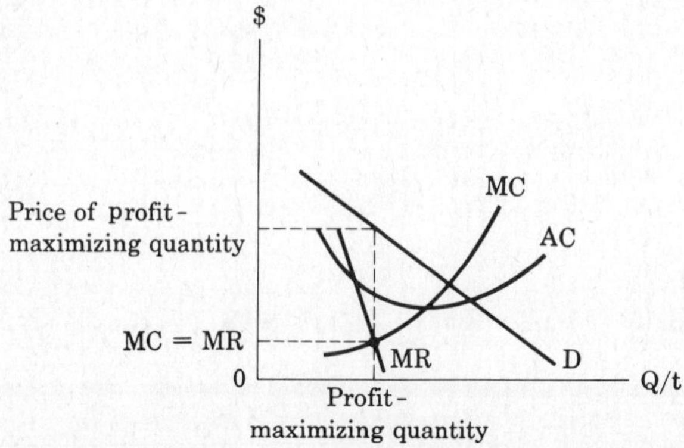

A profit-maximizing producer will offer that quantity at which marginal cost equals marginal revenue. The price at which this quantity can be sold is then read from the demand curve.

sold at price \$50, and 5 units will be sold at price \$45. The marginal revenue of the fifth unit is the difference between total revenues of 4 and 5 units: \$225 − 200 = \$25. Because this marginal revenue of \$25 is less than the price of \$45, we have an illustration of the point that the marginal revenue curve lies below the demand curve.

An interesting way of looking at this is to recognize that in order to sell the fifth unit, the price *had* to be reduced from \$50 to \$45 on the first 4 units as well. In the absence of price discrimination, there is only one price in the market at one time, and *each* unit sells for this price. The selling of the fifth unit permitted an additional \$45 to be taken in (the price of a unit), but it also required that \$5 be lost on each of the 4 units that could have been sold at a price of \$50. We must break the marginal revenue computation into two parts: the plus part from selling the extra unit, and the minus part from having to reduce price on all other units in order to sell the additional unit. In this case, the computation involves + \$45 and − \$20, for a marginal revenue of + \$25. This, of course, is the same marginal revenue we found by subtracting the total revenues from each other.

Look at one other example. We find that in order to increase sales from 8 to 9 units in Figure 9–3, the price must fall from \$30 to \$25. Therefore, the marginal revenue consists of, on the one hand, + \$25 gained from selling the ninth unit and, on the other hand, − \$40 representing the – $5 on each of 8 units that might have been sold at the higher price. The net result is a negative marginal revenue of – $15. Remember that negative marginal revenue is associated with demand elasticity that is less than one. When a reduction in price is accompanied by a reduction in total revenue (negative marginal revenue), the demand is relatively inelastic. This has an interesting connotation for the profit-maximizing decision.

What is the implication of negative marginal revenue for the profit-maximizing decision?

A profit maximizer attempts to produce at the output where marginal revenue equals marginal cost. If marginal revenue is negative, it means that a profit maximizer would produce at a quantity at which marginal cost is also negative. However, negative marginal cost is highly unlikely. It means that it costs less to produce a bigger quantity than a smaller one, or that as you raise total output, you reduce total cost. This just does not happen. A profit-maximizing producer will always offer a quantity that falls within the elastic (positive marginal revenue) range of the demand schedule.

How does a profit-maximizing monopolist select the level of output and price at which to produce?

The characteristics of the *cost curves* under monopoly are generally the same as those under pure competition. We shall see that an exception occurs in the case of "natural monopoly," but for the most part we assume a U-shaped average cost curve, with a marginal cost curve that intersects it from below and passes through its low point. A profit maximizer looks for the output at which this upward-sloping marginal cost curve intersects the downward-sloping marginal revenue curve. Although the *x* coordinate of this point of intersection gives the quantity, the *y* coordinate does *not* give the price. Price is not found on either the marginal revenue or marginal cost lines It is on the demand curve. Therefore it is necessary to project upward to the demand curve to find the price at which the profit-maximizing output will sell (Figure 9–4). It is safe to anticipate that at least one of you will make the error of trying to read price from the marginal revenue curve. This *is* an error and, being forewarned, you should make sure you are not the one who makes it.

Where is the monopolist's profit on the chart?

First, you should recognize that being a monopolist does not necessarily ensure a profit. Amtrak has proven that. Since taking over passenger

FIGURE 9–5. Profit and Loss of a Monopolist

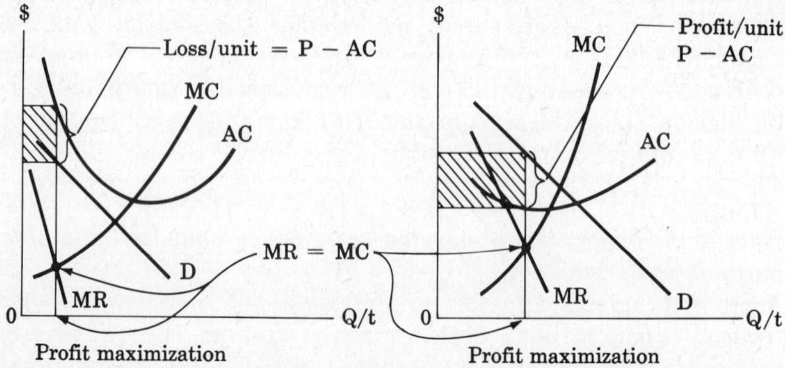

Profit (loss) is represented by the difference between total revenue and total cost. On our diagrams this is found by subtracting average cost (at the profit-maximizing output) from average revenue and multiplying this difference by the quantity sold. The rectangle bounded by quantity on one side and unit profit on the other represents total profit.

service on the railroads, Amtrak has incurred prodigious losses. It does this because the demand curve for its services lies below the average cost curve. At prices high enough to cover costs, few people use the trains. Most are priced out of the market. At prices low enough to attract passengers, costs exceed revenues. Amtrak, at the moment, is an unhappy monopolist.

However, loss or profit, as the case may be, are seen by comparing costs and revenues on the diagram (Figure 9–5). Average revenue is found on the demand curve. Average cost is found on the average cost curve. The difference, at any level of output, is the average profit (or loss). Multiplying by quantity gives the total profit or loss. This can be represented with the rectangle used in the earlier models.

A point to note is that regardless of whether there is profit or loss, the price in monopoly is always higher than the marginal cost, because marginal cost is set equal to marginal revenue for profit maximization, and price is always higher than marginal revenue. We do agree on that, don't we?

Is there any quantitative relationship between price and marginal cost? There is a very interesting and broadly used relationship. Let me give it to you before attempting to prove it. The relationship is

$$MR = P - \frac{P}{e}$$

or marginal revenue is equal to price minus the price divided by the coefficient of price elasticity of demand. One thing you can see immediately is that under pure competition, where elasticity is equal to infinity, the P/e term equals zero and MR equals P. This, of course, is the case of the horizontal demand curve.

What happens to the formula when elasticity is unitary?

Straightforward substitution into the formula says that the P/e term becomes $P/1$, or just P. Now the right-hand side of the equation is $P - P$ or zero. We know that a marginal revenue of zero occurs when elasticity is one. We also demonstrated in Chapter 3 that total revenue is maximized when price elasticity of demand equals one, and this means that marginal revenue is zero (Figure 9–6).

Additionally, we can note that when elasticity is less than one, that is, when demand is relatively inelastic, the P/e term becomes bigger than P. Therefore the right-hand side of the equation, $P - P/e$, is negative. We can examine other cases of elasticity, price, and marginal revenue, but these few applications using the formula to reach conclusions with which we are already familiar should confirm its validity and usefulness.

We started out to talk about the difference between marginal cost and price. The formula refers to marginal revenue and price.

That is true. Marginal cost comes in through the effort of a profit-maximizing producer to equate MC with MR. MC will take on the same value as MR at the profit-maximizing output. Most of the problems involve attempts to maximize profits, so this relationship proves to be quite useful.

Can you prove the formula?

I can try. We observed that it is necessary to reduce price in order to sell an additional unit of output and that the effect of this reduction in price on total revenue is twofold: It adds to total revenue through the proceeds realized on the marginal unit, but it also subtracts from total revenue because a reduction must be taken on the price of the other units that could have been sold at the former, higher price.

In Figure 9–7 P_1 and Q_1 equal the old price and quantity (high price, low quantity) and P_2 and Q_2 equal the new price and quantity (low price,

FIGURE 9–6. Applications of the MR = P − P/e *Formula*

(*a*) When total revenue is maximized, marginal revenue is zero. This occurs when elasticity is unitary.

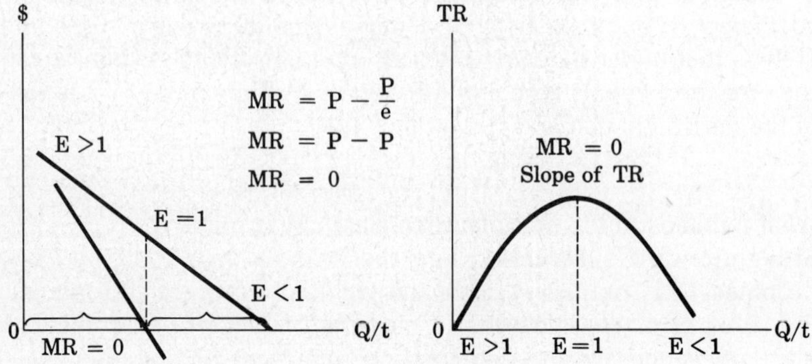

(*b*) When marginal revenue is negative, elasticity is less than one.

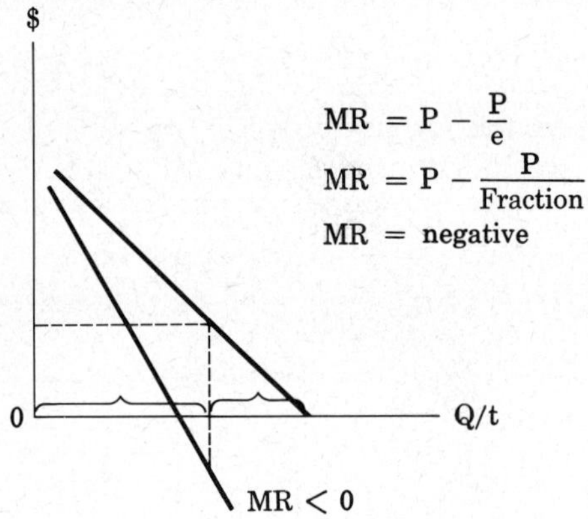

(*c*) Under pure competition MR = P.

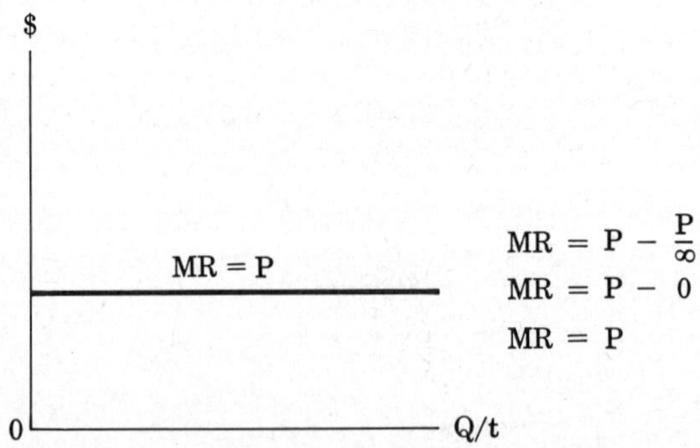

FIGURE 9–7. Derivation of MR = P − P/e *Formula*

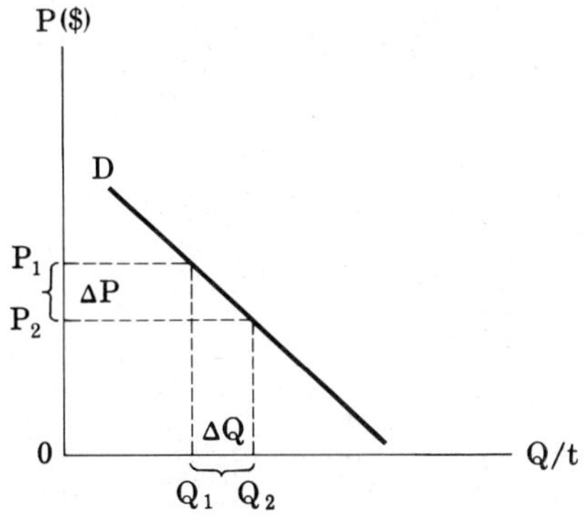

Lowering price from P_1 to P_2 causes total revenue to increase simultaneously by $P_2\, \Delta Q$ and decrease by $Q_1\, \Delta P$. The net effect is their difference:

$$\Delta TR = P_2\, \Delta Q - Q_1\, \Delta P$$

high quantity). We are interested in finding the change in total revenue per unit-change in quantity, that is, the marginal revenue. We know that a change in total revenue is equal to the new price multiplied by the additional units sold as a result of lowering the price, that is, $P_2\, \Delta Q$ minus the old quantity multiplied by the money lost on each unit as a result of lowering price, that is, $Q_1\, \Delta P$. Algebraically this expression is

$$\Delta TR = P_2\, \Delta Q - Q_1\, \Delta P$$

Since we are interested in marginal revenue, we divide the left side by ΔQ. However, the rules of algebra require that we do the same thing to the right side.

$$\frac{\Delta TR}{\Delta Q} = \frac{P_2\, \Delta Q - Q_1\, \Delta P}{\Delta Q}$$

$\Delta TR/\Delta Q$ is equal to MR by definition.

We break the right-hand side into two parts:

$$MR = \frac{P_2\, \Delta Q}{\Delta Q} - \frac{Q_1\, \Delta P}{\Delta Q}$$

The ΔQ's cancel, and we have

$$MR = P_2 - \frac{Q_1\, \Delta P}{\Delta Q}$$

Now you have to indulge us for a moment. Because the formula we want involves elasticity, and it is *point* elasticity rather than arc elasticity, we must think of the ΔP and ΔQ terms as being very, very small, and the P_1 essentially equal to P_2; similarly, $Q_1 = Q_2$. This permits the dropping of the subscripts. The next thing we want to do is factor out P from the expression on the right-hand side:

$$MR = P\left(1 - \frac{Q\,\Delta P}{P\,\Delta Q}\right)$$

It has been a lot of work, but it is worth it because $Q\,\Delta P/P\,\Delta Q$ is the formula for the coefficient of price elasticity, upside down, and we can rewrite the expression as

$$MR = P\left(1 - \frac{1}{e}\right)$$

This is another form of the formula which is frequently seen. We used earlier the form that results when you clear the parentheses by multiplying through:

$$MR = P - \frac{P}{e}$$

Can I use this formula for anything?

Sure. It has one very practical use. It can tell you how much markup to take, let us say, in a retail operation. If you work in a store for the summer and you trot out your formula and show the owner how to price his merchandise, he will bless you. Or then again, he may fire you as a wise kid. You will have to be the judge of what his reaction will be.

How can the formula be used for markup computations?

First, remember that for a profit maximizer, MC equals MR. The formula now becomes

$$MC = P - \frac{P}{e}$$

A little algebra allows you to get $P = MC\left(\frac{e}{e-1}\right)$*

---

* $MC = P - \frac{P}{e}$

$$MC = P\left(1 - \frac{1}{e}\right)$$

$$MC = P\left(\frac{e-1}{e}\right)$$

$$P = MC\left(\frac{e}{e-1}\right)$$

The meaning of this is quite clear. If the marginal cost is 100 and elasticity is, let us say 2, it means that the profit-maximizing price should be

$$P = 100\left(\frac{2}{1}\right) = 200$$

If the elasticity is higher, the price will be marked up less. For example, if elasticity is 5, the price would be $\frac{5}{4} \times 100$ or 125. This is logical because with higher elasticity there is more competition and you cannot mark up your prices as high.

But what merchant knows his elasticity of demand?
He may not think he knows elasticity, but there is a good chance that he knows the next best thing. He just uses another name for it. Any merchant should have a pretty good idea about what happens to his sales when he raises his price. Elasticity is simply the percentage change in quantity sold divided by the percentage change in price. Not unlike the man who spoke prose all his life and never knew it, the merchant deals with elasticity every time he runs a sale, and remains blissfully unaware.

What happens to monopoly in the long run?
As long as entry by other firms is blocked so the industry retains its monopolistic structure, the long run in monopoly is very much like the short run. If you recall, the presence of economic profits in the competitive model works to attract competition in from other industries, and their arrival means an increase in the supply of goods offered in the market. This greater supply exerts downward pressure on prices and induces profit-maximizing producers to reduce the quantity each offers. Under monopoly, we cannot even get started with this process. Although excessive profits may be present, there is no way that they can perform the function of attracting new capacity to the industry because entry is blocked, and the industry, by assumption, has but one producer. Therefore, the status quo is maintained. The long-run solution to a monopoly problem resembles the short run, except that the plant size that is selected by the profit-maximizing monopolist will be that at which marginal revenue equals *long-run* marginal cost (Figure 9–8). These considerations cast quite a shadow over the social desirability of monopoly.

What are the negative social connotations of monopoly?
The output of a monopolized industry will be smaller than might be expected if the identical industry were organized competitively. This

FIGURE 9–8. Long-Run Equilibrium Solution to Monopoly

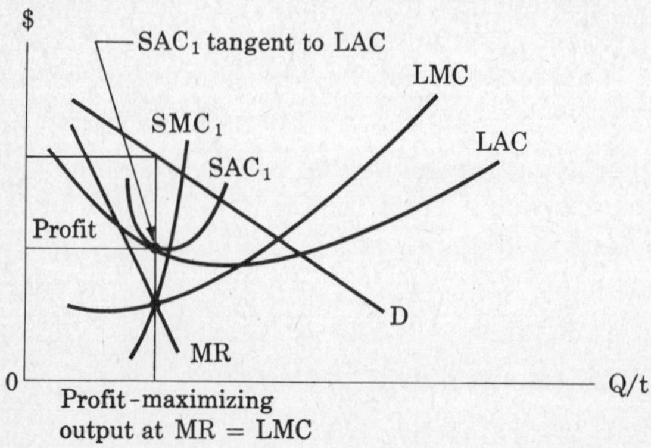

In the long run the profit maximizer produces the output at which long-run marginal cost equals marginal revenue. Because there is no entry permitted into this industry, the economic profit shown will continue to be earned, even in the long-run solution.

FIGURE 9–9. Monopoly Output is Less Than Competitive Because P *Is Less Than* MC

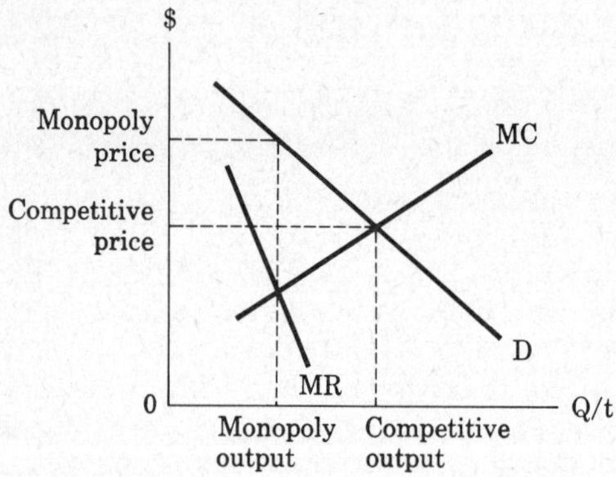

Under a monopoly organization output occurs where *MC* equals *MR*, and price exceeds both. If it were possible to organize this industry along perfectly competitive lines, the monopolist's marginal cost curve could be considered the industry supply curve. The market price and quantity would be that associated with the intersection of this supply curve with the demand curve. Therefore, production would occur at a level where price equals marginal cost.

occurs very simply because a profit maximizer equates marginal revenue with marginal cost. Under monopoly, marginal revenue is less than price, and so marginal cost is less than price. In a competitive model price and marginal cost are equated, and this occurs at a higher volume of output (Figure 9–9). When we say, therefore, that P is greater than MC, we are also saying that, due to the monopolist's desire to maximize profit, output is reduced below the socially desirable level that is attainable and indeed would be attained if price equaled marginal cost.

Why is the output where price equals marginal cost necessarily the socially desirable output?

It is socially desirable in the sense that the total utility derived from available resources is maximized under these circumstances. We begin by repeating the basic economic premise that the total resources of the society are limited in quantity. Any input used to produce one product will not be used to produce another, and any income spent on one item will not be spent on another. Thus the real cost of what is produced and consumed is measured by the value of what had to go unproduced and unconsumed as a result.

Let us consider a simple numerical example. Suppose that a monopolist producing product M maximizes his profit at an output where price equals 10 and marginal cost is 2 ($P > MC = MR$). Elsewhere in the economy, a firm in the competitive sector produces product C at price and marginal cost of 2 ($P = MC = MR$). This means that the price of the product in the monopolized industry is five times as high as the product in the competitive industry. People are willing to give up 5 units of product C in order to buy 1 unit of product M. However, the resources involved in the production of M and C have the same value at the margin, because the marginal cost of each is 2. In order to produce 1 unit of M, society sacrifices 1 unit of C. Here we have M valued five times as high as C but only costing the same as C to produce. Wouldn't society benefit if resources were redirected out of C and into M, so 1 unit of C was sacrificed and 1 unit of M worth five times as much was gained? The difficult is that there is no mechanism to reallocate these resources as long as the monopolist seeks maximum profit. Ideally, if price equaled marginal cost for all products, the opportunity cost of producing one unit of one product at the expense of another would just reflect their realtive values and there would be no way to improve total utility through a reallocation of resources. It could only be increased through an increase in total resources.

That sounds pretty convincing. Is there anything else wrong with a monopoly-structured market?

Another negative aspect of monopoly is that plant utilization is not

FIGURE 9–10. Long-Run Equilibrium Under Monopoly

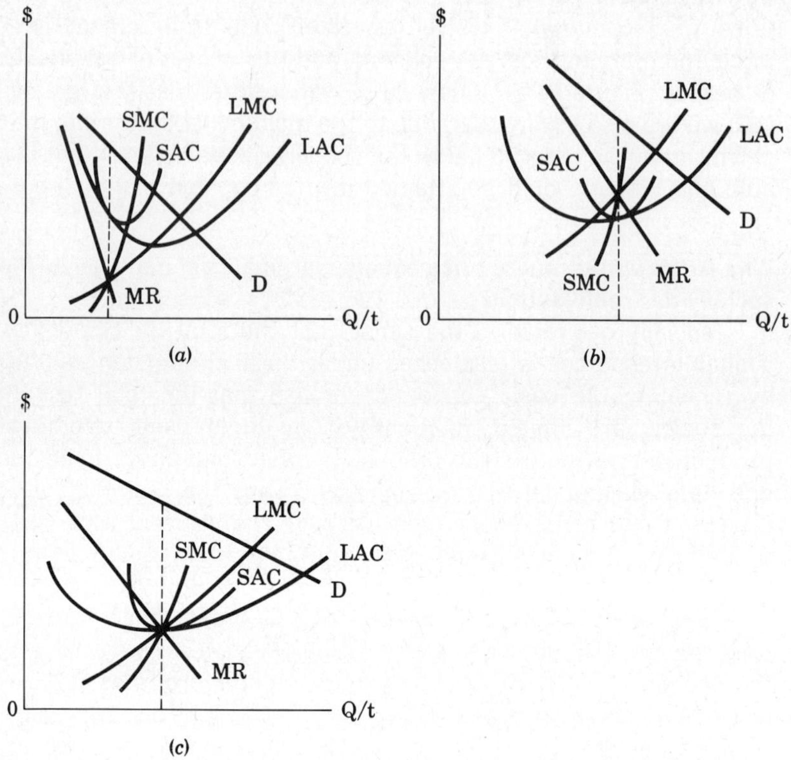

In the absence of entry by other firms, the long-run equilibrium condition under monopoly does not necessarily occur at the optimum plant size. Plant size might be less than optimum as in part (*a*), more then optimum as in part (*b*), or just equal to the optimum by coincidence as in part (*c*).

forced to the most efficient level as occurs under pure competition. Because there are no competing firms to force each producer constantly to seek more efficient methods lest he be priced out of the market, there is no pressure toward the low point on the U-shaped *LAC* curve. Profit-maximizing output may occur on the downward-sloping part of the long-run average cost curve, in which case the plant is too small for full exploitation of the economies of scale, or it might be on the upward-sloping section, in which case the plant is too large. It would only be a matter of coincidence if output were carried on at the most efficient level (Figure 9–10).

Finally, we note that economic profits may exist because of barriers to the mobility of capital into the industry. There is nothing wrong with economic profits as such. They do, however, reflect a misallocation of resources in the sense that the potential demand for the product in the monopolized industry is not being fully met.

Is there nothing good to be said of monopoly?

Yes, there are some saving graces. There is one line of thinking that points out that technological progress and its resultant increase in everyone's standard of living is dependent on the availability of funds that can finance research and development. Because research programs are risky affairs with no certainty of pay-out, a firm cannot undertake them unless it is capable of generating high, monopoly-like profits from its operations. The most spectacular success story in this class is the development of the transistor at AT&T's Bell Laboratories during the late 1940s. Unfortunately, the returns are not all in on this point. There is some evidence that, dollar for dollar, more basic discoveries are made by individuals working alone and in university-supported projects than through industrial research efforts. If this is so, monopoly profits should be redistributed either in the form of lower prices (which would follow from the industry being organized on a competitive basis) or taxation and subsidization of private research.

The other defense of monopoly involves the natural monopoly argument.

What is a natural monopoly?

A *natural monopoly* is said to exist if internal economies of scale are present in a *firm* operating at the level of total *industry* demand. Then, by concentrating total industry production in a single firm, average costs can be reduced below the level that would have to prevail if industry output were divided among a number of firms. The long-run average cost curve slopes continuously downward. Division of the total market output among two or more firms forces each to produce at a point to the left of, and at a higher cost than, the level that could be attained if one monopolized production. From the cost point of view, therefore, society would be better served if the industry were monopolized and output produced in the most efficient manner technologically possible (Figure 9–11).

In recognition of the advantages of natural monopoly, governments created the *regulated monopoly*. This is a private company that enjoys

FIGURE 9–11. Natural Monopoly

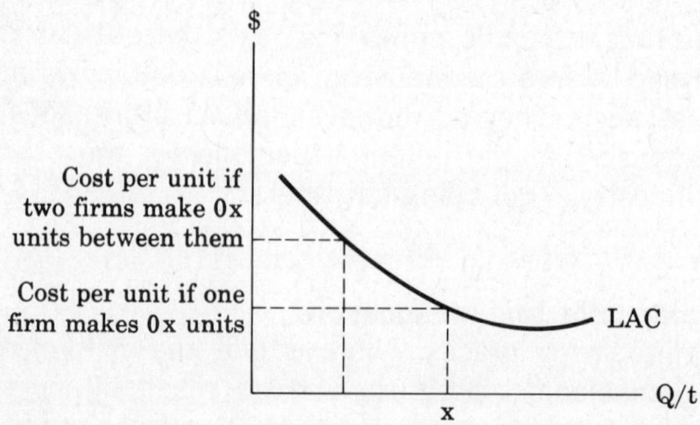

In the case where the *LAC* curve slopes down continuously to the left, production is more efficient if carried out by one large firm rather than a number of smaller ones. Remember that the *LAC* curve refers to costs of each firm. The greater the output, the lower will be its unit costs.

FIGURE 9–12. Marginal Cost Pricing for the Natural Monopolist

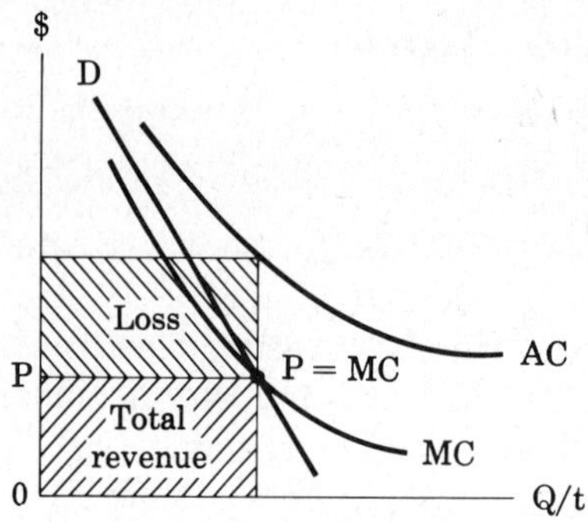

The marginal cost curve lies below the average cost curve for the natural monopolist, because his average cost curve is downward sloping. By setting the price equal to marginal cost, the natural monopolist will operate at a loss because price will then be less than average cost.

the full production economies of scale inherent in natural monopoly but that relinquishes to a governmental regulatory agency the power to set its prices. Such a situation occurs among our public utilities such as gas, water, electricity, and telephone. A public utilities commission rather than the free market or the monopolist himself sets the price at which these services are offered to the public Among the goals of the commission is the desire to provide the public with the needed services at a fair price, and also to give the investors in the public utility a fair return on their invested capital. We have seen that the marketplace will do this automatically in the case of a competitively organized industry. When regulators attempt it, the question of whether or not they succeed is open to considerable dispute. One thing that invariably accompanies public utility regulation, however, is *price discrimination.* We shall take a look at this practice now and see how it fits into the theory of the firm.

What is meant by price discrimination?

Price discrimination is defined as selling the same product or service in different markets at different prices.

Why does price discrimination always accompany public utility regulation?

This is one of the little ironies of our analysis. A short while ago we developed an argument that said that total utility in the community would be maximized if production proceeded to the point where price equaled marginal cost in each industry. Theoretically the regulators ought to strive to attain this result within the public utilities as well. Here is the rub. In a natural monopoly the average cost curve slopes downward at the output produced. This was the whole justification of permitting the monopoly to exist in the first place. Once again we return to the basic relationship between average and marginal values. When the average cost curve slopes downward, the marginal cost curve must lie *below* it. Therefore marginal cost is less than average cost for all possible outputs of the natural monopolist. Can you see the difficulty? If the regulatory agency attempts to maximize social welfare by pricing the service of the utility equal to the marginal cost of production ($P = MC$), the price will be lower than the average cost and the utility will operate at a loss (Figure 9–12). Regulators avoid situations like this by allowing utilities to charge different prices to different customers.

If you look back to Chapter 2 you will find our brief discussion of consumer surplus. The downward-sloping market demand curve indicates that some units of output could be sold at higher prices than others. Those that could be sold for more than the market price bring a consumer surplus in the sense of giving more utility to the buyer than he gives up in payment. A *perfect* price discriminator would charge the maximum amount for which each unit could be sold, thereby taking the entire surplus away. There would not be a single market price, but rather a series of different prices to the individual customers. If the consumer surplus thus usurped is big enough, it may enable the regulated monopoly to increase revenues sufficiently to turn its loss into a profit.

Is this really the way public utilities price their services?

The form of price discrimination just described, where each individual is charged the maximum price he is willing to pay for each unit, is called *first-degree discrimination*. This is the purest form, and as we saw, it involves a complete capturing of the total consumer surplus by the seller. Public utilities normally employ so-called *second-degree discrimination*. Rather than price for customer individually, they break customers down into groups such as residential consumer, industrial, commercial, high-volume, low-volume, and so on. Each group is charged a different price, so that although the discrimination is not perfect and does not capture all of the consumers' surplus, it is at least practical to administer. The actual mechanics of setting the rate structure are extremely complex and, unfortunately, frequently quite arbitrary. However, second-degree discrimination is the model.

Isn't price discrimination illegal?

The Clayton and Robinson-Patman Acts distinguish between valid price differentials and unlawful price discrimination. In order to be legal, the differential must reflect cost savings on the part of the seller. These savings may come from being able to ship in greater quantities to one buyer rather than another, thereby permitting less handling costs. They may come from having to ship shorter distances, again permitting cost savings in freight charges. Quality differences in the product may afford a chance to save some manufacturing costs which can be legitimately passed along to a buyer. Cost justifies discrimination, but if the price differentials exceed the savings realized by the seller, the practice may be held unlawful.

Price differentials to buyers of different *functional* natures are permissible. Thus manufacturers grant different discounts to retailers and wholesalers with the blessings of the law. Difficulty arises when it is not perfectly clear that a buyer is *exclusively* a retailer or wholesaler, and goods sold to him in one capacity tend to leak into the inventories he plans to sell in the other.

The major criterion in declaring price discrimination unfair, and hence illegal, is the question of whether or not it tends to lessen the extent of competition or hurt competitors. By this criterion you can see that this legislation applies to transactions within the channel of distribution, between seller and re-seller, rather than transactions involving the ultimate consumer. As far as the law of price discrimination is concerned, the final consumer is pretty much on his own. The law protects him from fraud and deceptive practices, but price discrimination toward consumers is so common that it is taken for granted. Thus we find doctors and dentists charging for medical services on the basis of the patient's income, theater tickets priced on the basis of where the patron sits and whether the show is in the afternoon or evening, personal services such as haircuts sold at one price to children and another to adults, bus rides offered at lower prices to senior citizens than to others, magazines offered at lower subscription prices to new readers than to old readers. All of these are instances of price discrimination, but they are legal and accepted, and very much a part of the business scene.

Why do sellers discriminate?

It is probably to make more money. We assume that all sellers behave in a manner that will maximize their profits, and if we find them discriminating, we must believe that this is consistent with profit maximization as well. Even the practice of physicians' pricing their services according to the ability of their patients to pay, which is defended by the medical profession as a form of private welfare program, has been vigorously attacked by critics as profit-maximizing behavior. Suffice to say, for most analyses, profits are higher with price discrimination than without it.

If profits are higher, why don't all sellers engage in price discrimination?

In order to discriminate, three conditions must be present in the market. First, there must be some control on the part of the seller over the prices charged. This requires an imperfectly competitive market. A pure competitor, after all, must accept the going market price for the product. He cannot sell any units at higher prices and would be acting contrary to his best interests if he offered merchandise to some customers below the market price.

A second requisite is that the different buyers in the market must be

FIGURE 9–13. Arbitrage

One opportunity for arbitrage exists in commodity markets, where identical commodities are traded in different geographic locations. For example, wheat is traded in Chicago and Kansas City. If the price in Chicago differs from that in Kansas City by more than the cost of transporting it, insurance while in transit, and similar other charges, an arbitrageur can buy in the low-price market (Kansas City) and sell simultaneously in the high-price market (Chicago), clearing a profit after shipping. Notice that the social function performed by arbitrage is to set up forces that will drive the prices closer together. The buying is done in the low-price market, thereby exerting demand pressures that will work to raise the price. The selling is done in the high-price market, thereby increasing supply and exerting pressures that will tend to reduce price.

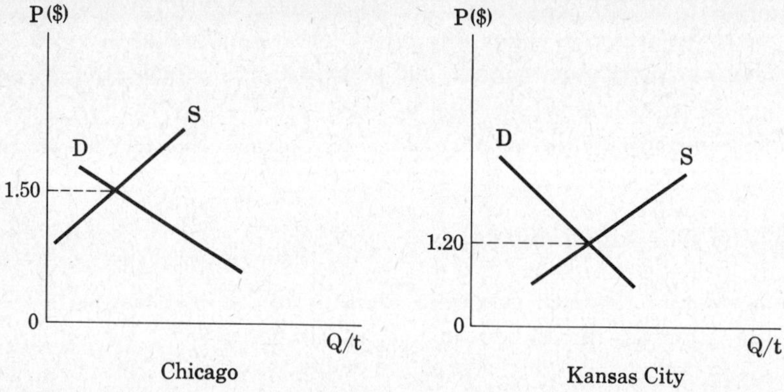

In this example the price of wheat is $1.50 in Chicago and $1.20 in Kansas City. If the cost of shipping a bushel of wheat is less than $.30, an opportunity exists for a successful arbitrage by buying in Kansas City and selling in Chicago.

prevented from trading with one another. If you sell aspirin to one customer for $.05 a pill and to another for $.50 a pill, the most natural thing in the world is for the $.05 customer to turn around and become a supplier to the $.50 customer. If they agree on any price between $.05 and $.50, it will be to their mutual advantage to trade and the discriminator will lose his high-price market. Therefore barriers must exist to prevent resale of the product. This is easily accomplished in the area of personal services. You cannot resell a child's haircut to an adult, nor can a poor man resell the medical services he has received to a rich one. We can sum this point up by saying that in order to discriminate it is necessary to prevent *arbitrage.*

What is arbitrage?

The process of *simultaneously* buying low and selling high is called arbitrage. There are professional arbitrageurs who make their living exploiting the fact that two different prices may exist at any one time for the same product. By buying in the low-priced market and turning around at the same time and reselling in the high-priced market, arbitrageurs lock in their profits in a riskless transaction. They look for the quirks that arise naturally in such competitive markets as the commodity, foreign exchange, and stock markets. Normally these opportunities occur because of a temporary lag in the flow of information from one part of the market to another. However, you can see how these opportunities would occur in markets where sellers discriminate if there were not some sort of barrier to prevent it from happening. One well-known case involved the sale of methyl methacrylate, a plastic molding powder that was useful for general industrial as well as specialized dental purposes. Industrial users were charged less than $1 per pound for the substance, while dentists paid $22 per pound for virtually the same product. An arbitrage market did develop in which the product sold to industrial users was "bootlegged" to the dental market. In an effort to erect a barrier between these markets, the manufacturer spread the rumor that the industrial version had been adulterated with arsenic. Although it was never definitely proven whether or not this had indeed been done, the rumor was enough to discourage would-be dental buyers from shopping the industrial market. Tariffs also serve as barriers between the frequently dumped export versions of products and the more highly priced domestic products. Industries do not lobby for tariffs only to protect them from foreign producers. They need protection from foreign re-sellers of their own products as well (Figure 9–13).

The third requirement for price discrimination to be practical is that there must be an opportunity to sell the product profitably in different markets at different prices. In technical terms, this means that there must be different elasticities of demand in the different markets.

Why must there be different elasticities of demand in the markets to permit price discrimination?

It all relates back to the formula we worked so hard to develop: $MR = P - P/e$. A discriminating monopolist wants to follow the $MR = MC$

criterion for profit maximization, just as does any other producer. The logic of producing only that which adds more to your revenue than to your cost still holds. Because a monopolist has the same average and marginal cost curves, whether he discriminates or not, we are working with a conventional analysis from the cost point of view. The cost of the last unit produced is the marginal cost, and this unit will not be sold unless the revenue received for it is at least equal to that marginal cost. In the case of the simple, nondiscriminating monopolist, we have seen that the price at which any sale occurs is found through the formula $MR = P - P/e$. We showed earlier that this formula can be expressed as

$$P = MR\left(\frac{e}{e-1}\right)$$

By substituting marginal cost for marginal revenue (because the firm is profit maximizing) and elasticity into the formula, we can compute the profit-maximizing price.

If there is to be discrimination, several different prices must be charged in the different market segments. Still, profit maximization calls for equating marginal revenue with marginal cost. Because all goods were *produced* together and only segregated for *sale* in the different markets, there is only one marginal unit from the production point of view and its cost is our *MC*. Marginal revenue in *each* market segment must equal this *MC*. Therefore we have a situation in which the marginal revenues in all the different markets are the same, but the prices are to be different. It follows from the formula that for this to be possible, *elasticities* in the different markets must differ. A discriminating monopolist will charge a higher price in a low-elasticity market than in one with a higher coefficient of elasticity. Obviously, if the elasticities are the same, the prices charged in the different markets will be identical, and no discrimination will occur.

Can you give an example of this price discrimination analysis?

We can use the diagram in Figure 9–14 to discuss price discrimination in a two-market situation. This is a so-called *third-degree discrimination* model. There we have demand curves drawn for two separate markets, with their accompanying marginal revenue curves. You should note that the quantities on each of these curves must be read from the origin. To get the total demand for the product (at least for these two markets), we must add the indivdual demand curves horizontally. The summed demand curve has a marginal revenue curve that is also equal to the horizontal summation of the individual marginal revenue curves. To select the total profit-maximizing output, we wish to equate this summed marginal revenue with the marginal cost of production. In this way, we can be sure that the marginal unit sold in either market will contribute at least as much to total revenue as to total cost.

The next problem is to allocate this total quantity produced among the different markets. If you think about it a bit, you will realize that we wish the marginal revenue in each of the different markets to be equal to each other and to the marginal cost. We have already pointed out why they must be equal to the marginal cost. The interesting thing is that the marginal revenues must be equal to each other; if they are not, total profit could be increased by a *reallocation* of product from one market to another until the marginal revenues are equal. Consider a situation in which output is distributed between two markets so that the marginal revenue is \$20 in one market and \$10 in the other. Total revenue can be increased by reallocating a unit of output from the \$10 marginal revenue market to the higher \$20 market. This works because the revenue lost by taking a unit out of the low marginal revenue market is (obviously) \$10. If you turn around and sell this unit in the other market, you increase total revenue by \$20. Thus, the gain in total revenue will be greater than the loss, and the total revenue will be increased on net. Because total cost was fixed once we selected a quantity to produce ($MC = \Sigma MR$), the increase in total revenue also represents a gain in total profit.

Having now selected the quantity to be produced, and having divided it up among the separate markets, it remains only to select the prices at which to sell in the different markets. These are found by reading from the respective demand curves, D_1 and D_2, the price at which each quantity will sell in each market. The formula relating price, marginal revenue, and elasticity suggests that the lower the elasticity, the higher the price that will be found.

We shall discuss the role of elasticity in demand analysis again when we come to oligopoly. Let us now turn our attention to the subject of monopolistic competition.

Why should we consider monopolistic competition here in the chapter on monopoly?

Some aspects of the monopolistic competition analysis are similar to monopoly analysis, and others fit better into the discussion we shall have under oligopoly. Rather than try to isolate monopolistic competition as a separate topic, it seems more helpful to break it up between these two discussions. At this point we are going to pursue the part of the analysis that resembles monopoly. In the next chapter we shall explore similarities between monopolistic competition and points raised in the oligopoly models.

FIGURE 9–14. Steps in the Discriminating Monopolist Analysis

Step 1. Add the demand curve and marginal revenue curve of each market segment to get the total market demand and marginal revenue curves.

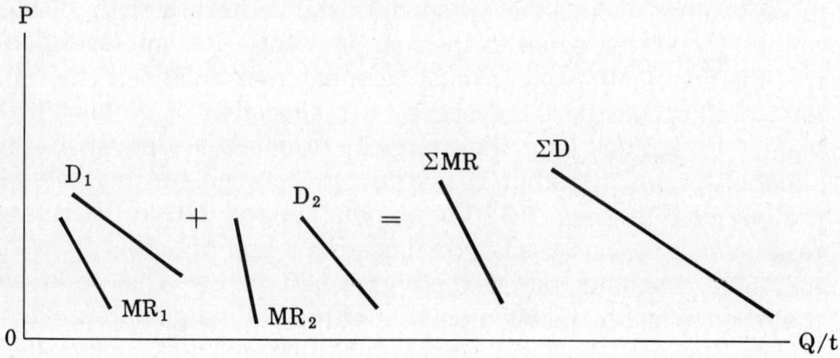

Step 2. Find the output at which $\Sigma\ MR = MC$. This is the total profit-maximizing output at which to produce.

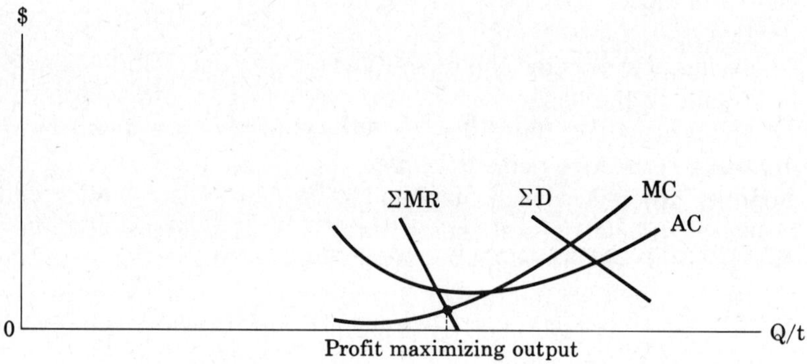

Step 3. Allocate the profit-maximizing output among the two markets so that the marginal revenue obtained from each is equal.

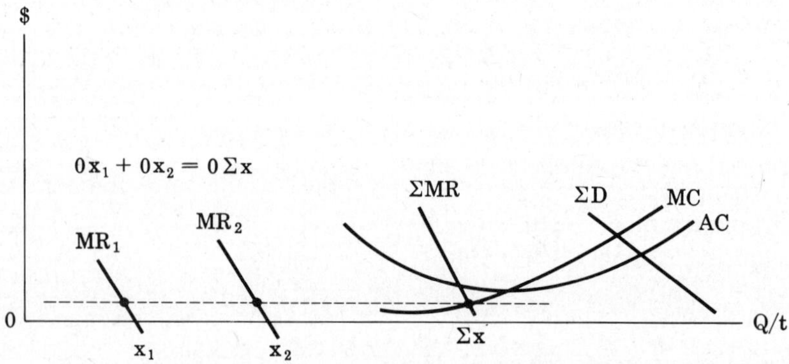

Step 4. Charge the price in each market that is indicated from its segment demand curve at the quantity allocated.

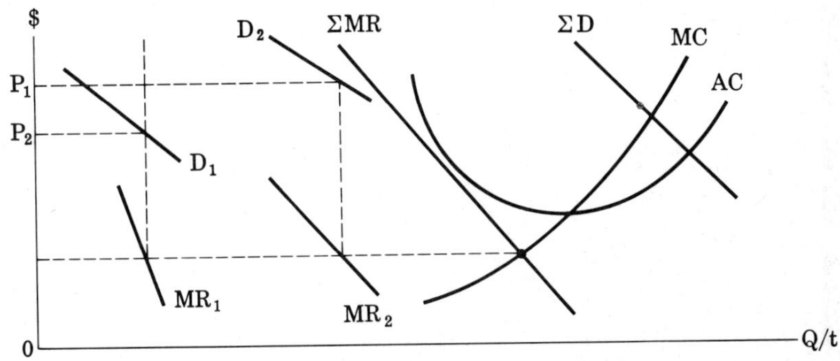

Review again the nature of monopolistic competition.

Monopolistic competition is the name given to a market situation in which a large group of firms offers more or less similar (but not identical) products. Generally the firms producing the products tend to be small (because there are large numbers of them), and entry into the industry is easy. One industry that has these characteristics is retailing. For example, we find a very large number of individual gasoline stations offering similar products: gas and oil. The offerings are differentiated by the brands of gas, the location of the station, the personality of the owner, the quality of service and mechanical repair work, the availability of credit cards, and a number of other factors. All of these considerations lead some customers to go to a particular gasoline station even if its prices are higher than those of a neighboring station. Others will not. As a result, the demand curve for any one gasoline station is highly elastic, but not perfectly so. A rise in price will result in loss of some customers, but not others. The result is that sellers in monopolistic competition have some discretion over the prices they charge, but not much. Individual firms can raise and lower their prices.

What happens if, when one competitor changes prices, another matches the price change?

That is the type of question we shall put off until next chapter. We know that each *oligopolist* considers the implications of what his fellow oligopolists will do in the event that he raises or lowers his price. Indeed, this is the basis of the economist's separating out oligopoly for

FIGURE 9–15. Profit Maximization Under Monopolistic Competition

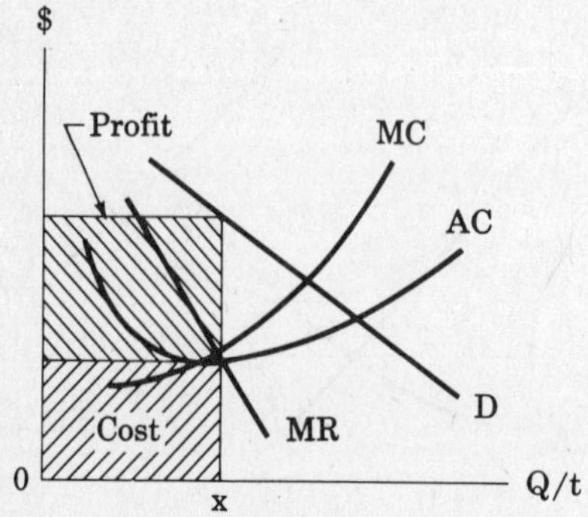

As long as competitors' prices remain constant, each seller has a stable, highly elastic, downward-sloping demand curve. The short-run profit-maximizing condition resembles monopoly in that marginal revenue and marginal cost are equated to determine the quantity to produce and price is read from the demand curve at that quantity.

study. Running through the oligopolist's mind are such thoughts as, What will my competitors do if I lower my price by $1? What will I do if they do what I think they will do? What will they do then, if I do what they think I think they will do, and so on, to an endless and paralyzing chain of reasoning. Oligopoly theory considers the manner in which economists cope with these difficult problems in market tactics. We shall discuss oligopoly in the next chapter, so we might as well defer our consideration of price competition under monopolistic competition as well. For the moment, let us deal with cases in which competitors' price behavior does not enter the picture. Instead, the *ceteris paribus* condition prevails, that is, all things remain equal, including the prices others charge in the market. As long as others do not change their prices, the demand curve of each firm will be *stable* and *highly elastic*, allowing for capture of some of the competition's customers through price reduction and loss of customers to competitors through price increase.

What happens in the* ceteris paribus *monopolistic competition model? First we want to examine the profit-maximizing behavior of the monopolistic competitor. We find that the demand curve he faces strongly resembles the monopolist's, but is more elastic. With its downward slope comes a marginal revenue curve that lies below it. The profit-maximizing position of the participant in this market is similar to that of the monopolist. He equates marginal cost and marginal revenue, and sets his price at whatever level the demand curve indicates this quantity can be sold. The short-run monopolistic competition diagram is identical to the monopoly diagram, with the same interpretations given to the total revenue, total cost, and total profit rectangles (Figure 9–15).

Then what is the difference between the analysis of monopoly and monopolistic competition?

The difference arises in the long run. Although entrance into the industry is blocked under monopoly, the door is wide open under the assumptions of monopolistic competition. If there are greater-than-normal profits generated, additional firms will come in and add to the total supply. The entry of additional participants into the industry causes the demand curve facing each seller to shift to the left.

Why does the demand curve shift to the left?

Remember that the total market demand is only so great. A limited number of permanent waves, haircuts, and gallons of gasoline will be sold in a neighborhood. Therefore the more firms there are selling these goods and services, the fewer units each one will be able to sell. The resulting reduction of each seller's market shows up as a shift of his demand curve to the left. This happens as long as entry continues, and entry will continue as long as there are economic profits to be earned. As in the case of pure competition, the shifting will stop once all the excess profit has been squeezed from the industry. This occurs when the price is finally equal to average cost, as is shown in Figure 9–16.

You say that this shifting of the demand curve is part of the long-run analysis. How do you know that?

The shifts we are talking about take place because new firms entering the industry add to total capacity by investing additional capital. That is a long-run phenomenon. We could, of course, also have these demand curves shift during the short run when competitors change their prices. Because the product offerings of each firm under monopolistic competition are substitutes for those of other firms, a change in the price by one firm will change the demand for the offering of another. There is nothing intrinsically long or short run about shifting demand curves.

FIGURE 9–16. Equilibrium Under Monopolistic Competition

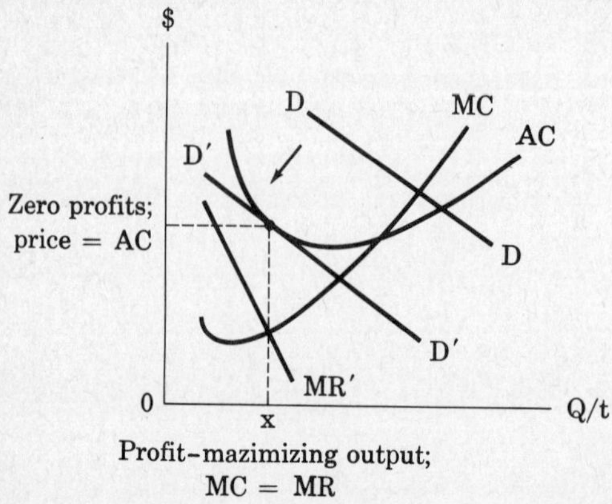

The initial demand curve facing this firm is shown by *DD*. Profits occurring in this industry attract new firms into it. Entry of these competitors reduces the demand facing each seller, and each seller's demand curve shifts to the left. This continues until all economic profits are eliminated from the industry and entry into the industry ceases. For this to occur, price must equal average cost at the profit-maximizing rate of output. Demand curve *D′D′* shows such a condition.

FIGURE 9–17. Comparison of Equilibrium Under Monopolistic Competition with Pure Competition

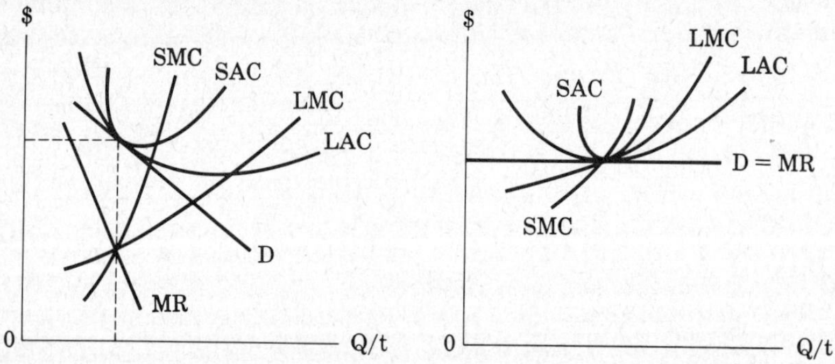

Both situations have zero long-run profits due to tangency of the demand curve and average cost curve at the profit-maximizing output. However, under monopolistic competition profit maximization occurs to the left of the low point on the average cost curve. Price is greater than marginal cost, and production takes place at less than the most efficient rate. Under pure competition price equals marginal cost, and production does occur at the most efficient rate.

The long- or short-run implications come from the reasons behind the shifts, not the shifts themselves.

Then long-run equilibrium occurs when the demand curve is tangent to the long-run average cost curve?
That is correct. It will, however, also be tangent to the short-run average cost curve of the plant designed to produce the zero profit output. What is more, long- and short-run marginal cost will equal marginal revenue at this output, just as they do in our other long-run equilibrium conditions. This case differs from pure competition in that although long- and short-run average costs are equal to each other and long- and short-run marginal costs are equal to each other, the marginal costs do not equal the average costs as they do in the long-run equilibrium under pure competition (Figure 9–17). The demand curve slopes down, and the marginal revenue curve lies below it. Marginal cost, which was set equal to marginal revenue, must also lie below price. Meanwhile, price is equal to average cost, a zero-profit situation.

It does not appear that you are producing at the low point on the long-run average cost curve.
Good observation. Equilibrium does not occur at the output where average cost is minimized. Each plant will be used at a level of production that is *smaller* than optimum. In a strict sense this is wasteful of resources, in that all of the economies of scale are not exploited. There are too many different suppliers, and each is too small for optimum efficiency.

How do you know they will be too small? Why not too big?
They will be too small because we have observed that entry into the industry continues until all profits have been eliminated. This requires that the demand curve be tangent to the long-run average cost curve, that is, price and average cost are equal. Because the demand curve slopes downward, it must be tangent to the average cost curve at a point where it too is downward sloping. Because the average cost curve

is U-shaped, its downward-sloping segment occurs to the left of the low point, or in a range where output is less than optimum.

Aren't economists upset about this tendency to have equilibrium occur at a point other than the most efficient?
Some are and some aren't. Certainly, it depends on your goals. If maximization of total output is the economic goal, as perhaps it should be in a poor, underdeveloped country, then monopolistic competition represents a burden that may be intolerable. However, if we recognize that one of the consequences of a monopolistic competition market structure is the availability of a *great variety* of convenient locations and a great plethora of colors and designs and models, we must acknowledge that monopolistic competition has its good points. A buyer has the possibility of finding a product that may come close to meeting his ideal specifications. However, the buyer pays for this opportunity by having the product made at higher cost and sold at still higher price than could be possible under standardized homogeneous production. If monopolistic competition is the characteristic structure of the capitalist society, these observations are quite pertinent. Once again, it is a matter of applying normative values when we come to evaluate the relative merits of competition versus monopolistic competition. Which do you value more highly: efficiency or variety?

CHAPTER HIGHLIGHTS

1. *We first considered how the strict requirements of the perfect competition model could be relaxed to give us monopoly, oligopoly, and monopolistic competition models, with or without price discrimination.*
2. *The monopoly model and the monopolistic competition models were discussed in some detail. The distinguishing analytical feature of all imperfect competition models was shown to be the downward-sloping demand curve facing the firm.*
3. *We recognized that the downward-sloping demand curve caused the marginal revenue to be lower than price. A formula,* $MR = P - P/e$, *was developed to show the relationships among price, marginal revenue, and elasticity.*
4. *Because profit maximization sees marginal cost and marginal revenue equated, price will exceed marginal cost in imperfect competition equilibrium states. We examined the social connotations of this.*
5. *Natural monopolies and the economics of public utility regulation*

were discussed. This led also to a lengthy consideration of the economics of price discrimination.

6. Finally, we took up those aspects of monopolistic competition that we could within the context of no price changes by other participants. We left the discussion of monopolistic competition with price competition for the next chapter.

QUESTIONS

1. Critics of advertising complain that advertising stifles competition because it permits firms to build up brand loyalty, thereby making it difficult for new firms to enter a market and compete effectively. Advertising's defenders say that advertising encourages competition because it permits a new firm to inform the public of its presence. Entry would be impossible without advertising. Which of these arguments seems stronger to you?
2. Economists working on antitrust matters in the late 1950s used to complain about the monopoly power in the publishing industry held by Life, Look, and The Saturday Evening Post magazines. Within a decade all three were out of business. Did these magazines really have monopoly power? If so, what put them out of business?
3. National Airlines in 1975 instituted a "no-frills" ticket. Where a first-class ticket from New York to Miami cost $150, and a coach ticket cost $98, the no-frills ticket was offered at $61—which was less also than train or bus fare. Where first-class travelers got steak dinners and unlimited liquor service and coach travelers got a modest meal and availability of cocktails, the no-frills traveler got no food and no liquor. Is this a form of price discrimination? Under what circumstances is it profitable for National Airlines?
4. It has been said that the Justice Department exercises its antitrust activities against bigness per se rather than monopolistic practices. Is bigness necessary in order that there be a monopoly present? Which do you think is a more important object of government antitrust action?
5. We have established the relationship between marginal revenue and average revenue (price), $MR = (P - P/e)$. Can you imagine a functional relationship that might exist between average cost and marginal cost and elasticity of supply? Give the formula.
6. Automobile manufacturing is commonly described as an oligopoly-structured industry. Does the structure of the automobile dealership industry alter your picture of the auto industry? To what extent is it monopolistic competition? Are the equilibrium results those called for by monopolistic competition?

7. *Irving Kristol has stated, "It was always assumed both by economic theorists from Adam Smith onwards and by public opinion that large aggregations of capital would be a temporary phenomenon and would not coalesce into permanent institutions. The reasons the laws of incorporation were made so simple and easy in the United States was because it was assumed that corporate competition would make the large corporation as we know it impossible." What went wrong? Are we better or worse off because things didn't work out as theorists from Adam Smith onward assumed they would?*

10 Oligopoly

Oligopoly is the most difficult economic model with which we deal. It involves all of the cost and market variables we have seen thus far, with their respective average and marginal curves, plus a new element. The new element is the possibility of retaliation.

What do you mean by retaliation?

In each of the market situations we have examined, there is little opportunity for anyone to do anything but accept the will of the "impersonal forces of supply and demand." In pure competition, a seller is completely anonymous. He cannot raise or lower his prices without hurting himself. Because everyone can sell as much as he wishes under the assumptions of the analysis, there is no theoretical reason why one seller would wish to retaliate against the competitive actions of any other. Action by one competitor has no effect whatsoever on the market.

In the case of the monopolist, there is no one against whom to retaliate. As a single seller, a monopolist sets his price and offers his product, fully cognizant of the shape of the demand curve he faces and assured that it will not shift out from under him. However, in the market structure called oligopoly—that is, relatively few, large sellers in direct competition with each other—an action by one very definitely affects the demand curve faced by another. If hurt, an oligopolist is likely to retaliate in an effort to regain his market position. This can set off a chain of actions and reactions, each of which affects the demand curves faced by the others.

FIGURE 10–1. Cournot Model—I

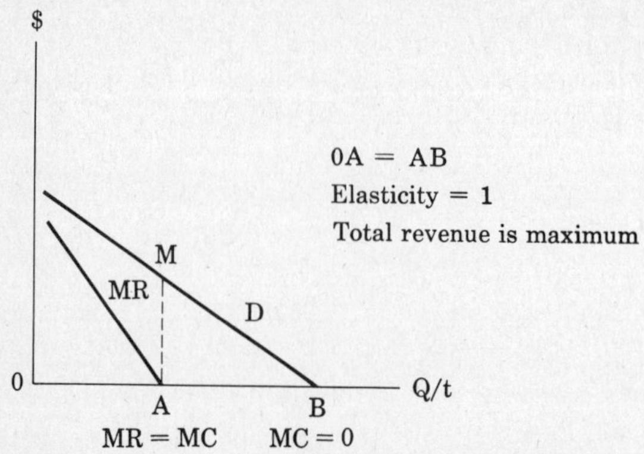

The first duopolist thinks that the total market curve belongs to him alone. He offers quantity $0A$ in the market, because this is the output at which marginal revenue equals the zero marginal cost. Output $0A$ is one-half of total market demand, $0B$. If $0B = 100$, duopolist A provides output of 50.

How does this possibility of retaliation make the analysis difficult?

A seller attempts to get the most out of a known market situation. He estimates the market demand curve and, in the light of his cost data, adjusts his output, production technique, and promotional effort to maximize profit. However, in oligopoly, no sooner does a seller make a decision in the light of one set of conditions, then the conditions change as a result of action taken by his competitor. Once again, the seller makes an adjustment and again retaliation causes the demand curve to shift. As economic analysts, we must watch this pursuit of the will-o'-the-wisp oligopolistic demand curves and try to jump ahead of events to see where it will all come out. Our task is to gain some insight into the manner in which oligopolists coexist and rapprochement is arrived at in oligopolistic markets. One analytical tool that is used is called the *reaction model.*

What is a reaction model?

Reaction models get right to the heart of the oligopoly problem. They attempt to portray how the conflict that arises among firms in the market will unfold by examining the interaction of the firms with each other and by tracing the sequence of actions and reactions over a period of time—firm A's profit-maximizing action; then firm B's reaction; then firm A's reaction to firm B's reaction; then firm B's reaction to firm A's reaction to firm B's reaction to firm A's action, and so on. If we follow such a sequence long enough, we should come to the long-run equilibrium solution to these conflict situations.

Can you give an example of a reaction model?

Undoubtedly the best-known model of this type is the Cournot duopoly model. It was published in 1838 and is considered a classic in economic literature. In Cournot's scheme, two sellers, A and B, each own a mineral spring from which water bubbles at zero cost and as a result of zero effort on their part. The water apparently has some medicinal powers and is in demand, despite the zero cost. Hence, we can picture a downward-sloping demand curve for mineral spring water.

In the beginning, duopolist A believes that he is a monopolist, that is, he is unaware that B has had the similar good fortune of finding a spring. He feels that the entire market is his to exploit, and like any good monopolist, he sets out to equate marginal cost with marginal revenue to determine the profit-maximizing output and charge whatever price is indicated on the demand curve. Cournot assumed a linear demand curve. The marginal revenue curve of such a demand curve is also linear, downward sloping. Because marginal cost is zero in our problem, a profit maximizer following the rules will produce the output at which marginal revenue equals zero, that is, intersects the *x* axis. In Chapter 3 we noted that marginal revenue was equal to zero at the output where elasticity was unitary. We also noted that elasticity was unitary at the midpoint between the origin and the output at which the demand curve crosses the *x* axis. Finally, to refresh one more old memory, we found that total revenue was maximized at the point where elasticity was unitary. This is perfectly consistent with profit maximization at this point, because when costs are zero, as in our mineral spring example, total revenue is the same as total profits. Therefore a monopolist following the *MR* equals *MC* (equals zero) profit-maximizing rule would offer enough product to satisfy half of the total market demand (Figure 10–1).

What do you mean by half of the total market demand?

The *total market demand* is the quantity at which the demand curve intersects the *x* axis. This is the quantity demanded at zero price. It can be thought of as the equilibrium quantity that would be produced under pure competition because it is a zero-profit output. And so if

FIGURE 10–2. Cournot Model—II

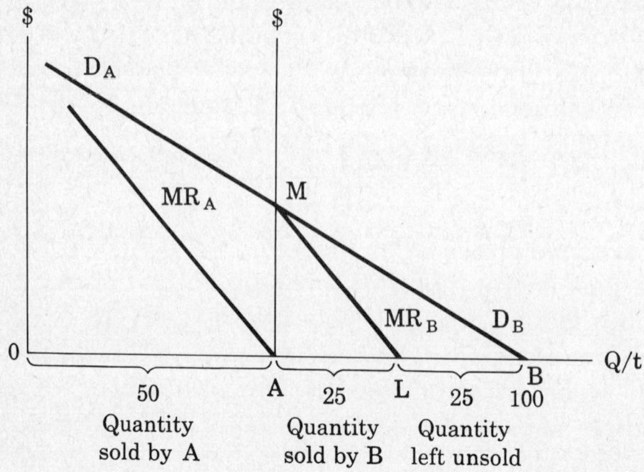

Duopolist B interprets *AB* as the quantity available to him because his competitor is already serving the market segment 0*A*. He treats line *AM* as the *y* axis and *MB* as the demand curve and offers the profit-maximizing quantity by producing half of *AB*, or *AL*. This is where the new original revenue curve, *ML*, equals marginal cost of zero.

the mineral spring water industry were a monopoly the market would receive half of the competitive output. But it isn't. Duopolist B also has a mineral spring.

What happens when duopolist B enters the market?
Under the Cournot assumptions, duopolist B will come along and, seeing half of the market served by A, will assume that as far as he is concerned, his own total market demand curve consists of the half left unserved. Let us take some numbers. Suppose that the *x* intercept (the amount demanded at price zero), which we have called the total demand, is 100 units. Duopolist A supplies 50 units. Duopolist B now thinks of the total demand curve as consisting of the segment running from quantity 50 to quantity 100, that is, the unserved part of the market. Applying the same reasoning as A, he will service half of the market as he perceives it, or 25 units (Figure 10–2).

This action by B is the heart of the Cournot system. Each duopolist assumes that the other will continue to sell the quantity he is selling regardless of what his competitor does. Hence he makes his profit-maximizing plans in light only of the *current* action of the other, not any anticipated future action. The profit-maximizing rule under these assumptions is, *Offer half of the market segment the other fellow is not covering* (Figure 10–3).

What does duopolist A do now?
Following the procedure outlined in the last paragraph, duopolist A will realize that he no longer has a total market of 100 units to exploit. Because B has come into the market and supplied 25 units of mineral water, the market segment not being covered and hence available to A has been reduced to 75 units. If A applies the "offer half of the market segment the other fellow is not covering" rule, he now has a total potential market of 75 units. He will maximize profit by reducing output and supplying 37½ units in the market.

What does duopolist B do next?
Duopolist B will become aware that the total market available to him, which he originally thought was a 50-unit market, has grown. Because A now produces 37½ units instead of 50, it leaves a potential market of 62½ units that are not offered by A. Duopolist B will see his total market as consisting of 62½ units and maximize profits by offering half of this, or 31¼ units.

What does duopolist A do next?
By now, the pattern should be familiar. Duopolist A will realize that his market is not 75 as he thought, but only 68¾. He will service half of that, or 34⅜.

And then . . . ?
This changes B's perception of the unserved market from 62½ to 65⅝. He accordingly offers half, or 32$^{13}/_{16}$.

It seems they never learn.
That's true. According to this line of reasoning, each participant attempts to maximize his profits by producing half of that part of the total market that the other does not serve. Such action is based on the assumption that the other will continue to behave exactly as he has

FIGURE 10–3. Schematic Sequence of Cournot Model

The distance AB represents total demand of 100.

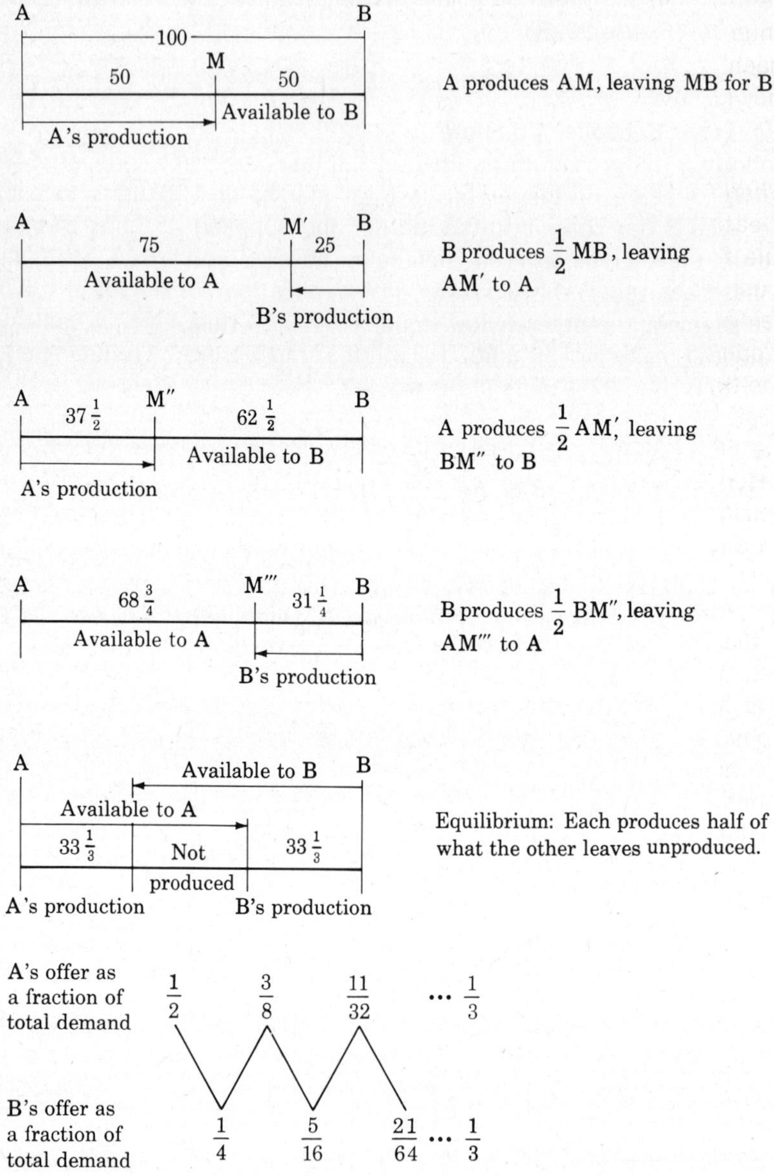

been behaving. This, of course, is a self-defeating assumption, because any action on the part of one changes the environment of the other, who changes his behavior accordingly. Thus, the Cournot model is extremely naive, assuming that no learning takes place despite the continuous buffeting each takes from the other. The model is like a machine. We put in the participants, turn the crank, and see where they end up.

Where do they end up?

If each can arrive at a quantity that also fulfills the profit-maximizing rule for the other, then both will be at a stable equilibrium point. We must have a situation in which A is producing half of the market not being produced by B and B is producing half of the market not being produced by A, and both are satisfied. This will be met if each produces one-third of the total market. When A produces 33⅓ units, it leaves 66⅔ units left unserved. If B profit maximizes by producing half of the 66⅔ units, he also will produce 33⅓ units. This leaves 66⅔ units unserved by him, so A's production of 33⅓ units is also profit maximizing and he will not change. Stable equilibrium occurs where each produces one-third of the total (Figure 10–3).

Is there a systematic way to analyze this case?

Yes. We can draw what are called *reaction curves*. These are graphs that show what one duopolist will do in the light of the other's actions. Construct a pair of axes with the vertical axis showing A's output and the horizontal axis showing B's output. Points on the map show combinations of output by A and B. Now plot the quantities each produces in the light of the other's output (Figure 10–4). Let A equal A's output, B equal B's output, and T equal the total output at zero price. Our rule says:

$A = \frac{1}{2}(T - B)$ *A*'s reaction curve

$B = \frac{1}{2}(T - A)$ *B*'s reaction curve

We want to bring these two functions together on the same pair of axes (Figure 10–5). Because the quantity A produces is a function of the quantity B produces and the quantity B produces is a function of the quantity A produces, the point at which they intersect is the point of equilibrium. This occurs with $A = B = \frac{1}{3}T$.

You can reach this conclusion graphically, or you can treat the reaction curve functions as a pair of simultaneous equations and solve them. This is the equivalent of finding the intersection on the graph, that is, the common values of A and B that satisfy both participants.

FIGURE 10–4. Construction of Reaction Curves

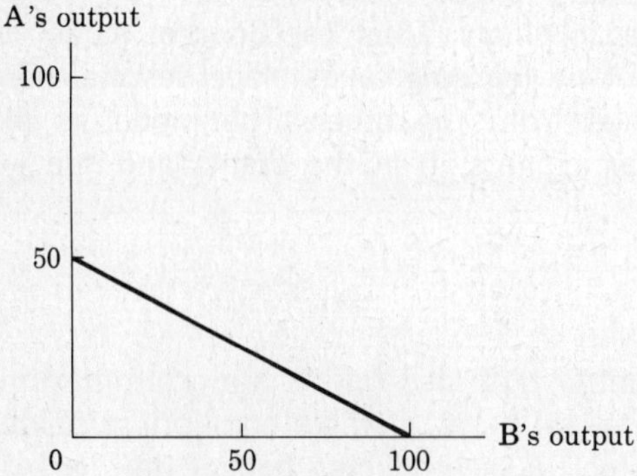

A's reaction curve

$$A = \frac{1}{2}(100 - B)$$

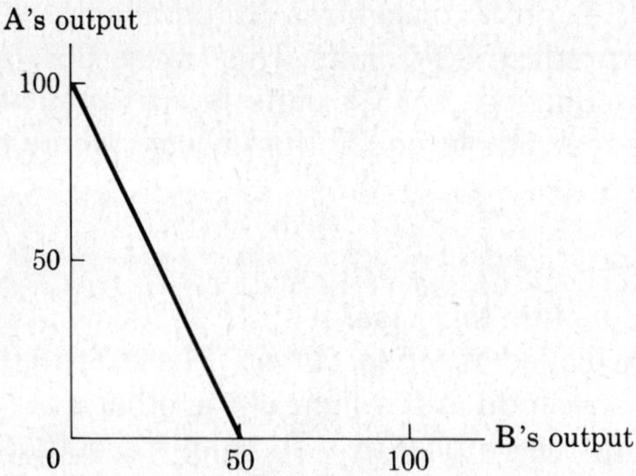

B's reaction curve

$$B = \frac{1}{2}(100 - A)$$

A reaction curve shows what one party will do in light of an action taken by the other. The Cournot model assumes quantity of output as the action variable. Here we put A's output on the vertical axis and B's output on the horizontal axis. A's reaction curve shows the output that he will produce as measured on the vertical axis if B takes the action indicated on the horizontal axis. B's reaction curve shows the output that he will produce as measured on the horizontal axis if A takes the action measured on the vertical axis.

FIGURE 10–5. Cournot Reaction Curves

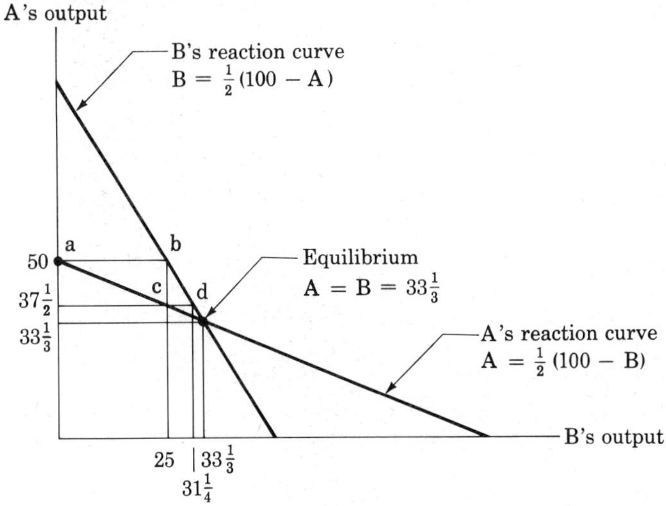

We read the reaction map as follows:

At point a, A thinks he is a monopolist; B produces 0 and A produces ½ (100 – 0) = 50

At point b, on the reaction map, if A produces 50, B's reaction is to produce
½ (100 – 50) = 25

At point c, if B produces 25, A's reaction is to produce
½ (100 – 25) = 37½

At point d, if A produces 37½, B's reaction is to produce
½ (100 – 37½) = 31¼

FIGURE 10–6. Bertrand's Equilibrium

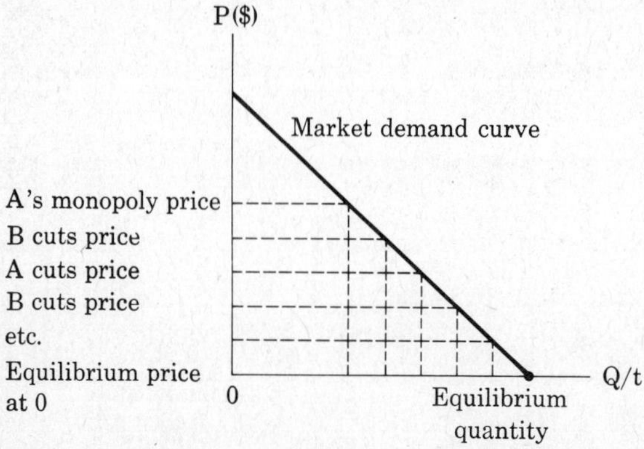

Can you show the solution step by step?

$$\begin{aligned} A &= \tfrac{1}{2}(T - B) \\ B &= \tfrac{1}{2}(T - A) \end{aligned}$$
(1) original equations

$$\begin{aligned} A &= \tfrac{1}{2}T - \tfrac{1}{2}B \\ B &= \tfrac{1}{2}T - \tfrac{1}{2}A \end{aligned}$$
(2) clear the parentheses

$$\begin{aligned} A &= \tfrac{1}{2}T - \tfrac{1}{2}B \\ -\tfrac{1}{2}A &= -\tfrac{1}{2}T + B \end{aligned}$$
(3) line up the variables under one another and multiply both sides of the second equation by -1

$$\begin{aligned} A &= \tfrac{1}{2}T - \tfrac{1}{2}B \\ -A &= -T + 2B \end{aligned}$$
(4) multiply the lower equation by 2

$$0 = -\tfrac{1}{2}T + 1\tfrac{1}{2}B$$
(5) add the equations

$$\begin{aligned} \tfrac{1}{2}T &= 1\tfrac{1}{2}B \\ \tfrac{1}{2}T \times \tfrac{2}{3} &= B \\ \tfrac{1}{3}T &= B \end{aligned}$$
(6) solution for B

$$\begin{aligned} A &= \tfrac{1}{2}(T - B) \\ A &= \tfrac{1}{2}(T - \tfrac{1}{3}T) \\ A &= \tfrac{1}{2}(\tfrac{2}{3}T) \\ A &= \tfrac{1}{3}T \end{aligned}$$
Substitute to solve for A

What does the Cournot model say about markets with more than two participants?

Obviously the solution becomes a bit more complicated. There are equations for each participant. If there are n participants, Cournot generalizes that in equilibrium each participant will offer $(1/n + 1)T$ units of output. Among them, n sellers will offer $(n/n + 1)T$, leaving a $(1/n + 1)T$ share unoffered. Again, remember that they each must think they are offering half of the total remaining after all the others make their offers. At equilibrium each participant thinks of the part not served by the others as consisting of the part he eventually gives plus the $1/n + 1$ share that is never offered. For example, suppose that there are nine oligopolists in a market where the total demand at zero price is 100. Here $n = 9$, and the share of each will be $(1/n + 1)T$, or $1/10$ of 100 or 10. Each gives 10 for a total of 90, and there is 10 that is not produced. However, when any one oligopolist looks at the total market, he sees the other eight producing a total of 80, leaving 20 not offered. He divides the 20 in half and offers 10. As long as they all do this, they are all in equilibrium.

Are there other reaction models in addition to the one by Cournot?
Others based on other sets of assumptions have been developed. Remember that the Cournot model requires each duopolist to believe that the other will continue to sell his quantity and never to anticipate a change, despite a history of experience to the contrary. Joseph Bertrand, a French economist writing late in the nineteenth century, criticized the Cournot solution by pointing out that a rational duopolist would not assume that the other would continue to service his share of the market, being content to take a part of the remainder, but rather would attempt to win away the opponent's share. Thus, if duopolist A started out, as suggested by Cournot, by selling half of the total monopolistic market, duopolist B would realize that, by cutting price, he could not only take away A's market but also sell to those lower down on the demand curve who stood ready to buy at a lower price. A, seeing his market taken away, would retaliate by cutting his price and taking away B's market. B would retaliate in kind, and the price war would continue down to the point of zero price. Because costs under the Cournot model are zero, this would be the breakeven point. In effect, Bertrand's equilibrium is the competitive solution where price just equals average cost and yields zero profit (Figure 10–6).

How can the two approaches differ so much?
Bertrand takes account of a point we shall be seeing again. Once an oligopolist sets a price, the demand curve becomes horizontal at that price as far as others in the market are concerned. They cannot sell anything at a higher price. At a price $.01 lower, they can sell all the competitor's volume. This is the same condition each firm faced under pure competition. The marginal revenue curve, rather than lying below the demand curve, actually coincides with it, and the Cournot rationale for the duopolists each producing half of what was left is destroyed (Figure 10–7). This depended on a downward-sloping demand curve.

FIGURE 10–7. Demand Curve for Duopolist B After Duopolist A Sets a Price

Duopolist A first maximizes profit in the customary way by producing $0M = (\frac{1}{2}0B)$ and charging P_1.

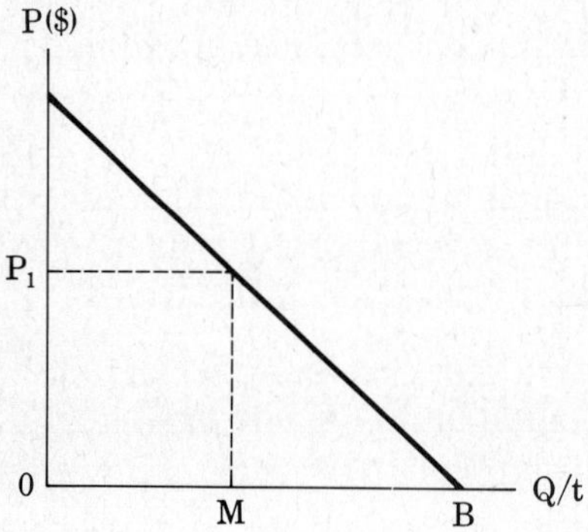

(*a*)

Once A sets the price at P_1, the demand curve facing B is perfectly elastic up to quantity $0M$. B cannot sell anything at prices above P_1. At \$.01 below P_1 he can capture the entire market up to $0M$ plus any increment that comes from reducing price. According to Bertrand, each will perceive the market in this way after the other has set the price, and set his own price lower.

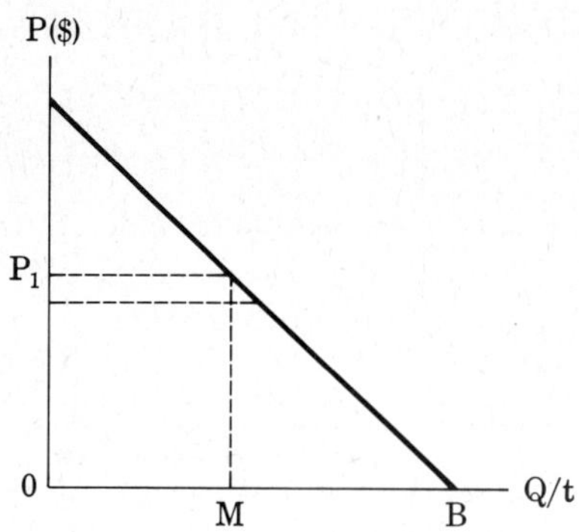

(*b*)

FIGURE 10–8. Bertrand Reaction Curve

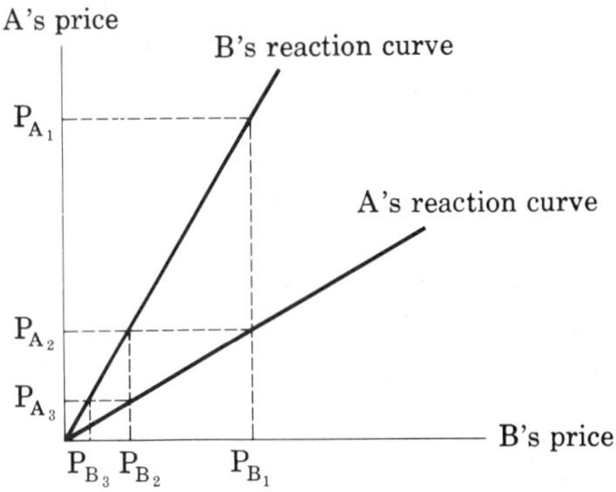

The formulas for the reaction curves are

$P_A < P_B$ A's reaction curve
$P_B < P_A$ B's reaction curve

Such a set of conditions is impossible to meet, but comes closest at price 0 for both A and B. The system will move in that direction, achieving equilibrium at the origin.

By cutting price, each duopolist can increase total revenue by the full sales of his opponent, plus whatever expansion takes place in total industry sales as a result of lower market price. Competition will become quite cutthroat under the Bertrand system, perhaps ultimately driving one duopolist out, and then leaving the other free to operate as a monopolist at the halfway point along the demand curve. The reaction curves for the Bertrand model are usually drawn with price on the axes (Figure 10–8). The formulas are

$P_A < P_B$

$P_B < P_A$

This is an impossible set of requirements. However, if we assume that there are no prices lower than zero, both prices crowd down to zero as the system attempts to satisfy the dictates of the functions.

Are there other reaction models?

The other classical model that we should mention in this context is that of Edward Chamberlin. We have already encountered the work of this relatively contemporary economist (1930s) when we examined the

FIGURE 10–9. Chamberlin's Duopoly Model

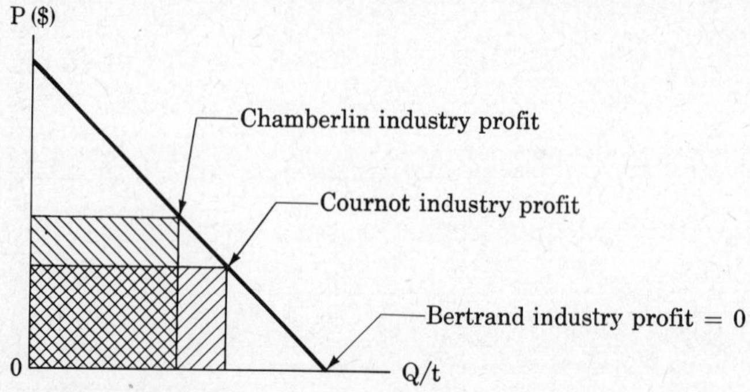

Recognizing that competition and retaliation were mutually destructive, Chamberlin felt that the duopolists would get together and agree to produce jointly the monopolistic output and divide up the profits. The industry output would be half the total demand.

FIGURE 10–10. Two Types of Demand Curve

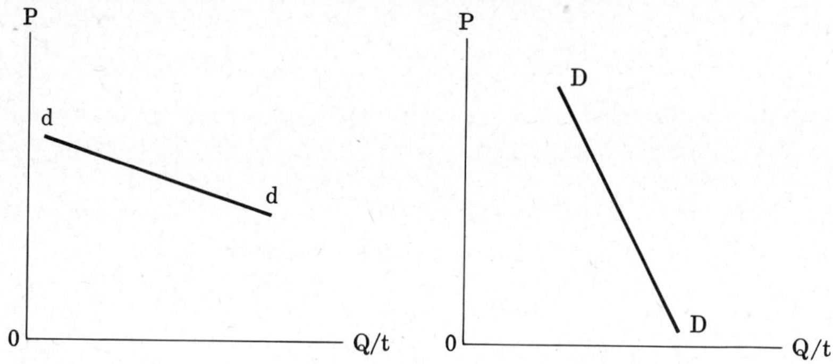

A *ceteris paribus* demand curve assumes that price changes will not be matched by competitors. As a result, each firm faces a highly elastic demand curve, *dd*. A demand curve in which all competitors match the price changes any one makes will be much less elastic. The curve *DD* is an example.

theory of monopolistic competition. In commenting on the duopoly problem, Chamberlin reasoned that the types of behavior Cournot and Bertrand envisioned were both irrational. Chamberlin granted that each seller would act as a profit maximizer in the light of the market conditions he saw. However, both would soon see that they would be better off if, instead of fighting, they got together and agreed to share the market at the monopoly price. This would lead to stability in price and quantity produced and increase *industry* profits to the maximum attainable. In effect, the appropriate diagram would be that of the monopolist maximizing total revenue by producing at the unitary elasticity point (Figure 10–9). Although Chamberlin did not deal with oligopoly at great length, his reasoning sets the stage for the next group of oligopoly models. The common element of these models is recognition by the oligopolists that market stability is necessary if they are to retain their sanity and their profits. These models deal with different forms of cooperative behavior on the part of oligopolists. We shall call these the *kinked demand curve* models.

How do the kinked demand curve models work?
One of the ground rules of the demand curves discussed in Chapter 2 is the *ceteris paribus* assumption. Price and quantity vary while everything else remains constant. When a firm sets a price, it assumes that all of the other variables will remain unchanged and it can read the quantity demanded from a *stable* demand curve. We have seen that as long as there are reasonable substitutes available, a *ceteris paribus* demand curve tends to be highly elastic. A reduction in price causes a relatively large increase in quantity demanded, and a rise in price leads to a sharp reduction in the quantity taken.

Let us now consider another type of demand curve. In this case any price change made by one seller is matched by a similar price change by his competitors. Such a curve tends to be less elastic. A reduction in price that is matched by all competitors does not lead to anyone winning away customers from anyone else. All that happens is that the total industry demand for the product rises as its price falls relative to other prices in the market, and each firm keeping its share of the market gains a proportionate increase of the industry sales. We can therefore visualize two demand curves designated as the *dd* curve and the *DD* curve, respectively. The *dd* curve shows quantities taken when price changes are not matched by competitors, and the *DD* curve shows quantities taken when price changes are matched (Figure 10–10).

How are these two demand curves employed in oligopoly models?
The best-known oligopoly model that employs these two curves is called the *Sweezy kinked demand curve analysis.* Suppose that Chevrolet has

FIGURE 10–11. Price Changes and the Two Demand Curves

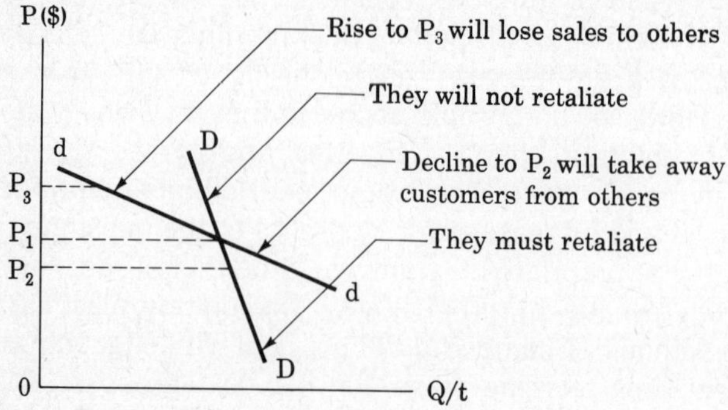

Price reductions from P_1 will be matched by other firms, thereby making *DD* the appropriate demand curve to use. Price increases will not be matched, thereby making *dd* the appropriate curve to use.

FIGURE 10–12. The Kinked Demand Curve

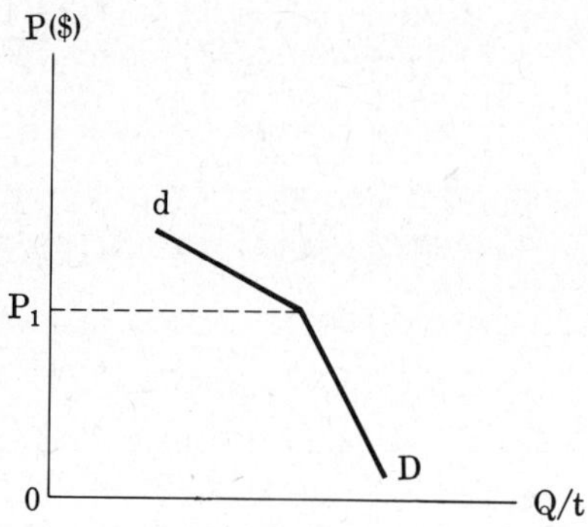

By discarding the upper portion of the *DD* curve and the lower portion of the *dd* curve, we end up with the kinked demand curve.

established a price of $5000 for a particular model auto. What happens to demand if it lowers the price to $4800? What happens if it raises the price to $5200? Before we can answer, we must decide which demand curve applies, *dd* or *DD*. We can see that if price is reduced and Ford and Plymouth do not match the reduction on their comparable models, Chevrolet's sales will increase markedly as shown on the *dd* curve. This should produce sizeable leftward shifts in the demand curves for other cars and reduce their sales accordingly. To avoid this, we may assume that competitors will be forced to match the price reduction with one of their own, thereby making *DD* the pertinent demand curve for price reductions.

On the other hand, what happens when Chevrolet's price is increased? Along the *dd* curve, we shall find that there is a sizeable drop in quantity sold as buyers flock to competitors whose prices have remained constant at the old price. Other firms will have their demand curves shifted to the right by the price increase on the part of their fellow oligopolist as long as they do not match his price rise. If they do match the price rise, they will not pick up any of his sales, and in fact will suffer a slight decline in volume as the quantity demanded from the total industry falls with the price rise. We may conjecture that oligopolists will not follow price rises too readily, but will hasten to match price reductions. That is, they will read their quantities from the *dd* curve for price rises and from the *DD* curve for price reductions (Figure 10–11).

How do we reconcile these two demand curves being used in different circumstances?

Assuming that we know the established price and quantity, we draw both demand curves passing through this point. For prices ranging below the present price, we use the lower part of *DD*, and for prices ranging above the present price, we use the upper part of *dd*. If we erase the unused portion of each curve, we find that the demand curve remaining has a kink in it at the established market price (Figure 10–12).

So what if it has a kink in it?

The kink produces a curious effect on the marginal revenue curve. In effect, marginal revenue simultaneously takes on two values at the quantity at which the kink occurs. One value is related to change in total revenue per unit-change in quantity as measured on the *dd* curve, and the other relates to change in total revenue per unit-change in quantity as shown on the *DD* curve Actually, each curve has its own marginal revenue curve. At the point where the demand curves inter-

FIGURE 10–13. Two Marginal Revenue Values at the Point of Intersection of the DD *and* dd *Curves*

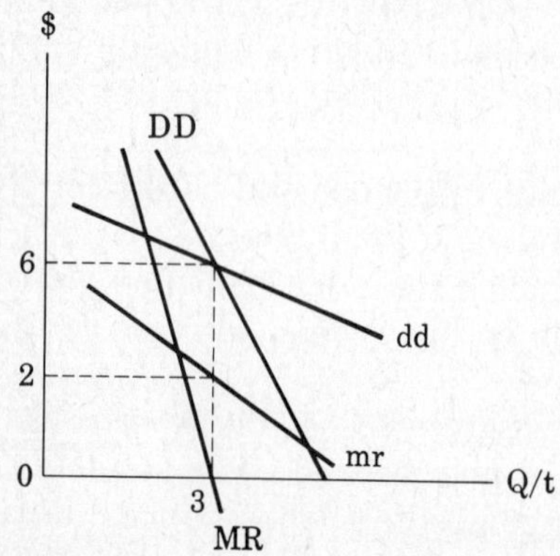

In the example here, data are tabulated for two demand curves that intersect at price 6 and quantity 3. Marginal revenue is zero on the *DD* curve, but 2 on the *dd* curve.

P	*Q*	*TR*	*MR*
12	1	12	
9	2	18	6
6	3	18	0
3	4	12	– 6
0	5	0	–12

DD

P	*Q*	*TR*	*MR*
10	1	10	
8	2	16	6
6	3	18	2
4	4	16	–2
2	5	10	–6

dd

FIGURE 10–14. There Is No Tangent to a Curve at the Kink

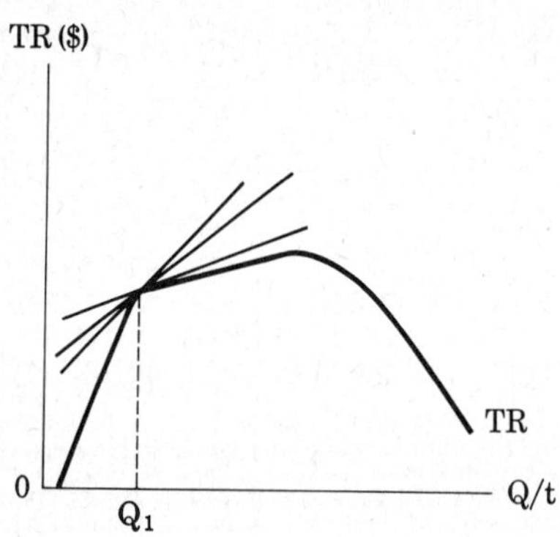

The total revenue curve has a kink in it at the quantity Q_1. If you try to draw a tangent to the curve at this point, you will find there are many lines that just touch the curve at the kink. Thus there is no one slope at this point, and no one marginal revenue.

FIGURE 10–15. Marginal Revenue Curve for Kinked Demand Curve

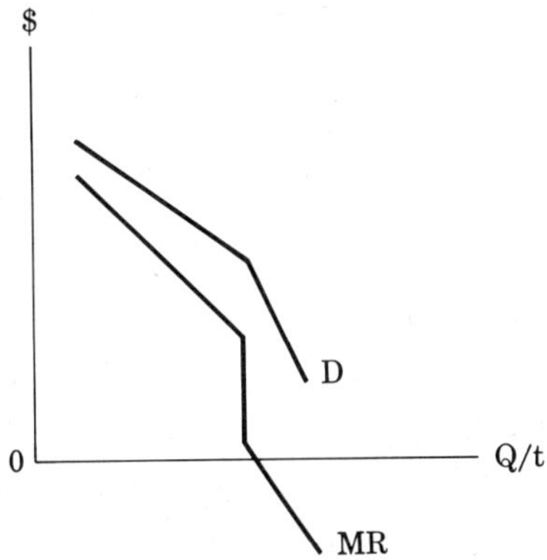

The marginal revenue curve drawn for a kinked demand curve consists of a segment of relatively small slope, a vertical segment at the kink, and a segment of relatively greater slope.

sect, the prices on both are equal, as are the quantities. However, the marginal revenues do not intersect there, and hence are not equal. The marginal revenue related to the less elastic *DD* curve is lower than that related to the *dd* curve at this price (Figure 10–13). The formula $MR = P - P/e$ will attest to this. At the point of intersection, *P* is the same on both demand curves. However, price elasticity is lower on *DD* than on *dd*. The lower elasticity indicates a lower marginal revenue associated with any given price.

How can there be two different marginal revenues at the same quantity? Strictly speaking, rather than two marginal revenues at this quantity, there are none. The marginal revenue, remember, is the slope of the total revenue curve, and the total revenue curve also has a kink at this quantity. You cannot draw a line tangent to a curve at a point where there is a kink (Figure 10–14). What happens is that we get one value as we approach the kinked point from above and another as we approach it from below. Exactly at the kinked point, there is a gap that is drawn as a vertical segment in the marginal revenue curve. Thus the marginal revenue curve consists of a sloping section, a vertical section, and then another, more steeply sloped section (Figure 10–15).

FIGURE 10–16. Marginal Revenue–Marginal Cost Conditions Under the Kinked Demand Curve

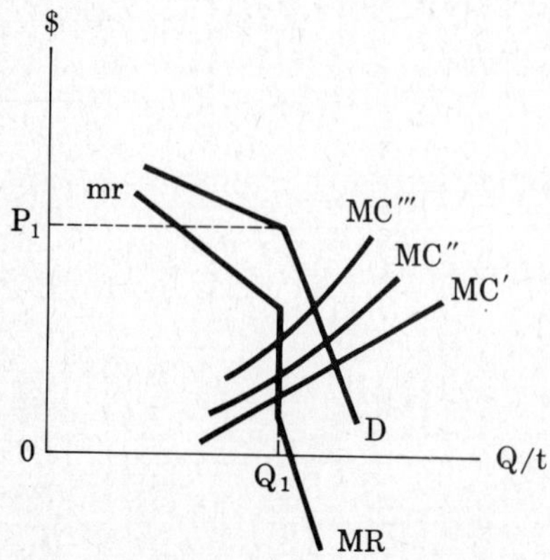

Even though the marginal cost curve shifts up or down, as long as it still intersects the marginal revenue curve in the vertical segment, it still leads to the same quantity and price as profit-maximizing conditions.

Why make such a big deal of the marginal revenue curve?

The big deal is made because if we pursue our marginal cost–marginal revenue criterion for profit maximization in the light of this marginal revenue curve, we find that there are a number of marginal cost curves that will give us the same profit-maximizing price and output. Notice that the marginal cost curve can shift up or down within the boundaries of the vertical segment of the marginal revenue curve and still intersect it at the same quantity. Then, of course, projecting up to the demand curve, we still find that this quantity is sold at the price at which the kink occurs. Therefore, price and quantity have a tendency to remain fixed at the profit-maximizing levels, even if there are changes in costs. Generalizing, we can state that oligopolists tend to keep their prices fixed longer than firms would under other market structures. The kinked demand curve says that if one lowers its prices, others will match, benefiting no one; and if one raises its price, none of the others will match, thereby causing loss of sales. It seems reasonable to stay where you are, and the marginal analysis we have just presented confirms that such an action will be profit-maximizing by the normal $MR = MC$

criterion as well (Figure 10–16). Oligopolists choose non-price forms of competition.

What determines the price at which the kink occurs?

This is one of the major weaknesses of this particular analysis. There is no explanation of how the kink occurs in the first place. We have a chicken-and-egg problem here. Prices will remain stable at the output at which the kink occurs, and the kink will occur at the output at which the stable price holds. However, it is hard to determine why this particular price comes into being. Additionally, there is no assurance in the analysis that this price maximizes the profits of the industry as a whole, thereby giving it at least the justification Chamberlin found in stability through cooperation. All the Sweezy kinked demand analysis tells us is that prices will remain fairly constant if profit-maximizing individual oligopolists follow normal maximizing principles.

Why doesn't the kinked demand curve arise in the case of monopolistic competition?

Interestingly enough, the concept of a *dd* and *DD* demand curve arose in Edward Chamberlin's original discussion of monopolistic competition. The Sweezy kinked demand curve came later, borrowing these two ideas and putting them to work in a specific application, that is, explaining why prices tend to remain stable under oligopoly. However, if we are to get a full picture of the workings of the monopolistic competition model as developed by Chamberlin, we ought to digress from our oligopoly discussion to take note of the role these two demand curves play in monopolistic competition.

How do the* DD *and* dd *curves work in the monopolistic competition model?

Remember that there are many suppliers of similar products in this model. Each thinks that he enjoys the anonymity of pure competition. The number of sellers is so great that even if one seller cuts price and consequently wins away customers from other sellers, he gets only a few from *each* of them. The effect is dispersed among such a great number that no *one* suffers more than a microscopic shift of his demand curve and feels no need to retaliate. Therefore, each participant perceives the market in terms of the *dd* curve with no price retaliation anticipated. If, because of a change in total demand or a change in cost or simply a reevaluation of the market, a producer decides that he is not equating marginal cost with marginal revenue, it is the marginal

FIGURE 10–17. DD *and* dd *Curves Under Monopolistic Competition*

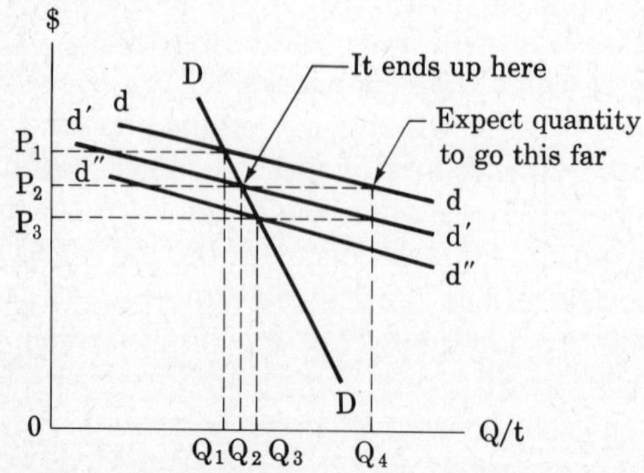

Each firm thinks that its demand curve is *dd*. It lowers price, expecting quantity sold to increase from Q_1 to Q_4. However, because other firms also lower their prices, the quantity changes only to Q_2. The new *dd* curve that the individual firm now thinks applies to his situation is *dd′*. However, lowering of price again is accompanied by other firms doing the same thing, so the effect is to cause *dd′* to slide further down the *DD* curve to *dd″*.

revenue of the *dd* curve he should consider and the price change he makes should relate to the *dd* demand curve.

If there is no matching of price under monopolistic competition, how does the DD curve come in?

Although there is no conscious matching of price in *retaliation* on the part of sellers in this market structure, Chamberlin pointed out that all of the firms in the group face similar cost and demand situations. The competitive nature of monopolistic competition forces each firm to adopt the most efficient technology that is available to any other competitor in order to compete on a price basis. We have already seen that the long-run equilibrium is a zero-profit condition because of easy entry. If efficient firms have zero profit, there is no room for inefficiency. Because the products are defined as only slightly differentiated, the demand curves are alike. Hence all firms have similar demand and production conditions. Any action taken *spontaneously* by one firm in an effort to maximize profits will also be taken *spontaneously* by the others. We emphasize the word spontaneously to point out that these matching changes are not in retaliation (as occurs in oligopoly), but rather they are simply mutual reactions to mutually perceived market opportunities. Nevertheless, the result is to produce a *DD*-type demand curve. When one firm sees an opportunity to lower price in order to increase profits, so too do the others. The result, of course, is to render each firm's action incorrect, because the quantity that was anticipated from the price change does not occur. Quantity was expected to respond to price changes along the *dd* curve, and instead the actual quantity change occurred along the *DD* curve.

Where does it all lead?
You should recognize now that, in the absence of a unique opportunity available to only one monopolistic competitor, the operational demand curve is the *DD* curve, even though each supplier thinks it is *dd*. We can therefore envision a demand curve family such as shown in Figure 10–17, whereby there is a *dd* curve radiating out from every point along the *DD* curve. Change of price is made in terms of *dd* expectations, but the result is merely to slide down the *DD* curve to a new position at the lowered price. Another *dd* curve is perceived to radiate out from this level.

Which demand curve shifts as a result of entry of competition into the industry?
We have said that when competitors are attracted by profit opportunities in the industry, their entry shifts the demand curve of the existing firms to the left. The question is, Which curve shifts, *DD* or *dd*? There is really only one curve that exists in the market, and that is the *DD*. The *dd* curves are hallucinations, seen by individual sellers but never actually operating. Therefore entry shifts the *DD* curve. Of course, wherever the *DD* curve goes, the *dd* curves go also, because they radiate out from it at the prevailing price levels (Figure 10–18).

Which demand curve is tangent to the average cost curve at equilibrium?
Here you will have to forgive me for an oversimplification in the previous chapter. There I asserted that entry of competitors would shift the demand curve until it eventually was tangent to the average cost curve, yielding zero profits and effectively cutting off entry. Before learning that there are two types of demand curves, this is a reasonable first approximation, and many explanations stop here. However, now that we

FIGURE 10–18. Entry of Firms Shifts DD *Curves*

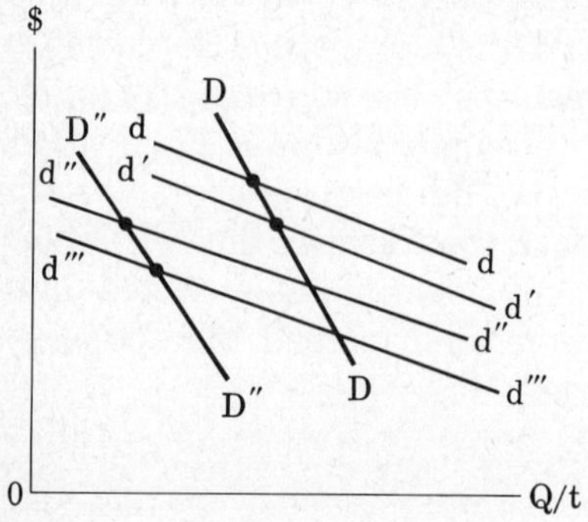

Wherever the *DD* curve shifts to, there is a *dd* curve radiating out from it at the existing price. Thus, entry causes both to move, but the *dd* curve is an artifact of the *DD* curve and the current price level.

FIGURE 10–19. The Long-Run Equilibrium—Monopolistic Competition

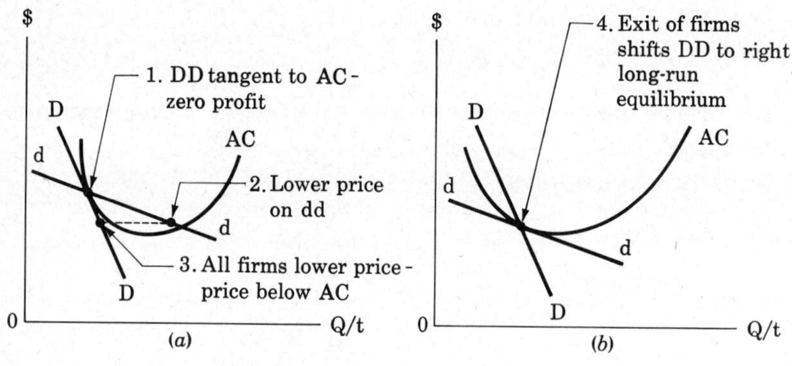

Economic profits attract competition into the industry, causing the *DD* curve to shift to the left. However, at the point where the *DD* curve is tangent to the average cost curve (zero profits), it still appears possible for a single firm to increase its profits by lowering price along *dd*. But, when all firms try to lower price, they find themselves on the *DD* curve at a point below the average cost curve (*a*). These losses induce *exiting* from the industry and shift the *DD* curve to the right. This continues until there is equilibrium with the *dd* curve tangent to the average cost curve and the *DD* curve intersecting it at this point (*b*). The steps are numbered in the diagram.

have somewhat more high-powered equipment, we can give a fuller explanation. *The long-run equilibrium must see the dd curve tangent to the average cost curve with the DD curve passing through the point of tangency* (Figure 10–19). The reasoning is as follows: As long as there are profits, firms will enter the industry. This will shift the *DD* curve. Also, as long as there are opportunities to improve profits through price changes, individual firms will change their prices. The only condition under which there is no incentive to attempt to improve profits through price change, nor for new firms to enter because of excessive profits, occurs at the point where the *dd* curve is tangent to the average cost curve and the *DD* curve intersects both. Here there are zero profits, and any different price produces loss because the *dd* curve lies below the average cost curve at all different levels of output.

Do the generalizations made about the efficiency of monopolistic competition in the previous chapter still hold?

Yes. The conclusion that monopolistic competition leads to so many small firms that not all of the economies of scale can be exploited still holds. The tangency still occurs on the downward-sloping portion of the demand curve. The firms are not big enough to exploit all the long-run economies of scale, but they are nevertheless run at a less-than-optimum rate of output in the short run. These twin sources of inefficiency are incurred in exchange for the benefits of having a diverse assortment of goods offered in the marketplace to a diversified population. Besides, the losses are not too great, because the demand curve facing each monopolistic competitor is very elastic, so its tangency is close to the low point on the *LAC*.

Let's get back to oligopoly. We noted that under the kinked demand curve, industry profits were not necessarily high. How can they made higher?

Under the Sweezy model, we accounted for stable prices in the face of possibly rising costs. This is certainly not the path to maximum possible industry profits. This behavior occurs simply because each firm is frozen to its behavior pattern by fear of retaliation on the part of the other firms in the industry. This pattern could be altered if the firms could eliminate their uncertainty regarding retaliation by opponents.

Remember that in each oligopolistic industry there are only a handful of competing firms. They know each other. It is possible that at some time during their careers managers of the different firms may have worked together. Certainly they meet at trade shows and fairs. They are also aware that each of them, in pursuing his own profit maximiza-

FIGURE 10–20. A Cartel

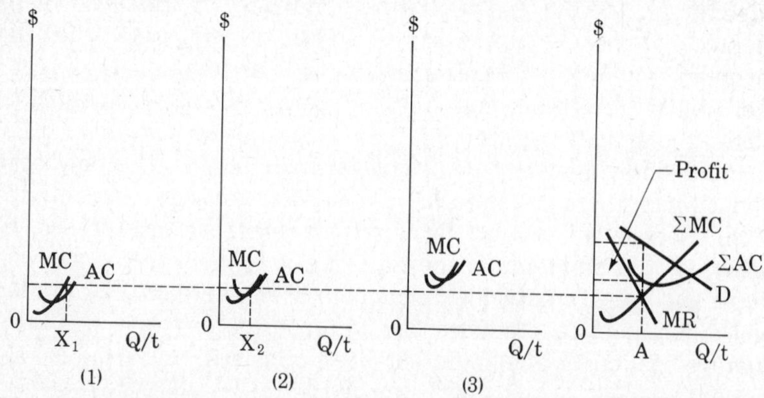

A cartel produces as a group of individuals but sells as a monopolist. Its aggregate marginal cost consists of the sum of the firms' individual marginal cost curves. Its demand curve is the monopolist's demand curve facing the total industry.

tion, will invite retaliation, with the result that all will suffer. Under these circumstances there is a great temptation to cooperate rather than compete, and establish a price level under which all can prosper handsomely. That way there is less work, less anxiety, and more profit. Certainly ideal for a utility maximizer.

Why don't oligopolists cooperate?

Price collusion seems like a natural and obvious way for oligopolists to find their way out of their dilemma. Indeed, wise old Adam Smith opined: "People of the same trade seldom meet together even for merriment and diversion, but the conversation ends in a conspiracy against the public, or in some contrivance to raise prices." This sentiment is echoed less elegantly by the electrical industry executive who stated that price fixing is a "way of life" in big business. Unfortunately, he was on his way to jail, since under the Sherman Antitrust Act such cooperation is illegal and subject to heavy fines and imprisonment. The executive mentioned above was involved in the electrical equipment price-fixing case, one of the biggest in recent times, in which some 29 different companies selling generators, transformers, and switching gear totaling $1.5 billion annually conspired to rig bids so as to divide up the market and allow all to prosper. The top management of General

Electric, Westinghouse, and the other giants involved denied all knowledge of the practice. The pressure was so heavy on middle management to produce that they felt compelled to risk fines, loss of job, and jail in order to avoid price competition. From this case we can get some feel for the anxiety and insecurity that can be generated among oligopolists in a free market.

If there were no antitrust laws, would it always be in the interest of oligopolists to cooperate?

First, let us see what cooperation involves. In order to begin to be worthwhile at all, prices must be held higher through cooperation than those that would prevail under competition. All sellers must thrive under the price umbrella. However, remember the law of demand. If prices are held high, the total quantity that the *industry* can sell is reduced. Some firms will see their total output drop below where it might have been if they had competed freely and independently. Of course, the rationale is that despite the lower volume, the firm is more profitable through cooperation than it would be under competition.

Is the firm more profitable under cooperation than it would be under competition?

Rather than simply answer this yes or no, let us develop an economic model and examine the problem. The most extreme form of cooperation (collusion) is formation of a centralized cartel. Under a cartel arrangement, all the individual producers agree to consolidate the sale of their output through a central sales agent. The DeBeers diamond cartel is the best-known and most successful in today's world. The diamonds mined in South Africa by the various private producers are all sold through a central agent. The purpose, of course, is to hold the world price of diamonds up by withholding supply from the market. When the cartel is complete, we have the following situation: Each firm retains its own internal marginal and average cost structure. However, the cartel faces a monopolist's demand curve. Because a single cartel is doing all of the selling, it is in effect a monopolist. Its downward-sloping demand curve has a marginal revenue curve that lies below it. By horizontally adding together the individual firms' marginal cost curves, the cartel computes its aggregate marginal cost curve and, in typical monopolist fashion, attempts to maximize the profits of the group by equating marginal cost with marginal revenue, asking the price indicated on the demand curve. Total profits are shown by the rectangle bounded by quantity on one side and the difference between average cost and price on the other (Figure 10–20). The question of whether

FIGURE 10–21. Assigning Cartel Output Quotas

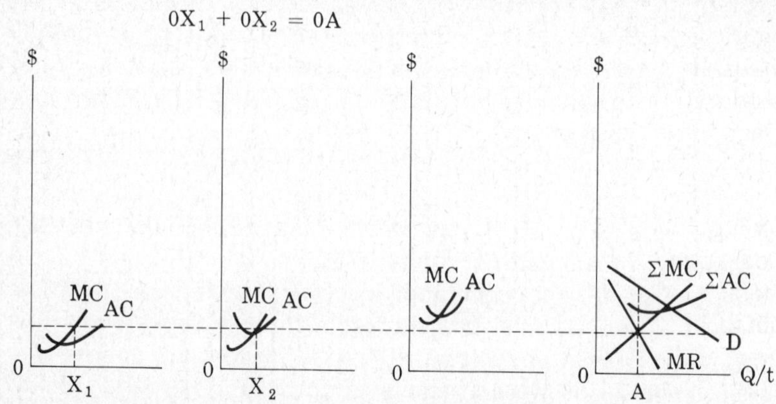

The cartel should allocate the profit-maximizing output among its constituent firms so that the marginal cost of each is equal. However, in this case, firm 3's lowest marginal cost exceeds the common *MC* value and it does not receive any quota, but it does share in the total profits.

or not a particular producer is better off depends on how the cartel allocates the aggregate profits among the individual producers.

Won't the cartel allocate profits in proportion to the output each firm produces?

Perhaps. But this raises the question of how the cartel allocates *output* among the members firms. Remember that the cartel sets a higher market price than would have occurred in its absence. This is the justification for its existence. Because the price is high, the quantity sold by the entire industry is lower than it would have been in the absence of the cartel. Some firms must be restrained from producing their normal output and assigned a quota instead, that is, some part of the total output. The profit-maximizing approach for the cartel is to divide up total production among its member firms so that the marginal cost of each of the different producers is identical. By now such a conclusion should begin to seem reasonable to you. The reasoning is similar to that used in the discussion of why a discriminating monopolist allocates output among the different markets with marginal revenue equal in each. In that discussion we found that any departure from equal marginal revenues caused the seller to lose more revenue in the market from which he took the unit than he gained in the market to which he redirected the unit. Here we find that if we depart from the equal marginal cost criterion, we take a unit from one plant where it is being produced at the common marginal cost level and reassign it to another plant where the cost of production will be higher because marginal cost increases with output. Hence cost minimization calls for an allocation of output that equates marginal cost in the different plants. Now, profits can be allocated in proportion to output, except for one thing. Some plants, such as firm 3 in Figure 10–21, may be such high-cost, inefficient operations that they won't be called upon to produce *any* output. Their lowest marginal cost is higher than the equalized marginal cost of the cartel. They will contribute no production. Should they get no profit? If they don't get any profit, they will not remain in the cartel. If they are given a share of the cartel's profit, the others cannot also be compensated for the full amount they produce, because the nonproducer's income must come from someplace. This impasse is one problem that the cartel faces.

What choice does the high-cost producer have if his cost of production is higher than price?

His cost of production is not necessarily higher than price. It is only higher than the marginal cost of the other producers at the output at which they are operating. Observe something very interesting about the cartel structure: As soon as the cartel fixes the price of the product, this price in effect becomes guaranteed to any one else who wishes to sell in competition with the cartel (Figure 10–22). Other, would-be producers can think in terms of a horizontal demand curve, whereby they can sell all that they wish at the fixed, cartel price. Note the similarity to Bertrand's model. When the demand curve becomes horizontal, so too does the marginal revenue curve. They coincide just as they do under pure competition. If the high-cost producer now thinks of the demand curve he faces as being horizontal at the cartel price and attempts to equate his own marginal cost with the higher marginal revenue (equal to price), he is able to produce and sell quite profitably under the cartel umbrella. In effect, he gets a free ride. His profit-maximizing output occurs at the output where his marginal cost equals marginal revenue. However, marginal revenue is now equal to price, whereas for the cartel it is below price due to the downward slope of the demand curve. This higher marginal revenue allows production of a greater level of output before marginal cost comes to equal it. A producer may find that the high volume he thus is able to sell will make him more profitable outside the cartel than are his more efficient com-

FIGURE 10–22. A Price Fixed by a Cartel

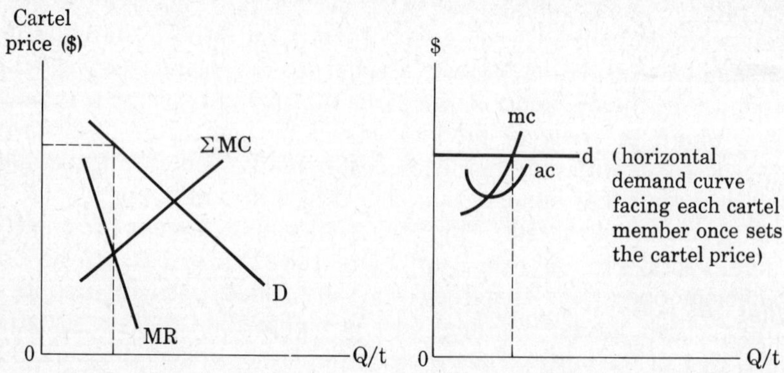

Once the cartel sets a price, it in effect creates a kinked industry demand curve with a horizontal segment running from zero to the quantity that can be sold at the cartel price. Because each firm operates at less than this quantity, they in effect would face the horizontal segment of the demand curve if they were outside the cartel. Firm 3 can produce and sell the output $0x_3$ if it leaves the cartel, whereas it is assigned no output if it remains within the group (Figure 10–21).

FIGURE 10–23. Cartel Results If All Firms Cheat

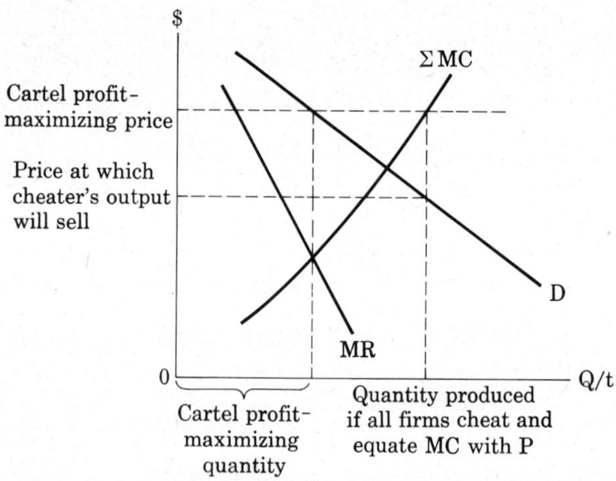

If all firms attempt to produce at the output where their marginal cost equals the market price, the result will be an overproduction in the market. The cartel will be unable to sustain this price, which will fall to the point on the demand curve at which such a quantity will be taken off the market.

petitors who remain within the cartel. How do you think this is going to affect the cartel members?

What will the cartel members do?

There is a possibility that they too will realize that if marginal revenue is as high as the price due to a horizontal demand curve, they can increase their output and sell outside the cartel. In effect, they will cheat, selling their normal quota within the cartel and then attempting to continue output up to the point where marginal cost equals price (Figure 10–23). The consequence of this, if the cheater is a sizable producer, or if there are a large number of cheaters, is to break the cartel. The market supply becomes too large for all goods to clear at the high cartel price (Figure 10–23). From this analysis, economists conclude that cartels may tend to be inherently unstable. There is a great temptation for firms operating within the climate of the high price created by the cartel, to try to get more than their share. However, by so trying, the environment of price shelter that the cartel created is destroyed.

Remember that cartels are illegal in the United States anyway, although there is evidence that they exist. What you should take away from this discussion is the notion of the different perceptions individuals can have of the demand curve and the consequences these perceptions have for production. As long as the demand curve is downward sloping and marginal revenue lies below it, producers are motivated to hold output down to a level at which $P > MC$. However, if the condition exists whereby they see their own demand curve as horizontal, they will increase output to the point where P equals MC. This is bad news for the cartel, but it can be good news for consumers. The increased quantities will drive prices down to clear the markets.

What can we conclude about oligopoly markets?

Having come this far in our study of oligopoly models, we conclude that:

1. Oligopolies are vulnerable to ruinous price competition.
2. Because of the threat of price retaliation, oligopolists tend to hold

their prices steady, even in the face of rising costs. The kinked demand curve model suggests that a profit squeeze will occur, but this is still the most acceptable outcome under the circumstances.

3. The profit squeeze can be avoided by forming a cartel in which all oligopolists share a market cooperatively and divide up the industry profits on some basis. However, the cartel, aside from being illegal in the United States, has certain inherent weaknesses that may inhibit its ability to sustain monopoly level prices.

Oligopolists are therefore left with market structures that they find unsatisfactory. In real life, industries go from one attempted solution to another. Some may try price leadership where there is a tacit agreement to follow the pricing lead of one member of the industry. The *tacit* nature of the understanding avoids the judicial pitfalls of collusion, but also produces uncertainties regarding the response of the presumed price followers. For example, consider the experience of the tin can industry during the 1950s. Here American Can Company, the traditional price leader, raised its prices on all products by 6 percent in September 1958. Continental Can, rather than accepting the role of follower, raised its prices by only 3 percent. At this point American Can retaliated by cutting price from 2 to 5 percent, which Continental matched and then some. By mid-1959 prices were 10 percent below the point they had been a year earlier, rather than 6 percent above as American had intended through its initial raise. Price leadership obviously has its shortcomings as a means of bringing orderly conditions to the market. This becomes particularly true during times of recession (as 1958 was), when demand is sluggish and competition goes all out. It is then, however, that the weaker firms most crave stability. Indeed, during the Great depression of the 1930s, the National Recovery Act sponsored by the Roosevelt administration attempted to impose officially sanctioned minimum price levels on entire industries, only to have them struck down by the Supreme Court as unconstitutional.

Finding price leadership ineffective, oligopolistic industries may attempt illegal cartels, only to have antitrust prosecution force dissolution of this effort and send them back to a period of timidly absorbing cost changes until one firm or another again becomes aggressive and institutes a competitive effort through price change.

The study of oligopolistic markets is the study of big business as it attempts to thread its way between adherence to America's antitrust laws and the rigors of market competition. There is extensive casework in this area, some from court proceedings and some from business historians, to which the student is recommended. For our own part, we must call this the wrap-up of the theory of the firm and go on in Chapter 11 to consider the theory of income distribution.

CHAPTER HIGHLIGHTS

1. *We identified oligopoly as a particularly difficult market structure to analyze because of the possibility of retaliation by one competitor to pricing initiatives taken by another.*
2. *To illustrate the types of problems found, we considered the duopoly models of Cournot, Bertrand, and Chamberlin. The reaction model was introduced as a tool for studying the behavior of oligopolists.*
3. *Two concepts of the demand curve were discussed: the* DD *curve, in which price changes taken by one firm are imitated by others; and the* dd *curve, in which they are not.*
4. *An outgrowth of the two demand curves was found to be the kinked demand curve. This curve shows demand facing an oligopolist to be more elastic for price increases than for price reductions.*
5. *The nature of the kinked demand curve, along with the discontinuity found in its marginal revenue curve, leads to the conclusion that oligopolists change price less frequently than firms facing more competitive market conditions.*
6. *Next we digressed from oligopoly to consider the long-run equilibrium condition in Chamberlin's monopolistic competition analysis. We saw the role played by the* dd *and* DD *curves.*
7. *Finally, we considered the possibilities of collusive behavior on the part of oligopolists. We examined how cartels operate, and evaluated their relative strengths and weaknesses.*

QUESTIONS

1. U.S. Secretary of State Henry Kissinger proposed that the oil-consuming nations form a cartel to counteract the oil-producing countries' cartel (OPEC). He proposed that the consumers' cartel should guarantee a price floor for oil. Commenting on this proposal, Economist Milton Friedman said, "In my opinion, this proposal would simply bail the OPEC cartel out of coming difficulties. . . . Far from solving the energy problem, it would convert a temporary shortage into a permanent waste of resources." Why do you suppose Kissinger recommended a price floor? Do you agree with Friedman's assessment that the OPEC cartel would soon face oversupply difficulties?
2. Many economists argue that the major effect of an increase in the federal minimum wage is an increase in the unemployment of people with low skills. They use the supply-and-demand analysis and point to a disequilibrium price above the equilibrium. Suppose

that the employer is an oligopolist with a kinked demand curve. Would the kink and its attendant discontinuous marginal revenue curve change this effect on employment? If so, how?

3. *A measure called the concentration ratio is used to determine the degree of oligopoly in an industry. The concentration ratio measures the percentage of total industry output produced by the four largest firms. Some economists suggest that a concentration ratio of 40 percent marks an industry in which oligopoly (recognition of price interdependence) is present. On this basis, 42 percent of all output was produced in oligopoly-like industries. Do you think that the concentration ratio is a good measure? Do you think that price interdependence occurs in more or less than 42 percent of the total national output?*
4. *Some years ago the American Basketball Association and the National Basketball Association engaged in a bidding war for top college basketball players. Can you describe this conflict in terms of a reaction model? Does the reaction model suggest that something akin to a Chamberlin-like accommodation would be a logical result?*
5. *A common practice during an inflationary period is for manufacturers to reduce the quantity of a product that they put into a package while holding the price constant. Can the kinked demand curve analysis explain this practice?*
6. *Following the success of the OPEC cartel, numerous other producers of primary materials considered forming cartels of their own to force price increases on the consuming nations. Among these are the bauxite producers and the banana growers. Evaluate the likelihood of each of these succeeding.*

11 The market for factors of production: demand

In Chapter 1 we pointed out our concern with markets for both goods and services and for factors of production. The circular flow of wealth diagram make it evident that the two markets were intertwined —the household sector provides the *demand* for a good part of the finished goods and services *supplied* by the business sector. In order to be able to buy the goods, however, households must have income. Their income comes from the *supply* of their labor and property to the business sector. The businesses, therefore, are on the *demand* side of the equation for these factor services, and they pay for these services with income gained from sale of products. We want to break into the circle at this point and examine the mechanics of business demand for factors of production. The major difference between the factor market and the goods and services market is that the demand for factors of production is a *derived demand*. This is sufficient to warrant separate treatment.

What is derived demand?

Consumer goods and services are demanded for their intrinsic ability to satisfy wants. They give utility directly. The demand for factors of production depends not on their own utility but on their ability to produce goods that in turn give utility. Factor demand is at least one step removed from the consumer. Although the immediate buyers of the factors of production are businessmen, factor demand ultimately is derived from consumers' purchases of finished goods and services.

FIGURE 11–1. Production Function

The schedules here show a hypothetical production function in which the amount of capital used is fixed at 1 unit and labor varies in 1-unit increments.

Labor units	*Total product*	*Marginal product of labor*	*Average product of labor*	*VMP_L if price of X is 2*	*VMP_L if price of X is 4*
0	0	0	0	0	20
1	5	5	5	10	20
2	11	6	$5\frac{1}{2}$	12	24
3	18	7	6	14	28
4	26	8	$6\frac{1}{2}$	16	32
5	33	7	$6\frac{3}{5}$	14	28
6	39	6	$6\frac{1}{2}$	12	24
7	44	5	$6\frac{2}{7}$	10	20
8	48	4	6	8	16
9	51	3	$5\frac{2}{3}$	6	12
10	53	2	$5\frac{3}{10}$	4	8
11	54	1	$4\frac{10}{11}$	2	4
12	54	0	$4\frac{1}{2}$	0	0
13	53	−1	$4\frac{1}{13}$	−2	−4

Think of the factors of production as a means to an end—the end of profit maximization for the firm. We must never forget that profit maximization from the sale of goods and services underlies the demand schedules for the factors of production.

Didn't we deal with this already in the chapter on the production function?

No, not exactly. The chapter on the production function describes how inputs are *technologically* related to outputs. When we *assumed* prices of labor and capital, we were able to establish a rule for combining the different factors most effectively. As you recall, we use inputs in combinations that permit the marginal product per dollar spent on one factor to be equal to the marginal product per dollar spent on each of the others: $MP_L/P_L = MP_K/P_K$ and so on. In that discussion we took the prices as given. They were established by "the impersonal forces of supply and demand in the factor markets." Additionally, even though the production function told us how to produce *any* output most efficiently, it did not tell us *which* output should be produced to maximize profit. We had to await the discussion on market structure in the last three chapters before we could conclude that under conditions of pure competition, profit maximization occurs at the output where marginal cost equals price; under imperfect competition, profits are maximized when marginal cost equals marginal revenue.

Study of the derived demand for factors of production requires that we combine our insights into production functions with what we know about the goods and services markets. It is a good opportunity to tie together some of the material we have been developing.

What does the demand curve for labor tell us?

The demand curve for labor tells us no more and no less than any other demand schedule; the number of units of an item that will be bought per unit of time at different market prices. In the case of the labor demand curve, the item is the labor unit and the price is the wage rate. The simplest case is the demand by a single firm for a particular type of labor. We want to show the number of labor units that a firm would employ at different wage rates.

By now you should be more-or-less familiar with the approach marginal analysis takes to problems of this sort. We examine the alternatives: what we get for what we give up. When a worker applies for a job, the employer asks himself what difference it will make to the total output of the firm if he hires the worker. Against this he must measure the wage that the worker will receive. If the wage is less than the worker's contribution, economics says that he should be hired. If the wage exceeds the workers contribution, it would not be in the interests of profit maximization to employ him. In order to make the comparison between what you give versus what you get, both must be stated in the same units. When we considered demand curves for goods and services, we compared the marginal utility of the item with the utility of the money that was asked for it. In the case of demand for factors of production, we compare the dollar value of the wage rate with the dollar *value of the marginal product* of the worker.

What is the value of the marginal product?

We just said that a firm should pay the marginal unit of labor a wage that does not exceed the benefit the marginal unit contributes to the firm. The term used for the gross dollar contribution of the marginal unit of labor to the firm is the *value of the marginal product of labor* *(VMP_L)*. It equals the *marginal physical product of labor* multiplied by the market *price* at which the *product* being produced sells. Look at the production function schedules shown in Figure 11–1. They show how output varies when different amounts of labor are applied to a constant quantity of capital. The *MPL* column shows the marginal physical prod-

FIGURE 11–2. Value of Marginal Product Curve

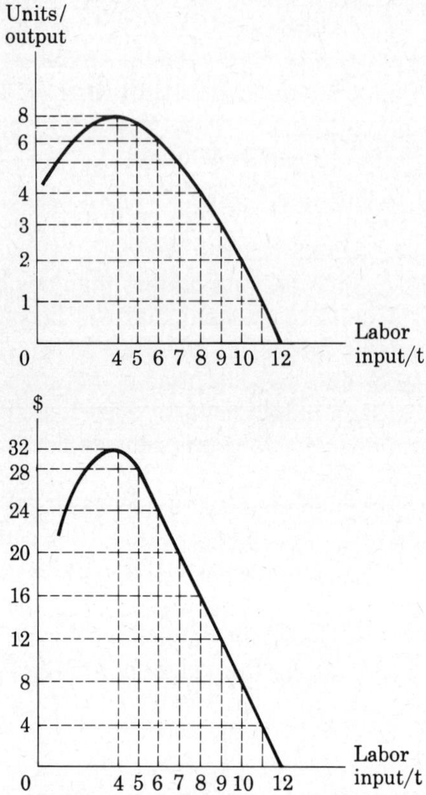

The value of the marginal product curve is the demand curve of the firm for a factor of production. It is found by multiplying the marginal physical product curve by the price at which the product sells in the market. In the figure here, price is assumed to be $4. The data are from Figure 11–1.

uct produced by successive increments to the work force while capital is held constant. The value of the marginal product is equal to this marginal physical product times the price at which each unit of product sells. Suppose that we are making a $2 item. To find the *VMP* schedule, multiply marginal product by $2. If the product sells for $4 in the market, the value of the marginal product is equal to marginal product times 4. Taking the case of a $4 product, we see from Figure 11–1 that employment of the eighth unit of labor adds $16 worth of output beyond what could be produced by 7 units of labor. If the eighth unit of labor adds $16 worth of output, it would not make sense to pay the eighth unit any more than $16 in compensation. But if we pay the eighth unit $16, we must pay every worker $16, in the absence of any form of discrimination. The *VMP* schedule is therefore a demand schedule, because it shows the average price at which different quantities of labor are bought (Figure 11–2).

If you pay labor the full value of the marginal product, what do you have left over to pay the other factors of production?

Good question. Oddly enough, it can be shown that even if you pay labor the entire value of its marginal product, you will have (under constant returns to scale) sufficient surplus left to pay all the other factors their value of the marginal product, including the entrepreneur who gets his normal profit. The surplus can be seen if we draw in the value of the *average* product (*VAP*) curve along with the *VMP*. Returning to our by-now familiar relationship between marginals and averages, we recall that when the average anything is falling, the marginal lies below it in value. In stage II of production, the average product is falling and the marginal product therefore lies below it. The *VAP* is what *each* worker *produces*. The *VMP* is what *each* worker is *paid*. Because all workers on the job get the same wage, and because that wage is low enough to justify employing the *least* productive workers, the others produce a surplus beyond what they are paid.

What do you mean—least productive worker?

Once the marginal worker is employed, he loses his identity as the marginal worker and becomes simply one of the total number of units of labor, each of whom receives the same pay. But that wage must be low enough to justify keeping the marginal worker. The pay rate is equal to the value of the marginal product, which is lower than the value of the average product. This difference between them (i.e., *VAP* – *VMP*), multiplied by the number of units of labor employed, leaves enough surplus to permit each of the other factors also to be paid at their value of the marginal product (Figure 11–3).

How do you know that the surplus created by paying one factor the value of its marginal product will be large enough to permit all others to be paid the value of their marginal products?

Of course, it is important that this be so if we are to generalize that the demand schedule for a factor of production is indeed equal to its value

FIGURE 11–3. Values of the Marginal and Average Product Curves

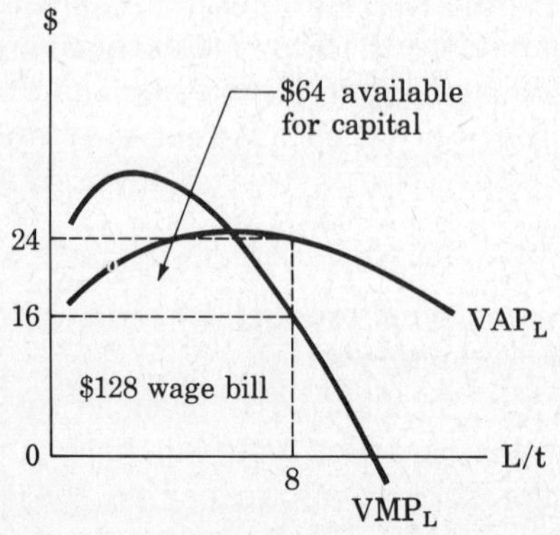

The value of the average product of labor curve lies above the VMP_L. It equals the average product multiplied by the market price of the good. In this example, for which the data were taken from Figure 11–1, 8 workers have a VMP_L of \$16 and a VAP_L of \$24. If each of 8 workers produces a *VAP* of \$24, the total product produced must be worth \$192. Since the workers' wage equals the VMP_L, the total wage payments are 8 times \$16 or \$128. This leaves \$64 with which to compensate capital.

of the marginal product schedule. If every unit of each factor, working cooperatively with all of the others, is to be paid its own *VMP*, then the value of the total product (*VTP*) that all working together produce must equal the sum of the values of the marginal products of the factors multiplied by the respective quantities employed. It turns out that under conditions of constant returns to scale, this will happen. Such a result has come to be called the *adding-up theorem* or *Euler's theorem*. Proof of this mathematical principle is beyond our present means, but the conclusion of the adding-up theorem is not. It states:

$$(VMP_L \times L) + (VMP_K \times K) = VTP$$

The value of the marginal product of labor times the number of units of labor employed, plus the value of the marginal product of capital times the number of units of capital employed, equals the value of the total prouct produced if there are constant returns to scale. All factors can be paid the value of their respective marginal products.

Can you demonstrate this?

Yes, but it is a little tricky. Look back at Chapter 5, where we discussed the symmetry of the stages of production. In Figure 11–3, which is based on the data in Figure 11–1, 8 units of labor are employed. Output is 48 units. At $4 per unit, *VTP* is $192. In order for the data in Figure 11–3 to be consistent with the adding-up theorem, the marginal product of capital must be 16, and because the product sells for $4 per unit, the value of its marginal product must equal $64.

How do you figure that?

If the value of the total product is $192, and if each of the 8 workers receives the value of his marginal product of $16, the total wage bill must be $128. This leaves $64 left to pay capital. The price of the product is $4 per unit, so the marginal physical product must be 16.

And is it?

Taking the data from Figure 11–1, and remembering that according to the ideas developed in Chapter 5 about the symmetry of the stages the average product of labor is equal to the total product of capital, we note that when the L/K ratio went from 7 to 8, the average product of labor went from $6\frac{2}{7}$ to 6. This means that when these figures are considered from the point of view of capital, the K/L ratio goes from $\frac{1}{8}$ to $\frac{1}{7}$ while the total product of capital (equals AP_L) goes from 6 to $6\frac{2}{7}$. In other words, when capital increased by $\frac{1}{56}$th unit ($\frac{1}{7}$ minus $\frac{1}{8}$), its total product increased by $\frac{2}{7}$ of a unit of output. Marginal product is stated in terms of output changes for each one-unit change in input, so we must multiply $\frac{2}{7}$ by 56 in order to get the change in total product if a full unit of capital were added to fixed labor. Fifty-six times $\frac{2}{7}$ equals 16. If the product sells for $4 per unit, we have a VMP_K of $64. Therefore the adding-up theorem states:

$$(VMP_L \times L) + (VMP_K \times K) = VTP$$
$$(16 \times 8) + (64 \times 1) = 192$$

Figure 11–4 shows this distribution of income from the vantage point of capital.

If a firm pays a factor of production the value of its marginal product, will this be profit-maximizing for the firm?

Yes. Up to this point we have defined the profit-maximizing output under pure competition as the output where marginal cost equals price. If we can show that paying a factor of production its value of the mar-

FIGURE 11–4. The Adding-Up Theorem from the Viewpoint of Capital

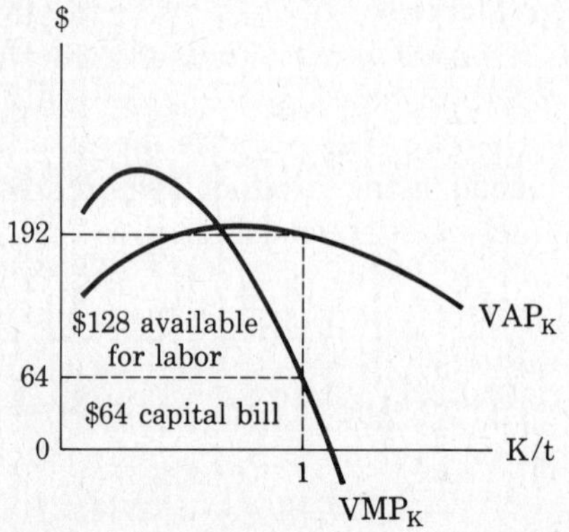

From the data in Figure 11–1, the marginal product of capital can be computed to be 16. The product sells for \$4 per unit, so the value of the marginal product of capital is \$64. Inasmuch as there is only one unit of capital employed, the total bill for capital is \$64. This leaves \$128 for labor, which is the same wage bill found in Figure 11–3.

ginal product is equivalent to producing where marginal cost equals price, we shall demonstrate that this is an alternative way of stating the profit-maximizing rule.

How do you show equivalence between the* MC = P *rule and the* P_L = VMP_L *rule?

We do it with a little algebra.

The value of the marginal product is defined as the marginal product multiplied by the price of X; that is,

$$VMP_L = (MP_L) \times (P_X)$$

We are asserting that profit maximization occurs when this is equal to the price of labor, P_L:

$$MP_L \times P_X = P_L$$

Dividing both sides by MP_L gives

$$P_X = \frac{P_L}{MP_L}$$

Now, notice that the P_L/MP_L is equal to marginal cost of a unit of X. If we employ an extra unit of labor and pay it P_L and it produces MP_L units of output, then *each* of these MP_L units costs P_L/MP_L dollars to produce. If the eighth unit of labor produces 4 units of product X, and we pay labor a wage of $16, the cost of each of the 4 units is $4. This equals the $4 price of X as well. Marginal cost is the cost of producing an extra unit. Each of the MP_L units can be considered the marginal unit and its cost of production is the marginal cost. Therefore, we can write in the last line,

$$P_X = MC_X$$

A profit-maximizing firm producing where MC equals P is paying its factors of production a price equal to the value of the marginal product.

The value of the marginal product curve is the firm's demand curve for a factor of production, correct?
Yes, for that part relating to stage II.

Do you get the industry demand for a factor by adding the marginal product curves horizontally?
Unfortunately it is not as simple as that. We run into a complication when trying to determine the industry's demand for a factor that is similar in nature to the external diseconomies of scale we found in Chapter 6 when examining the long-run average cost curve. There we saw that as an industry expands, the prices of the factors of production are bid up, thereby shifting the long-run average cost curve upward. We run into a similar external diseconomy when computing the industry demand curve for a factor. In this case it involves the price at which the finished product is sold in the market. Under the assumption of pure competition, each firm faces a horizontal demand curve and can sell as much output as it can produce without affecting the market price. However, when we look at the demand curve for the output of the total industry, we find that it slopes downward. In the absence of a shift in demand, the only way the industry can sell greater amounts of the product is through a lower price in the market.

What does the downward-sloping demand curve for the product have to do with the demand for factors of production?
We have seen that the value of marginal product curve can serve as a single firm's demand curve for a factor of production. It is, of course, a *ceteris paribus* demand curve. All other firms are assumed to employ a

FIGURE 11–5. Industry Demand for Factors of Production

Assume that the industry consists of 10 firms. Each has the production function used in Figure 11–1. If the wage rate is \$20, each firm employs 7 workers. The *VMP* of the seventh worker is \$20. Each firm produces 44 units, and the total industry output is 440 units.

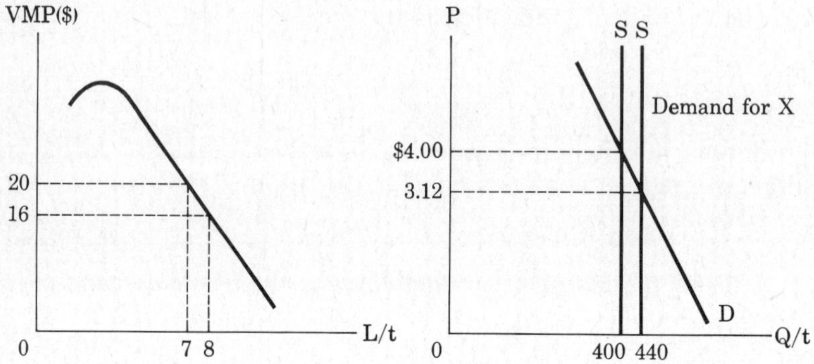

Assume that the wage rate falls to \$16. Each firm would raise its employment to 8 workers, because the *VMP* is \$16 for 8 employees. Notice, however, that the marginal physical product of the eighth worker is 4 units. Throughout the industry, total output would increase by 40 units if each firm hired one additional worker. Assuming demand elasticity for product X of 1/2, this 11 percent increase in quantity would reduce price by approximately 22 percent. If the price of X was \$4, it would decline by \$.88 to \$3.12. This reduction in the price of X reduces the *VMP* of 8 workers to \$12.48 (4 × 3.12). At a wage of \$16, the firms can no longer afford to hire 8 workers.

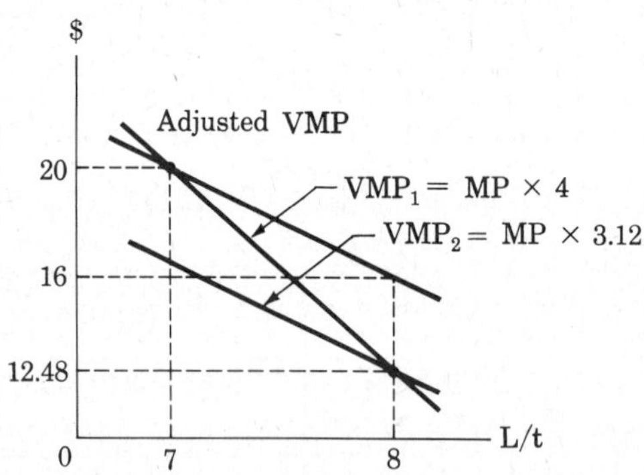

The industry demand curve is equal to 10 times the adjusted *VMP* curve for the firm.

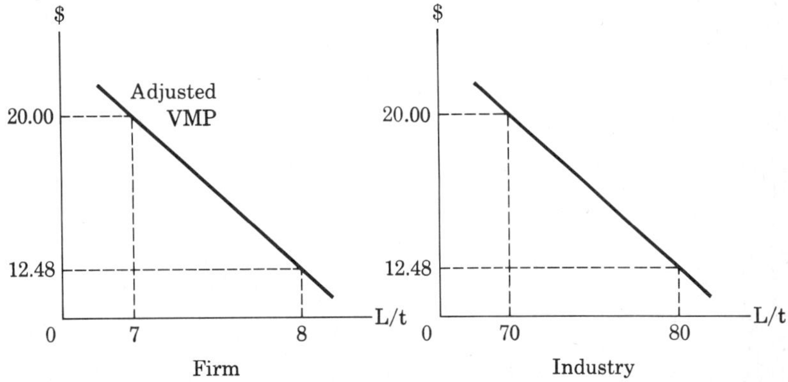

constant amount of labor, and the market price of the product is also assumed to hold constant while we examine factor demand at alternative wage rates. But there is something internally illogical about this idea when we attempt to examine an *industry* demand curve for labor. At points farther to the right along the industry demand curve, all firms employ more labor than they do on the left side of the curve. This means that none of the firms is in a *ceteris paribus* situation. The simple *VMP* demand curve cannot be used, because its underlying assumptions no longer hold. If one firm employs more labor when wages fall, so too will all the others. The result of all this additional employment of labor is greater output, which can only be sold at a lower market price. These lower market prices reduce the value of the marginal product below what would occur under *ceteris paribus* conditions. Speaking realistically, each firm must consider that if it employs more labor because of lower wages, the marginal physical product of labor will fall because of diminishing returns, and also the price of the product will fall because others also employ more labor. Each firm must calculate an *adjusted VMP* curve reflecting not only the falling marginal physical product but also the falling market price of the product. The curve slopes down more steeply than the *ceteris paribus VMP* curve. The industry demand curve for a factor is found by adding together these adjusted *VMP* curves (Figure 11–5).

Would you call that industry demand curve the long-run factor demand curve also?

No, once again there is a complication. Although we relax some of the *ceteris paribus* conditions in order to compute the industry demand curve for labor, there are other conditions that we still hold constant. We cannot say that we have a long-run demand curve until the analysis contends with variable quantities of other inputs, as well. If you will recall our discussion in Chapter 6, the long run is a period over which capital as well as labor inputs vary. We sought the ideal combinations of labor and capital for each alternative quantity of output. A long-run demand curve for labor shows the number of labor units bought at different wage rates while quantity of capital also varies. Similarly, we can develop a demand curve for capital under the condition that labor varies.

Why would varying the amount of capital affect the demand curve for labor?

Again we must draw together a number of elements of economic theory we have discussed in this course. The basic assumption underlying the law of diminishing returns is that for any *given* quantity of capital, the marginal product of labor decreases as more labor is used. That is, as the L/K ratio increases, the marginal product of labor falls. Recall also that an increase in the L/K ratio is also a reduction in the K/L ratio. An increase in the amount of labor using one unit of capital can alternatively be thought of as a reduction in the amount of capital using one unit of labor. We discussed these ideas in conjunction with the symmetry of the stages of production. Assume now that a firm is producing at some given rate of output under profit-maximizing conditions. Each factor of production is paid at a rate equal to the value of its marginal product. Now, assume that the price of labor falls. What happens?

Don't you move down the VMP curve to show the quantity of labor that will be bought at the new, lower price?

You do as a first approximation. But when the quantity of labor the firm employs increases in response to the drop in labor costs, it means that the L/K ratio rises. More important, it also means that the K/L ratio falls. The effect on the marginal productivity of capital is the same as it would be if part of the capital had been removed. MP_K increases, and you move up the marginal physical product of capital schedule. Of course, when that happens, the value of the marginal product of capital (VMP_K) also increases. This induces a disequilibrium with regard to employment of capital, because now VMP_K is greater than P_K.

Profit-maximizing rules say that you should employ more capital under these circumstances. reducing the VMP_K until it equals the price of capital. We therefore find that the reduction in the price of labor first induces an increase in the quantity of labor and then an increase in the quantity of capital used.

Is that all?

No, because the increase in the quantity of capital employed reduces the L/K ratio. And you know what happens when the L/K ratio is reduced: The marginal product of labor is increased. Each unit of labor has more capital with which to work, so the marginal product of labor rises. The MP_L curve shifts up. Now, in order to equate P_L with the value of the marginal product of labor, we must employ even more labor.

And then what happens?

This rise in labor again reduces the K/L ratio. It again raises VMP_K above P_K which again induces an increase in capital. This increase again reduces the L/K ratio, which again raises VMP_L above P_L, which again induces the employment of more labor. The new equilibrium situation will be arrived at through a series of successively smaller feedback responses first in one input and then in another. Eventually the changes die out. The firm will have moved to a new combination of labor and capital inputs and will be producing a new output (Figure 11–6).

How will the successive changes die out?

Profit maximization is still the goal. This requires that MC equal P. Marginal cost can be defined as the price of a factor divided by its VMP, and therefore we shall find that the VMP for each factor continues to shift until finally

$$\frac{P_L}{VMP_L} = \frac{P_K}{VMP_K} = P_X \quad \text{or} \quad MC_X = P_X$$

Can you sum up demand for a factor of production under conditions of pure competition?

We have concluded that if both the labor market and the product market are purely competitive: (1) The short-run demand curve of a firm for a factor of production is defined as its value of the marginal product schedule. (2) The industry demand for a factor is not simply the sum of the industry's VMP curves. Industry demand must consider the changes in the price of the product that occur as different quantities are produced and offered for sale. Each firm's VMP curve is adjusted

FIGURE 11–6. Long-Run Demand for Labor

In part (*a*) the firm starts out in short-run equilibrium with price equal to the value of marginal product.

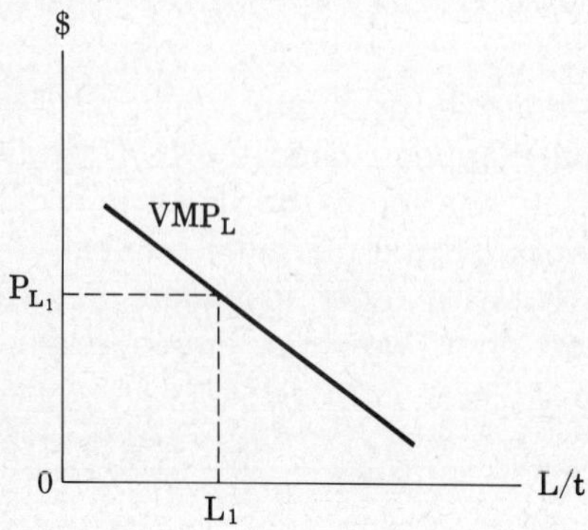

(*a*)

In part (*b*) the market price of labor falls and the firm moves along its *VMP* curve to restore the equilibrium condition. This increases the ratio labor/capital.

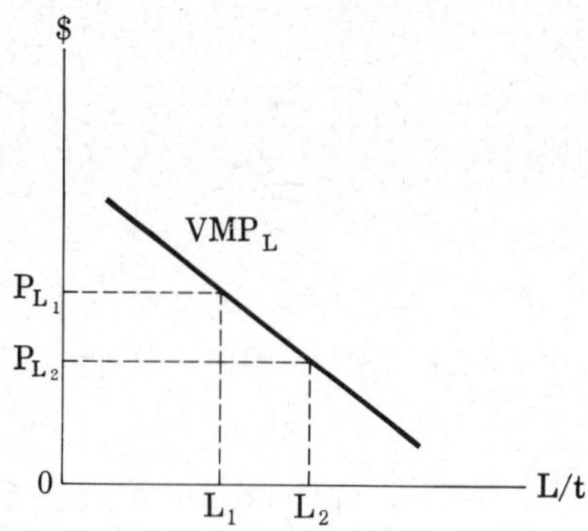

(*b*)

The increase in the labor/capital ratio is in effect a reduction in the capital/labor ratio. This increases the value of the marginal product of capital and causes the VMP_K schedule to shift up. As a result, P_K is less than VMP_K. In order to restore equilibrium, more capital must be employed (*c*).

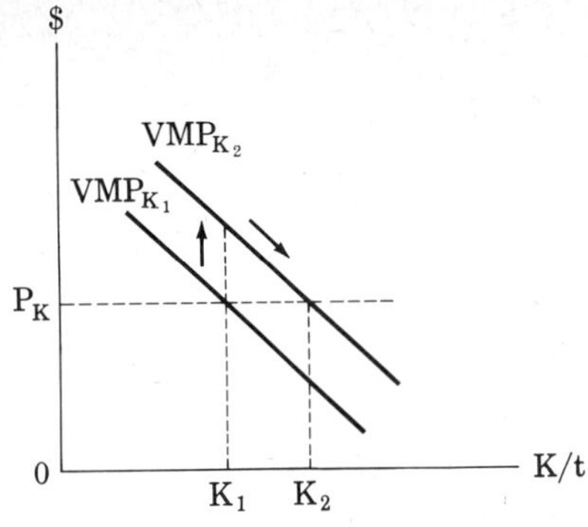

(c)

When additional capital is employed, the capital/labor ratio rises, which is the same as a reduction in the labor/capital ratio. This causes the MP_L schedule to shift up, resulting in P_L being less than VMP_L. In order for the equilibrium to be restored, the quantity of labor must be increased (*d*).

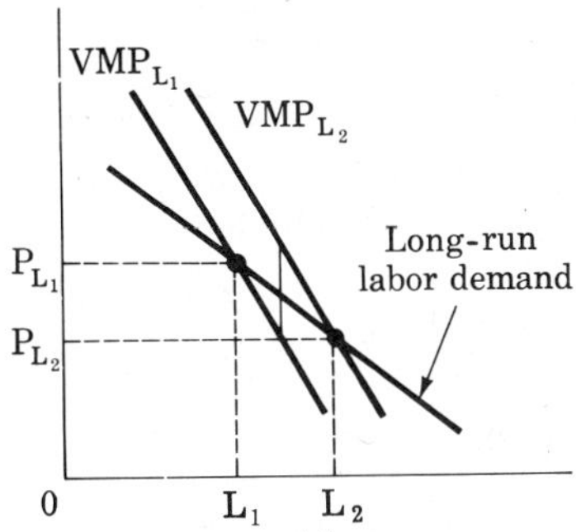

(*d*)

to be less elastic as a result of this consideration. The industry demand curve is the sum of these adjusted *VMP* curves. As different quantities of a factor are employed, its demand is affected by both changing marginal product and changing product price. (3) The long-run demand curve for a factor is more elastic than the short-run demand curve because changes in the quantity of each factor changes the marginal product of all other factors. This interaction among complementary factors increases the demand elasticity.

Frankly, these latter two considerations, the industry and the long-

FIGURE 11–7. Marginal Revenue Product

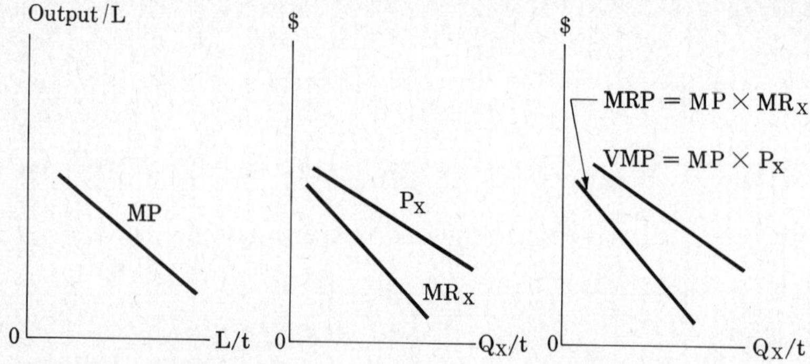

Under imperfect competition a firm must accept reduced market prices for its products if it wishes to increase its sales. Therefore, the contribution a marginal worker makes to the firm is equal to the marginal physical product multiplied by the marginal revenue.

run demand curves, are often omitted from quick discussions, and for simplicity's sake the demand curve for a factor under conditions of competition is said to be its *VMP* schedule. You should, however, be aware that this is an oversimplification.

What happens under conditions of imperfect competition?

The logic we have been employing is still appropriate. However, the details become a little more sticky. First, we should recognize that our analysis involves two markets: the factor market and the goods and services market. We can have imperfection in either or in both markets. The organization of this book puts off discussion of supply of factors until the next chapter, so let us limit this discussion to imperfection in the goods and services market. Recall what in our analysis distinguishes imperfectly competitive markets from those that are perfectly competitive.

Doesn't the demand curve facing each firm slope downward under imperfect competition?

That is correct. A firm operating under imperfect competition cannot sell as much as it wants without affecting the market price. Recall that this downward-sloping demand curve has a marginal revenue schedule that always lies below it. Each quantity of output has a separate price and marginal revenue associated with it. The relationship between them is

$$MR = P - \frac{P}{e}$$

What does this have to do with the demand for factors of production?
Under pure competition the factor demand curve for the firm is defined by the *VMP* curve, which is found by multiplying the marginal product by the price at which each unit of product sells. Because all quantities sell at the same price under pure competition, the firm does not concern itself with the thought that the employment of more workers causes greater output, which must be sold at lower prices if it is to clear the market. This outcome must be recognized under imperfect competition, however. Not only do diminishing returns reduce the marginal physical product; also, attempts to sell this added output force the market price on the marginal unit lower. Of course, by lowering the market price on the marginal unit, the firm must lower the price on all units. Thus the appropriate factor for monetizing marginal product is marginal revenue. Employment of the marginal factor of production under conditions of imperfect competition contributes an amount equal to the marginal physical product multiplied by the marginal revenue. This is called *marginal revenue product (MRP).*

How does marginal revenue product enter demand analysis?
We retain the approach we have been using. A firm does not wish to pay a factor of production any more than the factor contributes to the firm's revenues. Therefore, the marginal revenue product sets the maximum rate at which a firm can afford to pay the marginal worker. And, of course, in the absence of discrimination all workers are paid what the marginal workers gets. Therefore the marginal revenue product schedule is the demand schedule for labor under conditions of imperfect competition in the goods and services markets (Figure 11–7).

What is the consequence of using* MRP *instead of* VMP *for the factor demand curve?
The consequence is that at any given wage rate, fewer workers will be employed if the industry is monopolized than if it were organized as a large number of independent firms. The *MRP* curve is less elastic than the *VMP* curve. Reading out from the *y* axis, we arrive at the *MRP*

FIGURE 11–8. Monopolistic Exploitation

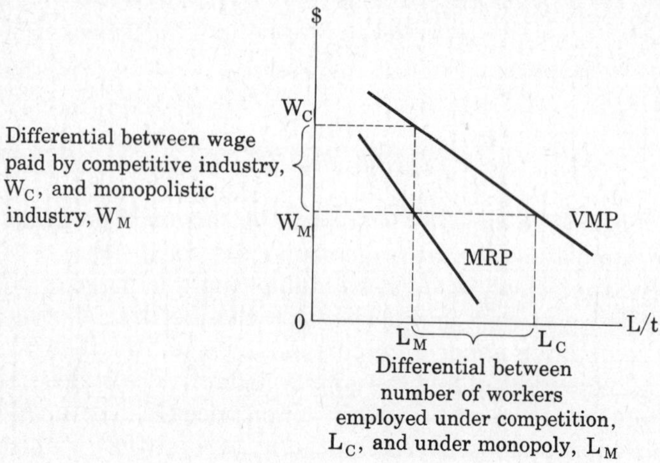

Imperfect competition reduces the number of workers that will be hired at any given wage rate and reduces the wage rate that will be paid to any given quantity of labor.

before the *VMP*. Reading up from the *x* axis, the same thing happens. Any given number of workers gets lower wages. Any given wage rate buys fewer workers. We have already observed in our study of the product markets that organization under a monopoly structure produces less output than would be forthcoming under a competitive structure. Here we have the analog of that finding. If output is lower, fewer workers find employment (Figure 11–8).

That sounds pretty bad.
Economists have given this underemployment a term that sounds really bad. Harking back to Marxian rhetoric, they call it *monopolistic exploitation*. Such a term is a bit much. It does refer, however, to the underemployment of factors in the monopolized market as compared to the competitive market.

Wait a minute. Didn't we decide that when examining the industry demand curve under pure competition, we had to consider lower prices at higher quantities as well? What's the difference?
That's true. We did decide that when determining the demand curve for

an industry, it is necessary to adjust the *VMP* curves of each firm for the fall in market price due to increased output. However, each firm still thinks in terms of a horizontal demand curve facing itself. This curve may shift down as industry output increases, but it does so without any obvious link to actions taken by the individual firm. Therefore the individual firm under pure competition continues to think of the *price* of the product as the factor by which it must mutliply marginal physical product. If this same industry were monopolized, however, and one overall management pondered the implications of changing output, it would recognize that its own decisions produce the different prices. It therefore recognizes marginal revenue as the appropriate factor by which to monetize marginal physical product. When considering the social implications of monopoly in Chapter 10, we pointed out that output would be lower than under competition. Additionally, we have just seen that fewer factors will be employed. Finally, each factor is paid according to his marginal revenue product, but the product is priced in accordance with the value of the marginal product. Thus the public gets fewer units of product and pays a price that exceeds the marginal cost of producing them. No wonder economists make monopoly the bogeyman!

Most of the discussion so far has been in terms of demand for labor. What about discussing the demand for capital?

You're right. We claimed to be discussing demand for factors of production, but have limited the discussion to labor. Of course, there is the need to analyze the demand for capital, and indeed for land as well, because these are the basic factors of production. The considerations behind the demand for capital are essentially the same as those underlying demand for labor. The maximum price that can be paid for a unit of capital cannot exceed the value of the marginal product (or marginal revenue product in the case of imperfect competition) of capital. The demand curve, therefore, is the VMP_K (or MRP_K). However, although the essential concept is the same, there is an important difference between the nature of capital and the nature of labor inputs, and this difference affects the analysis of demand for capital stock.

What is the big difference between labor and capital as inputs?

Although the demand curves for both labor and capital involve marginal product, they differ with regard to the period of time over which each produces its product. When a firm hires a worker, it agrees to pay him for an hour of work and gets it delivered—usually in advance of payment. In the case of capital, an investment by a firm involves the purchase of a durable good that will render its services over a number of years—the life of the machine. The firm pays in advance of receiving the services of the capital asset, and these services trickle in for perhaps the next 20 or 30 years. A single purchase of capital produces a stream of annual *VMP*'s. The demand analysis must compare the price of the capital with the stream of *VMP*'s.

So why not just add up the VMP's?

There are two problems that result from having to wait to get the returns on the investment in piecemeal fashion. The first is the uncertainty of how productive a particular piece of capital will be 10 years in the future. A lot can happen to alter the productivity of a particular investment that was not anticipated at the time the invesment was made. To draw on one event fresh in our memory, the cost of the energy used to run the equipment can triple overnight. Suddenly machinery that requires heavy energy inputs becomes less attractive. A rise in gasoline prices makes heavy automobiles obsolete before their expected life spans end. Under these circumstances the *anticipated* value of the marginal product will never come to pass. The first problem, therefore, is uncertainty about the future.

What is the second problem with having to wait?

The second problem involves a principle that is basic to many financial situations in which there is a stream of future income. Simply put, a dollar of income in the future is worth less now than a dollar of current income. Gertrude Stein not withstanding, a dollar is not a dollar. . . .

Why is future money worth less than present money?

It has to do with interest. Suppose that I earn a dollar this year. If I immediately lend it out at 10 percent interest, next year I will have \$1.10. However, if I didn't even get the dollar until next year, I would be poorer by \$.10. Therefore a dollar a year from now is worth less than a dollar now. It must be adjusted for the interest lost as a result of not having it for the year. This adjustment is called *discounting* the future income.

How do you discount future income?

Back in eighth grade, or before, you may have learned about compound interest. If you have \$1 principal and lend it at 10 percent interest, after 1 year you have

$$\$1.00(1 + .10) = \$1.10$$

After 2 years you have

$$\$1.00(1.10)(1.10) = \$1.00(1.10)^2 = \$1.21$$

After 3 years you have

$$\$1.00(1.10)^3 = \$1.33$$

And so on. Discounting is just the opposite of compounding. Assume that you will receive $1.10 one year from now. In order to calculate the present value of $1.10 to be received one year from now, we ask ourselves how much money we would have to invest now at current interest rates of 10 percent in order to have $1.10 next year. The answer, as we have seen, is

$$\frac{\$1.10}{\$1.10} = \$1.00$$

Thus the present value of $1.10 one year in the future is $1.00. Suppose that we were to receive $1.21 two years from now. What is the present value?

$$\frac{\$1.21}{(\$1.10)^2} = \$1.00$$

The formula for discounting a future income is

$$\text{present value} = \frac{\text{future income}}{(1 + i)^t}$$

where i is the interest rate and t is the number of periods in the future for which income is to be received.

Assuming an interest rate of 10 percent, the present value of $1.00 one year from now is

$$\frac{\$1.00}{(\$1.00 + .10)} = \$.91$$

The present value of $1.00 two years from now is

$$\frac{\$1.00}{(\$1.00 + .10)^2} = \$.83$$

If you invest $.83 for two years at 10 percent interest, you will have $1.00 at the end of the period.

How do you apply these ideas to investment demand schedules?

We must *estimate* the value of the marginal product for *each* year of the asset's life. Let us call these vmp_1, vmp_2, vmp_3, and so on. Then we must discount each down to the present value. Adding the discounted values gives the present value of the entire stream. This discounted

FIGURE 11–9. An Example of Discounted Cash Flow

Suppose that a machine is estimated to last 5 years. The first 2 years it will produce a *vmp* of \$500, then \$400 in year 3, \$300 in year 4, \$200 in year 5, and in year 5 the used machine will be sold for \$4000. What is its present value (PV) if the interest rate is 10 percent?

$$PV = \frac{500}{(1+.10)} + \frac{500}{(1+.10)^2} + \frac{400}{(1+.10)^3} + \frac{300}{(1+.10)^4} + \frac{200}{(1+.10)^5} + \frac{4000}{(1+.10)^5}$$

$$\$3980.00 = 454.50 + 412.00 + 300.40 + 204.90 + 124.20 + 2484.00$$

FIGURE 11–10. The Demand Curve for Capital Stock

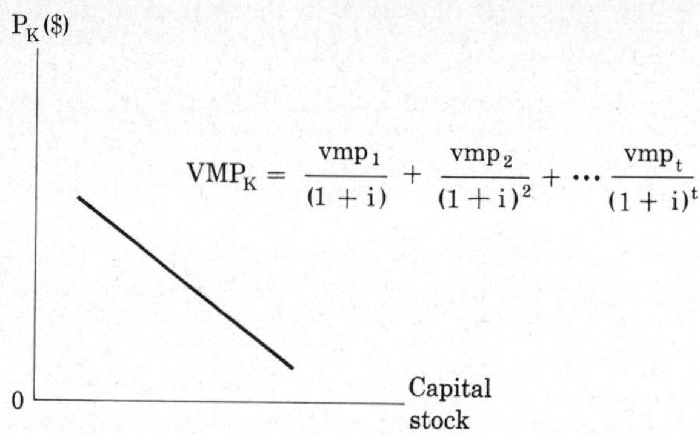

The demand curve for capital stock is the value of marginal product of capital. Before VMP_K can be found, however, each of the annual *vmp*'s must be discounted to the present period. The larger the capital stock, the smaller will be the annual *vmp*'s and also the VMP_K. This follows from the principle of diminishing returns and accounts for the downward slope of the demand curve.

present value of the *vmp*'s is the maximum price that should be paid for the unit of capital (Figure 11–9).

$$VMP_K = \frac{vmp_1}{(1+i)} + \frac{vmp_2}{(1+i)^2} + \frac{vmp_3}{(1+i)^3} + \cdots$$

Are all the annual* vmp's *the same?

Probably not. As the capital depreciates, its productivity will decline toward the later years. On the other hand, if you estimate that there will be continued inflation, you may want to raise your estimate of the price for which the finished products can be sold in later years as contrasted with current years. This rise in P_X will raise the value of the marginal product.

What does this calculation have to do with the idea of a downward-sloping demand curve?

This calculation has nothing to do with the idea of a downward-sloping demand curve. All this calculation does is define what we mean by the value of the marginal product of capital. The downward slope in the demand curve comes from the idea that higher quantities of a factor, other things being equal, have lower marginal physical products. I am sure you remember diminishing returns. If the capital stock were large, the value of the annual *vmp*'s would be smaller. Discounted, they would add up to a smaller VMP_K than if capital stock were small. This means that a large quantity of capital would be employed only if the price of capital were relatively small. On the other hand, if the quantity of capital were small, each of its *vmp*'s would be large and the VMP_K would be commensurately great. A high price could be paid. Alternatively, at high prices for capital, only small amounts would be used. At low prices, more would be used. These conclusions follow from diminishing returns and nothing else. The demand curve shows the maximum price that can be paid for alternative quantities of capital. This is equal to VMP_K (Figure 11–10).

What is the relationship between capital and investment?

This relationship causes a lot of confusion. Our production problems in *microeconomics* are oriented toward discussing the combinations of capital and labor that are used. We deal with capital-labor ratios, and so on. Hence we are interested in the amount of capital stock itself. Changes in capital stock, that is, addition of a marginal unit to or subtraction of a marginal unit from the capital stock, is called net investment or disinvestment. The demand curve we have drawn is a demand curve that shows the amount of capital stock that will be employed at any given price. *It does not show net investment*. The implication is that in equilibrium, net investment is zero. We are neither adding nor subtracting capital. Confusion arises because students of *macroeconomics* are more concerned with investment than with capital, because they want to know how many people will be employed in the

FIGURE 11–11. Demand for Capital as a Function of Interest Rates

The demand curve for capital is the VMP_K curve. This is the discounted value of the stream of *vmp*'s.

$$VMP_K = \frac{vmp_1}{(1+i)} + \frac{vmp_2}{(1+i)^2} + \frac{vmp_3}{(1+i)^3} + \cdots$$

The rate of interest enters the argument through the discounting process. If interest falls, the value of each $vmp/(1+i)$ increases (small denominator). For any given capital stock and stream of *vmp*'s, the VMP_K is increased. This shifts the capital demand curve to the right and permits a larger capital stock to be purchased at the same P_K.

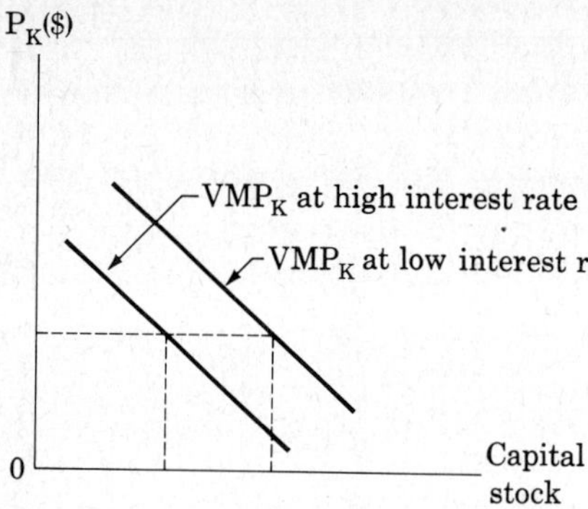

Alternatively, plotting the present value of any given stream of *vmp*'s against interest gives the following.

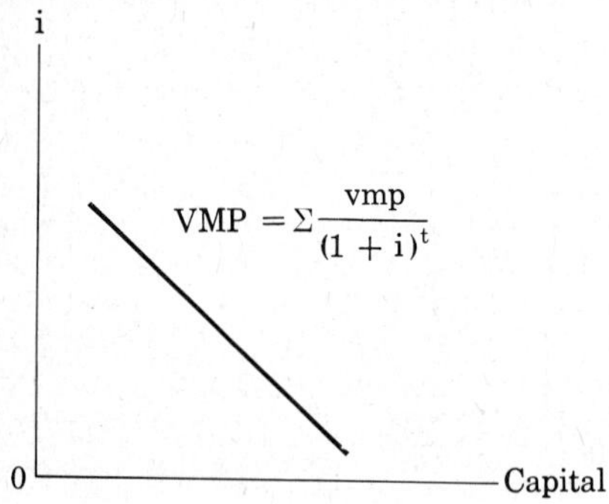

At a constant price of capital, the lower the interest rate, and the more capital stock you can afford to buy.

process of making machinery. Microeconomists are more likely to be interested in capital stock than investment, because they are concerned with where resources are allocated.

What role does the rate of interest play in the demand schedule for capital stock?

You may sometimes hear it said that the demand for capital is a function of the interest rate: The lower the interest rate, the greater the demand for capital. We, on the other hand, have treated demand as a function of price. In the case of capital price is the actual dollar amount that is paid for the machine or building or whatever the capital asset is. Like other demand schedules, the lower the price, the more capital will be demanded; the higher the price, the less capital will be demanded. We reconcile these two different demand functions for capital (i.e., demand as a function of price and demand as a function of interest) by noting the role of interest rates in the discounting process. The present value of a stream of annual vmp_K incomes is discounted more if interest rates are high, and less when they are low.

$$VMP_K = \frac{\sum vmp}{(1 + i)^t}$$

High interest rates shift the demand curve to the left, reducing VMP_K values. Low interest rates shift the demand curve to the right, raising VMP_K values. Therefore the amount of capital employed at any given price will indeed be higher when interest rates are low than when they are high. Demand for capital as a function of interest rates is perfectly consistent with demand for capital as a function of price. Both variables play major roles (Figure 11–11).

We have considered the demand for labor and capital. What about the demand for land?

Land is one of the classic factors of production. Back in the late eighteenth and early nineteenth centuries when the classical writers Smith, Ricardo, and Malthus were developing the bases of economic theory, agriculture rather than industry dominated a nation's production, and the theory of agricultural rents received a great deal of attention. Today there is a tendency to treat land analytically just like capital, examining its discounted value of marginal product to find the maximum rate of compensation that can profitably be offered for its use. It is interesting, however, to review some of the classical theory, now that famine resulting from population pressure on limited land areas is again making the economics of Reverend Malthus more than just a historical curiosity. We begin by focusing on the unique quality of land.

What is the unique quality of land?
Simply that the land is there. It is fixed in quantity. Its cost of production is zero. Its elasticity of supply is zero. The total quantity of land in existence is unrelated to the price offered for it. Therefore any rent received for its use, economically speaking, is a surplus, because the economic cost of producing the land is zero. Please note that we are referring to unimproved, raw land. Any improvements on it are part of *capital*.

Because of the fixed supply of land, the rent it earns is entirely a function of the demand for its use. And the demand for its use is determined by its value of marginal product. If the only use for a piece of New Jersey farmland is to grow tomatoes, the *VMP* will be a function of its productivity and the price of tomatoes. The demand curve for the land use will shift with the vagaries of the tomato market: left when the demand is low and right when demand is high. If, however, as happened to New Jersey farmers and many of their counterparts all over the country, developers see the land as practical for suburban residential use, the value of marginal product curve will shift sharply to the right. In fact, it is quite likely that the price of land for residential use will so far exceed the discounted *VMP* of land in agricultural use that farmers will sell their land to developers and it will shift entirely from agricultural to residential use. The market allocates the use of land. However, it cannot add to the total. That is fixed by nature.

Doesn't the location of the land make a difference?
Yes. Location of land is extremely important in determining rent. Farmers near the metropolitan areas can sell their land for higher prices than those who are farther from the city. Land along a major highway has a higher value of marginal product for industrial use than land far removed from any transportation. All of this is fairly obvious, perhaps, but in order to understand the classical rent theory of Ricardo, we must recognize the heterogeneous character of land.

What is the Ricardian theory of rents?
David Ricardo, arguing for abolition of the English Corn Laws around 1820, developed his differential surplus theory of rent. He pointed out that land available for agriculture varies in fertility, and that in a rational world the most fertile land would be brought under cultivation first. As a country grows, both in population and industrial strength, the demand for food increases, and farmers are forced to bring somewhat less fertile land under cultivation. The less fertile land requires more units of labor input to produce a bushel of corn, with the result

that the cost of production rises. If the cost rises, so too must the price at which the corn is sold. The price must be sufficiently high to cover the cost of production on the least fertile land in use. Meanwhile, production still continues on the *more* fertile land as well, and unit costs there are relatively low because it takes less labor to produce a bushel of output. The fortunate farmer who finds himself on the more fertile land produces at low cost but sells in the market at prices high enough to cover costs on less fertile land. He therefore earns a surplus over his cost, which Ricardo called *rent*. An increasingly infertile land is brought under cultivation in response to growing demand, the costs of production and hence market price continue to rise. Everyone working a piece of land that is superior in quality to the least fertile land will realize a surplus rent. The least fertile land is called the *no-rent land*.

We see, therefore, that the different farmers cover their costs, earn a *normal* profit, and in addition, earn a rental surplus ranging from zero on the no-rent land to very large rents on the most fertile land. Ricardo argued that all income beyond normal profit could be taken from the tenant farmer by the landlord, in the form of rent charge, without driving the farmers from the land or reducing the supply of food grown. Each farmer would be left with a normal profit that just matched the opportunities available to him elsewhere. Henry George, 50 years later, used the same argument to justify government taking the "unearned increment" as a single tax.

Ricardo summed up his rental argument as follows: "The value of corn is regulated by the quantity of labor bestowed on its production on that quality of land, or with that portion of capital which pays no rent. Corn is not high because a rent is paid, but a rent is paid because corn is high; and it has been justly observed that no reduction would take place in the price of corn, although the landlord should forego the whole of their rent. . . ."

Why do we spend time here on Ricardo? This isn't supposed to be a course in the history of economic thought.

We focus on Ricardo to explain why urban rents are higher in some locations than others and also to permit us to introduce *quasi-rents*. Comparing a prime retail location on Fifth Avenue in New York City, with its heavy stream of shopper traffic, against a location on, let us say, Tenth Avenue, far removed from shoppers, we find that the Fifth Avenue merchant pays more rent for his store. The difference is explained in Ricardian terms by noting that the Tenth Avenue location is analogous to the no-rent land. If a storekeeper can earn a living there, he must be able to earn 100 livings on Fifth Avenue. The landlord who owns the Fifth Avenue location may charge enough rent to reduce the merchant's profit down to the same level as that of the Tenth Avenue storekeeper. Once again the entrepreneur earns a normal profit, with the surplus accruing to the landlord. Property taxes based on assessed value serve to transfer part of that rent to the government as well.

What are quasi-rents?

Quasi-rents are a form of rentlike income that can accrue to factors other than land. It is through quasi-rents that we explain many of the incredible disparities in income seen in our society. Why do professional basketball players command six-figure salaries? Why do motion picture actors and actresses earn more in a year than most workers do in a lifetime? The explanation offered by economists is *quasi-rents*. Land earns a rent because of its uniqueness and its inelastic supply relative to demand. So too does talent. The kinds of talent possessed by professional sports and cinema performers are not commonly found in society. Audiences wanting to see these talents on display pay sizable revenues for the privilege. The performer *may* take as compensation the differential between the total revenue that comes in with him performing versus what would have been earned had he not been there. There is no doubt that Kareem Jabbar, with his million-dollar income, is underpaid by rent-theory criteria. His differential contribution to his team's revenue is probably four times as high.

What about table tennis players? They have talent but do not earn incomes that high.

That is true. The amount of quasi-rent income that can be earned depends on the effective demand to see the talent perform. Alas, professional table tennis players perform before small crowds. They may find that the opportunity costs of playing table tennis for a living are too high. Most performers in the sport are part-timers, and they have another activity at which they earn a living. Interestingly, these quasi-rent principles are reallocating the available athletic talent into new areas as the revenues to be earned in different sports grows. Golf was the first; tennis was next. Athletes who might have gone into professional baseball now opt for the greater quasi-rental income that comes from these other sports. It has been suggested that the best heavyweight fighter in the world probably isn't a fighter at all, but chose instead to go into football or basketball, where the quasi-rental income is as good, and the wear and tear are considerably less.

CHAPTER HIGHLIGHTS

1. We established that the demand for a factor of production is derived from the market demand for the finished good it helps produce.
2. We saw that in the case of competitive goods and services markets a profit-maximizing firm will employ the quantity of labor units that equates the wage rate with the value of the marginal product of labor, or in the case of imperfectly competitive goods and service markets, with its marginal revenue product. We also found that the VMP and MRP schedules are the demand schedules of a firm for a factor.
3. We examined the adding-up theorem, which states that payment of the marginal product to each unit of input will just exhaust the total product they jointly produce. This theorem assumes constant returns to scale.
4. We considered some of the complications inherent in constructing an industry demand curve for a factor of production. These difficulties stem largely from price changes occurring in the goods and services market.
5. Additionally, we noted other difficulties that occur when we consider the long-run demand for a factor of production. Complications arise because the quantity employed of one factor will vary with different prices of another. This alters the K/L ratios, thereby changing their marginal productivities.
6. Next we looked at the demand for capital. Its unique characteristic is that it delivers the value of marginal product as a stream of returns over a period of time, although it must be paid for in the present.
7. We explained what the discounting process is, and saw how it is used to find the present value of the stream of returns generated by a unit of capital.
8. We saw that demand for capital may be thought of as a downward-sloping function of either its price or the interest rate. The latter observation follows from the role of interest in the discounting process.
9. Finally, we took up demand for land as a factor of production. Ricardian rent concepts were examined briefly, and we saw how they apply to the theories of rent and quasi-rent in contemporary economics.

QUESTIONS

1. In the early days of automation, it was widely felt that the "automatic factory" would result in widespread unemployment as a result of substitution of capital for labor. Yet the United States economy now provides jobs for a work force that is roughly 20 million workers larger than it was when these fears were expressed. Can you explain this?
2. In writing about the derived demand for labor, Alfred Marshall spelled out four principles that would lead to a relatively inelastic demand curve for a factor of production. Demand would be inelastic if: (1) The factor is essential to the production of the product; (2) the commodity has a relatively inelastic demand; (3) the factor involves only a small part of the expense of producing the product, and (4) the other, substitute, factors have relatively inelastic supplies. Explain why each of these principles is valid. Cite some instances of factors in this position if you can.
3. In discussing his principles, Marshall used the role of plasterers in building a house as an example. Actually, since then the plasterers have virtually priced themselves out of business and there are very few still in demand. What went wrong for this group?
4. Capital theory states that investment should increase with a fall in interest rates. However, the historical record shows that over the business cycle, both interest rates and investment fall during periods of recession. In fact, the fall in investment contributes to the recession. How can you reconcile these findings with the theory?
5. The following appeared in a 1975 issue of Fortune magazine: "Manhattan now has a plethora, not only of empty office space, but dead capital as well. . . . Most new buildings are not earning enough to meet their mortgage payments. . . . The average valuation on all of the 55 million square feet produced in the 1970's is less than ¾ of cost. To determine value a building's cash flow is capitalized at the going rate for long term money—currently 10%." How did this all occur? What effect would a change in interest rates have on this statement?
6. We discussed the barriers to entry into the taxi industry that result from the requirement that New York City cabs display an official medallion issued by the City. What factors enter into the determination of what a medallion sells for? How is your answer affected by the price elasticity of demand for taxi rides during a period of rising gasoline prices?

12 The market for factors of production: supply

Supply in microeconomic theory refers to the amount of a commodity or factor that its owner will offer per unit of time in the market under various circumstances. The circumstances with which we are primarily concerned are different money prices per unit being offered in return. Because the market involves exchange of values and we deal with rational people, the customary assumption is that higher prices encourage more people to offer more supplies on the market. The higher the price, the greater the number of people who find their reserve supply price met.

What is a reserve supply price?

The *reserve supply price* is the price at which a potential supplier will just hold the marginal unit of a good or service off the market. In effect, at the reserve supply price the potential supplier becomes a demander instead. The alternative to offering a good or service in the market is to retain it. When a good is retained, the implication is that it is valued more highly than the money offered in exchange. Taking an opportunity-cost approach to the market, we can say that the potential supplier who decides to withhold his offering from the market is giving up the money he could have received in exchange. Because he ends up with the good and without the money, he in effect ends up in the same position as a demander who has bought something. He comes out of an exchange opportunity with the asset he values more highly. For example, if I am offered $3 for a hat and I refuse it, the result is the

FIGURE 12–1. Reserve Supply Price

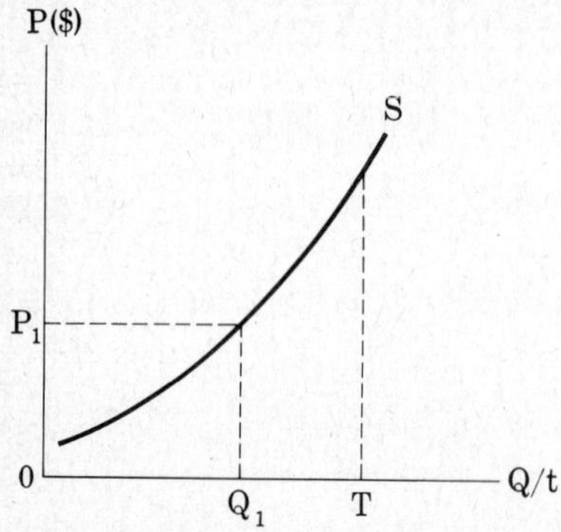

The reserve supply price is the minimum price at which a potential supplier will just hold the marginal unit off the market. It can be thought of as the price at which suppliers become demanders, because rejection of the price means that the utility of the marginal unit *not* sold is higher than the utility of the money offered. If $0T$ is the total quantity held by the supplier, $0Q_1$ units are offered at price $0P_1$. In effect, by withholding Q_1T units, our subject is in the market as a demander for that amount. The total amount offered plus the amount withheld equals the total available.

same as if I paid $3 for the hat. The reserve supply price is the borderline between being in the market on the supply or on the demand side (Figure 12–1).

What determines the reserve supply price?
This is the question with which we shall deal in this chapter. We have seen that in the goods and services market, the reserve supply price is determined by the marginal cost of producing an item. If someone offers a price below this cost, it should be refused. In fact, because it costs more to produce the item than the price offered, it may be well for the would-be supplier to turn about and attempt to buy the item for that price. This would be cheaper than making it. At any rate, we found that the marginal cost curve doubles as the supply curve in the competitive goods and services market.

In the factor market the considerations differ somewhat. Instead of the concrete world of dollars-and-cents costs, we are back in the more subjective areas of utility and disutility. For a worker to be induced to put in an hour on the job, he must be paid a wage that compensates for the utility he loses in giving up an hour of leisure. We therefore must consider the marginal utility of money, the marginal utility of leisure, and the marginal disutility of work in order to find the reserve supply price of labor. But before getting into that, there is a loose end from the previous chapter that must be tied up. In discussing the demand curve for labor, we noted the difference it made if the product market were perfectly or imperfectly competitive. We postponed our discussion of the effects of different degrees of perfection in the factor market. This is what we shall take up now.

What is the difference between a perfectly and imperfectly competitive labor market?

As you know, perfectly competitive markets are those in which there are many buyers and sellers of homogeneous goods and services. Imperfectly competitive markets are those in which, for one reason or another, there are relatively few buyers, or relatively few sellers, or nonhomogeneous products. A perfectly competitive labor market requires that there be many individual workers of comparable skills, not organized into unions or other collective bargaining groups, and many small employers located within a reasonably small geographical area. Any violations of these requirements renders the market imperfectly competitive.

What difference does it make if there are imperfections in the market?

Let's take the different market structures one at a time. Under pure competition, with its many buyers and sellers, no single employer is big enough to affect the market price of labor, nor can any single worker demand a price that is higher than the going wage rate. An employer will simply hire someone else, who under our assumptions has the same talents but is willing to work for the market price. Each *employer* faces a horizontal supply curve and each *employee* faces a horizontal demand curve, both at a wage level determined by the intersection of the market supply and demand curves (Figure 12–2).

I have trouble seeing the meaning of the horizontal supply curve of labor facing the firm.

The horizontal supply curve shows that a single firm can hire as many or as few workers as it wishes at a constant wage rate. The quantity

FIGURE 12–2. Competitive Factor Supply and Demand Curves

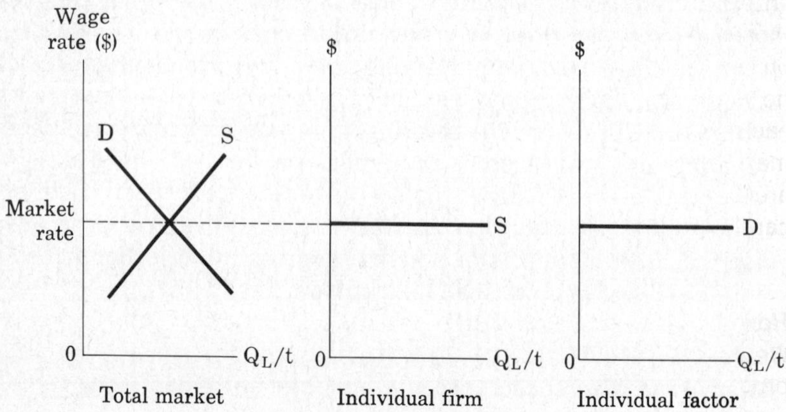

The intersection of the total factor demand and supply curves determines the market factor price. The implication of the competitive market is that any single firm can hire as many units of labor as it wishes at that factor price, and any seller of factor services can sell as many units as he wishes at a constant rate. (In the case of labor, we assume that a worker will be employed for an odd number of hours. We shall worry later about the fact that most jobs involve working 8 hours a day or none.)

FIGURE 12–3. Intersection of Factor Demand and Supply Curve

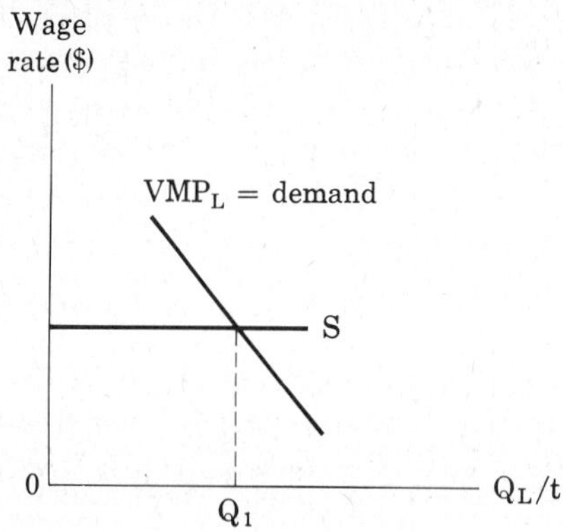

The horizontal supply curve shows the wage that must be paid to each worker by the individual firm. The *VMP* or *MRP* shows what the firm is willing to pay for different quantities. Their intersection determines the units of labor the firm will hire.

it employs relative to the size of the total market is insignificant. Consider, for example, the daily shape-up among longshoremen. There is an agreed hourly rate at which each class of longshoremen works. All those willing to work at that rate are present and available for work on any particular day. A single shipper can hire as many or as few as he wishes for that day and be secure that he will pay the same rate for each man, no matter how many he employs. The variations in total market demand caused by the presence or absence of a single employer are simply not large enough to shift the market demand curve significantly and cause a change in price.

How can this horizontal supply curve of labor be used in the analysis?
We have seen that a firm's demand curve for labor is value of marginal product schedule (or marginal revenue product in imperfect goods and service markets). The intersection of the firm's demand curve with the horizontal supply curve determines the number of workers who will be hired. At that quantity of labor, wage equals *VMP* (or *MRP*), and this was our rule for profit maximization. Don't forget that whether we use *VMP* or *MRP* depends on whether competition in the *product* market is perfect or imperfect. We are assuming for the moment that the *factor* market is perfectly competitive (Figure 12–3).

What happens if competition in the factor market is imperfect?
Let us consider the case in which there is only one employer, but the supply side of the market remains competitive. This situation arises in a company town where there is but one major firm. The fortunes of the town's residents vary with the fortune of the company. West Virginia is dotted with mining communities like this. Prior to the massive effort at unionizing farm workers, the agricultural industry in California had regions in which there was one major corporate farm standing as the potential employer of a large number of nonunionized migrant farm workers. These conditions comprise a *monopsonistic* labor market. If we had a few employers, we would have *oligopsony*.

Will a monopsonist in the factor market necessarily be a monopolist in the product market?
No, the two are not necessarily related. In fact, in the two instances cited, mining and agriculture, the employer is most likely to find himself selling his product in a competitive market while buying factors as a monopsonist. In order to be both a monopsonist and monopolist, a firm would have to be the only employer in a region and produce for

FIGURE 12–4. Labor Supply Curve Seen by a Monopsonist

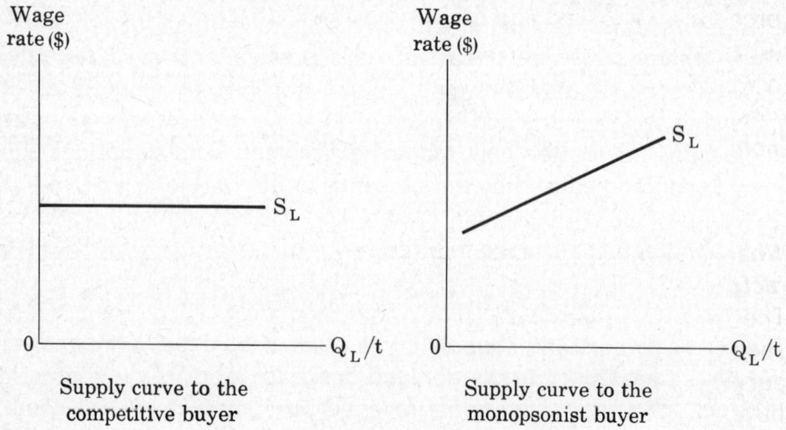

Under pure competition the labor supply curve to a firm is horizontal, although the total market supply curve slopes upward to the right. A monopsonist faces this total market supply curve.

FIGURE 12–5. The Marginal Factor Cost Curve

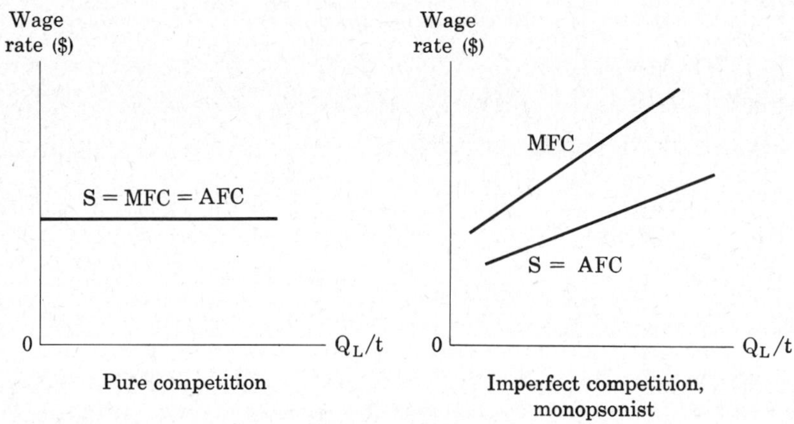

If it takes more money to induce the marginal labor unit to offer itself in the market, the inframarginal units will benefit also, because they too will get the higher pay rate. The total cost of hiring an additional worker is his wage plus the additional wages that go to the others who were willing to work for less.

local consumption, barring outside competitors. It is quite possible to visualize a monopsonist using its market power as a single employer to force local people to boycott competitors' products. It is quite possible, but not necessarily so. We will deal with cases of market imperfection in which the employer is a monopsonist in the factor market and others in which the employer is a competitor in the factor market facing a *monopolistic seller* of labor, that is, a trade union.

What happens in the case where the employer is a monopsonist in the factor market?

The important consideration here is how the supply curve of labor is seen by the employer. Remember that whereas the *total market* supply curve of labor is assumed to slope upward to the right, a *competitive* buyer of labor services sees the supply curve as a horizontal line. Such an employer can hire as many units as he wishes without affecting labor prices. However, if an employer is the *only* employer in the market, then he must face the *market* supply curve of labor. Therefore the labor supply curve, as seen by a monopsonist, slopes upward and to the right (Figure 12–4).

What difference does it make if the labor supply curve slopes upward to the right?

It makes a big difference in terms of the number of workers who are hired. The supply curve of labor shows the number of units of labor that will be offered at different wage rates. Each worker hired will receive the wage rate shown on the supply curve. Supply is an *average* wage curve, or an average factor cost curve from the point of view of the firm. Now, if there is an average factor cost curve, there must also be a *marginal* factor cost (*MFC*) curve. We know that whenever the average anything slopes upward, the marginal anything lies above it. Factor costs are no exception. We have a marginal factor cost curve that lies above the labor supply curve and slopes up to the right (Figure 12–5).

What does the marginal factor cost curve show?

This curve is quite analogous to the marginal revenue curve that lies beneath the demand curve. The marginal revenue curve shows the change in total revenue that occurs if one additional unit of output is sold. It is less than the price shown on the demand curve because we realize that if price were lowered to sell the marginal unit, the price

FIGURE 12–6. Monopsonistic Labor Market

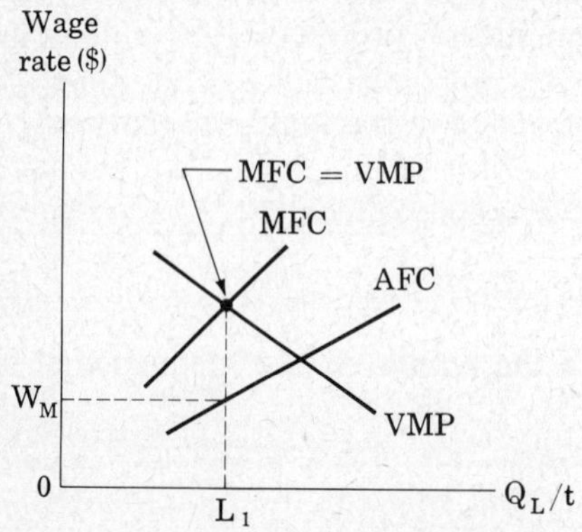

The firm uses the *MFC* = *VMP* criterion to determine the quantity of labor it will employ. However, the wage rate is indicated by the supply (*AFC*) curve.

on all the other units (inframarginal units) would be lowered as well. The change in total revenue received is affected by the combination of selling an extra unit and also receiving lower revenue on each of the inframarginal units. Here, on the labor side, we have a monopsonist who is faced with an upward-sloping supply curve of labor. This means that in order to employ an additional unit, the employer must increase the wage rate paid. We realize, however, that if the wage rate is raised for the marginal worker, it must also be raised for all the inframarginal workers as well. Wage rate is an average. If one gets it, all get it. Wages must be high enough to attract the least anxious worker to the market. The marginal factor cost curve, therefore, reflects the change in total outlay that the firm must make if it employs one additional unit of factor input. It equals the wage of the marginal employee plus the increased expenditure that had to be made on the inframarginal employees when their wages were increased also.

How does the marginal factor cost curve enter into the analysis?
The logic we have employed throughout this course says that a firm does not want to spend more to produce a marginal unit of output than it can take in from selling it. This is the rationale of the marginal cost–marginal revenue profit-maximization rule. From the factor point of

view, we can surmise that the firm will employ the number of workers at which marginal factor cost equals value of marginal product. Value of marginal product measures the revenue received for selling the output of the marginal worker. Marginal factor cost is the cost to the firm of employing the marginal worker. Equating them is equivalent to equating marginal cost with marginal revenue. It determines the number of workers to employ in order to produce the profit-maximizing output (Figure 12–6). Note, however, that whereas the quantity employed is found by reading from the *MFC* curve, the wage rate at which this quantity works is shown on the supply curve.

It appears that fewer workers are employed and at lower wages than if the industry were purely competitive.

True. Under monopsony fewer workers are employed and at lower wages than would be hired if the factor market were organized along purely competitive lines. Under pure competition each firm would view its labor supply curve as a horizontal line and employ labor up to the point where the market wage rate equals the value of marginal product. The total number hired and the wage rate are found at the intersection of the industry labor supply curve and the industry *VMP* curve. Under monopsony the number of workers hired and the wage rate are less because the single employer uses the marginal factor cost curve instead of the industry labor supply curve (*AFC*). This shortfall in employment and wage rate is known as *monopsonistic* labor exploitation (Figure 12–7).

What happens if the firm is a monopsonist as well as a monoplist?

Then we get the worst of both worlds. Not only does the employer read his marginal factor costs from the *MFC* schedule instead of the *AFC*, but he also uses the marginal revenue product instead of the value of the marginal product as the appropriate measure of gain from the marginal employee. You can see that the combined exploitations reduce employment in the monopolized-monopsonized industry even more sharply than either working alone (Figure 12–8).

What would be the effect of imperfection in the labor supply? That is, suppose that there is a labor union?

A labor union in the factor market is very similar in effect to a cartel in the product market. Although the individual workers do the work, the union is recognized as the exclusive marketing agent of their services.

FIGURE 12–7. Monopsonistic Exploitation

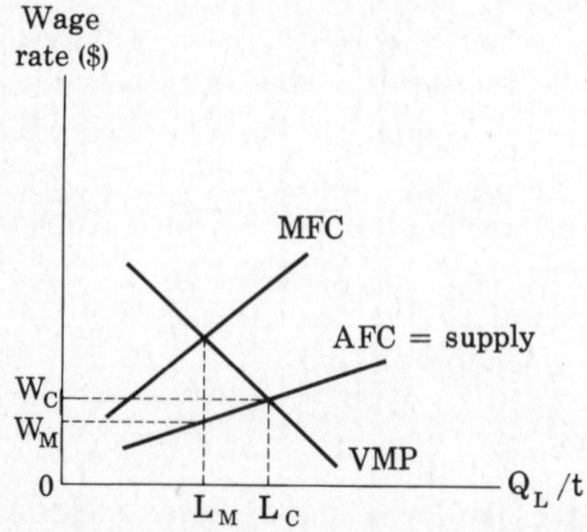

Under monopsony fewer workers are hired than would be under pure competition, and they are paid less than their value of marginal product. This condition is called monopsonistic exploitation. Under competition, $0L_C$ would be employed and the wage would be $0W_C$. Under monopsony, $0L_M$ would be employed at wage $0W_M$.

FIGURE 12–8. Monopsonistic and Monopolistic Exploitation Combined

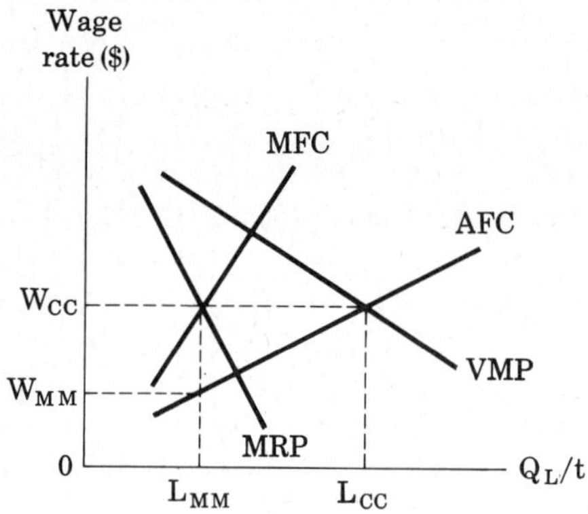

Under conditions in which an employer is a monopsonist in the labor market and a monopolist in the product market, he fixes the quantity of labor employed by equating marginal revenue product with marginal factor cost. This results in fewer units of labor being employed, and at a lower wage than would be the case under pure competition. Under the monopsony-monopoly condition, the number of workers employed is $0L_{MM}$ at a wage of $0W_{MM}$. Under pure competition the number would be $0L_{CC}$ at a wage of $0W_{CC}$.

FIGURE 12–9. Higher Wages Reduce Employment (All Other Things Being Equal)

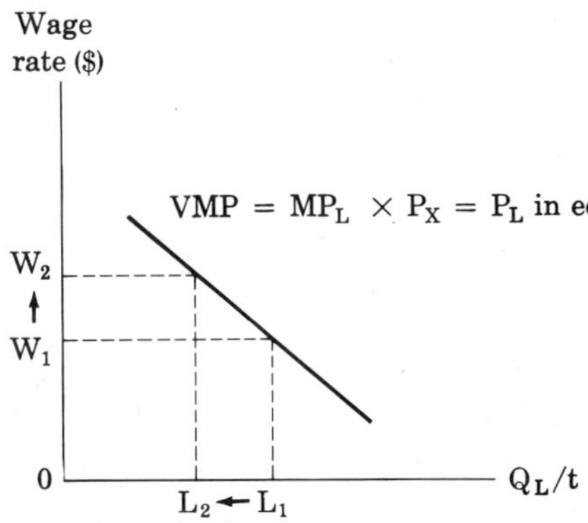

As long as the demand curve for labor does not shift, an increased wage, whether forced by a union or a minimum wage, must reduce employment. The higher wage can only be equal to the *VMP* at a lesser quantity of labor because of diminishing returns.

It wins this right through an election by the workers of a bargaining agent to represent them. The National Labor Relations Act requires the employer to deal exclusively with a representative once it has been duly elected. Therefore the union is in effect a monopoly seller of labor services. By now you should know what to expect when a monopolist is on the scene. There will be fewer units sold and the price will be higher than would have occurred otherwise.

How do you show the effect of the union on industry wages?

The demand curve for labor is derived from the marginal product schedule and the marginal product schedule slopes down as the quantity of labor increases because of diminishing returns, so we may anticipate that any increase in wage rates won by the union must result in a reduction in the number of workers that can be employed, all other things being equal. This is found by simply moving up along the *VMP* or *MRP* schedules and noting that higher wages can be justified only by higher marginal product—and that means fewer workers. Therefore, as a general rule, all other things being equal, increasing the wage rate by collective bargaining (or, alternatively, raising the government minimum wage) will cause employment in the affected industry to drop (Figure 12–9).

FIGURE 12–10. Higher Wages May Not Reduce Employment (All Other Things Not *Being Equal)*

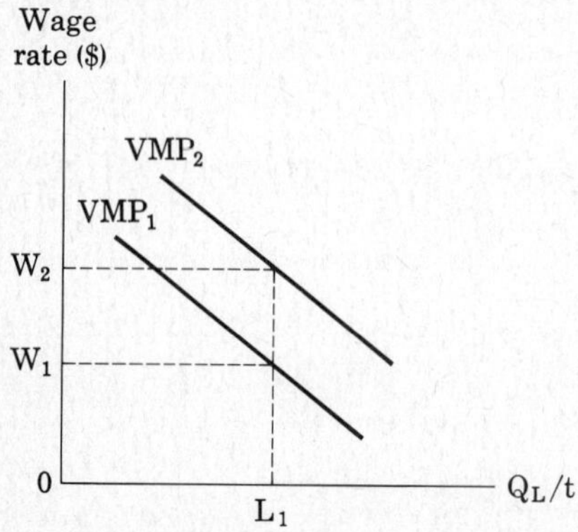

If the *VMP* curve shifts to the right as a result of an increase in either the price of the product sold or the marginal productivity of labor, the higher wage rate may not necessarily reduce employment levels. Wage rises from $0W_1$ to $0W_2$ at the same time the demand curve shifts from VMP_1 to VMP_2. Quantity of labor employed remains at $0L_1$.

Is there no way around this?

The *ceteris paribus* assumption can be eased. If the price of the product being sold were to rise, the value of marginal product curve could shift to the right. Also, if complementary capital equipment were added, the effect would be similar to that described in our discussion of the long-run factor demand curve. The marginal physical product of labor would increase, shifting the demand curve to the right (Figure 12–10). These offsets would allow a union to increase wages without measurably reducing employment. We sometimes find unions doing institutional advertising to promote the use of the product of the industry with which they bargain. The lithographer's union, for example, runs consumer advertising campaigns to promote the virtues of that particular printing technique. The garment workers encourage people to look for the union label in the clothing they buy. No one is more aware of the derived demand nature of labor employment than the labor unions. However, in the absence of an offsetting shift in the *VMP* schedule, a higher wage will reduce employment. The union is aware of this too, and must make its decision with regard to how high to raise its industry wage rate. The decision should be strongly influenced by the elasticity of the demand curve for labor. If the curve is relatively inelastic, an increase in wage rates will raise the total revenue realized by fewer union members employed. The more inelastic, the higher the total union wage bill and the smaller the reduction of employment will be.

What determines the elasticity of the demand curve for a factor of production?

The price elasticity of demand for a factor of production depends on the same things on which the price elasticity of demand for a product depends: substitutability. For demand to be relatively inelastic, the factor must be, first of all, essential to the production of the finished good. Even if the factor's price rises, there is little technical opportunity to substitute for it. Second, the supply of available substitutes for the factor should be highly inelastic. Therefore, even if an employer were technically able to substitute, it would be difficult to get substitute inputs. Third, the factor should represent a small part of the total cost of the finished good, so that even if the increased cost of a factor is passed on through to the market, the price rise will be so small that the consumer will not reduce his consumption of the finished product. These three qualities will make demand for a factor highly inelastic and enable a union to seek higher wages with relative impunity. The Airline Pilots Association provides an interesting example of these effects in practice. The presence of a pilot is obviously required for the plane to get off the ground. Federal Aviation Authority regulations specify exacting standards for the training of airline pilots, with the result that the supply of available substitutes can respond to market stimuli only after a sizable lag. Finally, the relative cost of the pilot's salary is insignificant in comparison with such other airline expenses as fuel, depreciation, and airport expense. Even if the pilots' increase in salary were passed along fully to the traveling public, the effect on each ticket would be small and demand would not be noticeably affected. No wonder the Airline Pilots Association has been able to make its members the envy of organized labor.

How do you know that the labor supply curve slopes upward to the right?

There are at least four labor supply curves that we ought to recognize as being separate and distinct from one another. These are (1) the individual's personal supply curve, that is, how many hours of work each person will offer in the market under different wage conditions;

FIGURE 12–11. Supply of Labor to a Single Industry

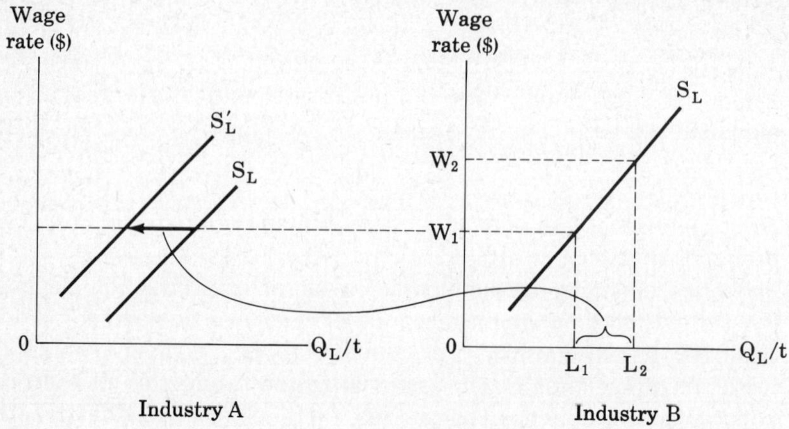

If industry B offers higher wages to machinists, more machinists will be willing to work there. They come from other industries, such as industry A, where they were employed. This leaving of industry A causes a shift in its labor supply curve to the left. The shift of the supply curve in industry A would equal the quantity increase in labor employed in industry B if all of the additional labor hired by B came from A.

(2) the labor supply curve facing a firm; (3) the labor supply curve facing an industry; and finally, (4) the aggregate labor supply curve. When we talk about *the* labor supply curve, we ought at least know to which one we are referring. All four will be discussed here, but there is only one that we can be certain slopes upward to the right. That is the labor supply curve facing an industry.

Why does the labor supply curve facing an industry slope upward? Industries compete with each other for available labor supply. Under the conditions normally associated with microeconomic analysis, all factors are employed. In order for one industry to bid factors away from another, it must offer a wage that is higher than the going rate. Consider the case of the automobile industry attempting to employ additional machinists. If the industry offers a relatively low wage, trained machinists will prefer to work elsewhere: construction, aircraft, machine tools, and so on. At higher wages in the auto industry there is an increase in the number of machinists finding work there to be attractive. The number of labor units supplied increases. Because these workers are diverted from employment in other areas, our observations of labor supply responding to changes in wage refers to individual industries, but not necessarily to the labor market in its entirety. Industry labor supply curves slope up to the right (Figure 12–11).

What about the labor supply curves facing individual firms?
We have already discussed this. The labor market under conditions of pure competition comprises many small employers. Each of these can hire as many workers as it can use at the going market rate. The going market rate, of course is an equilibrium rate determined by the industry supply and demand curve for the factor. Whereas the industry demand curve is the sum of the adjusted *VMP* curves of the individual firms as discussed earlier, the number of firms is so large that any change in demand by one of them will produce an insignificant shift in the industry demand curve against the industry supply curve and leave the market price unaffected. The supply curve to the firm under competitive conditions is perfectly elastic.

These two cases sound like old stuff at this point. Isn't there something new to discuss?
The other two cases of labor supply, the individual's supply curve and the aggregate supply curve, do involve new indeas. We shall take up the aggregate supply curve first. Although it involves new ideas, it does not really concern us too much in a course in *micro*economics. However, since we are dealing with labor supply, and since aggregate labor supply is a macroeconomic problem of great importance, it is worth a little of our attention. Its importance comes from the macroeconomic controversy over voluntary versus involuntary unemployment.

What is the controversy involving voluntary and involuntary unemployment?
As you know, macroeconomics deals with aggregate levels of economic activity. There is general agreement that unemployment rises when the level of aggregate demand for goods and services declines. This is a reflection of our old friend, derived demand. If there is less demand for what is produced, there is less demand for those doing the producing. The question is, Is this unemployment voluntary or involuntary?

FIGURE 12–12. Voluntary Unemployment

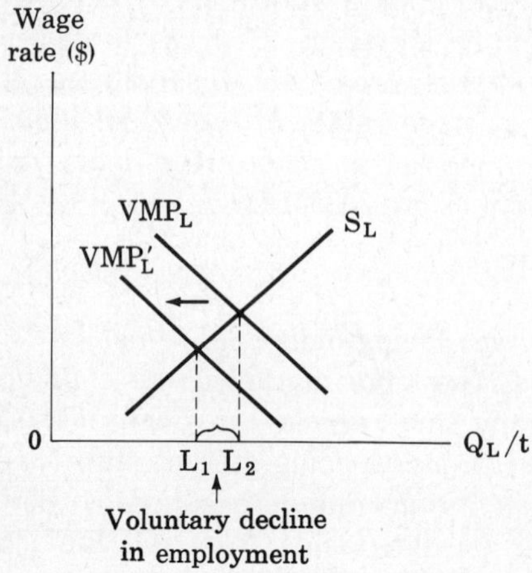

As aggregate demand falls, the labor demand curve shifts to the left. The new equilibrium has a lower wage and a lower level of employment. The upward slope of the supply curve suggests that workers voluntarily withdraw from the market if wages fall. The interval $L_1 - L_2$ is therefore voluntary unemployment, because these workers are not willing to work at the lower wage.

FIGURE 12–13. A Policy of Accepting the Lower Wage Caused by a Fall in Aggregate Demand

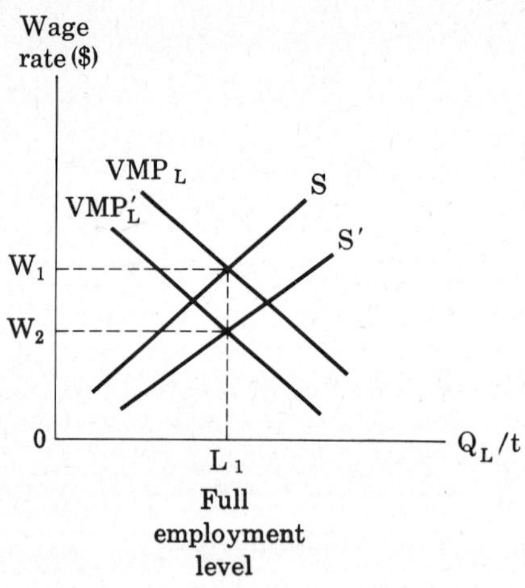

If labor generally reduced its wage demands, the labor supply curve would shift to the right. The full employment level could be maintained despite lower demand.

What is the difference?

Voluntary unemployment means that the workers have withdrawn from the market because the market price offered is not high enough. Involuntary unemployment means that some workers are willing to work at the going wage but cannot find jobs. The voluntary unemployment argument holds that market wages fall along the decline in aggregate demand, and as they do, the reserve supply price of some workers is passed and these workers drop out of the market. Such an argument presumes that the aggregate labor supply curve slopes upward to the right. Demand for labor is a downward-sloping aggregate *VMP* curve, and if it shifts leftward, the equilibrium point moves to a lower wage rate and labor quantity (Figure 12–12). The policy recommendation that follows from this picture of the labor supply curve is to try to induce labor to accept a lower wage. This would shift the labor supply curve to the right and establish a new equilibrium at the old (and presumably full) employment level and a lower wage level (Figure 12–13).

That seems reasonable. What's the other argument?

The other argument states that the unemployment that comes with a decline in aggregate demand is involuntary. It does not occur because labor has intentionally withdrawn from the labor market due to lower wages, but instead represents a disequilibrium condition where the same number of workers are willing to work at lower wages but are unable to work because there are not enough jobs for them. The statement that the same number is willing to work at a lower wage implies that the labor supply curve is perfectly inelastic at the full employment level (Figure 12–14). This model shows that when the demand curve for labor shifts to the left as a result of a drop in demand for goods and services, the employment level is not determined by the intersection of the demand and supply curves, but is instead on the new demand curve, at the same wage level as prevailed before. This is the position taken by the orthodox Keynesians. They argue that even though the aggregate demand falls, the real wage cannot, so there is no way for the lower demand curve to intersect the perfectly inelastic supply curve. The gap between demand and supply curves, therefore, represents involuntary unemployment in the sense that workers are willing to supply their services but are unable to find any demand for them.

Why isn't there a decline in wages that would allow the new demand to come into equilibrium with the supply?

The Keynesians make an interesting argument. They point out that the demand for labor is the VMP_L curve, which depends on the marginal

FIGURE 12–14. Involuntary Unemployment

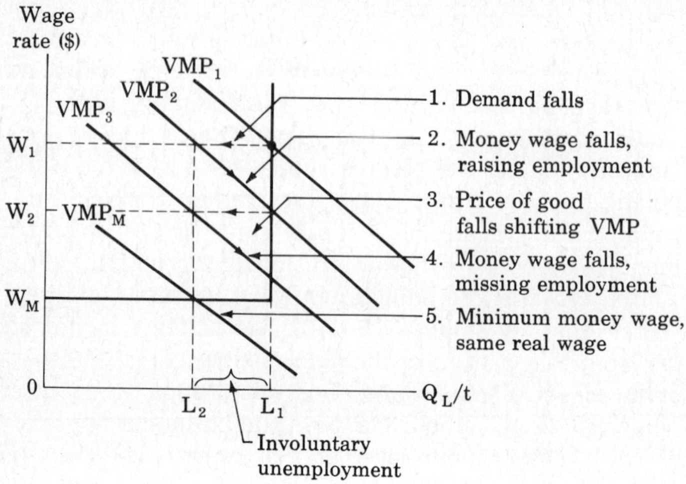

Supply is perfectly inelastic at full employment level $0L_1$. $0W_M$ represents the *minimum* acceptable money wage. The supply curve has a reverse L-shape, showing no one willing to work at a wage below $0W_M$, everyone willing to work at that wage, and no additional labor available to work once $0L_1$ units of labor are employed.

As demand falls from VMP_1 to VMP_2, the money wage may fall to $0W_2$. This reduction in wage induces a fall in the market price for the good being produced, thereby reducing the *VMP* of labor and shifting the labor demand curve to VMP_3. If wages are flexible downward, they can fall all the way to $0W_M$. However, each time they fall, the market price of the product falls as well, thereby shifting the *VMP* curve. Note that as long as prices follow the flexible money wage, the *real wage* is constant. It is the same at $0W_1$, $0W_2$, and $0W_M$, which means that reduction in money wage will not increase the number of workers employed.

physical product of labor, as well as on the price of the good being produced. If money wages were to fall as a result of a fall in demand for labor, the price of the good being produced by the labor would also fall. Because wages are a major part of cost and because, under long-run competition, economic profits are zero, price will follow costs down to restore the zero profit level. The price reduction following the wage reduction would work to shift the VMP_L curve to the left, thereby undoing any increase in employment that may have occurred because of the drop in money wages (Figure 12–14). The wage rate that is important for employment purposes is the *real* wage rate, or the money rate adjusted for changes in the prices of goods and services. The Keynesians argue that labor cannot voluntarily reduce its real wage rate, because prices will follow any reduction they agree to accept in money wages. If there can be no change in real wages, there can be no new equilibrium that equates supply and demand. The Keynesians counsel that the only effective policy to restore full employment is to shift the demand curve. If necessary this should be done through government purchase of goods and services financed by deficit in the federal budget.

Which is correct?
We shall leave it for your macroeconomic teacher to tell you. The subject is raised here merely to point out the possibilities, and what they mean.

What about the individual labor supply curve?
Now we get back to the most basic microeconomic unit, the individual. We must ask ourselves how rational, pleasure-seeking, fatiguable, mortal economic man behaves in the labor supply situation. The hours of each man's day belong to him alone. He must decide how to pass them. Under what conditions will he offer his time on the labor market, and under what conditions will he retain his time for other pursuits? We should recognize that offering labor in the market means giving up the ultimate scarce resource. Other assets may be replaceable, but time must be thought of as a wasting (and wasted) asset. It has alternative uses: sleeping, eating, playing, reading, talking. The alternative to work is summed up in the word *leisure*. Thus it becomes a question of examining the circumstances that will induce someone to trade leisure for work, and how much of each will be demanded. We must prepare a supply schedule.

What is the shape of the individual labor supply curve?
At the outset we should recognize that there are different types of personality that may be involved here, as well as different types of occupation. It is one thing to trade leisure for hours spent breaking rocks with a sledgehammer. It is quite another to be a winetaster at a vineyard. And, of course, it makes a difference if you are a professional athlete trying to work into shape by breaking rocks or a laborer trying

FIGURE 12–15. Three Possible Labor Supply Curves from the Individual's Point of View

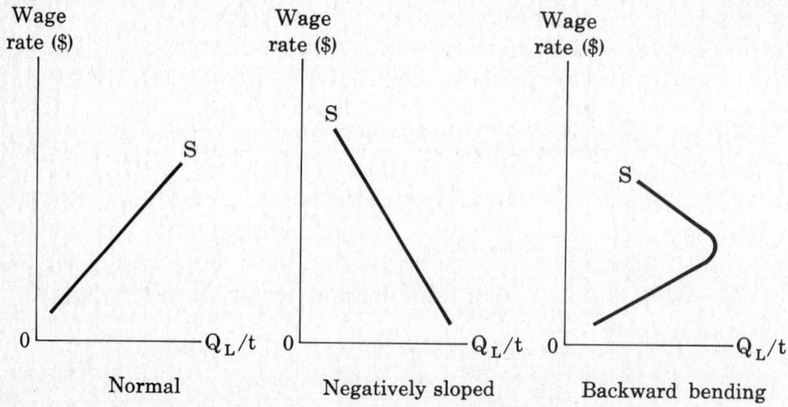

The normal supply curve slopes up to the right. However, the supply curve may also be negatively sloped over its entire range (unlikely), or backward bending over the upper portion of its range (highly likely).

FIGURE 12–16. Money–Leisure Indifference Curves

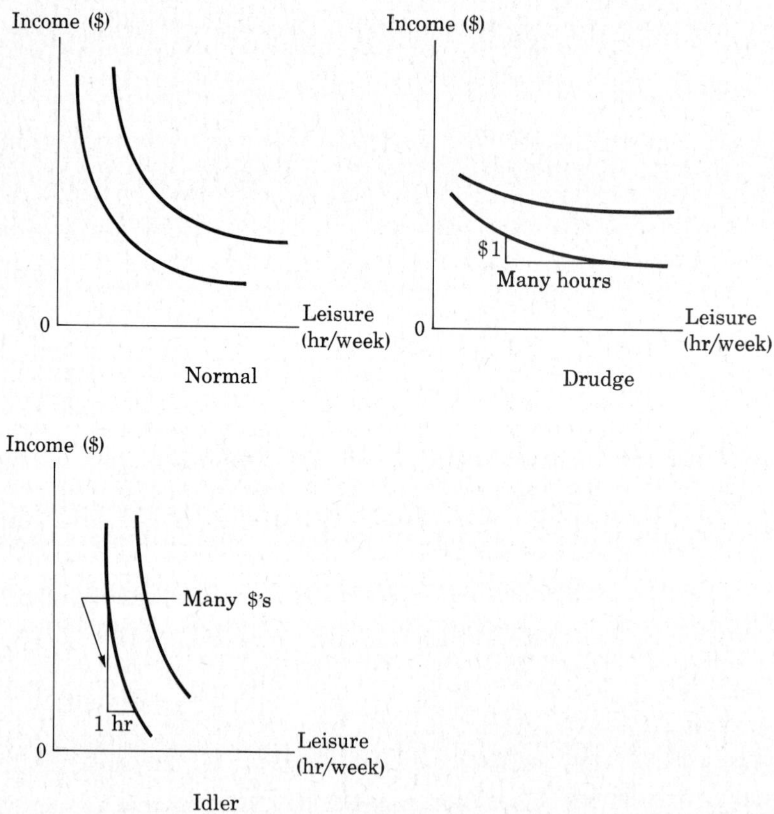

The indifference map shows total income on the y axis and hours of leisure on the x axis. Curves tending toward the horizontal show people with little inclination to trade money for leisure. Curves tending toward the vertical show people with a great willingness to do so.

to support a family of twelve. Obviously, there are many variables besides wage in this analysis, and generalization regarding the outcome is difficult. Isolating wage rate as the independent variable, we shall consider three possible outcomes. The individual supply curve can slope upward to the right, indicating that as the wage rate increases, more hours of work will be offered; or it can slope upward to the left, indicating that as wage rate increases, less labor effort will be offered; or it can do both, sloping right over one range and left over another. We refer to these three configurations as *normal*, *negatively sloped*, and *backward bending*. Let's consider the conditions under which these different supply curves may be found (Figure 12–15).

How can you determine whether an individual's labor supply is normal, negatively sloped, or backward bending?

We shall attack the problem with the same tool used to analyze consumer behavior: an indifference map—this one with money income on the y axis and hours of leisure on the x axis. Because neither leisure nor income is a nuisance when held in reasonable quantities, an indifference curve showing combinations of money and leisure slopes down to the right, and because both are subject to diminishing marginal utility, the curve will also be convex toward the origin. The slopes of the curves at any particular combination will certainly vary with the personalities and goals of the people involved. To get an idea of how this works, let us consider two groups at opposite personality poles. One group we can call the drudges, whose indifference curves tend towards the horizontal, and another we can call the idlers, whose indifference curves are practically vertical in orientation. The drudges are people who place little value on leisure. Because their indifference curves tend to be flat, with a low marginal rate of substitution of leisure for income, we conclude that they would willingly surrender a large number of hours of leisure for a small increment in income. At the other extreme, the idlers place very high value on leisure and require a large increment in income to induce them to surrender even a tiny bit of their leisure time (Figure 12–16).

FIGURE 12–17. Work vs. Leisure

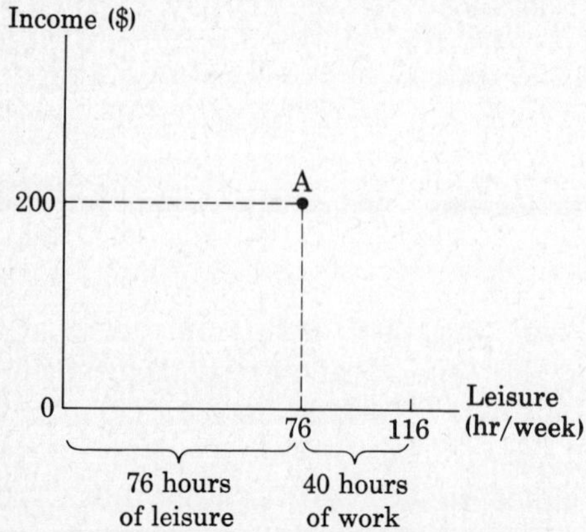

The x axis has a range running from 0 to 116 hours. These are the number of nonsleeping hours available for either work or leisure during the week. Points in between divide the 116 hours into periods of leisure and work. Point *A* on the map shows someone who works for 40 hours and earns $200.

FIGURE 12–18. An Indifference Map with Work and Income Measured on the Axes

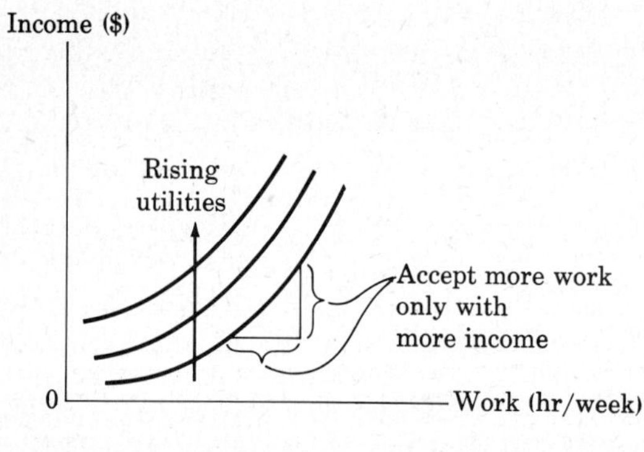

Because work is a nuisance good, the indifference curves slope upward to the right. This means that you will accept more hours of work only if you are given more income with it. Utility is greater for indifference curves farther to the left.

You have leisure and income on the axes. Where do we find work and wage rates, the ingredients of a supply curve?

Work enters the discussion through the back door. It is the opposite of leisure. Therefore any reduction in the amount of leisure held is considered to be an increase in the amount of work done. Let's put some numbers into the discussion. There are a total of 7 days with 24 hours in each or 168 hours in a week. If we allow time out for sleeping, we are left with, let us say, 116 discretionary hours that can be allocated to work or leisure. Mark off a point 116 hours out on the *x* axis as the maximum horizontal boundary of the map. Any point between the origin and this maximum of 116 hours divides the time into a leisure segment and a work segment. The portion between the origin and the point is leisure and that between the point and 116 is work (Figure 12–17).

Why go to all this trouble? Why not simply label one axis work?

We do it to keep this indifference map looking like the conventional ones with which we have dealt before. Both axes must represent goods or services that are desired, so we can affect a trade-off between them. If the *x* axis were to represent work rather than leisure, it would involve a "bad" instead of a "good." Work is what we called a nuisance good. If a consumer is to be induced to take an additional quantity of it, he must also be offered a sweetener in the form of the other good. In the case of an indifference map with income on the *y* axis and work on the *x* axis, the curve would slope upward to the right (Figure 12–18). Because we are not accustomed to reading indifference maps with this configuration, we instead resort to plotting leisure on the *x* axis and, working with its complement, work beginning at the 116-hour point and reading left.

How does wage rate come into the analysis?

Wage rate plays the same role that price does in the consumer analysis. It is the rate of exchange at which workers can convert their leisure time into income. It is the price that the market offers for leisure. We handled price in the consumer analysis through the construction of a budget line. We do the same here, first locating the *x* and *y* intercepts and connecting them. The *x* intercept reflects the condition of having zero income and 116 hours of leisure. It is the boundary point we have already marked on the *x* axis. The *y* intercept is the point at which all leisure has been exchanged for income at the going wage rate. If the rate were, let us say, $3 per hour, the *y* intercept would be 3 times 116, or $348. The slope of the budget line is found by taking the ratio

FIGURE 12–19. The Budget Line

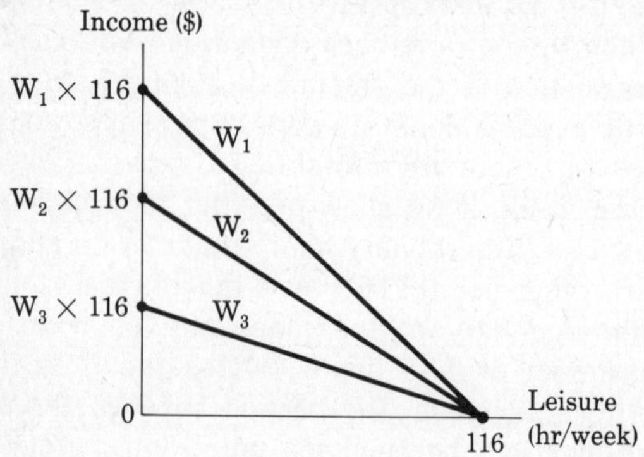

The budget line shows the combinations of income and leisure that are attainable at any given wage rate. The wage rate equals the slope of the budget line (ignoring the negative slope). In this diagram, $W_1 > W_2 > W_3$.

FIGURE 12–20. Equilibrium

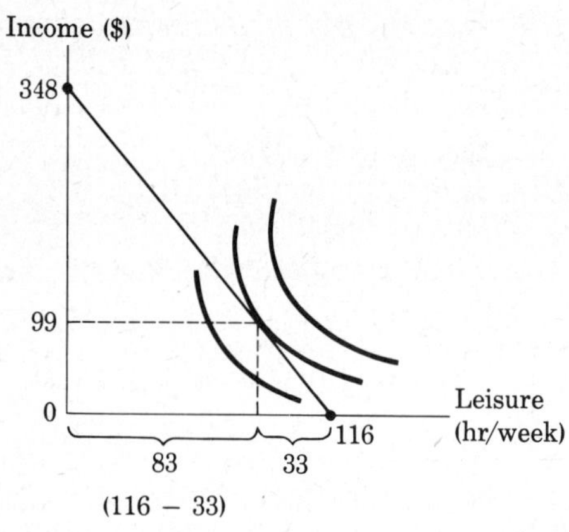

Assume that the wage rate is $3 per hour. In this case utility is maximized at 33 hours of work and $99 income.

of the y to x intercepts: $348/116 = 3$. The slope, therefore, is the wage rate. The budget line shows the combinations of hours of leisure and dollars of income that are attainable at a given wage rate when a maximum of 116 hours per week is available. Whereas the maximum number of hours is fixed, the wage rate can vary, and we shall get a different budget line for each wage. The higher the wage rate, the steeper the budget line (Figure 12–19).

How do you show different wage rates on the indifference map?
Regardless of wage rate, the 116-hour point is fixed on the map. It is analogous to the concept of income in the consumer demand analysis. In that analysis, the exchange process involved giving up dollars for commodity X at a stated rate, the price of X. Here, hours of leisure are what we have available to give up in exchange for dollars at a fixed rate, the level of wages. Starting at the 116, 0 point on the x axis, we read left along the budget line. If the wage rate is \$3 per hour, the next point is 115 hours and \$3 income, the next 114 hours and \$6 income, and so on. On the other hand, if the wage rate were \$4 per hour, starting at the 116-hour intercept, the first point to the left would be 115 hours and \$4 income, and the next 114 hours and \$8 income. The budget lines reflecting the different wage rates radiate out from the x axis. The y intercept equals $116W$, where W is the wage rate (Figure 12–19).

How do we get a labor supply curve from this indifference map?
As always, we assume that a rational person attempts to maximize utility within the constraints imposed by the market. In this instance, the individual will choose the combination of income and leisure hours that places him on the highest attainable indifference curve. This occurs at the point of tangency between the budget line and the highest attainable indifference curve. At this point, the rate at which a worker is willing to exchange hours of leisure for income exactly matches the rate at which the market requires that he do so, that is, the wage rate. Therefore we look to the point of tangency and read from the x axis the amount of leisure hours held. Subtracting this from 116, or if you prefer reading from the x intercept to this point, gives the number of hours of labor offered in the market at this price (Figure 12–20).

That still does not give us a supply curve.
True, but don't be impatient. If we draw the budget lines for a number of different wage rates and examine the points of tangency between

FIGURE 12–21. Labor Supply Curves

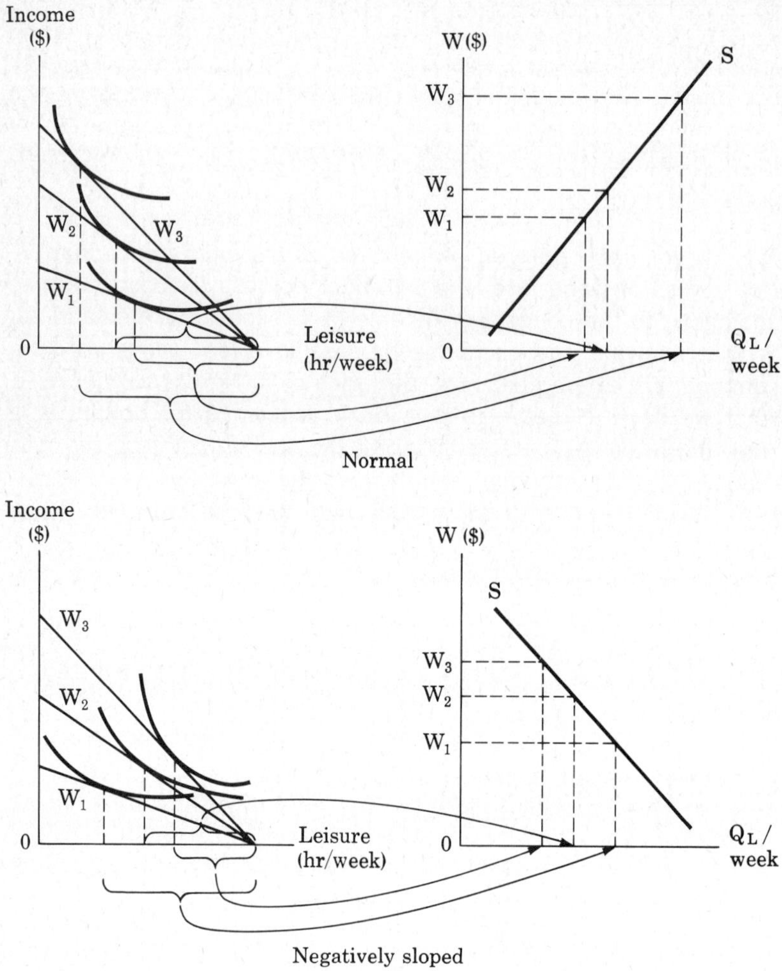

Labor supply curves can be constructed by drawing a number of budget lines, each representing a different wage rate. We plot on separate axes the number of hours worked against the wage rate. Depending on the shape of the indifference curve, these supply lines can slope upward to the right, or to the left.

each of them and the highest attainable indifference curve, we can discern the number of hours of labor offered at the different wage rates. Plotting the hours against the wage rates gives the individual labor supply curve for which we are looking.

Which way does it slope?

You can see from the ingredients of the analysis that it *does not necessarily* slope one way or the other. It depends on the shape of the indifference curves. Those running more in the direction of the drudge's configuration will produce a supply curve that slopes upward to the right. Curves running in an idler's configuration will produce supply curves running upward to the left. Other maps will have supply curves that slope upward over the low wage range and then bend backward. We can have all kinds. The underlying element involves our old friends, the income and substitution effects (Figure 12–21).

What do the income and substitution effects have to do with it?

Remember from the consumer indifference analysis that the total change in the quantity of an item that is taken when its price changes can be broken down into a substitution effect and an income effect. If the price of an item rises, the marginal utility provided by a dollar's worth of that item is less than before, and people will substitute other goods that provide greater utility per dollar. That is the substitution effect. The income effect refers to the fact that a rise in the price of any item reduces real income, and as a result less of every item is consumed, including that for which the price rose in the first place. These same ideas apply to the labor supply analysis. Think of leisure as the commodity in question and wage rate as the price paid for an hour of leisure. If the wage rate is $3 per hour, any hour spent at leisure is bought at the opportunity cost price of $3. If the wage rate is $4 per hour, an hour of leisure is bought for $4. Hence leisure is more expensive, and the individual tends to "buy" less leisure, that is, substitute more working hours. The substitution effect always leads to an upward-sloping labor supply curve with more hours of labor offered at higher wage rates. Work is substituted for the relatively more costly leisure.

The income effect, on the other hand, works in the opposite direction. If the wage rate rises, the effect is to make the worker more wealthy for any given number of hours worked. The increased wealth leads to purchase of more of the good things in life, including more leisure hours. Thus, the income effect induces the worker to offer fewer hours of labor supply with higher wages, and would tend to induce a negatively sloped supply curve of labor if it operated alone. The effect actually observed as plotted on the supply curve depends on how these two tendencies interact. When the income effect outweighs the substitution effect, the net result produces a negatively sloped supply curve. When the substitution effect outweighs the income effect, the result is an upward-sloping labor supply curve (Figure 12–22). In the aggregate, different people's labor supply curves must be combined to show the total labor hours that will be offered at different levels of real wage.

FIGURE 12–22. Income and Substitution Effects

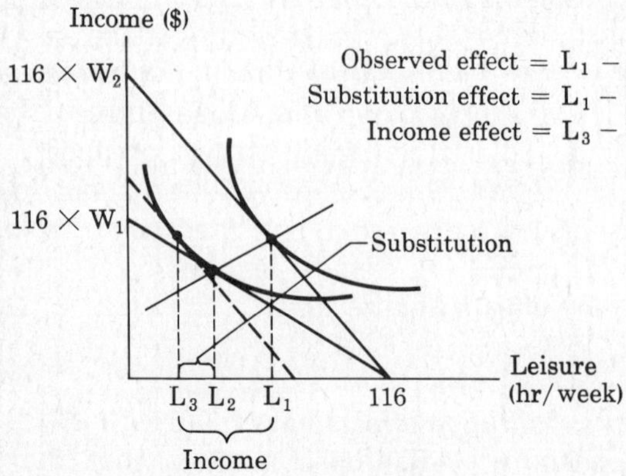

Negatively sloped

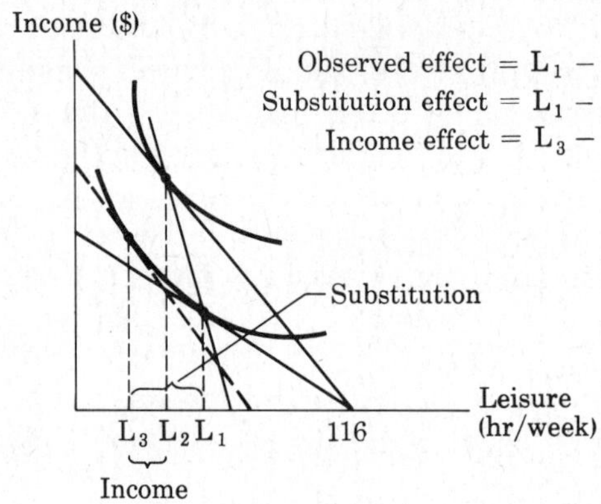

Normal

Separation of income and substitution effects takes place with the same construction used in the consumer demand indifference analysis. If income effect dominates, the supply curve will be negatively sloped. If substitution effect dominates, the supply curve will be normal.

FIGURE 12–23. Jobs in the Real World Involve Working in Clusters of Hours

Although a supply curve for an individual may be smoothly rising, his choice is frequently whether to work 40 hours or none. He will work none only if the utility of the total wage offered is below the marginal utility of his 40th additional hour of leisure.

At rates above the reserve supply price of the 40th hour, the entire 40 hours of work must be offered. This makes the supply curve appear as a reversed L, with 0 hours worked when the wage falls below a minimum level and 40 hours worked for all rates higher.

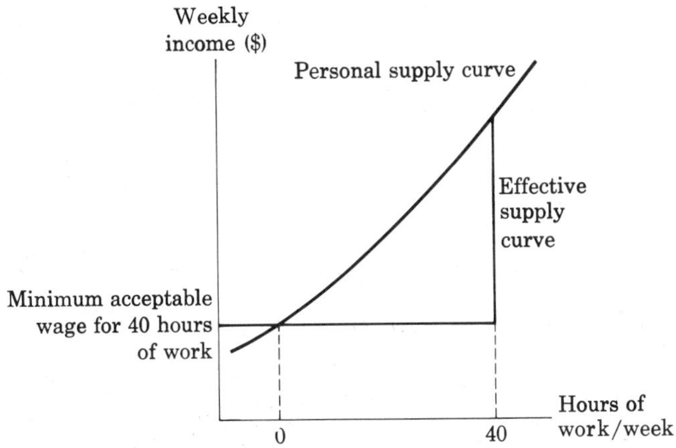

That is all very interesting, but how do you reconcile these individual forward- and backward-bending labor supply curves with the Keynesian concept of a perfectly inelastic labor supply curve in the aggregate?
These labor supply curves show the number of hours of labor service that a worker is willing to offer on the market at different wage rates. However, it frequently happens that jobs are available only in clusters of hours. For example, for a long time jobs have been offered in units of 40 hours per week or zero. Either work a full week or don't work at all. The demand curve facing the individual is not smooth and continuous. Now, when the wage rate drops a little, thereby reducing the utility offered in exchange for the marginal hour of leisure, the worker must ask himself if the utility of the offered wage is also below the utility of his 40th hour of added leisure. That is, if he withdraws 1 hour of labor supply, he must also withdraw 39 others, because he can find employment only in 40-hour units. Labor will be withdrawn due to falling wages only in the event that the offered wage rate gives so little utility that the 40th additional hour of leisure is worth more than the total wage offered (Figure 12–23). Of course, under this circumstance the time is not spent in leisure. Unemployed hours will be spent in search of a better-paying job.

Let's turn our attention to the supply of capital. What can you say about the nature of capital supply?

In the previous chapter we discussed the *demand* for capital equipment in terms of the price of the equipment as well as the market rate of interest. Interest rate entered the discussion through the discounting process. The higher the interest rate, the lower the present value of the stream of income generated by the capital over its productive life and the less you could afford to pay for the equipment. But our main focus was on the *price* and *quantity* of the *capital* equipment, because our microeconomic discussion deals with the quantities of factors, production functions, and factor costs.

For purposes of symmetry we could also deal with supply of capital equipment as a function of price. However, this approach would tell us nothing that is uniquely characteristic of capital as opposed to other goods and services. Producers of capital equipment are like other producers in that they operate under conditions of diminishing returns, have U-shaped average and rising marginal cost curves. We would come to the same conclusions about suppliers of capital goods as we have about suppliers of other goods: They maximize profits where marginal revenue equals marginal cost, employ factors where price equals value of marginal product, and so on. The more interesting capital supply concept concerns the offering of financial capital in the loanable funds market, as a function of interest.

Aren't you using the word* capital *in two different ways?

Yes, capital is one of those words in the English language that enjoys two legitimate but very different meanings in economics. Real capital stock describes the actual assets, plant, and equipment, that are used in production. Financial capital is used to describe the money that goes into the purchase of real capital stock. Because there may be a lag of several years between the time production on a piece of real capital is begun and the time it finally produces its total output, it is necessary that the capitalist have a surplus to pay in advance for the equipment and to support the group that builds it. Financial capital is used to buy sustenance for the producers of real capital stock during the construction and prepayout periods.

Where does the capital surplus come from?

Now we are getting to the nitty-gritty of economics. According to the circular flow, when goods and services are produced, incomes are created. To the extent that these incomes are spent on consumer goods, there is no capital surplus created. However, if a part of the income can be diverted away and not be spent on consumer goods, we can say that surpluses are being accumulated in the form of personal savings. The fact that some of the income earned by the owners of the factors of production goes unspent implies that some of the real goods and services produced in order to generate that income goes undemanded. When there is personal saving, there is also implicitly an excess of capacity beyond that needed for production of *consumer* goods in the market. This excess capacity is potentially available for the production of real capital stock, just as the savings are potentially available to finance its being built. The question of capital supply deals with the circumstances under which these surpluses can be created. Why does nonconsumption occur? How can it be induced to create surpluses that can be used to finance real capital stock?

Is that the same thing as asking how savings can be increased?
That is a straightforward question that is going to get a devious answer. We know that one way to increase savings is to increase the total income earned. If people, say, spend on the average 90 percent of their income, an income of $10,000 will produce $9,000 in consumption and $1,000 in savings. Increasing income to $20,000 will increase savings to $2,000, but will also raise consumption to $18,000. Thus, increasing income is one way to increase savings, but it doesn't do it at the expense of consumption. This is a macroeconomic solution to increasing savings: Increase income. The microeconomic problem is how to increase savings *relative* to consumption. It involves a reallocation of income from use as consumption to use as savings, and therefore, make it available for real capital expansion purposes. The macroeconomic discussion says that savings are a function of income level. The microeconomic discussion deals with savings as a function of interest rates. It examines how individuals allocate their income between consumption and savings.

Why are individual savings a function of interest rates?
We must ask ourselves why people save. After all, saving involves doing without goods and services, and we have assumed that rational people prefer having more to having less. Think about it. Perhaps you save toward some future event such as a trip, or toward purchase of some future, large-ticket item such as an automobile, or because you are afraid of losing your job in the future and want to be assured of having money, or because you want to leave a vast estate. There are many individual motives. The common element they share is that they all involve deferring consumption from the present to some time in the

FIGURE 12–24. Savings as a Function of Interest Rates

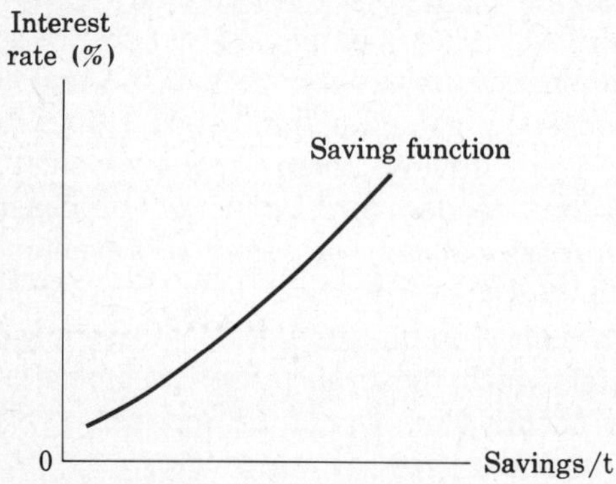

Interest income is the cost of consuming in the present, so a rational person will consume less as the cost rises. Thus savings will increase at higher interest rates.

future. By saving, people do not forego consumption. They merely postpone it, so that it takes place later on.

Interest rates play a role because some people who are anxious to spend money immediately are willing to pay a premium to borrow and use other, more patient people's funds. The saver, therefore, can earn interest income on the money he sets aside and then lends out. The higher the rate, the more he earns. Another way of looking at it, is to say that the higher the interest rate, the more consuming a saver can do in the future as a result of deferring a dollar of consumption today. If I have $100 and lend it for 10 percent for a year, at the end of that time I will be able to consume $110 worth of goods. The cost of spending the hundred dollars today, rather than waiting, is $10. Whether or not I choose to wait or spend depends on the marginal utility I get from current versus future consumption. If waiting reduces my satisfaction by more than 10 percent, I shall spend the money on current consumption. If, on the other hand, deferring consumption does not reduce my utility from marginal income by as much as 10 percent, I shall save.

The higher the interest rate, the more expensive present consumption becomes in terms of future consumption, because more of the latter is lost. Whereas spending $100 today rather than waiting a year costs an incremental $10 at 10 percent interest, it costs $20 at 20 percent, $30 at 30 percent, and so on. We know that the more expensive anything is, the less is demanded (old economic principle). In this case, as the relative cost of present consumption rises, less will take place. Or, in other words, at higher interest rates there is more saving (deferred consumption) than occurs when interest is lower. Because high interest rates raise the cost of present relative to future consumption, rational people *substitute* more of the latter for the former (Figure 12–24).

Did you say substitute? Is there also an income effect in this analysis?
Yes indeed. Whereas high interest rates will induce substitution of future consumption for present consumption, we should note that higher interest rates also raise *total* income when present and future incomes are aggregated. Of course, we know that when income rises, consumption of all normal goods tends to rise also. Therefore the increased income that results from higher interest rates will induce greater consumption. Hence, whereas the substitution effect suggests that savings rise with an increase in interest rates, the income effect says that savings fall under the same circumstances.

Well, which is it?
Generally, income effects are smaller than substitution effects. We normally figure that savings increase with higher interest rates. The supply curve of financial capital as a function of interest slopes up to the right.

Do the demand for capital and for supply of capital determine the interest rate?
Quite a bit of argumentation has occurred on this point, and at this date there is by no means universal agreement on what determines interest rates. The Keynesian economists hold that interest rate is strictly a monetary phenomenon and that interest rates are shaped by the supply and demand for *money*, rather than for capital. A more neoclassical view, however, holds that interest-rate determination is the outcome of the interaction of savings (the supply of financial capital) with *investment* (the demand or productivity of capital).

How does investment enter the discussion? Is that the same thing as capital?
Investment is certainly not the same thing as capital. However, they are closely related. But before specifying the relationship of investment to capital, we should clear up the ambiguities that surround the word

FIGURE 12–25. Investment as a Function of Interest

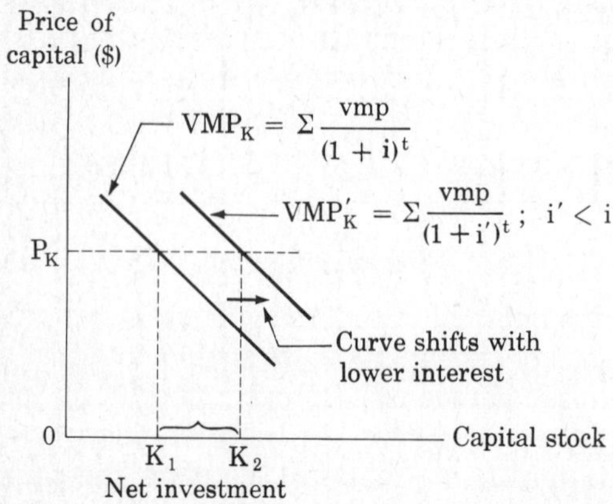

At any given price of capital (P_K) and interest rate (i), an equilibrium capital stock is established where the P_K equals the discounted value of marginal product. If the interest rate falls to i', the VMP_K schedule shifts to the right as a result of the discounting process. The present value of a given stream of income is higher at lower interest rates. Holding the price of capital constant at P_K, the equilibrium capital stock is increased from $0K_1$ to $0K_2$. The increase in equilibrium capital stock requires a net investment of $K_1 - K_2$ to reestablish equilibrium. The lower the interest rate, the greater the shift in VMP and the greater the net investment called for. Thus, net investment varies inversely with interest rate.

investment itself. These grow out of the fact that it has two common meanings, just as did the word *capital*. The more common meaning is the one we do *not* want in the present context; that is, the reference to purchase of common stock or bonds by one individual from another. This is a purely financial transaction involving the exchange of paper assets between buyer and seller. The "investor" gives up cash for a security, and the seller gives up the security (or is it insecurity?) for cash. The transaction is completely unrelated to real capital, buildings, and equipment, except in the sense that originally, when the security was first issued, the cash raised may have been used for that purpose. However, subsequent sale of the securities is a transaction that happens to be called investment but is of little interest here. Our concern is with what economists call *real investment*. Capital, in the form of existing factory buildings and equipment, is a *stock* concept. Investment is a *flow*. A stock of something is a quantity on hand at a moment in time. A flow refers to *changes* taking place in the stock *over* time. For example, a company may show a plant worth $1 million as an asset on its balance sheet. This is capital stock. If it adds a $10,000 machine to the stock this year, a flow of net investment has taken place. In other words, we use the term *net investment* for changes in capital.

What is gross investment?

Gross investment equals net investment plus replacement investment. A certain portion of capital stock wears out in the course of being used for production. This is called *depreciation*. Replacement investment is the creation of the capital equipment that is needed to offset depreciation and keep the capital stock at a constant level. Net investment, we have seen, refers to change in capital stock. If no replacement investment takes place, depreciation will cause net investment to be negative and capital stock will shrink. Happily, we are more likely to be concerned with increases in capital stock, or positive net investment. Whereas replacement investment varies as a function of capital stock, net investment is a function of the rate of interest, tending to be higher when interest rates are low and lower when interest rates are high.

Why is net investment a function of interest rates?

In our discussion of the demand for factors of production, we emphasized that the equilibrium, profit-maximizing quantity demanded was that at which the price of the factor equaled the value of the marginal product (or marginal revenue product in the case of imperfect competition). An individual firm faces a horizontal supply curve of capital equipment and seeks to equate the price of the capital (P_K) with the present discounted value of the marginal product of capital (VMP_K). As long as this equality holds, the firm has the proper capital stock and the only investment that occurs is *replacement* investment. Net investment will be zero. If, however, interest rates were to decline, the equilibrium condition of capital stock would be disturbed. The decline in interest rates would raise the value of the marginal product of capital, making VMP_K greater than the unchanged P_K. This occurs because of the discounting process whereby

$$VMP_K = \sum_{t=1}^{n} \frac{vmp_i}{(1+i)^t}$$

and *VMP* varies inversely with interest (Figure 12–25).

FIGURE 12–26. Savings and Investment Schedules Determine Interest Rate

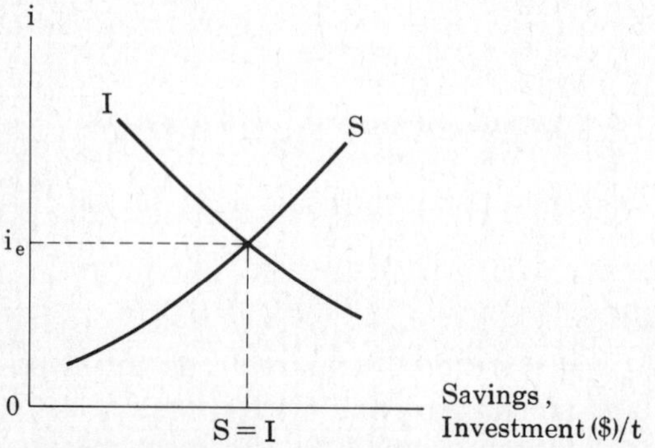

The aggregate savings function is an increasing function of interest rate. The aggregate investment function is a decreasing function of interest. Their intersection determines the market rate of interest.

Our model calls for increasing capital stock to restore the equation between P_K and VMP_K. As we have just seen, an increase in capital stock comes about through net investment. The lower the interest rate, the greater the increment called for in capital stock, and the higher the rate of net investment required. Net investment, therefore, is inversely related to the interest rate, and because replacement investment is a function primarily of the size of the capital stock and is not related to interest, their sum—gross investment—can be seen to be a downward-sloping function serving as a demand curve in the capital market. This demand interacts with the supply of loanable funds generated by savings to determine the market rate of interest (Figure 12–26).

The interest rate is free to fluctuate with market forces, rising when investors are more anxious and savers less plentiful, and falling when investors are less anxious and/or savers are more plentiful. Such an automatic mechanism gave neoclassical economics a built-in tendency toward self-adjustment, assuring its devotees that there could be no excess of aggregate supply because all income created would enter spending either as consumption or as investment. The Keynesians raised serious questions about the validity of this relationship, but once again we shall defer comment pending your exposure to more macroeconomics.

CHAPTER HIGHLIGHTS

1. We reviewed the idea of reserve supply price and saw that when potential suppliers withhold their offering because price is too low, they in effect become demanders of their own goods.
2. Next we digressed to consider what happens when there are different degrees of perfection in the factor-of-production market. We noted that the supply curve of the factor appears horizontal to the firm when competition is pure, but takes on an upward slope when the market becomes less perfect.
3. The marginal factor-cost concept was developed, and we saw its role in monopsonistic exploitation.
4. We also considered the effect a monopolistic seller of a factor of production, such as a labor union, would have on the market. The conclusion arrived at was that the quantity of labor used would be reduced and the wage rate raised.
5. The degree to which an increase in the price of a factor affects the quantity demanded depends on the elasticity of demand for the factor. We reviewed determinants of factor-demand elasticity.
6. Our focus returned to the supply of labor, and we noted that there are actually four different supply-of-labor concepts: the personal supply curve, the labor supply curve facing a firm, the labor supply facing an industry, and the aggregate labor supply curve.
7. We focused first on the aggregate labor supply, reviewing the voluntary-versus-involuntary unemployment controversy.
8. Then, using indifference analysis, we saw that the labor supply of an individual can be positively sloped, negatively sloped, or backward-bending. We considered the implications of this and discussed the role of income and substitution effects.
9. Investment and capital were revisited. We reviewed the dependency of demand for capital on interest rate.
10. Finally, the relationship of investment to capital was considered, and we distinguished between gross and net investment. We saw how investment and savings interact to determine interest rate.

QUESTIONS

1. In February 1975 there was a decline of 540,000 in the number of people at work relative to the number working in January. Nevertheless, the unemployment rate remained the same at 8.2 percent. This occurred because 580,000 people already unemployed stopped looking for jobs. Does this support the contention that the aggregate labor supply curve slopes upward to the right

or not? Would you term the 580,000 dropouts voluntarily unemployed?

2. *"African economies are dual . . . a modern exchange or money sector and a traditional village-oriented sector exist side by side. . . . Out of a total sub-Sahara African population of perhaps 160–170 million . . . only about 8 million work for wages during any part of the year." If only 8 million work for wages, are the rest unemployed? Is "leisure" the alternative to work in this situation?*
3. *The author of the statement in Question 2 concluded that the individual labor supply curve in Africa was backward bending but the aggregate labor supply was positively sloped as a function of money wages. How can you account for a backward-bending individual supply curve and a positively sloped aggregate labor supply?*
4. The New York Times *described the following: "Buck Rice is an oil field worker at Prudhoe Bay on the North Slope of Alaska. He works about 19 hours a day for one week and then has 7 days off. The wind-chill factor one day in February was 128 degrees below zero. By March it had warmed to −63 degrees. Mr. Rice earns about $35,000 per year." What do you suppose Mr. Rice's individual labor supply curve looks like? Do you think he earns his $35,000 a year? What accounts for his high wage?*
5. The Harvard Business Review *described an experiment in which employees could come to work at a factory whenever they wanted to and work for as many hours as they wished. What would the labor supply curve do in that case? How would the aggregate labor curve be affected?*
6. *Meyer and Kuh found a high correlation between the amount of money invested by corporations and the availability of internal funds generated by profits and depreciation, regardless of interest rates. In light of the opportunity-cost concept, does this seem like rational behavior?*

13 Putting it all together: exchange, equilibrium, and welfare

In our course so far we have examined a stream of comparatively unrelated analyses of supply, demand, costs, production, and income distribution. In this final chapter an attempt will be made to pull together these different elements of microeconomic theory into a single system. Although microeconomics deals with *individual* firms, factors, and consumers in the marketplace, we recognize that market transactions tie them all together and make the different elements of the economy dependent on each other. In this chapter we shall take a closer look at this interdependence.

We start by developing a piece of analytical apparatus that is particularly helpful in studying exchange transactions. This is the *Edgeworth box diagram*.

What is an Edgeworth box diagram?

Look at Figure 13–1. We have drawn two pairs of axes that serve as indifference maps for two hypothetical traders. The vertical axes on both diagrams are used to measure quantities of product Y and the horizontal axes are used to measure quantities of product X. The box diagram is formed when one pair of axes is bodily lifted, inverted, and set down on top of the other as shown in Figure 13–2. This gives us two indifference maps superimposed on each other. We have given our two traders a little personality by naming them Oscar and Felix. The diagram is read with the origin of Oscar's indifference map in the lower left-hand corner and the origin of Felix's in the upper right-hand cor-

FIGURE 13–1. Constructing the Edgeworth Box Diagram—I

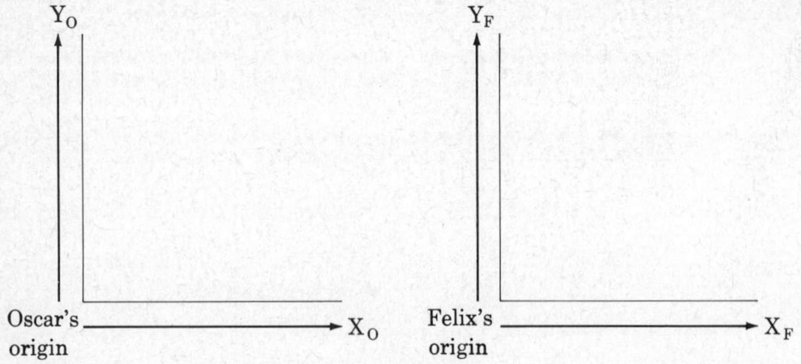

In a two commodity world, each consumer has his own pair of map axes. The horizontal axes all measure quantities of commodity X. The vertical axes all measure quantities of commodity Y. The axes for two consumers, Oscar and Felix, are shown below.

FIGURE 13–2. Constructing the Edgeworth Box Diagram—II

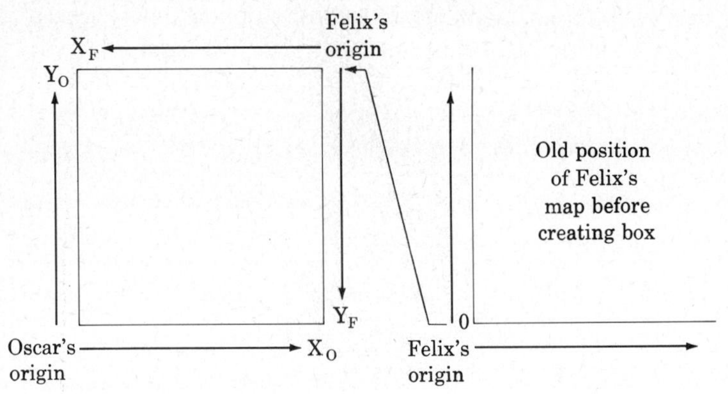

We physically lift Felix's indifference map, invert it so that the origin is in the upper right-hand corner, and put it down opposite Oscar's map. Now increasing quantities of Felix's holdings of X are read from right to left along the top side of the box, and increasing quantities of Felix's holdings of Y are read from top to bottom along the right side of the box.

FIGURE 13–3. Constructing the Edgeworth Box Diagram—III

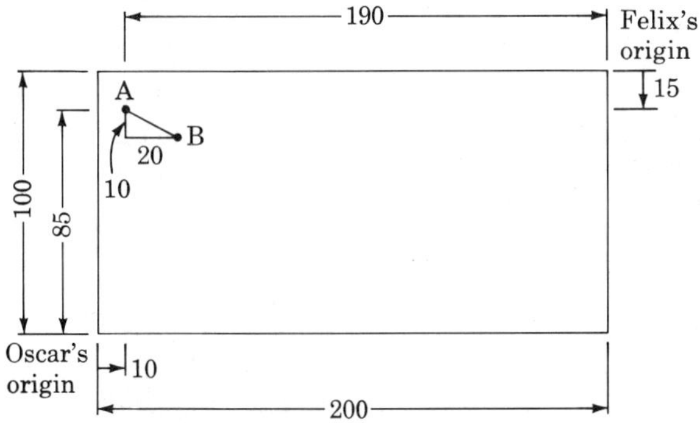

The length of the horizontal sides of the box measures the total amount of product X available to be divided between the two traders. The length of the vertical sides measures the total amount of Y available. Any point on the map divides the products. Here we see two possible divisions of 200 units of X and 100 units of Y. At point *B* Felix has less X and more Y than at point *A*. Oscar has more X and less Y.

ner. Felix and Oscar have between them a fixed aggregate quantity of products X and Y which they divide up. The quantities of commodity X held by Oscar are read from left to right along the bottom side of the box, whereas the quantities of commodity X held by Felix are read from right to left along the top side. In the case of commodity Y, we read Oscar's holdings from the bottom up along the left side, and Felix's holdings from the top down along the right. Thus, any point within the box divides up the total amounts of the two commodities between the two traders. In Figure 13–3, Oscar and Felix between them have 100 units of commodity Y and 200 units of commodity X. Point *A* shows that these quantities are divided between them so that Oscar has 10 units of X and Felix has 190 and Oscar has 85 units of Y and Felix has 15. Because Felix has most of the X and Oscar has most of the Y, they may want to trade. Suppose they agree, for example, to exchange X and Y at the rate of 2 units of X for 1 unit of Y. Point *B* represents their respective holdings after 20 units of X have been given up by Felix in return for 10 units of Oscar's Y (and similarly, 10 units of Y were given up by Oscar for 20 units of Felix's X). Between them Oscar and Felix

FIGURE 13–4. Indifference Curves on the Box Diagram

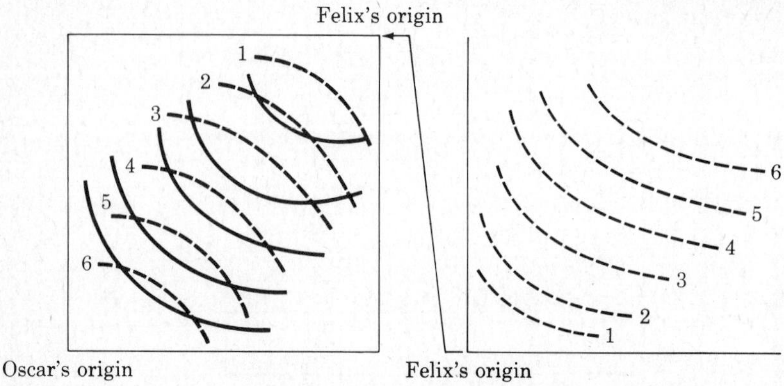

When the axes were shifted to form the box, the indifference curves that were drawn within the axes shifted as well. They retain their orientation to Felix's axes and now are convex to the upper right-hand corner increasing in utility as they go from right to left.

FIGURE 13–5. Utility in the Box Diagram

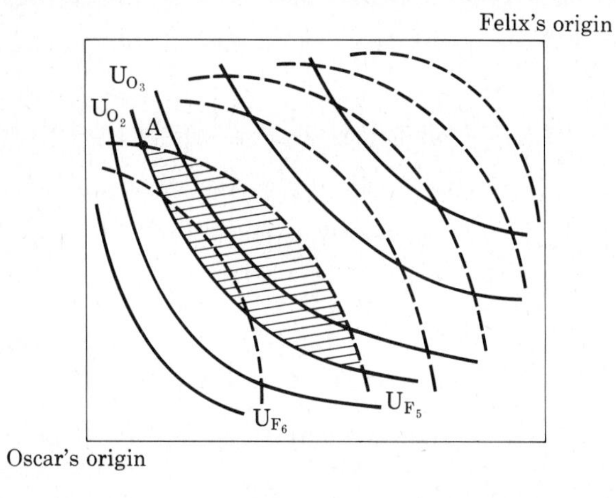

Every point in the box is intersected by two indifference curves, one for Oscar and one for Felix. Therefore, every point connotes a level of utility for each. In this case point *A* gives Oscar enough of product X and Y to bring him U_{O3} utility. It gives Felix enough X and Y to give him U_{F5}.

still hold the same total amounts of X and Y as before, 200 units of Y and 100 units of X. The outside dimensions of the box represent these joint holdings, and they remain constant. Each point in the box represents a different division of the two products.

How do the indifference curves enter the analysis?

When we picked up the axes to form the box, we also moved the indifference curves that were drawn in reference to the axes. Oscar's indifference map stayed in place, but Felix's is now oriented toward its upper right-hand origin. Utility increases on Felix's map as the curves go farther out from this upper-corner origin. Therefore, in Figure 13–4 we find Oscar's utility rising as the curves go up from left to right in the conventional manner, while Felix's utility increases as we trace the curves down from right to left. Oscar's and Felix's curves therefore intersect with each other all over the map. Every point has two curves passing through it.

It looks and sounds like a mess.

At first glance it does. However, if you remember that the curves convex to the lower left-hand corner belong to Oscar while those convex to the upper right-hand corner belong to Felix, it is all made much simpler. Every point on the map allocates so much X and so much Y to each participant. The indifference curves tell how much utility each one's combination gives him. In Figure 13–5 the distribution shown at point *A* gives Oscar U_{O3} level of satisfaction and it gives Felix U_{F5} level.

Does that mean that Felix's utility is greater than Oscar's?

No. Much earlier we established the fact that you cannot make *interpersonal* comparisons of utility. All you can say is that for Oscar, U_{O3} is higher than U_{O2}, and for Felix you can say that U_{F5} is not as high as U_{F6}. However, it is improper to infer who is happier, Felix or Oscar. These are ordinal utilities. They can be ranked only for the individual and not compared between individuals.

Okay, so the box diagram shows the different levels of utility each trader has in the light of his share of the total quantities of products X and Y. What next?

At point *A* in Figure 13–5, Oscar and Felix each enjoys the level of utility shown by the indifference curves containing their respective assortments of goods X and Y. For Oscar it is U_{O3} and for Felix it is U_{F5}.

FIGURE 13–6. Trade in the Box Diagram

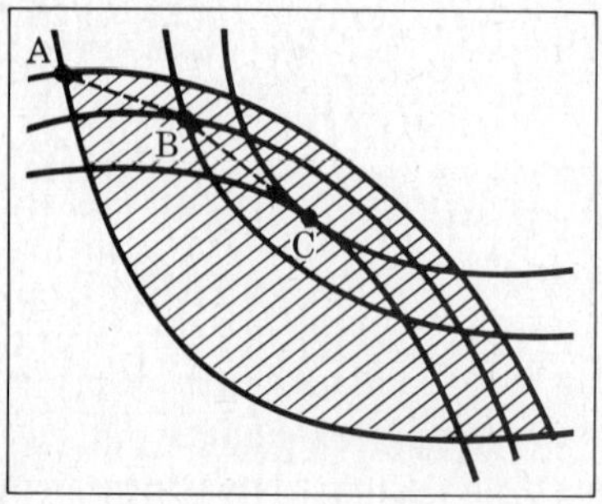

Both traders desire to maximize their own utility. Any point on the map within the shaded ellipse-shaped area is on higher-level indifference curves for both Oscar and Felix than is point *A*. Trade can continue until the distribution reaches a point where the two intersecting curves do not intersect at all, but are tangent to each other. In this figure, trade proceeds at a rate of only a few units of Y per unit of X from point *A* to point *B*. Felix is not willing to trade at the same rate beyond point *B*, because further trade would put him on a lower indifference curve. However, he would trade some more if he could get more units of Y per unit of X. This occurs between points *B* and *C*. At point *C* the indifference curves are back-to-back tangent, and trade ceases.

How they arrived at this distribution of goods is unimportant for the moment. What is interesting is whether or not there is some other distribution that *both* would prefer. If there is, they would tend to trade with each other to redistribute X and Y and improve their satisfactions.

How can you tell if there is some other distribution that both traders would prefer?

We go back to our basic understanding of indifference curves. Any combination lying on a higher indifference curve is preferred to combinations on lower curves. Remembering that Oscar's indifference curves increase in utility from left to right and Felix's increase from right to left, we must ask if there are any combinations that lie to the right of U_{O3} for Oscar and to the left of U_{F5} for Felix. Clearly there are. The sets of points lying within the shaded ellipse of Figure 13–5 all have this characteristic. Any of these combinations would be preferred by both parties to point *A*.

How can they get to any of these points?
Oscar and Felix should trade with each other. If Oscar gives up units of commodity Y to Felix and Felix pays for them with units of commodity X, both may improve their situations.

How do you know who should give up which product?
Very simple. Look at the slopes of Oscar's and Felix's indifference curves at point *A*. Oscar's is steeper. Remember that the slope of the indifference curve measures the marginal rate of substitution. Oscar is willing to give a lot of Y for a unit of X (and still have the same utility). Felix only wants a little Y to induce him to give up a unit of X and remain on the same level of utility. Because Felix is asking less for a unit of X than Oscar is prepared to pay, an opportunity exists for both to raise their utility by trading at some rate of exchange in between. As long as their marginal rates of substitution differ, some rate of exchange can be found that will be mutually beneficial. In fact, exchange will theoretically continue until the marginal rates of substitution of *both* Oscar and Felix for X and Y are identical. Once that happens, there is no longer room for mutual improvement of satisfaction through exchange.

How can you tell if the marginal rates of substitution are the same?
The slopes of Oscar's and Felix's indifference curves must be identical at the point designating the joint distribution of X and Y. This occurs at the points where the indifference curves are tangent to each other, that is, back to back as at point *C* in Figure 13–6. Once the distribution of goods X and Y reaches point *C*, there is no way for Oscar and Felix to trade at any ratio of exchange without reducing the utility enjoyed by one or both of them. Every other point on the map is on a lower indifference curve for either Oscar or Felix or both. Point *C* is what is called a *Pareto optimum* point.

What is a Pareto optimum point?
Economists, you will remember, are hung up on ideas like *efficiency*. They try to get the most return from a limited quantity of resources. Points such as *A* are inefficient in that the maximum possible utility is

FIGURE 13–7. The Contract Curve

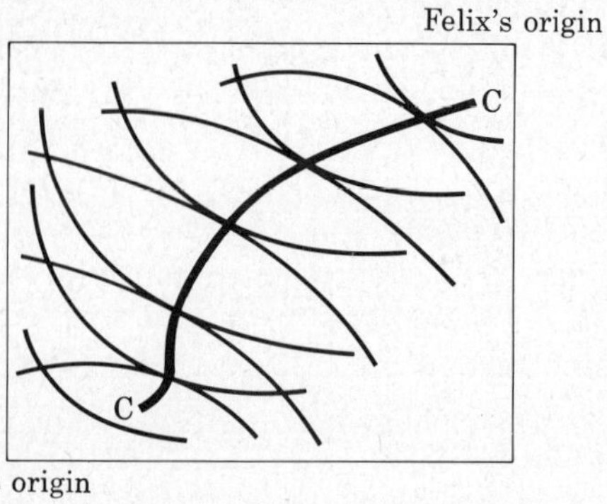

Trade can proceed until a point is reached where the marginal rates of substitution of the two traders for the two products are the same. When this occurs, there is no room for further mutually beneficial trade to occur. There are a number of combinations on the box diagram where this condition prevails. A curve connecting all points where the marginal rates of substitution are equal is called the contract curve. *CC* is such a curve.

not being derived from the 100 units of Y and 200 units of X that are available. It is possible to increase *both* Oscar's and Felix's utility without increasing the total quantity of goods available. As long as one person's utility can be increased without reducing someone else's, the society is operating inefficiently. At point C this is no longer possible. Such a condition is what we call a Pareto optimum.

***Does that mean that utility is maximized at point* C?**

Unfortunately, it is impossible to give a definite yes or no to this question. The answer again requires *interpersonal* comparisons of utility, which we cannot legitimately make. It may be that going toward Felix's origin will increase Oscar's utility more than it reduces Felix's. If so, that would be moving toward increased joint utility. On the other hand, utility may be increased by moving in precisely the opposite direction. You cannot say unless there are cardinal measurements on the indifference curves, and we can add and subtract utils to arrive at an answer. We cannot do this, so we can make no statement as to whether one point of Pareto optimality is better than another.

Is there more than one Pareto optimum point?

Yes. Wherever indifference curves are back to back, with identical marginal rates of substitution (*MRS*'s), a condition of Pareto optimum exists. In Figure 13–7 we can see that there is a set of such points connected by the heavy line *CC*. Such a line is called a *contract curve*. It gets this name because any contract made between two traders seeking to maximize satisfactions will normally distribute goods to some point at which the marginal rates of substitution are equal. Both parties can willingly negotiate to reach a point along the curve. However, any further attempts at trade place them in conflict, one gaining only at the expense of the other. For this reason some less optimistic economists call this the *conflict curve*.

The whole thing seems kind of abstract. Can you give a concrete example of how it works?

Let's see if we can make up a concrete example for which the box diagram is appropriate. Suppose that Oscar and Felix are business partners operating the F & O Pants Co., which manufactures a line of trousers and a line of jeans. In planning their activities for the year, they agree that between them they can afford to take 5 weeks (200 hours) of vacation. Additionally, they can put aside a fund of $1000 to be used by the partners in lieu of, or as a supplement to, the vacation time. At the time of drawing the agreement, Oscar didn't feel particularly in need of time away from the job, so he agreed to take only 1 week (40 hours) vacation and take instead $800 of the $1000. Felix found this agreeable and planned to take 4 weeks (160 hours) and the remaining $200 for his own. The situation as planned can be visualized in the box diagram shown in Figure 13–8.

The agreement was drawn in January. Suppose that by July Oscar is feeling much more tired than he had anticipated and would like additional vacation. Similarly, Felix finds himself in need of some additional money and is willing to relinquish part of his 4-week vacation period. Figure 13–9 shows the indifference curves that apply to each at this point in time.

How do you interpret the marginal rates of substitution for each?

It is obvious that Oscar's willingness to give up money for additional hours of vacation is higher than the amount Felix wants. Suppose that Oscar's marginal rate of substitution is 5. That means he will willingly sacrific $5 for each additional hour of vacation time. Felix, on the other hand, appears to have a marginal rate of substitution in the neighborhood of 2. This means that he demands $2 for an hour of vacation

FIGURE 13–8. An Example of Trade

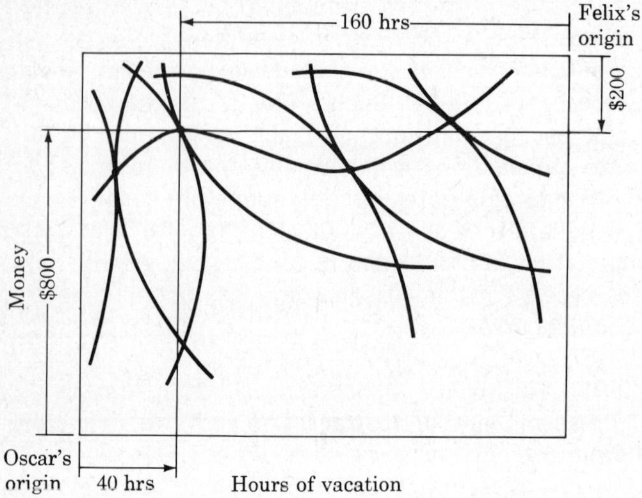

Felix and Oscar have divided up 200 hours of vacation time and a $1000 bonus so that Felix has 160 hours and $200 and Oscar has 40 hours and $800. According to the taste of the two at the time of making this agreement, the combination lies along the contract curve.

FIGURE 13–9. Consideration of Possible Rates of Exchange

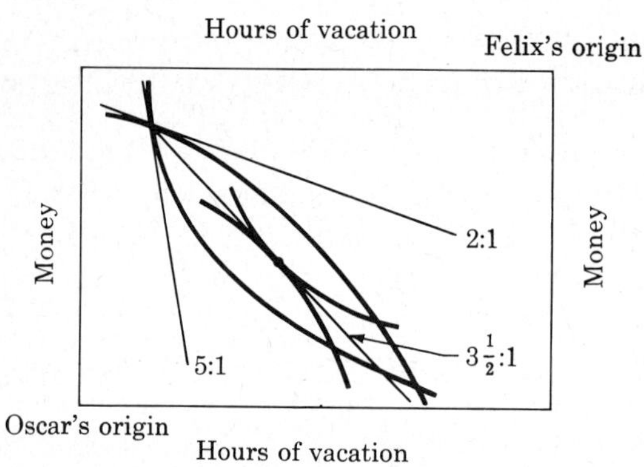

A change in tastes moves the contract curve away from the point Oscar and Felix had agreed on. They are now susceptible to mutually beneficial trade. The marginal rates of substitution of each measure the *least* favorable rate of exchange acceptable. Oscar is willing to give up 5 per hour of vacation, whereas Felix only wants $2 in exchange for an hour. They will eventually settle on some rate in between.

FIGURE 13–10. Sequential Trading at Different Exchange Rates

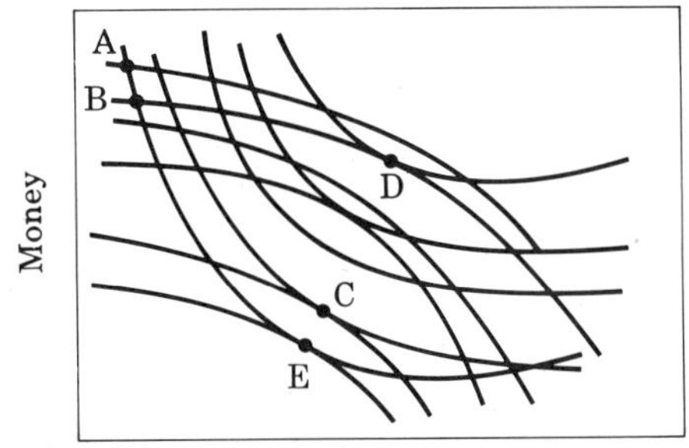

The rate of exchange is a matter of negotiation between the traders. In our case, if Felix is the stronger negotiator, the eventual contract curve equilibrium will be close to the initial indifference curve on which Oscar began. Virtually all of the gain in utility will belong to Felix (point *C*). On the other hand, if Oscar is the stronger negotiator, the equilibrium point will be close to Felix's initial indifference curve (point *D*). By constantly changing the rate of exchange to move right along the indifference curve of one of the traders, the other can act as a first-degree discriminator, effectively capturing the entire consumer surplus (i.e., increase in utility) for himself. Felix does this to Oscar if they end up at point *E*.

foregone. It certainly appears that they have an opportunity to trade. Any vacation time Oscar can get at a price less than \$5 per hour will increase his total level of utility. Any dollar income Felix can get in excess of \$2 per hour of vacation will increase his utility. They will probably agree to some price in between, perhaps \$3.50, and Felix will trade hours of vacation to Oscar at that rate.

How many hours will they trade at what rate?
They will trade until one or the other of the parties finds that he no longer wishes to trade. That will occur when the combination attained after the trade threatens to place him on a lower indifference curve than he enjoyed before the trade. For example, suppose that instead of splitting the difference and trading at \$3.50 per hour, Felix had gotten the better of Oscar and they traded at \$5 per hour, Oscar's *MRS*. How many hours would have been traded? If you look at Figure 13–10 closely, you

FIGURE 13–11. An Isoquant Map

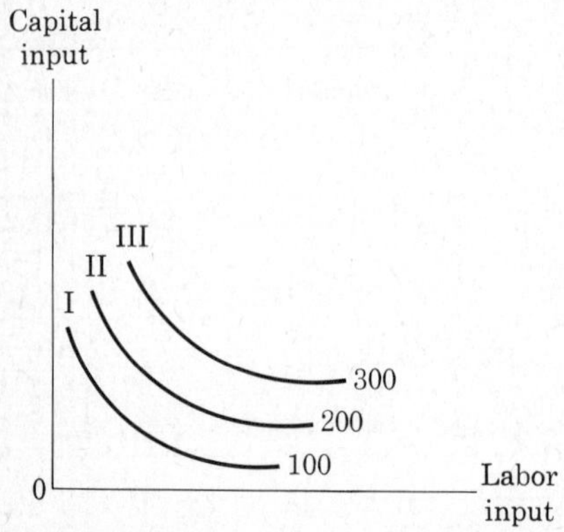

An isoquant is the graphical representation of a production function. Here we see the capital–labor combinations that can produce alternatively 100, 200, or 300 units of product X.

will see that only 1 hour would exchange at that rate. Although Oscar's *MRS* is $5 per hour at the existing distribution between Felix and him, he also has a *diminishing* marginal rate of substitution. After giving up $5 and gaining one additional hour of vacation, he finds himself on a point farther to the right along his indifference curve. The curve is flatter here, which means that he is no longer willing to trade at a 5:1 ratio. He will give up fewer dollars for the next hour of vacation. If you project further trade at the original $5 rate, the new hour–dollar combination lies on a lower indifference curve. Still, however, the rate at which Oscar is willing to exchange is different from Felix's. There is room for further trade, but it must be at a rate of exchange between the two marginal rates of substitution at point *B* in Figure 13–10. Exchange can continue until Felix and Oscar proceed to the contract curve where the marginal rates of substitution are identical and there is no opportunity for *mutual* benefit at any price. When this happens, the indifference curves are back to back, and all voluntary exchange ceases.

Okay, I think I understand how the box diagram works to show exchange. How can we use it to pull the overall analysis together?
We use the box diagram in two forms. One accounts for the distribution

of the goods and services bought and sold in the consumer market. We have already seen that given a willingness to trade, an ability to bargain, and rational behavior, competitive markets will allocate commodities until the marginal rates of substitution of the various traders (buyers and sellers) are equal. Competitive equilibrium sees each trader ending up on a contract curve.

The other form in which the box diagram is employed analyzes the uses of factors of production. Here we consider the other end of the circular flow of wealth, the buying and selling of land, labor, and capital in the factor markets. Because different producers must compete for factor use, and indeed each producer must decide for himself how to allocate factors among competing uses, we have a situation that is quite analogous to the consumer market. Here the object is to use the available resources most efficiently to produce the greatest volume of output.

How do you employ the box diagram to analyze uses of factors of production?

We draw a box diagram using isoquants instead of indifference curves.

Do you remember what an isoquant map is? If not, check Chapter 5. It is essentially a production indifference map, where the axes measure quantities of two inputs (such as labor and capital) used to make some product. Each curve shows the alternative combinations of the two inputs that can produce a given output. Figure 13–11 shows the isoquants for a production function. Isoquant I shows the combinations of labor and capital that can produce 100 units, isoquant II shows the labor–capital combinations that will produce 200 units, and so on. We can draw an isoquant *map* for every product, with each isoquant showing the inputs required to produce a different quantity of the product. The maps reflect the total production functions of the industries in question.

Yes, I remember what an isoquant is. How do you form the box diagram?

This is done in the same way we formed the utility box diagram. Take the isoquant map for one product and superimpose it on top of that of another, with the origins at opposite southwest and northeast corners. Let us pursue the example of our friends Felix and Oscar a bit further. The F & O Pants Co. makes both trousers and jeans. Figure 13–12 shows the isoquants for production of these two products. Assume that the total quantity of labor and capital resources available for production of trousers and jeans is fixed and, as before, is represented by the length of the sides of the box. Quantities of inputs used in trouser produc-

FIGURE 13–12. *A Production Box Diagram for Two Products*

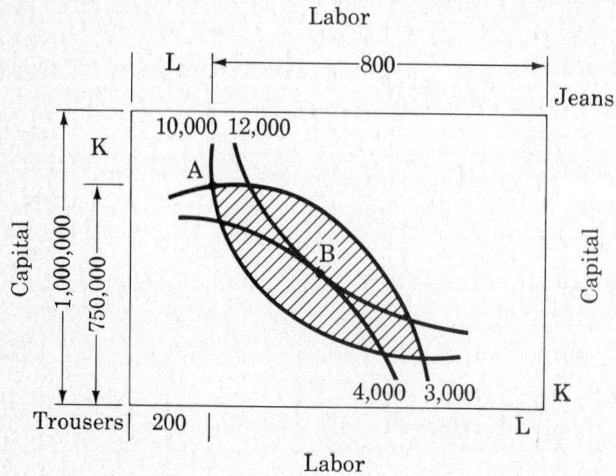

By orienting the isoquant maps for two products so that the origins are at diagonally opposite corners, we can see how factor inputs will be distributed in the production of each. In this figure, point *A* tentatively allocates resources among jean and trouser production to produce 10,000 trousers and 3000 jeans. This is not the best use of the resources available. Without increasing the quantities of inputs used, output can be increased by moving within the shaded area. Point *B* shows higher isoquants of both products, 12,000 trousers and 4000 jeans.

tion are measured from the southwest corner, increasing in an upward and rightward direction, while inputs used for jeans are measured from the northeast corner, increasing down and to the left. A point within the box, therefore, divides up the available capital and labor into one bundle of inputs used to produce trousers and the remainder for jeans. If there are 1000 workers and $1 million worth of capital available in the plant, point *A* divides it up so that 200 workers and $750,000 worth of capital are assigned to trousers and 800 workers and $250,000 worth of capital go to jeans. Thus, according to this distribution jean production is relatively labor-intensive, while trousers are capital-intensive. The isoquants at point *A* indicate that the plant is producing 10,000 pairs of jeans and 3000 pairs of trousers with this distribution of inputs.

Why should the distribution of inputs be so lopsided? Why should trouser production be so capital-intensive and jeans production so labor-intensive?
Perhaps they shouldn't be. The isoquant map will tell us. Point *A* is actually a random point selected for illustration. Remember that there are two isoquants intersecting at all points on the map and we could have selected any one as well as another, since we are not necessarily going to remain there. Just as in the case of the utility box diagram, we are going to see how a rational producer would distribute inputs among his products.

I see. How do you do that?
We employ the same criteria as before. Can a producer, using no additional inputs, increase the output of one product without reducing the output of the other? If so, and assuming that everything produced can be sold in the market, he should make the reallocation of resources called for. The *fixed* dimensions of the box show that the total quantity of inputs employed remains the same and that costs are therefore *fixed*. Thus, it makes economic sense to increase total revenue by increasing total output. Referring to Figure 13–12, it is apparent that by reallocating resources to points within the elliptical, shaded area, output of both products increases. Points within that area lie on higher isoquants than is shown at *A* for both trousers and jeans.

What is the limit to which production can be increased with the same inputs?
Once again the analysis runs parallel to the indifference curve box. Producers keep shifting inputs until they reach a point where two isoquants are tangent to each other, back to back. When this happens, we are once again at a Pareto optimum in the sense that there is no way to increase production of *both* products without adding to the inputs. Change from nonoptimal points, such as *A*, to the condition of Pareto optimally simply involves increases in efficiency, that is, getting more output from the same inputs. Any change occurring in the output mix once a Pareto optimum point has been reached involves a trade-off between trouser and jeans production. This entails a *marketing* decision. Would Felix and Oscar be better off making more trousers or more jeans?

How do you decide which of the Pareto optimum combinations to produce?
Each combination in the box can be produced with the same total quan-

FIGURE 13–13. Transformation Curve

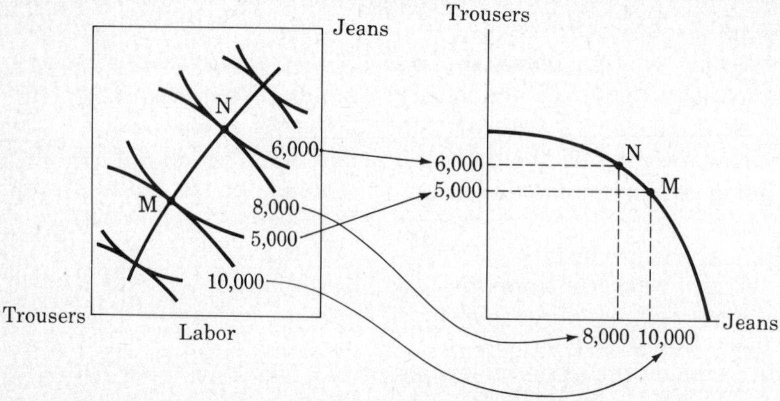

The contract curve shown on the isoquant box diagram gives the maximum quantities of one product that can be produced with some given quantity of the other. It is not possible to increase output of one without either reducing output of the other or else adding to total inputs. The information contained in the contract curve is conveniently transferred to another pair of axes that show the quantities of the products directly. This new curve is called the transformation curve or production possibility curve.

tity of inputs. We have already observed that under these conditions a firm maximizes profits by producing to earn the highest total revenue. Therefore we ask ourselves which combination of outputs maximizes total revenue. The choice has been narrowed to include only efficient points on the contract curve. Now one of the points on the contract curve must be selected.

How do you tell which combination maximizes total revenue?

The most simple arithmetic way would be to multiply the quantities of trousers and jeans at each point along the contract curve by their respective prices and, through trial and error, attempt to find the highest total revenue. However, there are a number of problems with this, not the least of which is its lack of elegance. It is just a sloppy way to do things in a classy subject like economic theory. Another difficulty is the fact that the isoquants drawn represent only a small sample of the total number possible. The contract curve is made up of an infinite number of points. Our trial-and-error process would calculate total revenue for only some of these, and we might well miss the combination that gives the maximum total revenue. For both of these reasons we must use a more roundabout approach and first construct two more pieces of apparatus: the *transformation curve* (sometimes known as the *production possibility curve*) and the *isorevenue curve*.

What are the transformation and isorevenue curves?

Transformation curve is a fancy name for a relatively simple idea. Take the quantities represented by the trousers and jeans isoquants at each point along the contract curve. If you plot these quantities on a separate pair of axes, one labeled trousers and the other labeled jeans, you will have a transformation curve. In Figure 13–13 trouser output is measured along the vertical axis and jeans output along the horizontal. Points *M* and *N* involve the same output data on the box and transformation diagrams. In the box diagram you can read the *input* data from the coordinates measured along the axes and the *output* data from the isoquant labels. The transformation curve permits you to read the output data directly from the axes themselves.

It is easy to see why this curve is sometimes called a production possibility curve. Along the contract line you cannot increase the quantity produced of one product without reducing the quantity of the other. Therefore each point shows the maximum number of trousers, given the jeans output, that can be produced from the available resources, and vice versa. It is the limit of production possibilities. These contract curve quantities are plotted on the transformation curve. It therefore shows the alternative maximum possible combinations of both trousers and jeans that can be produced from the available inputs.

I can see why it's called a production possibility curve. Why is it also called the transformation curve?

Transformation means that you change one thing into another. In the case of the transformation curve, the idea is that in order to move from one point on the curve to another, that is, in order to increase output of one commodity, you must reduce output of the other. In effect you *transform* one into the other. Some of the resources that were used to produce trousers are directed toward producing jeans. The result is a reduction in trouser output of a certain amount and an increase in jeans production. The rate at which trousers can be transformed into jeans by redirecting resources is called the *marginal rate*

FIGURE 13–14. Slope of the Transformation Curve

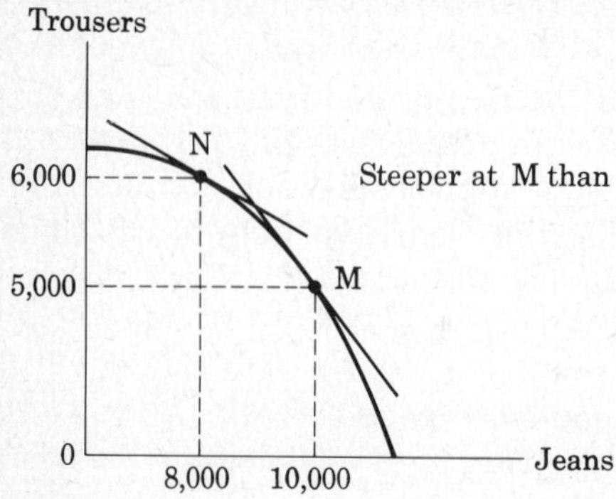

The marginal rate of transformation (*MRT*) shows the rate at which the resources used for trouser production can be converted into jeans manufacture. Between points *M* and *N*, 1000 pairs of trousers (6000 − 5000) get transformed into 2000 jeans (10,000 − 8,000). The formula is $\Delta T/\Delta J$, which is the slope of the transformation curve. The curve gets steeper as you go toward the right, indicating the increasing difficulty of converting factors from production of one product to that of another.

of transformation (*MRT*). Because this rate is shown by $\Delta T/\Delta J$, we see that the *MRT* is measured by the slope of the transformation curve. The marginal rate of transformation shows the *real* "price" of ΔT trousers that must be paid for every pair of jeans gained (Figure 13–14).

Why is the transformation curve drawn concave to the origin?

The concave-shaped curve reflects a condition known as increasing marginal rate of transformation. It occurs because the substitutability of resources from one use to another is not perfect. Following the curve around from upper left to lower right, we note that the *y* intercept shows the plant making all trousers and no jeans. This means that some resources that may really be quite ill-suited for trouser making are nevertheless employed in that effort. The result is that these resources make relatively little contribution to the total output of trousers. If we were to remove them from trouser making and apply them to jeans, we would lose comparatively little in trouser output and gain a relatively large increase in jeans production. The marginal rate of transformation is small in the upper left-hand corner because the "price" of a pair of jeans in terms of trousers is small. You have to give up only a little in the way of trousers to get an incremental pair of jeans. As you continue to take resources out of trouser production and put them into making jeans, you will switch them in the order of their qualifications to produce jeans. First you will take the resources best suited for jeans output. Then you will take those a little less perfectly adapted, then those that seem to do either equally well, then those that are well suited toward trouser production, and finally those that are almost exclusively designed to produce trousers rather than jeans. As you go from left to right, recognizing the difference in the nature of the inputs being switched at each point, you can see that the "price" of a pair of jeans in terms of trousers increases. The slope gets steeper. The *MRT* gets bigger as you transform more and more units of one product into the other.

How does the transformation curve help decide what quantities of each product to produce?

By itself it is not enough. We must also introduce the isorevenue line.

What is an isorevenue line?

Do you remember the isocost line? That showed the different combinations of inputs you could buy with the same total outlay. Well, the isorevenue line shows the different combinations of products you can *sell* to get the same total revenue. Once costs are fixed, the firm maximizes profit by maximizing revenue. Therefore we want to create a family of isorevenue lines, each showing a combination of products that will generate a different level of total revenue, and see which combination of outputs we are capable of producing will generate the greatest amount of revenue.

You're going too fast. How do you construct an isorevenue curve?

Total revenue is defined as price times quantity. Here we have two products, trousers and jeans. The total revenue received from selling some combined quantity of jeans and trousers is the price of trousers times the quantity sold plus the price of jeans times the quantity sold:

$$TR = P_T(T) + P_J(J)$$

If we want to hold total revenue constant and see what different quantity combinations will produce that total, we can specify *TR* and solve for the different *T* and *J* values. For example suppose that jeans sell for

FIGURE 13–15. Isorevenue Line

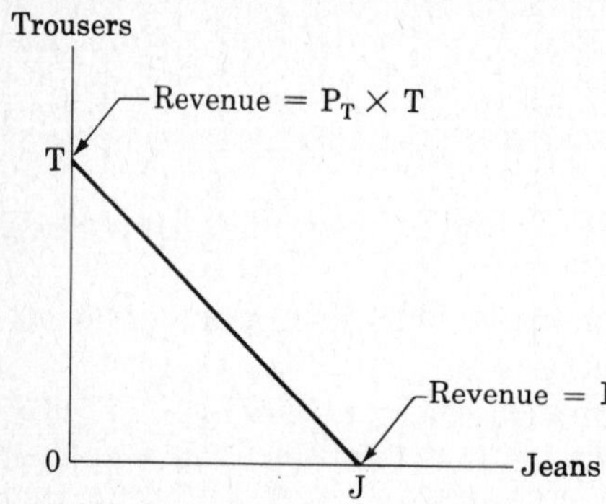

The isorevenue line shows the different combinations of trousers and jeans that will bring the same total revenue. If line TJ is an isorevenue curve, our analysis tells us that at point T there are no jeans being sold. All revenue comes from trousers, and the total revenue is price of trousers times quantity T of trousers, or $P_T(T)$. At point J, the same holds, and total revenue is price of jeans times J quantity of jeans, or $P_J(J)$. Since this is an isorevenue curve, these total revenues are equal:

$$P_T(T) = P_J(J)$$

$$\frac{T}{J} = \frac{P_J}{P_T}$$

The slope of the isorevenue line T/J equals the ratio of the price of jeans to trousers.

\$10 a pair and trousers for \$20. The isorevenue equation for total revenue of \$1000 would be

$$\$1000 = 20T + 10J$$

Solutions to this are 0J and 50T, or 10J and 45T, or 50J and 25T, and so on. Whatever values satisfy the equation are points on the \$1000 isorevenue curve. We can plot an isorevenue curve for any total revenue. As long as the prices are unchanged, they plot as parallel lines with a constant slope equal to P_J/P_T (Figure 13–15).

How do you maximize revenue?

If we superimpose a family of parallel isorevenue curves on top of a transformation curve, we have a diagram showing both the production possibilities and the total revenue each combination will bring. We are looking for that point on the production possibility curve that brings the highest total revenue. With a concave transformation curve, this is found at the point of tangency between the curve and one of the isorevenue lines. Higher revenues require outputs beyond the capacity of the plant.

Should you always produce the output at which the isorevenue line is tangent to the transformation curve?

Yes, if profit maximization is the goal. Notice also that at the point of tangency the slope of the isorevenue curve equals that of the transformation curve for reasons we have discussed many times earlier. This equality means that the market price of jeans relative to trousers (slope of the isorevenue line) is the same as the physical production "price" (*MRT*). The opportunity cost of a pair of jeans is the same whether incurred in the plant by redirecting resources or in the market by redirecting purchasing power. If we interpret this cost of producing an extra pair of jeans by transformation as the marginal cost of jeans, we can loosely observe that marginal cost equals the market price at this equilibrium, a result entirely consistent with our earlier criterion for profit maximization. The profit-maximizing goal thus determines which of the many points along the production contract curve should be produced by the firm, and thus fixes the distribution of resources among the alternatives (Figure 13–16).

We have developed the exchange box diagram, the production box, the transformation and the isorevenue curves, can you sum up how these tie the analysis together?

The exchange box diagram demonstrates how markets work to determine rates of exchange. In a competitive market buyers and sellers seeking to maximize their own utilities will negotiate until they end up along the contract curve. At each point along this curve both traders have identical marginal rates of substitution. These marginal rates of substitution can be thought of as prices, because they measure the number of units of one commodity that are given up for another. Naturally, in a money economy prices are expressed in terms of dollars per unit rather than pairs of jeans per unit of trousers. However, using the opportunity-cost idea, we can readily recognize that a price of $20 for trousers and $10 for jeans means that, in effect, two pairs of jeans are paid for one pair of trousers. Hence, each point on the contract curve involves a different distribution of commodities, as well as a different price that led to that distribution.

The total market sees tens of thousands of individuals interacting

FIGURE 13–16. Isorevenue Lines with Transformation Curve

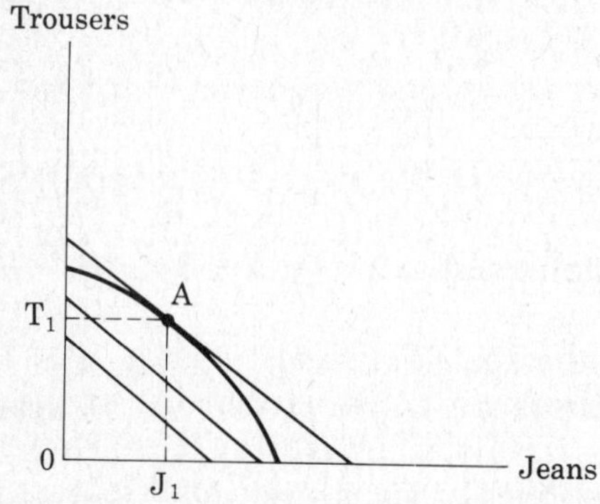

$$TR = T_1 \times P_T + J_1 \times P_J$$

By superimposing a family of isorevenue lines on the transformation curve, we can find the combination of products that is producible and also generates the highest total revenue. This is combination *A*, occurring at the point of tangency between the transformation curve and one of the isorevenue lines.

FIGURE 13–17. General Equilibrium

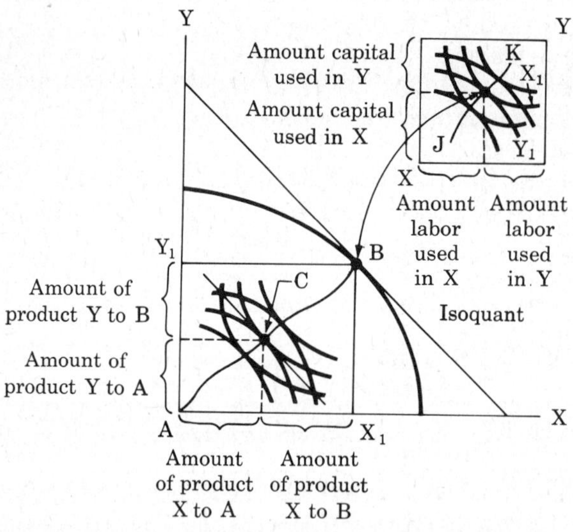

The total picture sees the point selected on the transformation curve at which *MRT* equals P_X/P_Y. A box diagram formed with these quantities and representing the total endowments of traders A and B will see them exchanging until curves from their indifference maps are tangent to each other, with *MRS* equal to the price ratio P_X/P_Y. The quantities, X_1 and Y_1 are the amounts shown on the isoquants in which we are interested. The labor and capital inputs going to each can be read from their point of tangency.

as suppliers and demanders to determine a market-clearing equilibrium price for each commodity. We used these equilibrium prices to determine the slope of the isorevenue curve. Of all the possible distributions of commodities shown along the contract curve, only one will occur in the market, and that is the one at which the marginal rates of substitution are equal to the ratios of the market prices of the commodities.

How do you know that?
This is shown in Figure 13–17, where a box diagram has been constructed to show how traders A and B distribute goods X and Y. Here the origin of the production possibility curve *LM* also serves as the origin of trader A's indifference map. Point *B* on the production possibility curve is determined by the curve's tangency to the highest isorevenue curve, and serves both as the point on the map showing total output (AY_1 units of product Y and AX_1 units of product X) as well as B's origin on the box diagram. The box diagram shows the distribution of these AY_1 and AX_1 units between traders A and B. We know that trade will lead them to *some* point along the contract curve *AB*. The point that does come out of trade is the one at which the marginal rate of substitution equals the price ratio of the products. We know this because each buyer in a competitive market is a price taker; that is, he can do nothing about the market prices but accommodate himself to them. Both traders will maximize their utilities by equating their marginal rates of substitution to the going prices. This occurs at point *C* on Figure 13–17, where $MRS = MRT = P_X/P_Y$.

How does the box diagram analysis tie production in with demand and distribution?
Remember that the production possibility curve in Figure 13–17 was not drawn at random. The combinations of X and Y plotted along it are the numerous Pareto optimum points found along the production con-

tract curve in the production box diagram. The combination of outputs that was selected for examination was the one market forces called forth through the price mechanism. The tangency of the isorevenue curve with the production possibility curve gave us the amount of X and Y to produce (X_1, Y_1). These amounts define which pair of isoquants we are interested in along the production contract curve (*J-K*). Going to those isoquants, we can read off the amounts of capital and labor that will be employed in the production of goods X and Y; and furthermore, by examining the slopes of the isoquants at the points of tangency, we learn the relative factor prices of capital and labor. In equilibrium, factors will be employed so that the ratio of their prices is equal to the marginal rate of technical transformation (the slope of the isoquant).

Therefore, given the market-determined prices of the outputs, we can find the marginal rate of transformation, the marginal rate of substitution, the relative distribution of goods, the relative distribution of factors of production, and the relative prices of the factors. That pretty well pulls it all together.

CHAPTER HIGHLIGHTS

1. *We began by explaining how to construct an Edgeworth box diagram by bringing the indifference maps of two traders together.*
2. *The box diagram can be used to demonstrate how trade will occur when people put relatively different valuations on different goods and services. Trade can continue until there is general agreement in the market with regard to relative values.*
3. *We defined a Pareto optimum as a condition where trade would no longer be beneficial to all parties, and one could only improve his utility if someone else's were reduced. This condition prevails along the contract curve where indifference curves are back to back and marginal rates of substitution are identical.*
4. *Next we noted that the box diagram was applicable to problems entailing allocation of factors of production to different outputs. A producer will shift factors until the ratios of their marginal physical products is identical for all goods. When this occurs, output of one product cannot be increased without reducing output of another. This distribution of factors falls along a production contract curve.*
5. *We pointed out that the transformation curve, or production possibility curve, plots the values of the tangent isoquants that lie along the production contract curve. Using a family of isorevenue curves, we picked the combination on the production possibility curve that generates the most revenue.*

6. Our conclusion was that in a freely competitive market, resources will be allocated so their respective price ratios equal the marginal rates of technical substitution. Trade will continue until the marginal rates of substitution equal the marginal rates of transformation, which, in turn, will equal the ratios of the market prices.
7. No statement was made regarding the social desirability of the distribution of the goods and services among the different traders. A conclusion in this area involves interpersonal comparisons which, in our final chapter as in our first, remain impossible to make in the absence of normative judgments.

Index

76 77 9 8 7 6 5 4 3 2 1